MW00929549

<u>Virtual Terror</u>

21st Century Cyber Warfare

Daniel Wagner

Copyright © 2017 Daniel Wagner

All rights reserved.

ISBN-10: 154484932X

ISBN-13: 978-1544849324

This book contains information obtained from authentic and highly regarded sources. Reasonable efforts have been made to publish reliable data and information; However, the author and publisher do not assume responsibility for the validity of all material, or the consequences of their use.

The author and publisher assume that both the advice and information in this book are true and accurate as of the date of publication. Neither the author nor the publisher gives a warranty (express or implied) with respect to the material contained herein, or for any errors or omissions that may have been made.

All rights are reserved. Except as may be permitted under US Copyright Law, no part of this book may be reprinted, reproduced, transmitted or utilized in any form by any electronic, mechanical, or other means, now known or hereafter invented, including photocopying, microfilming, and recording, or in any information storage or retrieval system, without express written permission from the author.

Cover image: Pixabay

Cover design: Anna Zayco (www.annazayco.com; aniazayco@gmail.com)

Also by Daniel Wagner

- Global Risk Agility and Decision-making

- Managing Country Risk

- Political Risk Insurance Guide

A repository of his published work (including more than 500 articles on current affairs and risk management) may be found at: www.countryrisksolutions.com.

This book is dedicated to everyone who has been or will be hacked, surveilled, threatened or harmed by Virtual Terrorism. Given the intrusive nature of the cyber-driven world we live in, where privacy and security are under constant threat—for individuals, businesses, and governments alike—it is probably only a question of time before anyone who is not already under surveillance, or has not yet been the subject of or impacted by a cyberattack, will be. This book is for you.

Acknowledgements

I am grateful to Aditya Ramachandran, who worked closely with me on this book. His additional research helped me tackle this extraordinary topic.

Throughout the course of my research, I met and/or spoke with a number of people who were willing to share their knowledge, including former (and first) US Department of Homeland Security Secretary, Tom Ridge; former (and first) US Chief Information Security Officer, Brigadier General Gregory Touhill; former Director of Cybersecurity Coordination for the DHS, Rear Admiral Mike Brown; President of Ridge Global, Chris Furlow; Jason Smolanoff, Global Cybersecurity Practice Leader at Kroll; Nicole Friedlander, Special Counsel at Sullivan and Cromwell; Attorney Matthew Meade of Buchanan Ingersoll Rooney; Andrea Bonime-Blanc, CEO of GEC Risk Advisory; reporter Josh Philipp of the Epoch Times; and Alex Kassirer and Ken Wolf of Flashpoint—all of whom work in the cyber arena daily and know much more about the subject than I ever will.

I am also grateful to Jennifer Ciotta—who shared her valuable and unvarnished editorial views—and to Nanette Norris, whose proofreading and indexing skills helped create a polished finished product.

Special thanks to Anna Zayco for her incredible design work on the book cover.

Contents

About the Author

Daniel Wagner is the founder and CEO of Country Risk Solutions, a cross-border risk management consulting firm, and has three decades of experience managing international risk in the private and public sectors.

Daniel began his career at AIG in New York and subsequently spent five years as Guarantee Officer for the Asia Region at the World Bank Group's Multilateral Investment Guarantee Agency in Washington, DC. During that time, he was responsible for underwriting political risk insurance for projects in a dozen Asian countries. After serving as Regional Manager for Political Risks for Southeast Asia and Greater China for AIG in Singapore, Daniel moved to Manila, Philippines, where he served in a variety of capacities in the Asian Development Bank's Office of Co-financing Operations, including as Senior Guarantees and Syndications Specialist. He then became Senior Vice President of Country Risk at GE Energy Financial Services.

Daniel has published more than 600 articles on current affairs and risk management and is a regular contributor to the *South China Morning Post and* Sunday Guardian, among many others. He is also the author of two previous books—*Political Risk Insurance Guide* and *Managing Country Risk*—as well as co-author of *Global Risk Agility and Decision-Making*.

He holds Master's degrees in International Relations from the University of Chicago and in International Management from the American Graduate School of International Management (Thunderbird), in Phoenix. Daniel received his Bachelor's degree in Political Science from Richmond College, in London.

daniel.wagner@countryrisksolutions.com.

linkedin.com/in/danielwagnercrs / twitter.com/countryriskmgmt

Praise for Virtual Terror

Virtual Terror is a thought-provoking and comprehensive look into the world of cyber threats. With national security, economic prosperity, and societal institutions reliant on information technologies in a globally-connected world, we must have our eyes wide open to the risks that accompany the benefits to being "always connected". Cybersecurity is a risk management issue, not just a technology problem. Daniel Wagner superbly sets the table for readers to effectively identify and assess the risk associated with today's evolving cyber threat landscape. *Virtual Terror* presents you with the information you need to better manage your cyber risk.

Gregory J. Touhill, CISSP, CISM
Brigadier General, USAF (ret) and US Chief Information Security Officer (2016-2017)

An inspired and fluid *exposé* of the emerging risks of virtual terrorism in the context of the evolving and faltering global order. Wagner underwrites his analysis with empirical data, with the potential to trigger a call to arms for policy and regulatory wings of government the world over. That Wagner makes such a dry, pithy and often geek-centered subject so palatable is a triumph of storytelling and exposition. A page turner.

Peter J. Middlebrook, CEO of Geopolicity (Dubai)

Daniel Wagner has produced a well-researched, informative, and insightful book that is loudly ringing the alarm bell about the threats posed by cyber warfare, touching on aspects that should be worrying to everyone. World War III will be a cyber war, and that war has already begun. *Virtual Terror* will help educate the world about the menace we already face, and what it may become in a short time if we fail to take the necessary actions to stop it. This is a great book and I recommend it to the lay person and practitioner alike.

Simon Smith, CEO of Official Intelligence (Australia)

Just as the carbon hungry robber barons of the Industrial Age unwittingly gave rise to man-made climate change, the Tech Titans of the Internet Age have unwittingly opened up a Pandora's box of cyber threats. With this new landscape comes the menace of virtual terrorism, which Wagner deftly defines in this important and at times disturbing book. The faceless, stateless, and borderless threat of "Virtual Terror" will not only redefine our lives but will redefine how the world must respond. This book is essential reading for anyone with an Internet connection.

Dante Disparte, CEO of Risk Cooperative and Chair of the Business Council for American Security

Wagner unpacks the critical topic of our age—cybersecurity—in its many forms. This important work tackles a diverse range of subjects in discrete and digestible bites. *Virtual Terror* makes an impactful contribution to the field and is recommended reading for anyone who wants to better understand how this phenomenon impacts us all.

Elad Yoran, CEO of Security Growth Partners and Executive Chairman of KoolSpan

Abbreviations

AML	Anti-Money Laundering
APT	Advanced Persistent Threats
AQ	Al-Qaeda
AQAP	Al-Qaeda in the Arabian Peninsula
ASAT	Anti-satellite
ASEAN	Association of Southeast Asian Nations
ATM	Automatic Teller Machine
C2	Command and Control
CBI	Computer-based interlocking
CCC	Chaos Computer Club
CCP	Chinese Communist Party
CEP	Counter Extremism Project
CCTV	Closed circuit television
CERT	Computer Emergency Readiness Team
CFAA	Computer Fraud and Abuse Act
CIA	US Central Intelligence Agency
CIO	Chief Information Officer
CISO	Chief Information Security Officer
COP21	Paris Climate Change Conference
CRISPR	Clustered, Regularly Interspaced, Short Palindromic Repeat
CSAC	Cybersecurity Association of China
CSCC	Center for Strategic Counterterrorism Communications
CSP	Content Security Policy
CTIIC	US Cyberthreat Intelligence Integration Center
DARPA	US Defense Advanced Research Project Agency

DDos	Distributed denial-of-service
DHS	US Department of Homeland Security
DIA	Defense Intelligence Agency
DNC	US Democratic National Party
DOC	US Department of Commerce
DoD	US Department of Defense
DOJ	US Department of Justice
DPA	Data Protection Administrators
DrDoS	Distributed reflection Denial of Service
ECTF	Electronic Crimes Task Force
ELINT	Electronics Intelligence
EMP	Electromagnetic Pulse
EU	European Union
FAA	US Federal Aviation Administration
FBI	US Federal Bureau of Investigation
FCC	US Federal Communications Commission
FEMA	US Federal Emergency Management Agency
FERC	Federal Energy Regulatory Commission
FISA	US Foreign Surveillance Intelligence Act
FISC	US Federal Intelligence Surveillance Court
FTC	US Federal Trade Commission
FTP	File Transfer Protocol
GB	Gigabytes
GDPR	General Data Protection Regulation
GEC	Global Engagement Center
GM	General Motors
GPS	Global Positioning System
GRU	Russian General Staff Main Intelligence Directorate
GSD	Chinese General Staff Department
GSM	Global System for Mobile Communication
HMI	Human-machine Interface
HP	Hewlett-Packard
HPM	High-power Microwave
HR	Human Resources
HUMABIO	Human Monitoring and Authentication using Biodynamic Indicators and Behavioral Analysis
HUMINT	Human spies and intelligence
IANA	Internet Assigned Names Authority
ICANN	Internet Corporation for Assigned Names and Numbers
ICBM	Intercontinental Ballistic Missile
ICC	Information Coordination Cell

ICIC	Improving Critical Infrastructure Cybersecurity
ICS	Industrial Control Systems
IFE	In-Flight Entertainment
IoT	Internet of Things
IP	Internet Protocol
IR	Incident Response
IRCs	Internet Relay Chats
IS	Islamic State
ISPs	Internet Service Providers
ISS	International Space Station
IT	Information Technology
ITU	International Telecommunication Union
LAN	Local Area Network
LED	Light Emitting Diode
MITM	Man-in-the-middle
NASA	US National Aeronautics and Space Administration
NATO	North Atlantic Treaty Organization
NCSF	US National Cybersecurity Framework
NERC	North American Electric Reliability Corporation
NGO	Non-Governmental Organization
NHS	UK National Health System
NIS	Network and Information Security Directive
NIT	Network Investigative Techniques
NPCI	National Payment Corporation of India
NRC	Nuclear Regulatory Commission
NSA	US National Security Agency
NTIA	US National Telecommunications and Information Administration
ODNI	US Office of the Director of National Intelligence
OECD	Organization of Economic Cooperation and Development
OPM	US Office of Personnel Management
OTA	Over the Air
OTP	One-time passwords
PC	Personal Computer
PCC	Prykarpattyaoblenergo Control Center
PIN	Personal Identification Number
PLA	Chinese People's Liberation Army
PPP	Private-Public Partnerships
PSN	Play Station Network

RADICS	Rapid Attack Detection, Isolation and Characterization Systems
RAT	Remote Access Tools
SCADA	Supervisory Control and Data Acquisition
SDI	Strategic Defense Initiative
SEN	Secure Emergency Network
SEO	Search Engine Optimization
SIBAS	Siemens Railway Automation System
SIGINT	Signals Intelligence
SIM	Subscriber Identification Module
SOCMINT	Social media intelligence
SSF	Strategic Support Force
SSID	Service Set Identifiers
SSL	Secure Sockets Layer
SWIFT	Society for Worldwide Interbank Financial Telecommunication
ToS	Terms of Service
TSA	US Transportation Security Administration
UK	United Kingdom
US	United States
USB	Universal Serial Bus
USG	US Government
USSS	US Secret Service
VEP	Vulnerability Equities Process
VPN	Virtual Private Network
VPS	Virtual Private Server
WMD	Weapons of Mass Destruction

Foreword

The Internet is an open system based on anonymity—it was not designed to be a secure communication platform. The ubiquity of the Internet is its strength, and its weakness. The Internet's malicious actors are known to all of us via disruption, sabotage, theft and espionage. These digital trespassers are motivated, resourceful, focused, and often well financed. Cyber soldiers are asymmetric fighters. They eschew traditional battlefield strategy and tactics. They camouflage their identity and activity in the vast, open, and often undefended spaces of the Internet. Their reconnaissance capabilities are both varied and effective. They constantly probe for weakness, an unauthorized point of entry, and a crack in defenses. They often use low-tech weapons to inflict damage, yet they are able to design and build high-tech weapons to overcome specific defenses and hit specific targets.

Holding your enemy accountable from the air, land or sea is easier than in the digital space. A military sentry on guard at a perimeter can eliminate an aggressor on sight. Attributing a digital breach to a specific actor, or holding it accountable in a meaningful way, is impossible. In the 21st century, there are only two kinds of organizations: those that have been hacked, and those that have been hacked but don't know it yet. The barbarians are no longer at the gate—they are inside and often exquisitely concealed.

The digital world is full of promise and peril. It has neither geographic nor political boundaries, but it has an ever-expanding cohort of attackers—nation states, hactivists, organized crime, and individuals. The attack surface expands every day, as does the level of complexity and sophistication of malicious code. Cyberattacks are a global menace and meeting the challenges to manage those risks, and build a culture of resiliency within an organization, is critical to the organization's survival and success.

Our digital age raises a variety of difficult and never-before asked questions, such as:

- When does a country interpret another's aggressive exploitation of its military or corporate secrets, or the clandestine insertion of malicious code in the industrial control systems of critical infrastructure, as either a precursor to an attack or an act of war?

- Does an infected country respond with an equally severe digital attack or does it use conventional military weapons?

- Should a private company unleash cyberattacks on its competitors as an accepted and ordinary manner of doing business?

The rules of the digital road are only just being established, but they are, and will remain, in a constant state of change and flux.

When you agree to the terms of service and privacy consent for so many of the goods and services we take for granted today, have you actually ever read one, or understood its implications? In doing so, you empower companies with the right to accumulate and sell the things you search, the websites you visit, the videos you watch, the cookies you leave behind, and other 'data exhaust'. With the advent of social media, those of us who use it surrender information about ourselves with astonishing regularity and without hesitation. Whether via an Internet Service Provider, a search tool, or a GPS-enabled app, all of the information we wittingly or unwittingly hand over to these data miners is used to profile and target individuals, groups, and even governments for economic, political, social, or national security reasons. And once it appears in cyberspace, it remains there forever— technically available for anyone with the means to acquire it to use it.

The real revolution we are all experiencing is not with the entities that acquire data, but with the existence of this tremendous volume of data and how we use it. Among its benefits are more efficient manufacturing, more productive agricultural production, improved health care, safer transportation, and a cleaner environment. Among the costs are an assault on privacy, an enhancement of intrusion into our personal lives, a heightened risk of cybercrime directed at each of us, and a false sense of comfort about just how safe we really are.

We are not going to put the data genie back into its bottle. It is exploding in the digital forevermore and will continue to do so exponentially. Limiting government's reach into the private domain of the citizen will be a permanent challenge in our digitally engaged and dangerous world. There will remain a persistent tension between safety, security, and privacy. Given the terabytes of information that exist between people, places, and things and the surveillance and sensor systems that have become more embedded in our communities and daily lives, we must remain forever mindful that we remain under constant threat as a result of their misuse.

No government, corporation, or entity can build an impregnable defense against cyberattacks, for the attackers have the first mover advantage—they need only penetrate one point of entry to launch their attack. Given their persistence, patience, and capabilities, it must be assumed that breaches will occur and that damage will ensue. Cybersecurity is now more frequently viewed as a business risk rather than an IT problem, but the impact of cyberattacks is very real.

Only those companies that adapt to cyberthreats by building a culture of resiliency will survive. A commitment to risk agility, continuous digital awareness, and perpetual security upgrades are the only means of combating ever expanding digital risks. The task is easily misunderstood. Digital risk must be managed before it manages you.

Tom Ridge
First Secretary of the US Department of Homeland Security
Former Governor of Pennsylvania

Preface

Shortly after John Kelly became US Department of Homeland Security Secretary (DHS) in 2017, he said that, if the average American knew what he knew about the threat of terrorism in the US on any given day, he or she would never want to leave the house. While conducting interviews for this book, former DHS Secretary Tom Ridge asked me if I was frightened by what I was learning. I said, "Of course." He then echoed what Kelly had said when he was Secretary, stating that, it did not matter whether his daily brief was 2 pages or 22 pages in length—he was also concerned by what he knew. The amount of concern he felt in 2005 when he left the DHS has been magnified by degrees, based on how the number of players in the terrorism arena has grown, and the extent of their sophistication and success.

Cyberterrorism has certainly magnified collective fear many times over because virtual terrorists have the luxury of operating in a borderless, anonymous, lawless world, where they can strike at will. These are some of the distinguishing factors between "terrorism" and "Virtual Terrorism", as it is defined in the book. You may not even realize it, but chances are very good that you have already been impacted, either directly or indirectly, by Virtual Terrorism. If you have not, it is simply a matter of time until you are. Knowing that is part of what makes this phenomenon so terrifying.

I wrote this book for several reasons. First, much of the literature that exists about terrorism is dated. The subject has been, and continues to be, widely written about, but much of its study has been undertaken from the perspective of the outdated belief that terrorists have a strictly *political* objective and seek to do harm through *conventional* means. That is clearly not the case today. Second, although cyberterrorism has also been broadly examined, cyberwarfare is such a relatively new phenomenon that comparatively little has been written about. Nothing has been written about Virtual Terrorism as I define it here, and not in a single volume, which, taken in its entirety, covers new ground. Third, I am very interested in helping to ensure that as many people as possible are informed about Virtual Terrorism—what it is, the harm it can do, and what we can do about it. Becoming educated about the topic is the first step toward combatting it.

My objective was to write a book that had inherent appeal to a broad readership. If you are new to the topic, you should be able to consider yourself informed after reading it. To the practitioner, you should be able to learn something new. To the academic community, I hope this will make a worthy contribution to the ongoing study of cyberterrorism. For the business decision maker, I want to encourage you to devote the resources necessary to fight this scourge and to reach out to those in government to jointly craft meaningful public-private partnerships. For those in government, law enforcement, and the intelligence community, my sincere hope is that this book will spur you to carry on with the tremendously important work that you do each day, and that you will be able to find a way to do even more together, and in partnership with the business community.

My approach was to be intellectually honest in attempting to corral a rather unwieldy subject. The definition of Virtual Terrorism I have crafted identifies a broad range of actors who contribute to this phenomenon—all of them bear some responsibility for what it has become. Although most Virtual Terrorism is conducted outside the scope of the law (because there is so little in the way of meaningful legal restrictions in cyberspace), some is conducted within its current scope. The end result is the same, however, because it has unleashed the ability to create fear among millions of people and cause enormous physical and psychological damage, at any time, in any place, and without warning.

A candid discussion about Virtual Terrorism raises some uncomfortable questions, such as, which is worse—an alleged Russian attack on the US presidential electoral process or the fact that America's electoral system is so vulnerable to a cyberattack? Is the unfortunate reality that critical infrastructure around the world remains vulnerable to cyberattack a greater problem than the threat of future attacks? Policy makers should be asking themselves such questions and doing what needs to be done to reverse the tide.

You can be forgiven if, after reading this book, you may never want to log on to the Internet or turn your smartphone on again. In truth, we would all be much safer if we did not, but that is not realistic. We are not going back to the days of typewriters and hand-delivered written messages. What we can do is be a lot smarter about how we use the Internet, for as frightening as Virtual Terrorism is today, it will become even more so in the years to come. That is why we must marshal our collective capabilities to fight it, with every tool at our disposal—today. If we fail to do so, the price we will pay in the future will become incalculable.

1. **The Era of Virtual Terrorism**

In Lithuania, more than 25,000 private photos and personal data—including nude pictures—were made public following the hacking of a chain of plastic surgery clinics. A hacking group called Tsar Team broke into the servers of Grozio Chirurgija clinics, in 2017, and demanded ransoms from the clinic's clients in Germany, Denmark, Britain, Norway. and other European Union (EU) countries. Following threats, several hundred images were released and the rest of the database was made public several weeks later. Dozens of patients came forward to report being blackmailed. Victims were asked to pay up to 2,000 euros (approximately US $2,200 at the time) to guarantee that nude images, passport copies, Social Security numbers, and other data would not be made public. The hackers had also demanded that the clinic pay 344,000 euros (US $385,000) in ransom, to prevent the data from being released, but it refused.[1]

A Borderless World

For cyberthieves, hackers, cyberwarriors, and others intent on committing acts of Virtual Terrorism, the world is a target-rich environment. The explosion in the growth of connected devices and data flows has made it extremely difficult to protect against advanced targeted attacks. By 2020, it is estimated that 4 billion people will be online, 50 billion devices will be connected to the Internet, and online data volumes will be 50 times greater than they were in 2016.[2] No wonder that, in 2014, the United States (US) government completed construction of a data storage facility in Utah larger than the Pentagon. Storing, reviewing, interpreting, and acting upon all that data is a mind-boggling task.

This explosion in connectivity has corresponded with a large rise in the number of malicious cyberattacks, a more profound security exposure, and enhanced requirements for ever more elusive, effective security counter measures. The number of entry points has grown exponentially, but the number of ways to protect data and data systems has not kept pace. In 2014, more than 70 percent of companies polled admitted they had become victims of successful cyberattacks, creating an estimated $170 billion spent in an effort to enhance security, as of 2015. That number grows every year. In 2016, more than 550 million people are estimated to have fallen victim to cybercrime—12 people every second—causing an estimated $3 trillion in global economic cost[3] and placing the cost of cybercrime within striking distance of that of the global, illegal drugs trade.[4]

Virtual Terrorism operates in a borderless world that is an unregulated land of opportunity for criminals and other actors intent on disrupting standard operating procedure and legal norms across the globe. Indeed, in the fast-paced and ever-changing nature of the virtual world, the term 'standard operating procedure' has already become a thing of the past. The virtual world is such a new phenomenon that most countries have no legislation addressing the virtual space and even fewer effective means of combatting criminal actions occurring within it.

At a time when financial resources are stretched so thin across governments, businesses, multilateral organizations, and non-governmental organizations (NGOs), the challenge is truly daunting and screams out for hyper risk agility, yet very few such entities have devoted the time, money, and resources necessary to thwart Virtual Terrorism. Those individuals, businesses, governments, and others who fail to adopt meaningful security measures and devote substantial resources to getting out in front of cyberthreats simply fall further and further behind the curve, with little hope of turning the ship around.

Defining Virtual Terrorism

Virtual Terrorism is distinct from terrorism. Despite decades of scholarly attempts to define what terrorism is, it remains an amorphous concept. Some of the best minds in the world have tackled the subject, but the most experienced among them admit that it is futile to attempt to wrangle the term into a single concept or definition. Terrorism can therefore be thought of like an amoeba that is forever in a process of

2

metamorphosis. Therein resides a central problem: if terrorism defies definition, how can we understand it, much less combat it, and what does that imply about our ability to do so in the future?

A widely acknowledged conventional definition of terrorism, from one of the subject's best-known thought leaders (from 2006), is:

- Acts or threats with <u>overt political objectives and motives</u> designed to have far-reaching <u>psychological repercussions beyond the immediate victim or target</u>,

- Acts conducted either by <u>an organization</u> with an identifiable chain of command or conspiratorial cell structure, or by <u>individuals or a collection of individuals directly influenced, motivated, or inspired by the ideological aims</u> of some existent terrorist movement and/or leader, and

- Acts that tend to be perpetrated by <u>a sub-national group or non-state entity</u>.[5]

That definition is somewhat opaque, as is the topic of terrorism, and has become dated because of the onset of the global War on Terrorism and the onset of the cyber era. Another well-known thought leader on terrorism updated the definition (in 2010) to specifically define cyberwarfare as, "the unauthorized penetration by, on behalf of, or in support of a <u>government into another nation's computer or network</u>, or any other activity affecting a computer system, in which the purpose is <u>to add, alter, or falsify data, or cause the disruption of or damage to a computer, network device, or the objects a computer system controls</u>."[6]

That definition does a good job of focusing in on the cyber component of terrorism, which was already a significant and growing problem at the time, even though most people were not yet aware of its importance. However, because of the explosion of conventional terrorism and cyberterrorism this century, and how they have come to impact the manner in which people all over the world live, a broader and deeper definition is now required. The Chinese have made an attempt to craft such a definition. Under China's Counterterrorism Law of 2015, terrorism includes "any thought, speech, or activity that, by means of violence, sabotage, or threat, aims to generate social panic, influence national policy-making, create ethnic hatred, subvert state power, or split the state."[7]

On one hand, that sounds Orwellian and appears to have been designed to enhance the narrative of the Chinese government and its *own* objectives. On the other hand, it encompasses a number of *direct* or *indirect* potential impacts of terrorism that are deliberately broad in scope and valid. Any definition of terrorism will be at least a little murky; the issue is whether it can be sufficiently broad to capture the scope and impact of terrorism. For that reason, the following definition should be used for **terrorism** in the context of this book (and beyond):

"Any action taken by an individual, group, business, government, or other entity that has the objective of promoting its interests while either attacking, snooping, causing harm, or sowing fear on intended or unintended targets."

As the nexus between terrorism and cyberspace, Virtual Terrorism is naturally also difficult to define. Unlike more conventional types of terrorism, in which the perpetrator usually seeks recognition and reveals his or her identity, the identity of the person(s), group(s) or government(s) responsible for initiating acts of Virtual Terrorism is deliberately hidden. Their motives and objectives may be unclear, and the length of the attack, and whether it will be repeated, are generally unknown.

What acts of Virtual Terrorism tend to have in common with more traditional acts of terrorism is the use of coercion and/or intimidation to achieve desired objectives. Both versions of terrorism encompass the achievement of ideological, political, religious, financial, "ethical", or other objectives, but unlike conventional definitions of terrorism, **Virtual Terrorism** is an even broader concept that may be defined as:

"Any action taken by an individual, group, business, government or other entity—whether having direct or indirect impact on intended or unintended targets, <u>whether it is within the confines of existing law or not, and whether visible to the intended target(s) or not</u>—that has the objective of promoting its interests while either attacking, snooping, <u>stealing</u>, causing harm, or sowing fear <u>through remote control or via the Internet</u>."

The net effect of an act of terrorism is, in the end, the same; however, Virtual Terrorism includes whether that act is within the confines of the law, is visible to the intended target, includes stealing, and is conducted via remote control or use of the Internet.

If the task of understanding and combatting Virtual Terrorism appears daunting, it will soon become insurmountable if sufficient resources are not devoted to the problem. This book is an effort to draw more attention to that challenge. Those opposed to Virtual Terrorism are going to need every shred of available political, financial, intelligence, law enforcement, and military resources, combined with an endless supply of determination, willpower, and perseverance to do battle with Virtual Terrorism. That battle has, of course, already begun, but if those individuals and organizations opposed to Virtual Terrorism do not give it the focus it deserves, the battle will soon be lost. Some may say it already has been.

Misperceptions about Terrorism

One of the most distinguishing features of terrorism is its ability to have a broad impact on not only the subject of the target but upon a whole host of actors that were not its intended target. Given how long terrorism has been at the leading edge of media coverage, most people have at least a basic understanding of what it is, but many of our perceptions about terrorism are flawed. For example, many people live in fear that they may ultimately become a victim of terrorism, but in fact, the chances of becoming a terrorism statistic are remote. Many people believe that a majority of Muslims share the radical views of Islamic extremists, but in fact, very few do. Many of the historical statistics that follow are truly surprising and should shatter a lot of misconceptions many of us have about who is impacted by terrorism, how frequently it occurs, and how acts of terrorism have changed over the last several decades.

Most of us have been acutely aware of the threats posed by global terrorism for decades—and particularly since 9/11—but even after everything we have seen, heard, and experienced for ourselves, **we still have many ill-conceived notions about what terrorism is all about**. Some of these are simply wrong. For example, there is *not* a strong statistical link between poverty and terrorism, and many individuals who join terrorist groups are well educated and come from middle class families.

The more you know about *non-virtual* forms of terrorism, the more you will realize that **you are personally unlikely to become a victim of terrorism,** even if you live in one of the countries most associated with terrorism, unless you happen to become a target by virtue of your nationality or profession. **The same cannot be said of Virtual Terrorism**. That should not serve to minimize the global threat, or how important it is to be prepared for the eventuality that an act of terrorism occurs in your country, but it should prompt everyone to think about other preconceived notions they may have about terrorism.[8]

While it is true that terrorism is a 'global' phenomenon, its most direct impact is felt in only a few countries. Since the beginning of the 21st century, there has been more than a nine-fold increase in the number of deaths from terrorism.[9] However, in 2013, 66 percent of all deaths resulting from terrorist attacks were claimed by just four terrorist organizations—Al-Qaeda (AQ), Boko Haram, the Islamic State (IS), and the Taliban—with more deaths being the result of attacks from Boko Haram than any other such organization.

Although much of the increase has been due to the ongoing Syrian conflict, it is worth pointing out that more than *82 percent of those killed in terrorist attacks died in just five countries*: Afghanistan, Iraq, Nigeria, Pakistan, and Syria.[10] The majority of deaths from terrorism do not occur in the West. Excluding 9/11, only 0.5 percent of all deaths have occurred in Western countries between 2000 and 2015, and only 5 percent of all terrorist deaths have occurred in Organization of Economic Cooperation and Development (OECD) countries since 2000.[11] This is a terrible tragedy for these countries, their people, and others that suffer from the direct impact of terrorism, but the impact felt by most of the world is limited to the ongoing metamorphosis in the manner in which governments address security protocols, how average citizens around the world are impacted by those protocols, and the economic costs associated with terrorism.

The Economist Cost of Terrorism

The economic cost of terrorism is estimated to have reached its highest ever level in 2014, at $53 billion, a 61 percent increase from the previous year and a ten-fold increase since 2000.[12] When considering these economic costs, bear in mind that the long-term *indirect* costs of terrorism can easily be up to 20 times greater than the *direct* costs. While the 'direct' cost of the 9/11 attacks was estimated at $55 billion, the secondary effects of increased security totaled nearly $600 billion, decreased economic activity was nearly $125 billion, and the cost of the Iraq War that followed has been estimated in excess of $3 trillion.[13] These indirect costs are truly significant.

Perception of risk clearly plays a significant role in how investors react to acts of terrorism. Terrorism in countries perceived to have higher risk can prompt a severely negative result with traders, investors, and lenders. This is an important reason why acts of terrorism often have a more negative impact on developing countries than developed countries.

Since individual, business, and government interests and approaches to addressing the problem of terrorism are often not in sync, all parties need to have incentives and guidelines in place so that they may act in a consistent fashion. Increasing safeguards and enhancing general awareness are precursors to meaningfully addressing the persistent nature of the threat but can have unintended consequences. For example, for many years following the 9/11 attacks, the US was on 'orange' alert, meaning that an attack could happen at any time and that the threat was ever present. However, after the passage of some time, average citizens began to pay little attention to the threat level, particularly if no attacks occurred.

Reducing the possibility that an attack can occur, will be successful, or will cause significant damage by enhancing security protocols, goes hand-in-hand with changing perceptions that an attack may occur at all. There is a risk that constantly increasing security spending may both enhance the cost of an attack and reverse any gains made in changing risk perceptions if an attack occurs and is successful.

Spending the money necessary to reduce vulnerability to attack is perhaps the greatest challenge facing developed country governments and businesses. This is because most developed countries did not construct infrastructure and buildings with the type of security safeguards necessary to thwart terrorist attacks. When power transmission sub-stations, railroad tracks, or office buildings were constructed, security was not a foremost consideration. Most developed countries remain highly vulnerable to attack on soft targets. One of the ironies in the terrorism landscape is that this same type of unease is not the case in many developing countries, where security was always a primary concern.[14]

Terrorists' ability to shut down or substantially reduce tourism in a country from a single act of terror, no matter how significant in terms of loss of life or property damage, only invites more such attacks to occur. Depending on the country, it may be days or years until another attack occurs, or it may not occur at all, but the impact on tourism is usually profound. Given that anyone with a car, knife, or gun can easily perform an act of terror, and that the IS and other extremist groups have called on their followers to pursue low-tech soft target attacks, it is surprising that more such attacks do not occur with greater frequency. This is a tribute to law enforcement and intelligence agencies, which do a remarkable job behind the scenes thwarting conventional terrorist attacks.

Why Virtual Terrorism is Different

Thwarting Virtual Terrorism is another type of battle entirely, given that the perpetrators usually do not wish to reveal their identities, they operate in a stealth manner, and victims' ability to either identify or punish the perpetrators is limited, at best. Since Virtual Terrorism attacks may occur undetected and persist for years, the opportunity for a virtual terrorist to inflict a particularly high degree of damage and cost is unrivaled. Given that so few governments either have laws specifically protecting against Virtual Terrorism, or useful means of enforcing them, most of the time, virtual terrorists are free to operate at will.

Depending on the context, Virtual Terrorism may overlap more generally with terrorism, cybercrime, and even cyberwar.[15] Large-scale cyber weapons, such as the Flame Virus and NetTraveler, are akin to biological weapons because, in our interconnected world, they have the potential to be equally destructive.[16] If Virtual Terrorism were to be treated similarly to more conventional forms of terrorism, then it would only include attacks that threaten property or lives, but Virtual Terrorism goes quite a few steps further, with its adherents seeking to obtain vast amounts of information, disrupt infrastructure and information networks, and steal state secrets.

Various forms of Virtual Terrorism have shades of gray within shades of gray. For example, Virtual Terrorism typically seeks to inflict damage on a specific target while sowing *fear* among a group of people in the process. By contrast, cybercrime requires committing *crime*, which may or may not include the use of fear as a tactic of intimidation.[17] Cybercrime will, by definition, be illegal, but given the absence of laws against Virtual Terrorism, it is not necessarily illegal. The absence of enforceable laws against Virtual Terrorism and a general inability to prosecute the perpetrators are important distinctions between Virtual Terrorism and cybercrime versus more conventional acts of terrorism.

Categorizing Virtual Terrorism

While Virtual Terrorism is a largely amorphous concept, it is useful to categorize acts of Virtual Terrorism so as to distinguish between levels of capability, since the levels of sophistication of perpetrators is as distinct as the amount of damage they are able to inflict:

- Simple-Unstructured: The ability to conduct basic hacks against individual systems using tools created by someone else. The perpetrator possesses basic target analysis, command and control, or learning capability;

- Advanced-Structured: The ability to conduct more sophisticated attacks against multiple systems or networks and to modify or create basic hacking tools; and

- Complex-Coordinated: The ability to conduct a coordinated attack capable of causing mass-disruption against integrated, heterogeneous defenses (including cryptography). The perpetrator has the ability to create sophisticated hacking tools, highly capable target analysis, command and control, and organization learning capability.[18]

Given how many aspects of Virtual Terrorism are, and will remain, unknown, in some respects it may not matter to the individual(s) or organization(s) on the receiving end of an attack whether the perpetrator has a basic command and control ability or is advanced in that regard. *The 'unknown unknowns' enable perpetrators to create uncertainty, which is part of what makes Virtual Terrorism such a powerful utensil of fear.*

Virtual Terrorism attacks have distinct advantages over physical attacks, since they can be conducted remotely, anonymously, inexpensively, and do not require significant investment in weapons or personnel. Virtual Terrorism also enables smaller, under-financed, and lesser-known terrorists to participate on a more level playing field with larger, better known groups, and to intrude and disrupt organizations much larger than itself—even entire nations. That is why the Virtual Terrorism phenomenon is in the process of creating a paradigm shift, taking the advantage away from large scale, well-financed, and heavily armed entities toward smaller, more nimble opponents who have the advantage of operating in the dark and under cover of anonymity.

Virtual Terrorism and Hybrid Warfare

Virtual Terrorism is an important component of what is known as Hybrid Warfare, another difficult term to define, but perhaps best understood as a complex set of interconnected threats and forceful means used to further political motives. The term Hybrid Warfare appeared at least as early as 2005 and was subsequently used to describe the strategy used by Hezbollah in the 2006 Lebanon War. Since then, the term "hybrid" has dominated much of the discussion about modern and future warfare and has become a foundation for modern military strategy. Modern adversaries make use of conventional/unconventional, regular/irregular, and overt/covert means, and exploit all the dimensions of war using hybrid threats to exploit the full-spectrum of modern warfare—not being restricted to conventional means. In practice, any threat can be hybrid as long as it is not limited to a single form and dimension of warfare.

Renowned military strategist Colin Gray convincingly argues that modern warfare is essentially more of the same, since most conflicts throughout history have been defined by the use of asymmetries that exploit an opponent's weaknesses, thus leading to complex situations involving regular/irregular and conventional/unconventional tactics. Similarly, the rise of cyber warfare has not fundamentally changed the nature of warfare but expanded its use in a new dimension.[19] It is the interconnected nature of Hybrid Warfare that defines it, while at the same time defying an absolute definition of what Hybrid Warfare actually is. In that regard, Virtual Terrorism and Hybrid Warfare share commonality of purpose and exploitation.

A hybrid adversary can be state or non-state. In the Israel-Hezbollah War and the Syrian Civil War, the main adversaries are non-state entities within the state system, which can act as proxies for countries but have independent agendas as well. Iran is a sponsor of Hezbollah, but it was Hezbollah's agenda (rather than Iran's) that resulted in the kidnapping of Israeli troops that led to the Israel–Hezbollah war. By contrast, Russian intervention in Ukraine is a state actor waging Hybrid Warfare by using a local hybrid proxy to project power. Hybrid adversaries deploy a combination of methods of attack, including conventional capabilities, irregular tactics, terrorist acts, indiscriminate violence, and criminal activity to achieve their objectives. Hybrid adversaries also use clandestine actions to avoid attribution or retribution. These methods are used simultaneously, across the spectrum of conflict, with a unified strategy.

Hybrid adversaries are flexible and adapt quickly. The IS's transnational aspirations, blended tactics, structured formations, and use of terror are all part of its arsenal. One of the IS's responses to US aerial bombing campaigns has been to quickly reduce the use of checkpoints, large convoys, and cell phones, dispersing its fighters into civilian populations, and to use civilian collateral damage from airstrikes as a recruiting tool.[20] However, the objective of Hybrid Warfare need not necessarily be military victory—regime change, misinformation or disinformation, and swaying elections in one direction or the other are all examples of Hybrid Warfare.

Where an opponent cannot be matched militarily, the asymmetrical tools deployed in Hybrid Warfare have the benefit of being unleashed where they are not expected, so the element of surprise is prominent. Russia uses the tactic of *maskirovka*, which, loosely translated, means subterfuge— the elements of surprise, diversion, and deception, and a readiness to act outside post-war operational norms within which the West has built its military and political response mechanisms. Cyberspace is a primary theater of Russia's asymmetrical activity because it offers a way to easily combine fighting arenas, including espionage, information operations, and conventional combat, and to do so behind a curtain of plausible deniability (for example by taking advantage of proxy operators).

A perpetrator can stealthily cross great distances without physical barriers to reach a target, removing the need to emphasize speed. Rapid, decisive victory is unnecessary because the ebb and flow of combat can exhaust a target's resources, or generate confusion, and trigger a response that serves the perpetrator's goals just as well. Active combat can be followed by frozen conflict, which also can serve the original political purpose and constitute "winning". Autocratic societies such as China and Russia are best positioned to engage in Hybrid Warfare. As centralized decision-makers, they can move fast, unhindered by democratic checks and balances, such as an independent legislative branch. They can prolong operations without the need to publicly justify the use of resources or explain battlefield casualties. For these and other reasons, they can easily wage Hybrid Warfare in perceived peacetime, when it is harder for Western liberal democracies to build public and legislative support for the government expense and risk to troops.

Russia perhaps best personifies the preconditions for successful Hybrid Warfare, having the strong political leadership needed to order an attack, a sophisticated intelligence apparatus to identify vulnerabilities, control over a wide array of resources that can be rapidly deployed, and a highly developed information and propaganda capability for both internal and external communications. In practice, Russian hybrid attacks have employed diplomacy, cyber and information warfare, the threat of, and actual use of, military force, economic inducement and coercion, and legal tactics such as utilizing court systems.[21] With such an array of options at its disposal, it is no wonder that Russia has mastered the art of Hybrid Warfare.

Hybrid Warfare is no longer considered unusual, given the difficulty of distinguishing civilians from combatants, the tendency to combine direct and indirect approaches to fighting, and the ambiguity in conflict classification in the contemporary combat environment. States counter this confusion created in the process by blending law enforcement, intelligence, and military actions into a single comprehensive governmental response. Today's conflicts are therefore defined by the blurring of traditionally distinct lines, making Hybrid Warfare the norm.[22]

The Enormity of the Problem

US Office of Personnel Management

13

There are numerous examples that serve to exemplify the potential damage and costs associated with Virtual Terrorism and how it can both sow fear in a large population while breaking the law (these will be explored later in the book), but the breach of data from the US Office of Personnel Management (OPM) stands out for several reasons. First, the sheer scope and significance of the theft of data is staggering. Second, it illustrates how vulnerable are data systems that would ordinarily have been thought of as 'secure'. Third, it demonstrates how powerless even the US government (USG) is to retrieve the captured data. Fourth, the question of just how severe the damage will be, and for how long, will never be known. The OPM case also reveals how gaps, inconsistencies, and outdated security protocols, combined with managerial incompetence and institutional sclerosis, can collide to create a perfect Virtual Terrorism storm.

The OPM first noticed that it had been the subject of a data breach in April 2015, a breach which was originally thought to have resulted in the theft of personnel records of approximately 4 million current and former government employees (and applicants). That number was subsequently revised upward to more than 22 million—the largest data breach of government data in US history. The data targeted included names, dates, and places of birth, home addresses, Social Security numbers, and detailed security clearance-related information. The depth of information stolen as a result of the cyberattack was staggering, including military records, veteran status, job and pay history, insurance and pension history, and more than 5 million sets of fingerprints, compromising the identity of some clandestine agents.[23]

It took the USG several months to send letters out, to all those known to have had their identities and personal information compromised, about complimentary identity theft protection and monitoring services that were being provided to them until December 1, 2016. Through the OPM's Cyber Resource Center, the government opted to use a 25-number Personal Identification Number (PIN), intended to ensure security; however, it failed to include any special characters in the PINs, which did not help make the case for security. Many of the impacted individuals undoubtedly opted to pay for identity monitoring services themselves.

With a database of information derived from the OPM and other data breaches, the Chinese government is believed to have created a systematic roadmap of Americans and their connections, as well as information it can use to blackmail government employees, recruit insiders as spies, and monitor people who speak out against its policies. With the database, the Chinese Communist Party (CCP) is in a position to monitor some foreigners in much the same way it does its own citizens (this will be explored in greater detail in subsequent chapters).

One of the leading Chinese organizations apparently involved in creating the database was the 61 Research Institute, one of four known research institutes under the Third Department of the General Staff Department—the branch of the People's Liberation Army (PLA) that oversees military hackers. The organization is led by Wang Jianxin, a son of Wang Zheng, who helped establish the CCP's signals intelligence operations under Mao Zedong. While the 61 Research Institute's role in the project ties it to global cyberespionage, many other Chinese domestic security branches were also involved in building the system—including various branches of the police and some half dozen branches of the secret police.

This database is believed to have been developed since 2013 and commanded from the highest levels of the Chinese government. The functions of the spy system, and the departments involved, suggest that it was designed not only to be used as a database on foreigners but also as a system to better monitor Chinese citizens. One of its functions is to gather information on individuals from all available sources, in and outside of China, that can be used for criminal trials.

The software used for the database was originally a big data analytics program for smart city measurements, which the CCP altered for its own purposes. What made the software attractive were its powerful functions for gathering information and showing relationships between data. It is also believed to be scalable enough to hold the credentials on every Chinese citizen and to display everything, from their personal data, to data on their family members, relations, and personal background. The database displays data in nodes, which can be displayed by themselves, in relation to other data or events. A security service using the system could conduct deep data mining on personal files in the system, to show how individuals relate to one another, even over set time frames.

The Chinese spy system takes this information and organizes it in a form that departments of the Chinese regime can then use—whether for industrial espionage or other purposes. Although the most visible Chinese cyberattacks feeding this database have targeted US federal employees, the system can potentially affect every American. Many citizens of the US have extended family members working in the federal government, and every American is listed in numerous federal databases, so the OPM breach, in conjunction with other data breaches believed to have been orchestrated by the Chinese government, should really be viewed as a gateway into the lives of most Americans.[24]

OPM Breach Fallout and Reaction

The OPM breach was serious on a variety of levels. The very idea that the heart of the USG could be penetrated and sensitive data stolen without its knowledge was bad enough, but that it was done with relative ease made it seem even worse. The OPM had apparently been warned multiple times about its security vulnerabilities, including in a March 2015 OPM Office of the Inspector General semi-annual report to Congress, which warned of "persistent deficiencies in OPM's information system security program," including "incomplete security authorization packages, weaknesses in testing of information security controls, and inaccurate Plans of Action and Milestones".[25]

The Report's assumption was that the breach would presumably never have happened if these systemic weaknesses had not existed, operating on the assumption that, with a more robust system of encryption, multiple step authentication procedures, and the ability to accurately detect intrusions, early attempts to penetrate OPM's data banks would have proven unsuccessful. The problem with that assumption is that anyone who may have obtained user credentials can enter a system; encryption cannot protect data that is accessed by walking through the front door. Herein is the multi-faceted nature of cyber-hacking: it can be done through the front door or the back door, legally or illegally, in full view or in the shadows.

A 2016 House Oversight Committee Report[26] concluded that the series of attacks was probably coordinated by two Chinese government-sponsored groups, and that a successful initial intrusion enabled hackers to do greater damage at a later time. The Report concluded that evidence of cyberattacks existed as far back as November 2013. The US Computer Emergency Readiness Team (CERT, part of the DHS) discovered malware that had been in OPM's computer system since 2012. CERT determined that an intrusion had netted manuals and other information about the agency's information technology (IT), which provided a roadmap for hackers. Shortly thereafter, the OPM shut down compromised networks, but by then, another attacker had established a foothold in OPM's systems. The discovery of the breach "should have sounded a high level multi-agency national security alarm" to take more dramatic steps, the report concluded, but the agency had neglected many of the inspector general's security recommendations.

It was not until April 2015 that OPM discovered the intrusion by the second attacker. The report concluded that the breach discovered in 2014 was likely carried out by a hacker organization called Axiom Group and that the breach discovered in 2015 was likely conducted by another hacker group called Deep Panda—both thought to be affiliated with the Chinese government. The source of the attack may indeed have come from these groups but it is worth pointing out that among the revelations noted by WikiLeaks in its Vault 7 release of documents in 2017 is that the USG (and presumably other governments) mask some of their own hacking by using computer code to disguise the origin of a given cyberattack. The Central Intelligence Agency's (CIA's) Marble software can forensically disguise viruses, trojans, and cyberattacks.[27] On that basis, if, for example, the Russian government operated in a similar manner, it could have made it appear that China was the culprit, although it may not actually have been. Only the perpetrator and the intelligence agencies know for certain.

The Report includes several other noteworthy findings, including that the OPM had access in the summer 2014 to a tool from cybersecurity firm Cylance that eventually played a key role in discovering the 2015 attack but it chose not to purchase the company's services until much later. The Report made 13 common sense recommendations, including calling for federal agencies to reduce reliance on Social Security numbers, improve cybersecurity acquisition practices, and increase pay to recruit higher caliber security personnel.

Members of Congress called on Congress to pass legislation (H.R. 451[28]) requiring agency Chief Information Officers (CIOs) to certify security for websites that handle highly sensitive personal information before making them public, pass bills (H.R. 4361[29], S. 2975[30]) that would ensure agency officials are not required to collectively bargain with unions in order to secure their networks, and that contract requirements for sharing information with private sector companies that handle sensitive data be strengthened.[31] *Astonishingly, while all of these resolutions were introduced in the US Congress, none of them was enacted.*

Following the OPM breach, and despite the failure of the US Congress to act on significant legislation in its wake, the Obama Administration did implement some important initiatives. Sixteen infrastructure sectors were subsequently deemed 'critical' by the USG as obvious targets for Virtual Terrorism and are now regulated under the US National Cybersecurity Framework (NCSF)—including financial services, telecommunications, and food production and distribution.

President Obama also issued an Executive Order entitled Improving Critical Infrastructure Cybersecurity (ICIC), intended to enhance the security and resilience of America's critical infrastructure by encouraging efficiency, innovation, and economic prosperity. The ICIC is an attempt to set industry standards and best practices to help organizations manage cybersecurity risks. Yet, in spite of companies' knowledge of the existence of this threat, only 17 percent of

600 IT security executives surveyed[32] from 13 countries, in 2014, (including the US, the United Kingdom, and Brazil) said their companies had achieved what they would regard as a 'mature' level of cybersecurity (i.e. actually had IT security programs in place to thwart an attack).

Both the NCSF and ICIC are intended to be guidelines rather than a mandate for corporate behavior—and herein lies a problem which is familiar to government attempts to address man-made risk more generally. As is the case with the COP21 (the Paris Climate Change Conference) guidelines, there is no law requiring compliance, nor any penalties for a failure to comply (although COP21 was hailed as a 'breakthrough' agreement, most people do not realize this). The same may be said about the fight against terrorism. How many governments and companies have implemented strict security protocols to protect themselves against terrorism without having experienced an attack?

Part of the issue here is that both governments and companies are reluctant to take measures that will slow their economies down or interfere with their ability to operate efficiently. Implementing sufficient IT countermeasures takes time, sucks up resources, and cuts into profit. Not factored into many organizations' thinking process on this subject is how to put a price on Virtual Terrorism or the inevitable loss of reputation that goes along with it when an attack becomes public (which can, of course, be significant). If corporate executes were thinking more along these lines, perhaps more companies would be taking the risk more seriously.

As the online world meets the physical world, the risk of Virtual Terrorism can only rise, and this applies not only to governments and companies but to individuals, as the use of "smart" devices, including phones, home alarm systems, televisions, appliances, and other electronics becomes more popular. All of these items can be hacked, implying that our homes can be accessed remotely, and our televisions and computers monitored remotely, not just by governments, but by hackers. Few consumers consider this 'darker' aspect of living the "smart" life.

One advantage individuals have is that they tend to upgrade their computers and other electronics (every 3-5 years)—more frequently than companies tend to upgrade theirs (which is every couple of decades in the case of control systems). On that basis, it is easy to see why control systems are targets of choice for virtual terrorists—their software is typically outdated and often light years behind current technology in relative terms. Surprisingly, some critical infrastructure systems are even using software that is more than a decade old.

The enormity of the challenge in determining the nature of the threat and monitoring vulnerability at the government level was summarized by a 2015 report[33] from the USG Accountability Office, which noted that *most federal agencies overseeing the security of America's critical infrastructure still lack formal methods for determining whether those essential networks are protected from hackers. Of the 15 critical infrastructure industries examined—including banking, finance energy and telecommunications—12 of them were overseen by agencies that did not have proper cybersecurity metrics.* These sector-specific agencies had not developed metrics to measure and report on the effectiveness of all of their cyber risk mitigation activities or their sectors' basic cybersecurity posture. If that is the case 16 years and after hundreds of billions of dollars have been spent to enhance security of all types following 9/11 in the US, the advantage clearly resides with those intent on implementing Virtual Terrorism.

The Cyberwarfare Ecosystem

One of the things virtual terrorists have in common (whether they be terrorists, spies, governments, businesses, individuals, or criminals) is that they rely on cyber-based technology to support their objectives. To a victim, a cyberthief may be indistinguishable from a cyberterrorist—whether that is a person, corporation, or government—because the victim may view anyone using Internet-based technology to do something illegal, disrupt the normal flow of operation, or otherwise cause harm as having the same net end effect. In setting the stage for the rest of the book, it is useful to broadly categorize these virtual terrorists:

- Cyberterrorists are state-sponsored and non-state actors who engage in cyberattacks to pursue their objectives. Transnational terrorist organizations, insurgents, and jihadists use the Internet as a tool for planning attacks, radicalization, and recruitment, a method of propaganda distribution, a means of communication, and for disruptive purposes.

- Cyberspies are individuals who steal classified or proprietary information used by governments or private organizations to gain a competitive, strategic, security, financial, or political advantage. These individuals often work at the behest of, and take direction from, foreign government entities.

- Cyberthieves are individuals or organizations that engage in illegal cyberattacks for monetary gain.

- Cyberwarriors are agents or quasi-agents of nation-states who develop capabilities and undertake cyberattacks in support of a country's strategic objectives. These entities may or may not be acting on behalf of a government with respect to target selection, timing of the attack, and type(s) of cyberattack, and are often blamed by the host country when accusations are levied by the nation that has been attacked.

- Cyberactivists are individuals who perform cyberattacks for pleasure, philosophical, political, or other nonmonetary reasons. Examples include someone who attacks a technology system as a personal challenge (a "classic" hacker) and a "hacktivist," such as a member of the cyber-group Anonymous, which undertakes an attack for political reasons.

The activities of these groups can range from nuisance-related denial of service attacks and website defacement to disrupting government and private corporation business processes. The threats posed by these cyber-aggressors and the types of attacks they can pursue are not mutually exclusive. For example, a hacker targeting the intellectual property of a corporation may be categorized as both a cyberthief and a cyberspy. A cyberterrorist and cyberwarrior may be employing different technological capabilities in support of a nation's security and political objectives.

The concept of attribution in the cyber world entails an attempt to identify, with some degree of specificity and confidence, the geographic location, identity, capabilities, and intention of the cyber-aggressor. Mobile technologies and sophisticated data routing processes and techniques often make attribution difficult for intelligence and law enforcement agencies. There are no clear criteria for determining whether a cyberattack is criminal, an act of hactivism, terrorism, or a nation-state's use of force equivalent to an armed attack. Likewise, no international, legally binding instruments have yet been drafted explicitly to regulate inter-state relations in cyberspace[34] (this will also be addressed in subsequent chapters).

Consistent with the notion that virtual terrorists are, to borrow Winston Churchill's famous phrase (originally used to describe Russia), "a riddle wrapped in a mystery inside an enigma"[35], Virtual Terrorism, and the tools to combat it, are, and will remain, enigmatic, and in an embryonic stage, for many years to come. Using the amoeba analogy noted earlier, the phenomenon is in a constant state of evolution. This poses an incredible challenge to those fighting Virtual Terrorism, for, as soon as new technology and intelligence is deployed to reduce its impact, new adaptations of Virtual Terrorism will be generated that defy them. There can be no denying that Virtual Terrorism has become, and will remain, a permanent element of life in the 21st century and beyond. Better understanding it is half the battle to getting out in front of it.

2. The Dark Web and Remote Control

In January 2017, guests were locked out of their rooms at the picturesque Alpine hotel, Romantik Seehotel Jaegerwirt, in Austria, because the electronic key system at the hotel had been infiltrated. The hotel was locked out of its own computer system, leaving guests stranded in the lobby, prompting confusion and panic. An e-mail ransom demand to the hotel's manager required two Bitcoins (approximately $1,800 at the time) and warned that the cost would double if the hotel did not comply with the demand by the end of the day. The e-mail included details of a "Bitcoin wallet", the account in which to deposit the money. As the reservation system for the hotel in the village of Turracherhöhe was 90 minutes away by car, the hotel decided to pay the ransom. To guard against future attacks, the hotel considered replacing its electronic keys with old-fashioned door locks and keys.[36]

Data—The World's Most Valuable Resource

A century ago, a new, hot commodity—oil—spawned a lucrative, fast-growing industry, prompting antitrust regulators to step in to restrain those who control its flow. Similar concerns are today being raised by the giants that deal in data, the oil of the Digital Era. These titans—Alphabet, Amazon, Apple, Facebook and Microsoft—appear unstoppable. They are the five most valuable listed firms in the world and their profits are surging, having collectively racked up more than $25 billion in net profit in the first *quarter* of 2017. Amazon captured half of all dollars spent online in America; Google and Facebook accounted for almost all the revenue growth in digital advertising in the US in 2016.

These Internet companies' control of data gives them enormous power. Old ways of thinking about competition, devised in the era of oil, look outdated in what has come to be called the "data economy". Smartphones and the Internet have made data abundant, ubiquitous, and far more valuable. Today, virtually every activity creates a digital trace—more raw material for the 'data distilleries'. Artificial Intelligence (AI) techniques such as machine learning extract even more value from data. Algorithms can predict when a customer is ready to buy, a jet engine needs servicing, or a person is at risk of a disease. Industrial giants such as GE and Siemens are undergoing a digital transformation process and already sell themselves as "data" firms. By collecting more data, a firm has more scope to improve its products, which attracts more users, generating even more data. Vast pools of data can thus act as protective moats.

These Internet giants' surveillance systems span the entire economy. Google can see what people search for, Facebook what they share, and Amazon what they buy. They own app stores and operating systems and rent out computing power to startups. They have a "God's eye view" of activities in their own markets and beyond. They can see when a new product or service gains traction, allowing them to copy it or simply buy the upstart before it becomes too great a threat. By providing barriers to entry and early-warning systems, data can therefore stifle competition.

There needs to be more transparency about data collection and its uses. In 2017, the sensitive personal details of almost 200 million US citizens were accidentally exposed by a marketing firm contracted by the Republican National Committee. The 1.1 terabytes of data included birthdates, home addresses, telephone numbers, and political views of nearly 62 percent of the entire US population. Although the data was available on a publicly accessible Amazon cloud server, anyone with a link to it had access to the data. The information was stored in spreadsheets uploaded to a server owned by Deep Root Analytics, which had been updated in January 2017 when President Donald Trump was inaugurated and had been online for an unknown period of time.

Apart from personal details, the data also contained citizens' suspected religious affiliations, ethnicities, and political biases, such as where they stood on controversial topics ranging from gun control to abortion and stem cell research. It was the largest breach of electoral data in US history and raised fears that leaked data could easily be used for nefarious purposes, from identity fraud to harassment of people under protection orders, to intimidation of people who hold an opposing political view.[37]

In the future, companies could be forced to reveal to consumers what information they hold and how much money they make from it. Governments could encourage the emergence of new services by opening up more of their own data vaults, or by managing crucial parts of the data economy as it would public infrastructure, as India already does with its digital-identity system (Aadhaar). They could also mandate the sharing of certain kinds of data, with users' consent— an approach Europe is taking in financial services by requiring banks to make customers' data accessible to third parties. Data collection and storage entails new risks, vis-à-vis anti-trust legislation, privacy, and the risk of cyberattacks.[38]

The era of Big Data meshes nicely with the Era of Virtual Terrorism, creating a target-rich environment, and raising fundamental questions about the potential value of data. It also raises questions about a subject never before considered necessary to address, such as who controls the Internet and whether any laws that can be implemented to attempt to control the flow of data are worth the paper they are printed on, since they are very likely not enforceable, given the borderless and anonymous world of cyberspace.

<u>Who Controls the Internet</u>?

In 2013, the Obama administration announced plans to relinquish USG control over the Internet. Pressure to release the final vestiges of authority the US maintained over the system of Web addresses and domain names that organize the Internet had been building for more than a decade but revelations of US National Security Agency (NSA) surveillance by Edward Snowden that year had made the move appear necessary. The relationship between the US and the Internet Corporation for Assigned Names and Numbers (ICANN) had drawn wider international criticism, also, because big American companies such as Google, Facebook, and Microsoft play such a central role in the Internet's global functioning. Ceding US oversight ended a conflict between the US Department of Commerce (DOC) and the ICANN that had been in place since 1998.

Some proponents called the move consistent with other efforts the US had been making to promote a free and open Internet and advance the notion of a multi-stakeholder model of global Internet governance. Business groups and some others had long complained that the ICANN's decision-making was dominated by the interests of the industry that sells domain names and whose fees provided the vast majority of the ICANN's revenue. The USG contract was a modest check against such abuses.

Opponents wondered what would happen if control of the Internet got into the wrong hands, since the USG's oversight position enabled it to spy on the rest of the world. Any other power that had similar control would undoubtedly desire to do something similar. Critics of the move called the decision hasty and politically tinged and voiced significant doubts about the fitness of the ICANN to operate without US oversight and beyond the bounds of US law. Some wondered whether the ICANN could be accountable to the whole world —the equivalent of being accountable to no one.[39]

The truth is that, when the ICANN was founded in 1998, it had intended to become independent by 2000, but the Internet simply became too important for the US to let go. Being shielded by the US, the ICANN resisted attempts by the United Nations' International Telecommunication Union (ITU) —a governing body in charge of telecommunications—to take over its job. The Internet Assigned Names Authority (IANA, the part of ICANN that addresses country codes, Internet numbers, and protocols) continued to be part of the ICANN, even as other countries were certain the US had to be abusing its power behind the scenes. As the millions of dollars of business transacted over the Internet became trillions, and billions of people began using the Internet, more people, businesses, and governments objected to the USG having *de jure* control over a large chunk of the Internet, particularly given that this oversight was done via a procurement contract.

Under pressure from the EU and others, the ICANN and the USG took small steps toward their eventual breakup. They would probably have muddled along together for another decade if it has not been for the outrage sparked by the Snowden revelations.[40] Only months after the first Snowden disclosures confirmed long-suspected global Internet surveillance by the US, technical organizations around the world issued the Montevideo Statement, reinforcing the importance of globally coherent Internet operations, warning against Internet fragmentation at a national level, identifying the need for ongoing efforts to address Internet governance challenges, and agreeing to catalyze community-wide efforts toward the evolution of global multi-stakeholder Internet cooperation. They called for accelerating the globalization of ICANN and IANA functions—towards an environment in which all stakeholders, including all governments, participate on an equal footing. [41]

In October 2016, the US formally ceded its role as overseer of the ICANN. By allowing the IANA contract to expire, and by relinquishing its oversight authority, the USG essentially gave other countries direct influence over what is included in the root zone—a standardized file previously hosted by the US that serves as the first step in the process of finding any particular website. Countries such as China and Russia already censor the Internet domestically but the expiration of the IANA contract has made it easier for these and other governments to vote in the ICANN to limit global access to certain sites by removing them from the root zone through the ICANN.

Internet freedom advocates remain concerned that standard operating procedure in countries such as China and Russia will become the new global norm. Removing sites from root zones is one problem; the inability to add something new is another. The new structure could enable oppressive regimes to take control of the global Internet and restrict access outside their borders—for individuals and organizations that use the Internet legally—implying that *there is an incentive for those who do not use it legally to flourish.*

Another risk with the new ICANN structure is that, as is the case in multilateral organizations such as the UN, countries may be inclined to 'horse trade' their votes and throw their support behind Russia or China (for example) in return for those nations' support in another issues of interest. In this way, the new structure could enable oppressive regimes to take control of the global Internet and restrict access outside their borders.

The expired contract does not permit the US to exercise any control over the Internet; rather, it allows the NTIA to ensure that ICANN continues to manage domain names in a manner consistent with free speech and the First Amendment of the US Constitution. The US DOC should be given more credit for the fact that it never attempted to prevent any domain names from being added to the root zone. The US effectively maintained its minimal oversight role from 1998 and never hampered a "global consensus" or undermined the global Internet community. What it did was prevent malicious actors from exerting oppressive influence over the world's use of the Internet. That could well now change.[42]

Cybersecurity versus Cybergovernance

As noted previously, governments do much of the lurking, probing, and stealing of information without our knowledge. Russia is clearly prominent among the dark private marketplaces and China has been one of the most prominent government actors. As any Chinese citizen or visitor to China knows well, the Chinese government's attempted control of the Internet within China is legendary. Knowledgeable people inside China believe that the Chinese government has ambitions to govern the Internet on a global scale.

In March 2016, China founded its first national nonprofit organization for cybersecurity, the Cybersecurity Association of China (CSAC). Led by Fang Binxing, who helped build the Chinese Communist Party's (CCP) system for censoring the Internet, the Great Firewall, the CSAC had 275 founding member organizations, including major Internet firms, cybersecurity companies, scientific research institutions, the National University of Defense Technology, Alibaba, Baidu, and many others. The organization's declared goal is to organize and mobilize forces in all aspects of society to participate in building China's cybersecurity.

This ties back to a push that was brought to the surface in November 2014, when the CCP hosted its first World Internet

Conference, which had the slogan, "An Interconnected World Shared and Governed by All". At the time, the US had already announced its plans to relinquish federal control over the Internet through the ICANN. The Great Firewall's secretary-general is Li Yuxiao, a research fellow at the Chinese Academy of Cyberspace and a major proponent of Chinese governance of the global Internet. Li has publicly questioned who will take the baton from the US and how the Internet will be run in the future. He sees China as transitioning from merely being a participant in the Internet to playing a dominant role in it. He believes China has a right, as the country with the most netizens, to make the international rules of cyberspace governance.

The CSAP carries the same overall message. The Association is not so much about *cybersecurity* it is about *cybergovernance* and about extending law to the Internet (and if Li has his way, specifically, the laws of China). The CCP would like to impose its approach to 'cybergovernance' globally, with its model of strict government control over all facets of the Internet, including all companies involved in the Internet. For the CCP, the word "cybercrime" refers to more than just hackers; it is also about an ongoing crackdown on online rumors, pornography, gambling, and other "crimes", which tend to be a major focus of the CCP's systems for Internet control—which include suppression of free speech, religion, and the promotion of democracy in China. The 2016 assessment of global Internet freedom from Freedom House[43] ranked China dead last, behind even Iran and Syria.

The Council on Foreign Relations reported in 2015[44] that the CCP would likely do more to gain influence over the UN's ITU and is trying to gain more power over the global Internet. As two of the permanent members of the UN Security Council, China and Russia have pushed major programs in the past designed to direct the ITU's role in global Internet governance in their favor. Some of the authoritarian programs proposed for global Internet governance through the ITU were outlined by the Center for Democracy and Technology while the ITU was holding its meeting on rules for the Internet in November 2012. These included programs to decrypt information passing through the Internet.[45] The CSAC appears to be a continuation of these efforts but using the term "cybersecurity" to give Chinese ambitions a more benign appearance.[46]

The New Internet

At the dawn of the Internet age in 1992, global Internet traffic was approximately 100 gigabytes (GB) of information per *day*. By 2002, it was approximately 100 GB per *second*. By 2013, it was approximately 29,000 GB per second. And by 2018, it is predicted to be 50,000 GB per second. As a result of this astonishing growth in the generation and flow of data, 90 percent of all the data that has ever been created was generated in just two years (2014 and 2015). As of 2015, the world produced 2.5 quintillion bytes of data per *day* (that is 1,000 raised to the power of six, or 10^{18}).[47]

As a result of the sheer volume of raw data, we actually only 'see' about 4 percent of the Internet. The 'next' Internet, currently being built by the Pentagon's research and development branch, intends to view the Internet in its entirety. A program called Memex is being developed by the US Defense Advanced Research Project Agency (DARPA) (with the help of 18 partners, including the US National Aeronautics and Space Administration's (NASA's) Jet Propulsion Laboratory) and is being designed with new search functions that will change how we use the Internet.

First created in 2014, Memex seeks to do with raw data what social media did to online chat rooms—connecting everything, making relationships more visible, and making it easier for users to find whatever it is they are looking for. DARPA's key interest in Memex, at least initially, is to help map the 'Dark Web'—the Internet beneath the Internet—that exists on peer-to-peer networks. Memex is already being actively used for law enforcement, focused initially on finding bad people doing bad things on the Dark Web. The Dark Web is home to a great many things in addition to terrorism, such as human trafficking, drugs, firearms, pedophilia, hitmen, and hackers.[48]

The goal of Memex is to invent better methods for interacting with and sharing information, so users can quickly and thoroughly organize and search subsets of information relevant to their individual interests. The technologies developed in the program should provide the mechanisms for improved content discovery, information extraction and retrieval, user collaboration, and other key search functions. Among the envisioned benefits of the program are:

- Development of next-generation search technologies to revolutionize the discovery, organization, and presentation of domain-specific content;

- Creation of a new domain-specific search paradigm to discover relevant content and organize it in ways that are more immediately useful to specific tasks;

- Extension of current search capabilities to the deep web and non-traditional content; and

- Improved interfaces for military, government and commercial enterprises to find and organize publicly available information on the Internet.[49]

Memex is of particular interest to governments and law enforcement since networks are not indexed by traditional search engines. Memex may be able to change the nature of the Dark Web. *It is designed to do two key things: examine pixels to try to determine what small things mean and search metadata—the information behind all images and videos that already exist but is invisible to current search engines.* Metadata is particularly important because it is associated with images and videos and enables connections to be drawn between them and individuals.

Law enforcement will, therefore, soon be able to tell if a picture or video was taken with the same device and to see other content that was created by the same individual. *It should also allow for connections to be made between drugs and the people selling them and images of abducted people and the people who took the pictures.* Some social networking sites already scrub metadata for such things as image location (those tend not to be the sites that terrorists use) and other sites that lawbreakers use.

Some parts of Memex are open source (publicly available and without licensing fees) and are already being used by some major private sector Internet organizations. Apache Web (whose servers power nearly 53 percent of the Internet) is already using it, as is another core Internet technology (Drupal), and Google. Internet users will undoubtedly already have noticed improved search results, with more meaningful information, particularly for multimedia content. The main problem with current search engines is that they tend to use a centralized, one-size-fits-all approach that searches the Internet with the same set of tools for all queries. The current model remains a heavily manual process that does not save sessions, requires nearly exact input with one-at-a-time entry, and does not organize or aggregate results beyond a list of links. While that model has been successful commercially, it does not yet work as well for many government uses. That is what Memex aims to change.[50]

Underground Markets

Governments have a huge task on their hands in attempting to control or remove underground markets for virtual data which have existed since the dawn of the Internet era in the 1990s, when Internet Relay Chats (IRCs) were first created. IRCs facilitate text communication, with the chat process functioning on a client/server networking model and computer programs that a user can install on his or her own system. These 'clients' communicate with chat servers to transfer messages to other clients. IRCs are mainly designed for group communication in discussion forums but also allow one-on-one communication via private message, as well as chat and data transfer, including file sharing.[51]

The appearance of cryptocurrencies and anonymous communications like Bitcoin and Tor have allowed these markets to develop far past their genesis. Dark Web forums (the encrypted network that exists between specific servers and their clients) are a very efficient platform through which to conduct illegal business. Some forums are accessible only via the Tor network while others are only accessible via traditional web browsing. These forums offer a plethora of real world and digital items, ranging from illicit drug sales, counterfeit items (such as passports, driver licenses, and bank notes), and weapons, to services such as carding (credit card fraud), personal identifiable information (PII) fraud, zero-day exploits, botnet services, and bulletproof hosting.

Gaining access to some of these forums can be difficult, with those using more extreme vetting tending to have a higher caliber of malicious activity. A user may need to compromise and deface a web site of the forum's choice to gain a full profile, or create a new variant of ransomware (which is suspected to be a primary cause of some recent outbreaks of ransomware). Due to the illicit nature of the content and services offered, it is not uncommon for a site to be populated with decoy users from both criminals and law enforcement personnel.

Not surprisingly, the virtual underground has developed its own jargon and slang. Among the most commonly used are:

- Black Hat SEO: The use of aggressive search engine optimization (SEO) strategies and techniques focusing only on search engines (not a human audience), which usually do not obey search engines guidelines.

- Crypters: Tools that encrypt malware in order to bypass detection by antivirus software.

- Binders: Tools used to "trojanize" a legitimate program with a malware sample.

- FUD: "Fear, Uncertainty, and Doubt" in the normal security world means "Fully UnDetectable" in the virtual world.

- Rippers: Actors in forums identified as scamming other users without delivering useful services or contraband.

- Zero-Day exploits: Techniques that exploit previously unpatched vulnerabilities (used by attackers to gain unauthorized access to computing systems).

Regular users of the Dark Web interact with one another much as gangs do, with their own accepted methods of communication, protocols, and gossip. They know which sites are preferred for which purposes, the hottest new trend, who to stay away from, and which actors they want to be like. Like any other service providers, they vary significantly in quality and desirability. Examples of virtual forums offering a range of illegal services include:

- Sky-Fraud: A Russian underground forum that has been in operation since 2014. Its user base consists of approximately 26,000 active users in Russian and English. It is free for users but easy for scammers, non-reputable members, law enforcement, and security researchers to access. Among the services it offers are bulletproof hosting services, PII, credit card data, botnets, exploits, malware, Black Hat SEO, and even web design. Sky-Fraud accepts payment through PayPal, Webmoney, and Entropay. Data found on this forum is believed to be of low fidelity, given the number of amateur hackers that operate on the site.

- Lampeduza Underground Marketplace: Lempeduza is a Russian forum first referenced in 2013, when one of the forum members ('rescator') was involved in the sale and distribution of breach-related data of a large retailer. Lampeduza also appears to be strongly related with the notorious carding forum 'rescator[.]cm', where credit card data related to the massive series of 2013 retailer breaches was offered for sale. Access to the site costs just US $50 and among the services it offers are carding (trafficking of credit card, bank account, and other personal information), data dump services, credit card fraud, hacking, anonymization practices, spam, and Black Hat SEO. Data offered on Lampeduza is believed to be of moderate value as the site challenges prospective buyers in an attempt to determine which vendors are credible. Users can voice complaints and action can be taken against a vendor (common among many of the anonymous marketplaces).

- Exploit.in: A Russian language based hacking forum, in operation since 2007, with approximately 35,000 users. Some areas of the site that discuss noncriminal activities are accessible to the public (including discussions on web-design, programming, and hardware), while topics such as security, hacking, virology, and anonymity require a valid user account. Exploit.in is free of charge but first-time users must be vouched for by an existing member who can communicate in the forum's Russian Internet slang. Due to a closed registration process, this forum is less polluted with fake accounts than some others. Among its service offerings are carding services, bulletproof hosting, malware distribution services, zero-day software vulnerabilities, and malware. Much of the value derived from this marketplace is based on the relationships between highly connected users, many of whom have multiple profiles on other forums. Successful vendors appear to have strong relationships with one another in other forums or venues, allowing each of them to vouch for one another.

- LeakForums Marketplace: This platform began in 2011 and has approximately one million users. The Marketplace is an initial source of many leaks and is known as an easy platform for obtaining copies of well-known malware such as ORCA or Adwind. LeakForums specializes in leaks related to PII, social media accounts, and the trade of paid hacker tools. The forum is free of charge and has no vetting. Its service offerings include malware (which is free for registered users), serial keys for commercial programs (including Microsoft Windows, Microsoft Office, and antivirus engines), stolen credentials, hacked databases, and well-known trojan programs. The quality of the data found here is low and the quality of the forum itself is debatable, due in part to a high number of amateur criminals attempting to increase their profile but selling very low-quality tools. This site also lacks the reputation system that the more mature markets such as AlphaBay and TheRealDeal have, which makes it harder for a potential buyer to trust in the vendor.

- HackForums: One of the longest running hacking forums of the Internet, notorious for housing a large number of amateur hackers. Founded in 2006, it has approximately 600,000 users. The forum addresses hacking, programming, computer games, web design, and web development, as well as the sale of hacking tools and services. It is free of charge, without vetting, and prone to a high number of fake profiles, amateur criminals, scammers, and law enforcement personnel. Among its service offerings are stresser services (i.e. DDoS), RAT (Remote Access Tools), stolen social media accounts, crypters, VPS (Virtual Private Servers), VPN (Virtual Private Networks), and hosting services. The quality of the data found here is very low due to the absence of a reputation system or initial vetting of users.

- AlphaBay: This marketplace grew quickly after its start in 2014 until it was shut down in 2017 (along with the Hansa Market—a small victory for the good guys). AlphaBay had approximately 240,000 clients (who constituted a considerable number of suspected security researchers and non-reputable users), an estimated 40,000 vendors, 250,000 listings, and in excess of $1 billion per year in revenue (which is presumably why it was targeted by the US Department of Justice (DOJ)). AlphaBay was free of charge and its services included dumps (databases containing credit card data), bank drops, Card Verification Value numbers, credit card data, illicit drugs, weapons, counterfeit items (such bank notes, passports, and driver's licenses), malicious software, and even courses on how to make money through illicit activities. Some of that site's data came from compromised e-commerce sites and point of sale terminals. AlphaBay ensured that transactions were secure and seamless by offering the "multisig" transaction method and two-factor authentication process to access the marketplace. AlphaBay also offered digital contracts (a system that utilizes the user reputation system to decrease the risk in transactions).

As is the case with other types of marketplaces, underground markets provide a variety of services designed to cater to their target market—in this case, all types of criminals. Underground economies operate with anyone who has access to a web browser and Tor. Most of the known market places are of questionable value but some 'reputable' criminals operate within them. The most useful markets are discriminating, exclusive, and hard to access, but the open markets offer real insight into how the underground world operates. It is difficult to come to any conclusion other than that they operate at will and with impunity.[52]

A Wall of Anonymity

In August 2016, a hacking group calling itself the Shadow Brokers announced an online auction for what it claimed were cyberweapons produced by the NSA. Based on never previously published documents provided by Edward Snowden, the arsenal of information contained what were believed to be authentic NSA software used to covertly infect computers around the world. The evidence that tied the Shadow Brokers dump to the NSA came in an agency manual for implanting malware, classified top secret, provided by Snowden, and not previously available to the public.

The draft manual instructed NSA operators to track their use of one malware program using a specific 16-character string, which appeared throughout the leak in code associated with the program SECONDDATE. SECONDDATE plays a specialized role inside a complex global system built by the USG to infect and monitor what is believed to be millions of computers around the world. Its release, alongside dozens of other tools, marked the first time any full copies of the NSA's offensive software had been made available to the public, providing a glimpse at how an elaborate spying system looks when deployed.

SECONDDATE intercepts web requests and redirects browsers on target computers to an NSA web server, which is, in turn, designed to infect them with malware. SECONDDATE helps the NSA portray itself as a "man-in-the-middle" (MITM) against users on a wireless network, tricking them into thinking they are talking to a safe website when in reality they have been sent a malicious payload from an NSA server. The tool focuses on the greatest vulnerability to your computer—the web browser.

Executed correctly, the target continues normal webpage browsing, completely unaware, lands on a malware-filled NSA server and becomes infected with as much of that malware as possible. SECONDDATE is just one method that the NSA uses to get its target's browser pointed at other servers. Other methods include sending spam that attempts to exploit bugs in popular web-based e-mail providers or entices targets to click on malicious links that lead to other servers. The NSA often lurks on systems that are supposed to be controlled by others.[53]

The danger of such tools is that they can be used to target anyone who is using a vulnerable router, the equivalent of leaving lock picking tools lying around a high school cafeteria. The person or persons who stole the information can use them and, once they are released, so can anyone else. In April 2017, the Shadow Brokers released another cache of extremely potent and previously unknown software capable of breaking into systems running Windows. The software could give nearly anyone with sufficient technical knowledge the ability to wreak havoc on millions of Microsoft users.

The leak included a litany of typically codenamed software "implants" capable of breaking into—and in some cases seizing control of—computers running versions of the Windows operating system earlier than Windows 10. The crown jewel of the implant collection was a program named FUZZBUNCH, which automated the deployment of NSA malware and would allow a member of the agency's Tailored Access Operations group (discussed later) to more easily infect a target from their desk. As a result of the breach, nation-state attack tools became available to anyone who cared to download them—in essence, becoming a cyberweapon for hacking into computers.[54]

Upon first becoming visible in 2016, posts from the Shadow Brokers raised broad speculation that the Russian government was the source. One cyber investigation firm believed that, rather than being the work of secretive government agents or a sophisticated cybercrime syndicate, the Shadow Brokers was a single hacker in Russia whose poor choice of an alias led to his unmasking. A private intelligence company was able to trace the origins of this 'group' to an account on VK (a popular European social network) belonging to a man in Kurgan, Russia. Once discovered, the Shadow Brokers account then went quiet and the account belonging to the Russian national believed to be behind it was subsequently deleted.

One theory at the time was that this individual did not hack the data at all; rather, the files were sold to him by NSA contractor Harold T. Martin III, who was arrested that same month, apparently having stolen tools matching the description of what the Shadow Brokers was selling. The private sector operative who was investigating the Shadow Brokers analyzed connections between its name and other linked accounts, including the image it used on Twitter of a multi-eyed creature from the video game "Mass Effect". The fictional creature was part of a group called the "Shadow Brokers" and worked as a "Galactic Information Broker".

The operative contacted other online accounts using similar names and images and tried to elicit a response akin to the official account of the Shadow Brokers. Eventually, the operative found another Twitter account that had actively promoted the auction and appeared connected to an account on the VK social network that used the same imagery and broken English. The VK account belonged to a young man whose first name is Kirill, a high school graduate from Kurgan who ran a video game marketplace. After locating the account, the operative then went back to the main account of the Shadow Brokers and tweeted a simple "Hi Kirill". Almost immediately after the tweet, the person on the social network deleted his personal VK account and his profile picture. By October, bids for the information had only totaled 1.76 Bitcoins (approximately $1,100 at the time).[55]

Subsequent attacks claimed to have been undertaken by the Shadow Brokers raised additional questions about whether the group was Kirill, a cybercrime syndicate, or a government. The group's identity remains a mystery. This case demonstrates how Virtual Terrorism can, and often does, originate in the deepest, darkest corners of the Internet—literally in an individual's bedroom or garage—and how one person can come into contact with dark forces that can enable him or her to punch well above his or her weight to become an information, arms, or drug dealer.

The case also illustrates how someone who is clever and armed with the right skills, imagination, and tools can identify and do "business" with others who occupy those crevices of the Internet. The example is also noteworthy because of the openness with which Kirill brazenly attempted to sell such a highly secretive and valuable commodity. The unfortunate reality is that this type of action is not uncommon in the virtual world.

In April 2017, the Shadow Brokers reappeared and leaked data highlighting some of the NSA's most potent hacking tools, targeting most versions of Microsoft Windows, with evidence of sophisticated hacks on the Society for Worldwide Interbank Financial Telecommunication (SWIFT) banking system in several banks around the world. The data dump also contained code for hacking into banks, particularly in the Middle East. EastNets, the largest SWIFT service bureau in the Middle East, provides anti-money laundering (AML) oversight and related services for SWIFT transactions in the region. Apart from data concerning specific servers, the archive also included reusable tools to extract information from Oracle databases, such as a list of database users and SWIFT message queries. The objective appears to have been to gain insight into the AML activities of regional banks and their potential ties to terrorists. None of the implants were apparently detected by antivirus programs, with the ability to remain invisible being central to the success of any such software.[56]

Remote Control

Virtual attacks by remote control (that is, from a distance and using an electronic device) can be unleashed by anyone, at any time, for any reason, and can be swift or painfully slow. A person, organization, or government may never know it has been targeted, or may be made to know immediately, so as to maximize fear and impact. In 2016, one of the most powerful known cyberweapons was posted online for anyone to use. Strong enough to take down portions of the Internet for specific countries, the malware known as "Mirai" was strong enough to challenge Internet Service Provider (ISP) systems that were otherwise capable of processing hundreds of gigabytes of data per second. The malware was significant because it meant that cybercriminals and nation-states had access to a tool capable of taking nearly any system offline and it drove home concerns cybersecurity experts had warned about for years—that connecting so many objects in our lives to the Internet, with so little attention to security, would eventually come back to haunt us.

The malware pulled its strength from an army of hacked "Internet of Things" (IoT) devices and included everything from Internet-connected cameras and digital video recorders to Internet routers, baby monitors, children's toys, home alarm systems, refrigerators, and even smart bras. The infected devices were then used to build "botnets" which could then be utilized to launch attacks. The release of the Mirai tool meant that a home refrigerator could be used to attack a major network without the owner's knowledge. In the rush to release products into the marketplace, many manufacturers bypass security protocols that would either add cost to a product or make it less competitive because its security may be less robust than that of competitors. Most consumers have no idea that these 'smart' products have vulnerabilities, can be hacked, or even put their own homes at risk.

The drama leading up to the discovery of Mirai began when a cybersecurity blog was hit by an extremely large and unusual form of cyberattack known as a distributed denial-of-service (DDoS) attack. DDoS attacks are common methods used by hackers and can take websites offline by overloading them with fake traffic. This attack was unique because the website was bombarded with 620 gigabytes per second of fake data, making it one of the most powerful DDoS attacks ever recorded. The security service that temporarily protected the website said it was nearly twice as powerful as the previous record attack, experienced earlier in the year, at 363 gigabytes per second. The release of Mirai guaranteed that the Internet would be flooded with attacks from many new types of botnets.

Mirai spread by continuously scanning the Internet for IoT systems that still had their factory default protections or default usernames and passwords (common in IoT devices). This differed from existing botnets which often used networks of infected computers. To bring computers into a botnet, cybercriminals typically seek to infect them by tricking people into clicking infected links that will then install a form of malware. Running a scanning tool, a cybersecurity professional was able, in a short period of time, to identify and locate, across the world, 32,000 digital video recorders that could be compromised. With the advent of Mirai, the world's collection of 'smart' devices could theoretically be infected or seized by literally anyone with the technical knowledge to use the cyberweapon to "reset" the botnet.[57]

The Internet can also be used against itself. A cyberattack that took down large swaths of the Internet around the world in October 2016 was carried out, in part, by unsuspecting devices connected to the Internet. Digital video recorders and webcams in homes were taken over by malware and then, without the owners' knowledge, used to help execute the massive cyberattack. Hundreds of thousands of devices appear to have been infected with the malware (a DDoS attack). Hackers were able to flood a website with so much traffic that it impaired normal service, overwhelming the servers of New Hampshire-based Dyn, one of the Internet's middlemen that helps provide connection to sought after sites.

The attack interrupted connection to a variety of popular websites, such as Twitter, Netflix, and Spotify, in some parts of Europe and the US. The methods used in the attack were similar to others aimed at Internet service providers, such as France's OVH. Following one such attack, the source code used to carry out the strike was released online, enabling other hackers to use the same malware to carry out their own attacks.[58]

The Internet is also used by organizations employing "virtual plotters" and "cyber planners" in frequent contact with the individuals who will carry out terror plots. This is distinct from "lone wolves" who may have been inspired by organizations but are not actually guided by them. Some remote-controlled terrorists are trained and guided by organizations that micromanage the entire process.

A good example is Mohammed Ibrahim Yazdani, a young Indian engineer who was groomed by IS to carry out its first strike on Indian soil. When IS identified him as a recruit willing to carry out an attack in one of India's major technology hubs, it arranged everything, down to the bullets he needed to kill victims. For 17 months, terrorist operatives guided him through every step of the planned attack, including providing the weapons needed to do so. The organization's only identifiable connection to the would-be attacker was the Internet.

The operatives conceiving and guiding such attacks do so from behind a wall of anonymity. When the Hyderabad plotters were arrested in 2016, they could not so much as confirm the nationalities of their interlocutors in the IS, let alone describe what they looked like. The recruits are instructed to use encrypted messaging applications so that the guiding role played by the group remained obscured. As a result, many remotely guided plots in Europe, Asia, and the US in recent years were initially labeled the work of lone wolves, with no distinct or verifiable operational ties to the IS.[59] Only after forensic investigations have definitive links been established. *Anyone can claim responsibility for an act of terrorism but, in the world of Virtual Terrorism, such a claim does not necessarily mean anything.*

Another distinguishing characteristic of Virtual Terrorism is its unpredictability—literally anything and anyone can become a target or a victim via remote control. Examples of large and small-scale acts of remote control terror have become so frequent and commonplace that it is difficult to keep track of them and we are quickly becoming desensitized to these random acts of terror because of their commonality. That is, when we become aware of them. Many such attacks go undetected for months or even years.

Healthcare

In some industries, attacks have reached epidemic proportion. None is better exemplified than those in the healthcare industry. Hackers breached hospital computers at the Hollywood (California) Presbyterian Medical Center in February, 2016, rendering them unusable, and then demanded payment to unlock the computers. Believing it had no choice, since normal operations needed to be restored as quickly as possible, hospital administrators agreed to pay almost US $17,000 ransom in Bitcoin.

At the time, experts believed it was just a taste of what will ultimately become a ransomware epidemic, even though many such attacks undoubtedly go unreported, for fear of damage to an organization's reputation and future income stream. An investigation by The Institute for Critical Infrastructure Technology (a nonpartisan organization working with the private sector, federal agencies, and legislative community on threats to critical infrastructure) found that malware had been installed in hospitals throughout the US. One security firm ran a test with more than 40 hospitals, setting up fake networks in place of their actual networks to determine whether hackers would try to breach them. They did.[60]

Cyberattacks have become a significant problem for the healthcare industry, leading to an influx of attacks against hospital networks that have successfully penetrated security defenses and compromised medical devices, which are often vulnerable to attackers. Hackers have evolved and are now increasingly targeting medical devices that use legacy operating systems that contain known vulnerabilities. By camouflaging dated malware with current versions, attackers are able to successfully bypass traditional security mechanisms to gain entry into hospital networks, and ultimately, to access sensitive data.

Healthcare is now the most frequently attacked industry, even more so than financial services and retailers. Persistent medical device attacks targeting hospital networks have gone completely undetected for months. Sophisticated attackers are highly motivated to target healthcare institutions to gain access to valuable patient records that can net a lot of money on the black market. The attacks typically target medical devices deployed within hospital computer networks that contain a multitude of backdoors and botnet connections, providing remote access for attackers to enter.[61]

On May 12, 2017, as part of the largest global ransomware attack ever experienced, hospitals across the UK were hit by a large-scale cyberattack; 39 hospital trusts as well as health practices and dental services in the National Health System (NHS) were targeted across England and Scotland by spreading a virus through internal computer systems. Targets were sent an encrypted, compressed e-mail file that, once loaded, allowed the ransomware to infiltrate. Some doctors could not access patient files. Some emergency care patients had to be diverted to other facilities. Doctors throughout the country received ransom messages demanding money.

The malware 'Wanna Decryptor' ("WannaCry") was identified as the likely cause of the problem, part of the stolen trove of NSA data released by the Shadow Brokers. It is presumed that patient data had been accessed, though it was difficult to confirm. Entire hospitals had to be shut down as a result of an inability to operate essential systems. Some hospital administrators made the decision to shut down operations in an attempt to preserve any uninfected machines and systems. Phone calls could not be accepted nor prescriptions dispensed. A Bitcoin pop-up message appeared on some network screens, stating that important files had been encrypted and demanding that users pay $300 to be able to access their computers.[62]

The malware typically propagated by attackers is not detected by healthcare industry endpoint security software. Some of the malware used specifically targets older versions of Windows software. Since newer versions of Windows are not vulnerable, workstations with more recent software eliminates the need for endpoint security software to be activated, but not doing so also ensures that the worm goes undetected while it continues to search for older Windows systems. Since most medical devices do not have additional endpoint security software, the attack goes undetected. In order to ensure success, the attackers intentionally repackage and embed new, highly sophisticated tools and camouflage them. Once the attackers are inside a network, a variety of medical devices become easy targets. Attackers are intentionally moving to old variants of attack vectors to specifically target medical devices, knowing they have no additional security protections.

The challenge for healthcare providers is immense. Some medical care facilities have found it necessary to 'clean' (replace software, reload, or rebuild) multiple devices at the same time, to prevent them from being re-infected by another medical device that still contains malicious code. In some cases, hospital staff have had to manage shutting down dozens (or even hundreds) of medical devices at the same time—a potentially catastrophic task that can result in the death of patients. Most of these organizations cannot detect such attacks until their systems are fully compromised; they may be unaware of ongoing data breaches, and they ordinarily lack an adequate strategy or the funding to identify the problem, remove the malware, or prevent it from happening again.[63]

Cars

In July 2015, a 29-year old hacker revealed a gadget of his own making that enabled him to take over operation of any GM vehicle with the OnStar system. Called "OwnStar", his hack allowed him to do exactly what the OnStar system does —locate, unlock, and start a car using his gadget. In order for the device to work, however, a hacker must first place a small wireless device somewhere on the car he or she wishes to breach. Once the vehicle came within Wi-Fi range of the device, which in this case he built for about $100, he was able to gain access to the car. The hacker actually posted a video that demonstrated how the device works. In it, he demonstrated how he was able to penetrate a security flaw in OnStar's mobile software by intercepting communications after the OnStar user opens the app. The OwnStar device then gains the user's credential and notifies the OnStar user that he had indefinite access to the vehicle.[64]

The hacker had, ironically, purchased a General Motors (GM) vehicle for his mother earlier in the year and, shortly thereafter, began to look for vulnerabilities in the OnStar system. It only took him a few days to identify a flaw and create a way to exploit it. The device was comprised of only a few key components, including a $40 "Raspberry Pi" computer and three radios. The device not only intercepted all of the information necessary to log into a targeted car, but it also sent that information to the hacker wirelessly, allowing him to locate the car at any time and unlock it at his convenience. Even after GM said it had fixed the vulnerability, the hacker remained able to perform the breach, prompting the company to issue an app to fully mitigate the risk.

GM was unlucky enough to have been targeted by a capable hacker but the truth is that such vulnerabilities are prevalent in most connected devices. After this story became public, other hackers found a security flaw in Chrysler's jeep that enabled them to commandeer the vehicle wirelessly from a remote location using their computer. The vulnerability they discovered enabled them to take over functions such as brakes, the steering wheel, and the accelerator. While these types of car breaches have attracted a lot of attention from the media and lawmakers, the attacks were carried out in controlled environments by "white hat hackers" (hackers who help discover security flaws so companies can fix them). However, as more cars have become connected to the Internet, malicious hackers have begun to target vehicles, leaving car manufacturers scrambling. Until vulnerabilities are discovered and patches released, all consumers can do is wait.[65]

Most of the time, these vulnerabilities stem from automakers' lacking the right expertise to secure their computer systems from cybercriminals. Cars are vulnerable because they were never built with such defenses in mind. By 2020, it is estimated that up to a quarter of a billion connected vehicles will be on the road.[66] Security researchers have been testing auto vulnerabilities for some time, presuming that breaches could possibly occur when a car was within a certain physical range of a hacker, or if special hardware had previously been installed in the cars. The white hat hackers have shown that certain makes and models of cars with wireless connectivity can be breached without such stipulations.

Also in 2015, two security researchers discovered a vulnerability in Chrysler's Fiat that allowed for some vehicles to be controlled remotely over the Internet from thousands of miles away.[67] The vulnerability existed in Uconnect, a feature found in Fiat vehicles that enables phone calls to be made, controls entertainment and navigation, and powers a Wi-Fi hotspot. When exploited, the hackers were able to use Uconnect's cellular connection to learn the car's Internet Protocol (IP) address and gain access from anywhere in the country. Hackers were then able to gain access to the chip controlling entertainment and rewrite firmware to implant code to take over such things as the engine and brakes. A security flaw also enabled hackers to remotely open the locks in BMW and Rolls Royce vehicles using blank car keys to fool the cars into thinking their owner was trying to unlock the door.[68]

It is only a matter of time before nefarious hackers become incentivized to devote substantial resources to hacking autos and make money by exploiting systemic vulnerabilities. One way a hacker might attempt to do so, for example, is to use a car's Global Positioning System (GPS) to locate someone in a remote area and install a ransomware-type virus on their car's computer so that it will not work until money is transferred to the criminal's account. Another might be to force a car to speed up or make its brakes fail and deliberately cause an accident. Who would ever be able to prove what happened, or why, particularly if it were a single car accident? A driver might effectively be held hostage to a hacker simply by virtue of a threat to do so.

While auto makers are doing a better job of getting out in front of the problem and staying on top of it, the very fact that such vulnerabilities exist, in the Era of Virtual Terrorism, is somewhat surprising. As is often the case, it is only when manufacturers are threatened with monetary losses that they devote more attention to such issues. As a smart-car owner, the most important thing to do is keep your car's software up to date. While some companies regularly produce wireless updates, most do not. Following its travails, Fiat produced a patch to download, but owners must themselves install the update via a Universal Serial Bus (USB) drive or visit their local dealer to have the update installed. That seems a small price to pay to have a higher degree of confidence. Consumers can reward vendors who are transparent about security issues by buying their product but they may never even know there is a problem.[69]

Trains

Modern railways rely on a wide range of digital equipment which are tempting targets for hackers, including cab signaling, traction control systems, automatic train control (ATC) systems for controlling the train and directing operators, protection systems, and passenger information and entertainment systems. Train stations rely on digital systems for computer-based interlocking (CBI, a signaling system designed to prevent the setting up of conflicting routes), centralized traffic control, level crossing protection, and switching yard automation. Digital systems are also used in traction substations and in ticket and passenger information systems.

Over a three-year period culminating in 2015, researchers identified security vulnerabilities in several interlocking and train control devices and in more than 10 transport network devices. They determined that railway systems are not difficult to hack but doing so requires specific knowledge in railway automation. The researchers highlighted that, while the software used for railway systems is generally not publicly available, their tests were conducted on real world installations; the conclusion was that these systems are a problem.

A train protection system that is widely used in many European countries is Siemens Railway Automation System and researchers have noted that it uses Siemens SIMATIC components, such as the WinAC RTX controller, which is designed for (PC) personal computer-based automation solutions. WinAC RTX has several security weaknesses, including the ability to control the device without authentication and the use of known protocols such as XML over HTTP, which makes it possible to create tools for controlling the device.

Experts believe there are three types of threats when it comes to CBIs: safety, economics, and reliability. If an attacker can gain access to such a system, he can cause physical damage by changing a switch while a train is passing over it, or by setting up conflicting routes. Attacks against CBI can be conducted by a malicious actor who has physical access to the system or by using social engineering to trick someone with access to the system into executing malicious code (such as by inserting a malicious USB drive into the system). Using publicly available information, experts determined that, in many cases, physical security was terrible. In addition, access passwords were sometimes displayed on written notes pasted to the control dashboard that anyone can see. An attacker can also target the communications systems that connect various components of the CBI with each other and with the outside world.

In some countries, such as India and Germany, some companies specialize in telecommunications for railways. In Germany, one company provides special Global System for Mobile Communication (GSM-R) Subscriber Identification Module (SIM) cards that are used to connect trains to control centers. These SIM cards have good encryption but a malicious actor could attempt to jam the connection between the train and the control center using a GSM jammer. Researchers have pointed out that, in areas where certain levels of the European Train Control System are used, trains automatically stop if the connection between the train's modem and the control center is lost, which means that an attacker who can jam the connection can cause a train to stop.

Another problem with GSM-R is that some handsets have a feature that can be used to manage the devices via Short Message Service (SMS). An authentication feature that relies on a PIN is used to prevent abuse but the default code provided by the manufacturer is rarely changed. Over the air (OTA) management features present in some GSM-R equipment also introduce security risks, especially since some support OTA firmware updates. The modems used for GSM-R could also be vulnerable to the types of mobile modem attacks wherein an attacker can compromise a modem, for example, by using a malicious firmware update pushed via OTA, and could also hack the host the modem is connected to.

In the case of railway systems, an attacker who can compromise the modem could also hijack the ATC system, which can allow him to control the train. Modern trains also have entertainment systems, passenger information systems, intercoms, IP cameras, and wireless access points that pose a risk because they all operate via a single communication channel. Researchers have analyzed devices from a variety of vendors used in railway systems and one concern that has arisen is that their firmware, in many cases, includes hardcoded private keys for Secure Sockets Layer (SSL) certificates and remote administration features. This exposes supposedly secure communications to MITM attacks and allows attackers to remotely log in to a device. Attackers can also use the exposed keys to fingerprint devices and attempt to find equipment that is accessible over the Internet. Some of the devices that have a USB port also have the Autorun feature enabled, which is designed to allow engineers to easily perform software and configuration updates but introduces additional security risks.[70]

Play Stations

What follows are some examples of attacks that have occurred, or could certainly occur, in online games and further illustrate the variety and unpredictability of current (and future) remote control attacks. The hunt for those responsible for the terrorist attacks in Paris, in 2015, led to a number of raids in Brussels, where Belgian officials learned that Sony's Play Station 4 (PS4) was being used by IS agents to communicate and was selected specifically because it was notoriously difficult to monitor. When the PS4 was first launched in 2013, security professionals were concerned that there was insufficient focus on security and that PS4's camera could give the government or hackers the ability to 'spy' on users. It turned out that the non-peripheral based communication on consoles provided terrorists with a channel to effectively converse with one another without being detected. The low-tech system may offer a more secure means of communication than encrypted phone calls, texts, and e-mail.

In an effort to strengthen its ability to fight terrorism, in 2010, the US Federal Bureau of Investigation (FBI) pushed lawmakers to gain access to all manner of Internet communications, including gaming chat systems. The US Federal Communications Commission (FCC) did not grant the

FBI access to peer-to-peer communications but the FBI did end up building its own rigs to record their communications in pursuit of criminals in organized chats, like a pedophile trying to lure kids via Xbox Live. Most consoles today come equipped with such capabilities, since nearly anything that can be done on the games can be recorded.

On that basis, terrorists can easily put their own Play Station Network (PSN) together and chat, free from the fear that anyone is listening because of the difficulty and infrequency of governments eavesdropping on those forms of communication. It remains unclear just how much access governments have managed to obtain on PSN and Xbox Live, but whatever it is, it is probably short of its ability to track more traditional forms of communication, such as cell phones and computers.

While government agencies can often build profiles of suspected terrorists based on their Internet or communication history, it is much harder to profile individuals based on console usage (PSN has in excess of 110 million users and two thirds of them are active). Very few of those users would presumably visit extremists' sites in the PSN Web browser, or brag about future attacks in a public game lobby. At a time when terrorism-inspired titles such as 'Call of Duty' are the best-selling games every year, can there really be any way of easily identifying potentially problematic games and users?

In addition, there are any number of ways that terrorists could send messages to each other without speaking a word. An IS agent could spell out an attack plan in *Super Mario Maker*'s coins and share it privately with a friend, or two *Call of Duty* players could write messages to each other on a wall in a disappearing spray of bullets. There are also many methods of non-verbal communication that would be almost impossible to track. To do so would require the FBI or NSA to tap *all* the activity on an entire console, not just voice and text chat, and that may not even be technically possible, or desirable, from a resource allocation standpoint.

Burner phone manufacturers were once criticized for making it easier for criminals to communicate. Should companies like Microsoft and Sony be similarly criticized? If they have not already done so, electronic game manufacturers may be inclined to volunteer to make it easier for governments to monitor specific accounts or consoles in the future. As it is now, the most popular gaming devices also happen to be a very effective way to connect not just the world's friends but its enemies as well.[71]

Emergency Management Systems

In April 2017, hackers set off emergency sirens throughout the city of Dallas; all 156 of the city's sirens were activated more than a dozen times. It took nearly an hour for city officials to stop the sirens from blaring in the middle of the night, after deactivating the system, which remained shut for several days, fearing another attack would occur when the system was reactivated. The city's 911 emergency call system was overloaded as a result, impacting the ability of emergency services to respond. As a result, Dallas officials worked with the US Federal Emergency Management Agency (FEMA) to create an alert system that would send messages to all cell phones in the area when there is an actual emergency. The City Council subsequently allocated more than $500,000 to upgrade emergency sirens over a 6-year period. The net benefit is that Dallas will have upgraded infrastructure and a better ability to avoid and respond to any future attacks.[72]

Aircraft

Given that cars can be cyber-jacked, how realistic is it for computer hackers to be able to interfere with aircraft while they are in the air? While hijacking and fully controlling an aircraft by remote means would appear to be much more difficult to achieve, interfering with an aircraft's operational systems, including inducing a catastrophic failure in order to extort money, is a distinct possibility. This could be done via a cyberattack, which is increasingly easy to imagine, given the amount of Internet connectivity for computers, electronic games, and entertainment. Internet signals are routed through existing communications architecture, such as the Aircraft Communications Addressing and Reporting System, which is used for short messages, or the Automatic Dependent Surveillance-Broadcast (ADS-B), an anti-collision system. As these both send and receive information, they can, in theory, be targeted.

Yet such an attack from outside is less likely due to the technical challenges of overcoming software architectures that, unlike in banks, are relatively unfamiliar and largely bespoke. It would be far easier to pay a disgruntled employee to implant malware, either directly into the aircraft during a maintenance routine or through the jetway when the aircraft docks, to upload into the In-Flight Entertainment (IFE) system (surprisingly, the IFE system on one of the world's newest commercial aircraft, the Boeing 787, was originally linked to the aircraft's flight control system but Boeing subsequently addressed this oversight). That said, even the threat of activating such a program when a flight is in the air could be enough to trigger a ransom.

The reason this has apparently not yet occurred is that the airlines and law enforcement authorities are aware of the danger and are actively taking steps to address the threat, including designing fallback systems to revert to basic manual control in the event of an anomaly discovered in the system. In addition, the integration of aircraft systems, which increases the chances of finding a pathway through the entire architecture, is a relatively new development, brought about by the move to fiber optic cabling and data buses. That said, if such an attack had occurred it is most likely that an airline would never want to make such an event known publicly.[73]

In 2017, Germany's military enhanced its aviation cyber expertise in response to government-funded research revealing that hackers can seize command of military aircraft with equipment worth just a few thousand dollars. In order to avert future cyberattacks, the government ordered that its military aircraft be fitted with protective systems. The German Aerospace Centre (Germany's state-funded authority for aerospace, energy, and transportation research) determined that hostile hackers would need equipment worth no more than 5,000 euros to perpetrate an attack that would disrupt a military plane's operations.[74] Germany will be spending considerably more than that to attempt to avoid the threat.

Nuclear Submarines

54

A 2017 report by the British American Security Information Council had a sobering message for the world's fleet of nuclear-armed submarines—and in particular, for the UK's operational fleet of Vanguard-class submarines armed with nuclear-tipped Trident II D-5 ballistic missiles—about the growing potential for cyberattacks. It said that a successful attack could neutralize operations and possibly lead to an exchange of nuclear warheads (directly or indirectly). The very possibility of a cyberattack against ballistic missile submarines (SSBNs) could have a severe impact upon the confidence of maintaining an assured second-strike capability and, therefore, on strategic stability between states.

Suggestions that the fleet was vulnerable had previously been met with complacency and claims that the submarines' isolated 'air-gapped' systems cannot be penetrated were found to be false. The report found that the exponential growth in the complexity of cyberattack techniques outmatched defensive capabilities, which has a transformative impact upon all forms of warfare. Malware injection during manufacturing, mid-life refurbishment, or software updates, and data transmission interception all allow potential adversaries to conduct long-term cyber operations— potentially without being detected.

Emerging technologies have already enhanced the ability to detect the existence and location of global submarines. Future weaponized underwater drones may facilitate close proximity kinetic and cyberattacks on SSBNs. Advanced nano and bionic technologies (such as implantable and subdermal data storage and communication devices) can be smuggled onto vessels and activated autonomously, manually, or remotely. The report confirmed that it takes sophisticated, well-resourced, and sustained cyberattacks to exploit the vulnerabilities in remote submarine subsystems and provides illustrative attack vectors aimed at disrupting, destroying, or endangering operations.

The overall submarine network architecture is physically isolated from the Internet and any civilian network, thus severely limiting the possibility of real time external access into the command network by remote hackers. But this does not prevent attacks from inside the submarine or the prior injection of malware into submarines, missiles, warheads, or other infrastructure at the manufacturing, construction, and maintenance stages. The vessel, missiles, warheads, and all the various support systems rely on networked computers, devices, and software, each of which must be designed and programmed. All of them incorporate unique data and must be regularly upgraded, reconfigured, and patched. Regular radio-transmissions from ashore could be used for limited bandwidth cyberattacks, spoofing, or activating pre-installed malware programs. Such highly covert, adaptive, and targeted programs could be designed to trigger in response to specific events. The risks can be reduced by significant, vigilant, and continuous cyber protection but cannot be eliminated.[75]

Sex Toys

Since literally anything connected to the Internet can, in theory, be hacked, cybersecurity experts have warned that some dildos are vulnerable to hacking. Some vibrators connect to a smartphone app via Bluetooth, allowing a person's sexual partner to provide pleasure from anywhere in the world. Hackers are able to intercept the web connection, raising the prospect of a total stranger being in control during a couple's most intimate moment. One such vibrator manufacturer has sold more than two million dildos worldwide, specifically because it can be controlled remotely. The vibrator sends data back to the company for "diagnostic purposes" and data is collected when the app is actually in use. This raises a number of issues ranging from violation of privacy to a form of sexual assault. If any such 'attack' has occurred, it is not documented, though it must be assumed this has occurred.[76]

Hotel Rooms

In January 2017, guests were locked out of their rooms at the picturesque Alpine hotel, Romantik Seehotel Jaegerwirt, in Austria, because the electronic key system at the hotel had been infiltrated. The hotel was locked out of its own computer system, leaving guests stranded in the lobby, prompting confusion and panic. An e-mail ransom demand to the hotel's manager required two Bitcoins (approximately $1,800 at the time), and warned that the cost would double if the hotel did not comply with the demand by the end of the day. The e-mail included details of a "Bitcoin wallet", the account in which to deposit the money. As the reservation system for the hotel in the village of Turracherhöhe was 90 minutes away by car, the hotel decided to pay the ransom. To guard against future attacks, the hotel was considering replacing its electronic keys with old-fashioned door locks and keys.[77]

Orange is the New Dark Overlord

After stealing and releasing 10 episodes of the fifth season of the Netflix series "Orange is the New Black" a month before its official premiere because Netflix had refused to pay ransom to prevent its early release, the hacker group "The Dark Overlord" threatened to release shows by four other networks unless ransom was paid (they had demanded 50 Bitcoin, which was valued at $66,000 at the time). The Overlords released episodes to the general public online and held unreleased shows from ABC, Fox, IFC, and National Geographic for possible future release.[78]

The Overlords had apparently hacked a post-production company associated with the series in order to gain access to 10 of the full 13 season episodes (the other three had not been completed at the time). The incident raised questions about what else could be hacked in the entertainment arena—the winners of the Oscars and Grammys, or the commercials for the Super Bowl? It was a wake-up call for large television and production companies of the need to enhance cybersecurity protocols for themselves and third-party vendors, implying it will not be too long before such vendors must demonstrate that they have robust protocols in place before being hired in the future.

Candid Cameras

Governments once had a relative monopoly on cameras used to monitor people but today closed-circuit television cameras (CCTVs) are more prevalent more generally than ever before. The UK—the most monitored country on earth per capita—was estimated to have had as many as 6 million cameras installed throughout the country to monitor its citizens and visitors[79] as of 2015 and it was estimated that the city of Chongqing in China had installed as many as 500,000 cameras at that time. Today, cameras are installed in every conceivable type of business, home, and mode of transportation. That also applies, as well, to computers, tablets, phones, televisions, game consoles, nanny cams, and home security systems, among others.

The degree of surveillance has reached unprecedented proportions. Cameras are inexpensive and easy to install and monitor. The capability and quality of these cameras has matched their explosive growth. Military drones already have cameras that can view targets as small as six inches in size from an altitude of 20,000 feet. By being linked to sensors, they also contribute to the collection and analysis of data. Cameras read our license plates, our faces, and our movements.

While contributing to a false sense of security, cameras are themselves vulnerable to remote control attack. Without the knowledge of those being surveilled, virtual terrorists happily share the images of their prey online for anyone to see, whether it is a person in a laundromat, someone watching football on his couch, or patrons at a bar—anywhere in the world. It is common knowledge that phone and computer cameras can be turned on remotely (which is why it is highly recommended to cover their lenses with paper when not in use), but many people either do not know it or fail to prevent it from happening. There are plenty of examples of individuals who have found out the hard way that. when their laptop is on and the camera is not covered, they are exposed.

One of the best-known examples is former Miss Teen USA, Cassidy Wolf, whose bedroom-based laptop was hacked, capturing nude photos and videos of her walking around, getting out of the shower, and dressing. After recording images for months, the hacker revealed himself by sending a 'sextortion' e-mail demanding that she either perform a series of sex acts for him or he would upload all the images of her that he had shared with her (and a lot more). Three months later, the FBI identified one of her schoolmates as the extorter. He used a tool kit easily available for purchase on

Crimazon and used the malware to target eight other women in Southern California.

Hackers and pedophiles often target baby cams, the majority of which do not require a password (or use the same manufacturer-designate password for all of their devices). There is a lurid trade in nanny cam images for sale in the digital underground, which includes young mothers breast-feeding their infants. Since the cameras include a speaker and microphone so parents can listen and speak to their children, hackers sometimes use them to terrorize their victims verbally.[80]

So, virtual terrorists have the ability to use or hijack almost any system or gadget linked to the Internet, with or without the knowledge of its owner or designated user. As will be discussed in subsequent chapters, variants of remote control terrorism have the ability to impact literally anyone connected to the Internet in any way. Some of the applications are staggering in terms of their potential impact on governments, businesses, and individuals.

3. **Governments and Geopolitics**

In 2015, German writer Christoph Rehage uploaded a YouTube video that referred to Mao Zedong as "China's Hitler". A Chinese Communist Youth League website then called for him to be punished for violating Chinese law, even though he lives in Hamburg. It argued that Rehage, who speaks Chinese, made the video to circulate in China, which the League said undermined the sovereignty of its Internet.[81]

Paradiplomacy is a form of international relations conducted by subnational or regional governments intent on promoting their own interests but without interaction with or assistance from other governments. Paradiplomacy may be performed both in support of, and in complementarity with, official state-level diplomacy, or come in conflict or compete with it. Otherwise known as 'substate diplomacy' and 'intermestic affairs', it speaks to *the growing trend of the internationalization of domestic issues*, bringing local, regional, and state-level concerns and objectives to the center stage of international affairs. It raises interesting questions about the relevance and applicability of international law and has opened a debate about the future of the state system that has provided the foundation for the international political order for centuries.[82]

In the Era of Virtual Terrorism, the lines governing what is conventional "statecraft" versus new and alternative forms of it are becoming more and more blurred. Where does a legitimate concern of a government for its own welfare (and that of its citizens) cross the line between being an acceptable form of cross-border relations as opposed to being illegal and unacceptable? The distinction between what is best for a government rather than for its people is important, given that many of the world's governments function to ensure that they continue to exist in their present form (examples include China and North Korea).

To what extent does the perpetuation of a leader's power and wealth drive official versus non-official policy (examples include Russia and the US)? How much more convoluted is the web that is weaved when multiple objectives are being achieved at the same time by a given action? How much more objectionable is that tangled web likely to become when only part of it is visible to those outside a government? What is clear is that, *in the Era of Virtual Terrorism, the world is not only increasingly borderless, but without boundaries—in terms of what is known to the public, what is deemed acceptable in the body of public opinion, what is within the scope of the law, and what can be stopped.*

Governments spy on one another, and on their people—that is what governments do. They always have and they always will. But *spying has been taken to a whole new dimension, wherein access to other nations' secrets, their businesses, and their people have intersected with the promotion of state interest as a new art form.* Intrusion and theft beyond the reach of the law have made deception all the more possible because of anonymity. Those nations with the greatest financial, military, and cyber resources are naturally the most prolific at perpetrating Virtual Terrorism; The countries which are the most adept at this, and have been the best documented as such, are China, Russia, and the US.

China

Unrestricted Warfare

Chinese military doctrine has long articulated the use of a wide spectrum of warfare against its adversaries. Much of what is known outside of China about its approach to asymmetric warfare is contained in a book first published in 1999 and translated with the title *Unrestricted Warfare. The first rule of unrestricted warfare is that there are no rules and nothing is forbidden.* The book advocates tactics known as *shashou-jian* (Assassin's Mace), the concept of taking advantage of an adversary's seemingly superior conventional capabilities by "fighting the fight that fits one's own weapons" and "making the weapons to fit the fight". It proposes ignoring traditional rules of conflict and advocates such tactics as manipulating foreign media, flooding enemy countries with drugs, controlling the markets for natural resources, joining international bodies so as to be in a position to bend them to one's will, and engaging in cyberwarfare (the doctrine was quite ahead of its time, given that it was written in the early days of the advent of the Internet).

Having had nearly two decades to develop this philosophy, Chinese military strategists are, of course, prepared to use conventional weapons to fight their enemies, but, especially where it lacks a competitive advantage—such as not having a large or effective blue water navy—*one of its tactics is to use cyberwarfare to make up the difference.* Since the turn of the century, China has set in place an impressive cyberwarfare infrastructure that includes citizen hacker groups, military units. and an extensive cyberespionage network around the world. This includes an aggressive effort to obtain advanced Internet network technology.

Noteworthy in that regard was China's threat to ban government procurement of Microsoft software, hardware, and technology unless Bill Gates agreed to provide China with a copy of its proprietary operating code, which he had refused to reveal to Microsoft's largest US commercial clients. *After Gates agreed to provide it, China then copied the Cisco network router found on almost all US networks and most Internet service providers. China then sold counterfeit routers at cut-rate discounts around the world. The buyers apparently included the Pentagon and a host of other US federal agencies.* A subsequent report by the FBI concluded that the routers could be used by foreign intelligence agencies to take down networks and weaken cryptographic systems.

Armed with intimate knowledge of the flaws in Microsoft's and Cisco's software and hardware, China's hackers had the ability to stop most of the world's networks from operating. Chinese networks would also have been vulnerable but, *as part of its deal with Microsoft, the Chinese modified the version of Microsoft software sold in China to include a secure component using their own encryption. They also developed their own operating system (Kylin) and secure microprocessors for use on servers and Huawei routers.*

By 2003, the Chinese government had created cyberwarfare units with defensive and offensive capabilities with weapons that had never been seen before, including the ability to plant information mines, conduct information reconnaissance, change network data, release information bombs, dump information garbage, disseminate propaganda, apply information deception, release clone information, and establish network spy stations. By 2007, China was penetrating US and European networks, successfully copying and exporting huge volumes of data.[83] China has since developed its cyberwarfare capabilities into a finely tuned and largely unrivaled machine.

The CCP, PLA, and GSD

China is extremely adept at waging economic warfare. One way to estimate the damage done in this war is by the cost of intellectual property theft. The Commission on the Theft of Intellectual Property has estimated that such theft costs the US $300 billion and 1.2 million jobs per year. Other organizations believe the cost is closer to $500 billion worth of raw innovation that is stolen from US companies annually, which would otherwise generate revenue, profits, and jobs. *The Chinese government's theft of intellectual property for economic gain is just one piece of a larger strategy to fight a war while avoiding troop-to-troop combat.*

China's spy and cyberoperations are orchestrated under the PLA General Staff Department (GSD), the Chinese military's highest-level department dedicated to warfighting. Under the GSD, three departments work on its spy campaigns for unconventional warfare. The Second Department focuses on human spies and intelligence (HUMINT), the Third Department focuses on cyberespionage and signals intelligence (SIGINT), and the Fourth Department focuses on electronic warfare, intercepting satellite data and electronics intelligence (ELINT). The GSD also oversees China's military regions, the army, navy, and air force, and the Second Artillery (the home for China's nuclear weapons).

The Chinese government's applications of Hybrid Warfare are broad, enabling it to deploy a large array of tactics and methods to achieve its objectives. This includes capabilities in areas as all-encompassing as trade, finance, ecology, psychology, smuggling, media, drugs, Internet networks, technology, economic aid, culture, and international law. Estimates on the number of soldiers in each GSD varies; most only focus on cyberspies. The Project 2049 Institute estimated, in 2011, that there were 130,000 personnel in the Third Department, while the Wall Street Journal estimated, in July of that year, that the Department had 100,000 hackers, linguists, and analysts in 12 operational bureaus. Others have estimated that there are 20 operational bureaus with between 250,000 and 300,000 soldiers dedicated to cyberespionage (the New York Times has also reported 20 bureaus). Under the Second Department, between 30,000 and 50,000 spies are believed to be working on insider operations targeting US and other foreign companies. No estimate is publicly available on the number of operatives in the Fourth Department.

According to a report from the US Congressional Research Service, the PLA is not a national army belonging to the state, but serves as the Party's armed wing. The soldiers deployed in the GSD's spy departments are used to further the financial and political ambitions of the CCP. The PLA is, in essence, a state within a state, completely devoted to the survival of the CCP, which provides the PLA with financial and material resources. State-run cyberattacks and China's use of more conventional spies are part of a larger, coordinated effort under the GSD that answers to China's top leaders in the Central Committee of the CCP.

The orders governing China's spy departments are derived from the CCP's Five-Year Plans, which often include targeted industries and economic goals of the Party. One of the clearest links between the Five-Year Plans and the campaigns of economic theft by the Chinese military is Project 863, set in motion by former leader Deng Xiaoping in 1986, which mandated theft of intellectual property from foreign businesses. The Project was emblematic of the CCP's drive to "catch up fast and surpass" the West, according to a 2011 report from the US Office of the National Counterintelligence Executive. It provided funding and guidance for efforts to clandestinely acquire US technology and sensitive economic information.[84]

Originally, an Attempt to Maintain Control

China's first publicly known cyberattacks began in 1999. The media was under the CCP's control, the Internet was already tightly censored, and the Party's history of campaigns against its own people, and its use of pervasive surveillance, left a residual environment of fear that ensured a level of self-censorship among the masses. However, the Party wanted to plug a gaping hole—the friends or family of Chinese citizens who lived abroad that it could not control. The Chinese government's first state-run cyberattacks coincided, in July 1999, with an attempt to silence Falun Gong practitioners and other Chinese living overseas.

The first known Chinese state-run cyberattacks against the West targeted networks in four countries—two in the US, two in Canada, one in the UK, and one in Australia. All of the targets were websites that explained what Falun Gong is and how it began to be persecuted in China. According to a January 2002 RAND Corporation report, the attacks took place within a close time frame that aligned with the persecution of the group in China and several of the cyberattacks were traced to networks under the Chinese Ministry of State Security.

As the government continued using cyberattacks to try to quell the free flow of information abroad, it recognized that the new tool could have other applications. Security researchers began seeing cyberattacks originating from China that served multiple uses. They were used to spy on dissidents and the same methods were used to steal from Western companies and gain intelligence from foreign governments. Google revealed, in January 2010, that China was targeting its networks but documents later leaked by WikiLeaks revealed that the attacks were part of a larger campaign that had been occurring since 2002. The Chinese regime was also targeting government networks of the US and its allies, as well as networks belonging to the Tibetan Dalai Lama and e-mail accounts of Chinese artist Ai Weiwei. An attack from 2006 to 2007 breached computers of two US congressmen and stole documents about dissidents critical of the Chinese regime.

Mastering the Game

With US intelligence agencies focused on terrorism in the first decade of the 21st century, Chinese spies and their hackers were not a primary focus. Chinese hackers launched successful attacks in Taiwan and, in 2005, were able to carry out the Titan Rain cyberattacks that targeted everything from military contractors to the Pentagon and NASA. In 2007, *Chinese hackers were able to carry out the Byzantine Hades cyberattacks with little more than a peep of condemnation from US officials. The attacks, which were traced to the Chinese military, ended up getting broad media attention years later, in part because part of the theft of designs of the F-35 fighter jet (which enabled China to produce its own stealth fighter, the Chengdu J-20).*[85]

During the Obama administration, the US devoted more resources to the problem and began to respond more robustly. In May 2014, the US Justice Department indicted five Chinese military hackers from Unit 61398 for their alleged role in economic theft but Chinese cyberespionage has grown to become a goliath. *The whole system runs through a corrupt nexus among government officials, military officers, business executives, and academics throughout China. It makes money back by developing products based on the stolen information.* The system even extends to "transfer centers" that process stolen information and transforms them into usable designs.

Many of the Chinese products based on stolen American research and development are resold back in the US at a fraction of the price of the original American product. Chinese law states that any company greater than 50 people in size must have a government liaison assigned to it, blurring the lines separating government from private industries, military from government, and the private sector from the military. The systems in place to accommodate economic theft take place across all three of these sectors.

During the Cold War, if a Soviet spy had stolen designs for a US spy camera, for example, the designs would have been transferred to a research facility where Soviet engineers would have attempted to directly reproduce the technology. China's approach was different, given its acknowledgement about its technological gap with other countries at the time. While the Soviets would start their counterfeit process from the top, the Chinese started theirs from the bottom.

If a Chinese spy were to get her hands on the same hypothetical spy camera, she would similarly transfer it to a research facility but, rather than try to duplicate the camera, the researchers would find earlier generations of the technology and build those first. They would send spies to gather publicly available information for the earliest models of the targeted technology, buy the next generations in stores, and send students to study and work abroad in the targeted industry. The process would give them a foundation of knowledge and, when they were ready to reverse engineer the modern generation of the gadget, they could easily see which parts had been upgraded and which changes had been made from the technology's previous generations. The Chinese approach was significantly faster and more cost effective than the Soviet approach.

Unbridled Access to Technology

The Chinese government's current system for processing and reverse engineering stolen designs has grown significantly larger than it was during the Cold War and has developed from a strictly military operation into a system permeating the entire Chinese government. *It is an elaborate, comprehensive system for identifying foreign technologies, acquiring them by every means imaginable, and converting them into weapons and competitive goods.* The departments in charge of reverse engineering are officially called China's National Technology Transfer Centers (or National Demonstration Organizations) and became established by policy in 2007. Among their names are the State Administration of Foreign Experts Affairs (under the State Council), the Science and Technology Office (under the Overseas Chinese Affairs Office), and the National Technology Transfer Center (under the East China University of Science and Technology).

These organizations do not attempt to hide their purpose; their charters explicitly name 'domestic and foreign technology' as targets for 'commercialization'. The transfer centers play several roles, which include processing stolen technology, developing cooperative research projects between Chinese and foreign scientists, and running programs designed to 'encourage' Chinese nationals who have studied abroad to become part of the organizations. *China's meteoric economic rise can, in part, be attributed to this system of minimal investment in basic science through a technology transfer apparatus that worked to suck in foreign proprietary achievements while most of the countries which they were stealing from had no idea what they were doing.*

China could not have experienced the dramatic economic transformation it has experienced in the 21st century, nor have sustained its progress, without inexpensive and unrestricted access to other countries' technology. A 2010 report from the US Defense Threat Reduction Agency noted that modernization in the Chinese military depends heavily on investments in China's science and technology infrastructure, reforms of its defense industry, and procurement of advanced weapons from abroad. It added that the Chinese regime's theft of technology is unique in that, under the system, autonomy is given to research institutes, corporations, and other entities to devise collection schemes according to their needs.

State Theft as a Business

The PLA is required to cover a portion of its own costs. Its decades-long focus on building external sources of cash has made its military leaders some of the most powerful people in China. With only 70 percent of its operating expenses covered by the state budget, the PLA must make up the difference and generate supplemental funds for its modernization. Just as is the case regarding the nexus between government and private business, the lines between the military and the state and the military and the private sector are thin. The PLA maintains thousands of front companies in the US, whose sole reason for existing is to steal and exploit US technology. According to the US Defense Threat Reduction Agency, the Chinese regime operates more than 3,200 military front companies in the US dedicated to theft.

Project 863 (also called the 863 Program) was started by former CCP leader Deng Xiaoping in 1986. According to a report from the US Office of the National Counterintelligence Executive, it provides funding and guidance for efforts to clandestinely acquire US technology and sensitive economic information. Project 863 originally targeted seven industries: biotechnology, space, IT, automation, laser technology, new materials, and energy. It was updated to include telecommunications and marine technology.

The Chinese government also runs the Torch Program to build high-tech commercial industries, the 973 Program for research, the 211 program for "reforming" universities, and countless programs designed to attract Western-trained scholars back to China. Each of these programs relies on foreign collaboration and technologies to cover key gaps, encouraging Western-trained experts to help China's technological development by returning to China or "serving in place" by providing needed information gained while working for their Western employers. Project 863 maintains a library of tens of millions of open source articles in scores of databases that contain more than four terabytes of information gleaned from American, Japanese, Russian, and British publications, military reports, and standard specifications.

One of the most powerful organizations behind economic theft is the 61 Research Institute, under the Third Department of the GSD. The man in charge of it, Major General Wang Jianxin, has some powerful connections at the most senior level of the Chinese government. The names of many known military hacker units in China begin with the number '61', and there are at least 11 units under the GSD's Third Department with that designation, including Unit 61398, under which five military hackers who were indicted by the DOJ in 2014 operated.[86]

Attacks Against Japan

Since November 2013, China is believed to have targeted Japan in a large-scale hacking operation similar to campaigns against the US. Among the hundreds of victims targeted were the Japanese pension system and government organizations, as well as companies in the research, manufacturing, and finance arenas. Dubbed "Blue Termite", the CCP was thought to be responsible, based on similarities to its attacks against the US. The Japanese pension service was consistent with previous targets of CCP hackers—while their primary target used to be intellectual property and data used for monetary gain, their preferred target shifted to personal information useful for spies.

The CCP had not long before stolen an estimated 80 million records on Americans from health care company Anthem, which preceded the OPM breach. Modeled after its domestic spy program (the "Social Credit System"), the CCP was believed to be creating a database on US citizens; the attacks on Japan suggest the CCP was expanding its database to include Japanese citizens. The hackers gathered geopolitically and technologically significant information on Japan during the attack. The hackers targeted Japanese industries in construction, robotics, manufacturing, communication, media, information services, satellites, electricity, and energy.

The methodology used corresponded with changes made in Chinese state-run cyberattacks at the time. The hackers were using spear phishing attacks (by infecting e-mails tailored for each victim) to gain access to computers in targeted networks. A few days prior to the start of the attack, a group of hacker activists leaked information on an Italian company which provides hacking services for governments. The leak included was a zero-day vulnerability—a type of cyberattack that cannot be stopped since it has not yet been identified by security companies—that the group had used in its own attacks. This attack involved infecting websites frequented by the intended victims (known as a "watering hole attack") and included code to filter out unwanted targets.

Shortly after the zero-day vulnerability used was revealed, CCP hackers obtained it and began using it in their attacks. The malware they used was a specific remote access trojan (RAT), which gave them full control over the computers, previously used by the Chinese group in other targeted attacks against governments. The hackers behind the Blue Termite attack then installed a RAT on the computers of their victims, which allowed them to monitor all activity on the computers and control the computers at will. Many of the documents and tools used by the hackers were written in Chinese. The hackers used a graphical user interface for their command and control server and had technical documents related to the malware used in the attacks—both of which were in Chinese.[87]

Containment?

According to the NSA, nearly 700 Chinese cyberattacks designed to steal corporate or military secrets in the US had already occurred between 2009 and 2014.[88] When, in 2015, the US signed a cyber agreement with China, it sent a list of Chinese hackers identified as having stolen commercial secrets from US businesses to President Xi, requesting their arrests. Chinese authorities made some arrests but *by passing evidence against Chinese hackers to Chinese authorities, the US unintentionally helped the Chinese government close gaps in its system of economic theft.* The Chinese authorities presumably took this information as a road map for how US investigators detect attacks and used the information to adjust their methods and make cyberattacks progressively more difficult to identify.

The agreement stated that neither country would "conduct or knowingly support cyber-enabled theft of intellectual property, including trade secrets or other confidential business information, for commercial advantage. The cyber agreement also established a system for high-level dialogue between the US and the CCP, which, on the US side, included the Secretary of the DHS and the attorney general.[89] However, *it only prohibited "cyber-enabled theft of intellectual property", which did nothing to address intellectual theft through other means, rendering it relatively toothless. And it failed to forbid economic theft more generally—only one method of economic theft—while leaving unmentioned that the CCP itself is behind so many of the attacks against the US.*[90]

Acknowledging America's own capabilities in this arena, President Obama said at the time that, "although the Chinese and Russians are close, we are the best at this, and if we wanted to go on the offense, a lot of countries would have some significant problems, but we don't want to see the

71

Internet weaponized in that way. We are preparing a number of measures that will indicate to the Chinese that this is not just a matter of us being mildly upset, but is something that will put significant strains on our bilateral relations if not resolved. We are prepared to take countervailing actions in order to get their attention, but my hope is that something can get resolved short of that."[91] It was a little late for that by 2015.

Buyer Beware

In terms of government actions, it is also worth pointing out that, in 2016, the Chinese government passed new laws enforcing its national security abroad by including Chinese law in the terms of service (ToS) of Chinese name brand products. For example, *by purchasing a Xiaomi smartphone, the buyers agree to assume full legal liability not to engage in activities China has banned. The terms ban purchasers from opposing the principles of the Constitution of the People's Republic of China, from leaking state secrets, or subverting the government. Some of the terms of the agreements have actually been there for several years but broadened in scope in 2016.*

By being a citizen of Tibet, Taiwan, or Hong Kong, a purchaser is technically violating Xiaomi's user agreement, which forbids "undermining national unity". An author writing about Tibetan Buddhism may violate its rules on "cults". The agreement also forbids "spreading rumors" by discussing news. And by using Xiaomi's products, buyers give Xiaomi the right to access their accounts. Other Chinese tech firms, such as Huawei, Foream, Condenatcenter, Adbox, and Decathlon, have similar user agreements. Under Decathlon's agreement, users are not allowed to do anything that could "damage the reputation of government organizations".

In 2015, German writer Christoph Rehage uploaded a YouTube video that referred to Mao Zedong as "China's Hitler". A Communist Youth League website then called for him to be punished for violating Chinese law, even though he lives in Hamburg. It argued that Rehage, who speaks Chinese, made the video to circulate in China, which the League said undermined the sovereignty of its Internet. In

2015, the National People's Congress Standing Committee passed the National Security Law, which emphasized that "China must defend its national security interests everywhere" and would "affect almost every domain of public life in China". The law's mandate covers politics, the military, finance, religion, cyberspace, ideology, and religion.

The Counterterrorism Law was also passed in 2015, which requires foreign tech firms to cooperate with Chinese investigations and its brand of "counterterrorism", the definition of which includes "any thought, speech, or activity that, by means of violence, sabotage, or threat, aims to generate social panic, influence national policymaking, create ethnic hatred, subvert state power, or split the state". Any company that wants to do business in China must uphold these rules.[92] This raises the larger issue of ToS agreements, how few consumers actually read them, how few thereby necessarily legally abide by them, and whether governments are willing and able under international law to pursue those who do not (wittingly or unwittingly).

The Chinese government will completely block access to much of the Internet inside the country as part of its effort to suppress dissent and maintain the CCP's control on power. In 2017, the government ordered China's three telecommunications companies—China Mobile, China Telecom, and China Unicom (all state-owned)—to block access to VPNs by February 2018. Millions of Chinese citizens have for years circumvented China's censorship system, known as the Great Firewall, by using a VPN, which allows unfettered access to any website. Beijing's directive follows a year-long effort to promote its version of "Internet sovereignty".[93] In doing so, the Chinese government is doubling down on its effort to maintain control of the Internet within its borders, while also endeavoring to increase the amount of control it has over the Internet outside of its borders.

Russia

Sly as a Fox

No discussion of Russia and its involvement in state-sponsored Virtual Terrorism would be complete without reference to the US presidential election of 2016 and the allegations of cyber intrusion surrounding it. The USG began an exhaustive search into those allegations prior to and following the election of Donald Trump, after many months and many millions of dollars spent to attempt to identify a "smoking gun" that would corroborate accusations that the government of Russia purposely sought to influence the results of the election.

In January 2017, a US Intelligence Community Assessment was released; it gave its best assessment of how and why Russia had interfered in the US election. The CIA, FBI, and NSA believed that Vladimir Putin ordered an influence campaign, in 2016, to undermine public faith in the US democratic process, denigrate Hillary Clinton, and harm her electability and potential presidency. The agencies believed (with a high degree of confidence) that Putin and the Russian Government aspired to enhance Trump's chances of winning the election by discrediting Clinton and publicly contrasting her as less desirable. It believed that Moscow's influence campaign followed a Russian messaging strategy that blended covert intelligence operations such as cyber activity with overt efforts by Russian Government agencies, state-funded media, third-party intermediaries, and paid social media users ("trolls").

The Assessment added that Russian military intelligence (the General Staff Main Intelligence Directorate (GRU)) used the Guccifer 2.0 persona and DCLeaks.com to release US electoral data obtained in cyber operations publicly, in exclusive releases to media outlets, and via relayed material to WikiLeaks. Russia's intelligence services conducted cyber operations against both major US political parties and obtained and maintained access to elements of multiple US state or local electoral boards (though the types of systems Russian actors targeted or compromised were not involved in vote tallying). Russia's state-run media contributed to the influence campaign by serving as a platform for Kremlin messaging to Russian and international audiences.[94]

In May 2017, the NSA issued a classified document that analyzed intelligence from a months-long investigation into the alleged Russian cyber interference in the US election and its voting infrastructure. The report indicated that Russian hacking may have penetrated further into US voting systems than was previously understood and stated unequivocally that Russian military intelligence (specifically, the GRU) conducted the attacks.[95] It stated that the GRU carried out a cyberattack on at least one US voting software supplier and sent spear phishing e-mails to more than one hundred local election officials days before the poll.

A July 2017 report by *Time* magazine claimed that among the actions that had apparently been taken by Russian hackers was an unsuccessful attempt to download the identities of all 15 million Illinois voters (90,000 voter files had actually been stolen). The Illinois state government had managed to identify and retain the IP addresses of the attackers, which the FBI confirmed led back to the GRU. This resulted in concern by the USG that the Russian government could attempt to subtly alter voter rolls by amending voter ID information (for example, making some voters ineligible to vote on voting day), interfering in the election reporting system, and in that way having an impact on the outcome of various state election results.

The NSA assessment acknowledged that there remained much uncertainty about how successful the Russian operatives were and it did not reach a conclusion about whether their actions affected the outcome of the presidential election.[96] *This serves to emphasize just how difficult it is to produce definitive evidence of wrongdoing in cyberspace. The cloak of anonymity cyberspace provides gives any actor confidence that they may never be discovered or punished.*

One of the things that makes successful detective work in cyberspace a real challenge is that any hacker can spoof an attack by using the same tools and methodology of a known hacker. Malicious actors can easily position their breach to be attributed to whomever they wish. Based on the malware deployed to achieve the breach of the Democratic National Committee (DNC), for example, it is easy to attribute blame to any entity. Perhaps Russia really did do it, but the Kremlin can easily point the finger at the CIA, given that, under its UMBRAGE Group (revealed by Wikileaks in March 2017), the Agency maintains a digital library of attacks and techniques from a variety of hacker groups, so that it can use the same methods to launch attacks while framing known hacker groups. Wikileaks noted that UMBRAGE files included attack profiles of Russian hacker groups, which could be used to leave falsified 'fingerprints' for cyber forensic investigators.[97] For that matter, *in theory, any other government, hacker group, or individual could be the guilty party.*

Cyber Meddling in Europe

The UK government was concerned that Russia (and China) may have interfered with the EU referendum website prior to the BREXIT vote in June 2016. A report by the Commons Public Administration and Constitutional Affairs Committee did not specifically identify who may have been responsible but that both Russia and China use an approach to cyberattacks based on an understanding of mass psychology and of how to exploit individuals. Ministers were forced to extend the deadline to register to vote in the EU referendum after the collapse of the government's website on June 7th, just 100 minutes before the deadline.

At the time, the government said it was the result of an unprecedented spike in demand, with more than 500,000 people apparently attempting to register on the final day. The report said there were clues that a DDoS attack using botnets was used to overwhelm the site. While the incident, as in the alleged Russian hacking in the US election, had no material effect on the outcome of the referendum, the Committee expressed grave concern about interference in the election process. A Cabinet Office spokeswoman said there was no evidence to support the Committee's claim of possible interference from foreign governments;[98] yet another riddle wrapped in a mystery inside an enigma.

In May 2017, in France, a large trove of e-mails from the campaign of then-presidential candidate Emmanuel Macron was posted online less than two days before the election, with some nine gigabytes of data posted by a user called EMLEAKS to Pastebin, a document-sharing site that allows for anonymous posting. Macron's En Marche! (Onwards!) political movement said that the documents released online only showed the normal functioning of a presidential campaign but that authentic documents had been mixed on social media with fake documents to sow "doubt and misinformation". Given that Macron's opponent, the National Front's Marine Le Pen, in previous weeks had been warmly embraced by Vladimir Putin in Moscow, Russia was the presumed culprit. Macron's team had noted several previous attempts to hack its systems during the campaign, and that it had been the target of a series of attempts to steal e-mail credentials since January. In February, the Kremlin denied that it was behind any such attacks. Until May, the perpetrators failed to compromise any campaign data.[99]

According to the NSA, Russian hackers were responsible for the Macron breach, and left a trail of evidence, but it was not enough to prove for certain they were working for the Russian government. It was, however, strongly suggestive that they were part of Putin's broader "information warfare" campaign. In December 2016, after Macron had emerged as the most anti-Russian, pro-NATO (North Atlantic Treaty Organization), and pro-EU candidate in the presidential race, the phishing e-mails started. They were of high quality and included the names of members of the campaign staff and, at first glance, appeared to come from some of them. The final e-mail encouraged recipients to download several files to protect themselves. The campaign opted to a deploy a classic "cyber-blurring" strategy, well-known to banks and corporations, creating false e-mail accounts and filling them with phony documents the way a bank teller keeps fake bills in the cash drawer, in case of a robbery. They did so, on a large scale, to create the obligation for the perpetrator to verify the information in order to determine whether it was a real account. This slowed the attackers down and bought the campaign some time.

The Russians did a poor job of covering their tracks, which made it easier for private security firms to search for evidence. In mid-March, a private cybersecurity firm watched the same Russian intelligence unit believed to have been behind some of the DNC hacks start building the tools to hack Macron's campaign. They set up web domains mimicking those of En Marche! and began dispatching e-mails with malicious links and fake login pages designed to bait campaign staffers into divulging their usernames and passwords or to click on a link that would give the Russians a toehold onto the campaign's network. The attack was characterized by haste and a trail of digital mistakes, which burned their entire operation. They were forced to start anew.

The hackers also made the mistake of releasing information that was, by any campaign standard, pretty boring. The 9 gigabytes worth of purportedly stolen e-mails and files from the Macron campaign were spun as scandalous material but turned out to be almost entirely the humdrum of campaign workers trying to conduct ordinary life in the midst of the election maelstrom. The metadata tied to a handful of documents (code that shows the origins of a document) demonstrated that some passed through Russian computers and were edited by Russian users. Some Excel documents were modified using software unique to Russian versions of Microsoft Windows. Other documents had last been modified by Russian usernames, including one person researchers identified as a 32-year-old employee of Eureka CJSC, based in Moscow, a Russian technology company that works closely with the Russian Ministry of Defense and intelligence agencies and which had received licenses from the Russian Federal Security Service to help protect state secrets.[100]

From Mother Russia, With Love

Many people are familiar with Russia's more recent well publicized election-oriented cyberattacks but Russia has a long and well documented history of involvement in other forms of cyber meddling. Some of the lesser-known examples are:

- April–May 2007: Estonia angered Moscow by planning to relocate a Russian World War II memorial and Russian soldiers' graves. Russia retaliated by temporarily disabling Estonia's Internet—in one of the world's most Internet dependent economies. The DDoS attack focused on government offices and financial institutions, disrupting communications.

- June 2008: Lithuania was punished for outlawing the display of Soviet symbols when Russian hackers defaced government web pages with hammer-and-sickles and five-pointed stars.

- August 2008: After Georgia's pro-Western government sent troops into a breakaway republic backed by Moscow, Russia invaded the country, and Russian hackers attacked Georgia's Internet, marking the first time Russia coordinated military and cyber action. Georgia's internal communications were effectively shut down.

- January 2009: As part of an effort to persuade the president of Kyrgyzstan to evict an American military base, Russian hackers shut down two of the country's four ISPs with a DDOS attack. Kyrgyzstan subsequently removed the military base and then received $2 billion in aid and loans from the Kremlin.

- April 2009: After a media outlet in Kazakhstan published a statement by Kazakhstan's president that criticized Russia, a DDOS attack attributed to Russia shut down the outlet.

- August 2009: Russian hackers shut down Twitter and Facebook in Georgia to commemorate the first anniversary of the Russian invasion.

- May 2014: Three days before Ukraine's presidential election, a Russia-based hacking group took down the country's election commission, and a back-up system, in an overnight attack. The attack was aimed at creating chaos and hurting the nationalist candidate while helping the pro-Russian candidate (Russia's preferred candidate lost).

- March 2014: For the second time, the Russian government coordinated military and cyber action. A DDoS attack 32 times larger than the largest known attack used during Russia's invasion of Georgia disrupted the Internet in Ukraine while Russian-armed pro-Russian rebels were seizing control of the Crimea.

- <u>May 2015</u>: German investigators discovered hackers had penetrated the computer network of the German Bundestag, the most significant hack in German history at the time. The BfV, German's domestic intelligence service, later said Russia was behind the attack and was seeking information not just on the workings of the Bundestag but on German leaders and NATO, among others.

- <u>December 2015</u>: Hackers believed to be Russian took over the control center of a Ukrainian power station, locking controllers out of their own systems and leaving 235,000 homes without power (discussed in Chapter 9).

- <u>October 2015</u>: Security experts believe that the Russian government tried to hack into the Dutch government's computers to pull out a report about the shooting down of Malaysian Airlines Flight MH17 over Ukraine. The Dutch Safety Board headed the investigation and concluded that the passenger plane was brought down by a Russian-made missile fired from an area held by pro-Russian rebels.[101]

It is worth pointing out, also, that Chinese products are not alone in being accused of potential security risks because of deliberate flaws or being infected with malware. Top US intelligence officials have publicly expressed doubts about the sanctity of Russian made Kaspersky software because of its founder's previous service in, and presumed ongoing links to, the Russian military. Kaspersky's antivirus programs regularly rank in the top five for personal and business computers but US officials believe the firm is linked to Russian defense and intelligence bodies and are concerned about the threat that foreign hackers could penetrate US infrastructure via suspect software and malware.[102] In July 2017, the Trump administration removed Kaspersky from two lists of approved vendors used by the USG to purchase technology equipment. Surely, users of US-made software must have similar concerns.

<u>What can be Done?</u>

Since cyber meddling in other countries' electoral processes is well established, and there appear to be a variety of means and incentives to engage in it, what if anything can be done to discourage it? If Russia is any example, imposing sanctions is not particularly effective. Another alternative may be to convince adversaries that any future meddling will either be ineffective or too costly to be worthwhile. Such meddling could be rendered less effective by seeking to reduce or counter its influence on electoral debates by swiftly exposing and/or ignoring them. That is largely what occurred with the 2017 French election.

Enhancing cyber network defenses with an 'active' defense would also certainly help—something President Trump declared a commitment to do shortly after he became President. Demonstrating both a capability and a willingness to strike back and punish those states and actors engaged in cyber meddling might also act as a deterrent but any nation wishing to discourage cyber meddling must adopt a stronger declaratory posture by robustly emphasizing (publicly and privately) the importance placed on the integrity of each democratic process. Using existing military-grade cyber tools would no doubt be seen as escalatory and is perhaps better reserved for wartime but it cannot hurt to let adversaries know that they exist and could be used if deemed warranted and necessary. Ultimately, effective cyber deterrence can only emerge out of a consistent set of actions, policies, and declarations implemented consistently over time.[103]

The US

<u>War Short of War</u>

In May 2016, the RAND Corporation released a report[104] stating that China, Iran, and Russia were using "short of war" methods to erode the influence of the US in Asia, Europe, and the Middle East. Each country uses some combination of measures short of war—including economic leverage, terrorism, limited military incursions, aggressive diplomacy, and covert action—to achieve their objectives, requiring an effective counter-strategy from the US that seamlessly incorporates measures short of war into a long-term globally integrated plan. The Report cited as examples of "short of war" actions Russia's use of propaganda and limited military action to seize parts of Ukraine, China's use of diplomacy, finance, and subtle military action to expand into the East and South China Seas, and Iran's use of covert action, investments, and pressure through religion to promote its interests in the Middle East. No doubt, from the USG's perspective, these countries were specifically listed because they are perceived to be the greatest potential threat to the US but, of course, the US can certainly be accused of doing a variation of the same thing to them.

It also made specific reference to Hybrid Warfare and Unrestricted Warfare being used to fight the US through unconventional means. As noted earlier, Hybrid Warfare involves using combinations of unconventional methods to advance strategic goals while avoiding traditional combat. Unrestricted Warfare refers to individual unconventional tactics, including political, economic, cultural, legal, and propaganda warfare, among others.

The report points out that US strategies to counter these moves have been largely ineffective because strategists in the US continue to use outmoded and ineffective linear models of war, while its most significant adversaries are approaching war by subtler and more sophisticated means.[105] While the US military may indeed be guilty of not adopting a cutting edge and more nimble posture from a purely military perspective, what the report failed to acknowledge is that the US has military and cyber capabilities that can either match or exceed anything that any other country can muster against it —and the US has been a leader in cyberwarfare.

The Day the World was Hacked

That capability was amply demonstrated on May 12, 2017, the same day that the hospital system in the UK was shut down, when more than 74,000 computers in 99 countries were estimated to have been impacted in the space of 10 hours. The total number of computers estimated to have been infected globally was in excess of 250,000, in approximately

150 countries. In what was believed to have been the first global use of a 'ransom worm', the malware WannaCry was identified as the likely cause of the problem. If ever there was a question about US capability in the cyber arena, this dispelled such doubt. The victims included more than 29,000 institutions in China, Russia's central bank, and several government ministries, Spain's Telefonica, Portugal Telecom, Fedex, Renault, a German railway, Nissan, Hitachi, Sandvik, some major universities, and a host of others.

The attack was initiated through SMBv2 remote control execution in Microsoft Windows. Codenamed "EternalBlue", it was made publicly available on April 14th, 2017. This application of the malware extorted Windows users by blocking their personal files and demanding payment to restore access, exploiting a vulnerability that was discovered and concealed for future use by the NSA. The ransomware automatically scanned for computers it could infect whenever it loaded itself onto a new machine using Windows. *It spread so quickly because it was delivered by a special digital code developed by the NSA to move from one unpatched computer to another*, having a 'hunter' module which seeks out computers on internal networks. If a laptop were infected and opened in a new network, it would spread to other computers in that network, and from there to others.

Microsoft scolded the USG, stating that an equivalent scenario would be like the US military having some of its Tomahawk missiles stolen, and reminded the government that cybersecurity is a shared responsibility.[106] The NSA found a flaw in Microsoft software that made the hack possible and reported it to the company only after a security breach was discovered. Consumers were advised of a patch to protect against that malware in March of that year. Those that had downloaded a patch were protected but computers that were already infected remained so. The day after the May 12th attack, Microsoft took the unusual step of issuing a new patch for its XP operating system—three years after it had been discontinued. The sheer scale of the attack is illustrative of how many companies and individuals fail to update their anti-virus software on a routine basis. The worm demonstrated the vulnerabilities that lie in the backdoors built into operating systems. Once the software to access these systems is obtained, it can be used any way a hacker may wish to.[107]

In the days following the attack, security firm Symantec discovered a code used in the malware that "was historically unique to Lazarus tools". The Lazarus Group is believed to be behind numerous high-profile hacking attacks on banks' SWIFT servers, including the theft of $851 million from the Bangladesh Central Bank in 2016, and was deemed to be responsible for the 2014 Sony Pictures hack (blamed on North Korea). Evidence uncovered by Kaspersky Labs supported that conclusion. It had traced some of the IPs used by the Lazarus attackers back to North Korea, for the first time establishing a direct link between the suspected cyber criminals involved in the Lazarus operations and the rogue state.[108] Could that have been a false flag operation, courtesy of the NSA, or was North Korea (or another nation) the real culprit?

Zero-days

The USG is an avid user of undiscovered software bugs and US intelligence agencies stockpile them as part of an expanding global cyber arms race. Routinely disclosing such vulnerabilities to the companies that make the products they want to penetrate, such as Apple, would mean unilaterally disarming themselves in cyberspace. The biggest use for zero-days is to hack phones, since that is what terrorists use as their primary computing platforms. The flip side, of course, is that if the government keeps these vulnerabilities a secret, there is nothing to stop criminals and hackers from targeting innocent people when they obtain them, as the Shadow Brokers did.

A zero-day vulnerability is a bug in software code that could allow access to that system and that has not been disclosed to the vendor. There is zero-days' notice before it becomes public—hence the name; it means that there is no patch or fix available when it becomes public. Zero-day vulnerabilities can impact any software and, with estimates suggesting anywhere from 3 to 20 bugs per 1,000 lines of code, there is a lot of potential for problems. Consider, for example, that Apple's iOS operating system is thought to consist of over 8 million lines of code and the US Army Future Combat Systems contains more than 60 million lines.

Most of these bugs are relatively harmless. A vulnerability is a special kind of bug that creates a security weakness in the software's design, implementation, or operation. Zero-day vulnerabilities are created or discovered by hackers, researchers, governments, and companies that specialize in developing cyberweapons to sell to intelligence agencies and law enforcement. Companies and governments discover their own vulnerabilities but they also rely on a network of independent researchers to identify flaws in lines of code. These are highly skilled engineers who reverse-engineer source code to find vulnerabilities that can be exploited.

The FBI is reported to have spent $1 million for a zero-day that allowed the agency to hack into the iPhone used by the San Bernadino shooter in 2015. The high price makes the market for zero-days limited, since only governments and intelligence agencies can generally afford to pay for them. The USG (and other governments, of course) is in the business of acquiring zero-days. The USG prefers to buy vulnerabilities from its own citizens (no doubt other governments prefer to do the same) and typically buys well-developed, robust exploits that have been thoroughly tested and that easily integrate with the other hacking tools they use.

That said, most undiscovered software bugs stay secret. A RAND report[109] in 2017 concluded that there is just a 5 percent chance of someone else independently discovering the same vulnerability, meaning that the risk associated with failing to disclose them would be limited. The report offered the first real glimpse into the world of zero-days after researchers gained access to a database of more than 200 zero-days owned by a company that sells them to governments and other customers on the so-called gray market. The research reveals that up to 25 percent of zero-day vulnerabilities persist for more than a decade, with the average life expectancy of such flaws estimated at 6.9 years —the time from the vulnerability being found to when the vendor discovers it and issues a patch or when a software upgrade inadvertently fixes the mistake. No one knows how many zero-days exist, which pieces of software they target, how often they are being used, or against whom. [110]

Under the vulnerability equities process[111] (VEP) established by the USG, US intelligence agencies are supposed to collectively determine whether to disclose a vulnerability it has obtained or discovered—so that software developers have an opportunity to fix the problem—or withhold the information to use the flaw for offensive or defensive purposes. The NSA is the designated agency to lead the VEP, with all the other government agencies, to ascertain their collective interests and weigh offensive capabilities against defensive concerns for the private sector and US interests more generally. The WannaCry attack clearly demonstrated that the NSA did not reveal the vulnerability it had discovered before it was stolen.

The USG has consistently indicated it is predisposed to releasing vulnerabilities and leans toward taking a defensive position. In congressional testimony, the NSA has said the intelligence agencies revealed close to 90 percent of the vulnerabilities they discover. But the Shadow Brokers case and the release of Vault 7 have led to increasing suspicion that the way VEP is 'supposed' to work may only be true given a narrow definition of 'vulnerability'. In this case, their hand was forced. The NSA knew the vulnerability was online and was obligated to act.

A Smorgasbord of Options

WikiLeaks has not been kind to the USG. With each new data dump, more revelations are revealed about what the US has done in the cyber sleuthing arena—and it is truly impressive. In its 2017 "Vault7" series, several previously unknown CIA malware frameworks were revealed. Two of them, dubbed 'AfterMidnight' and 'Assassin', target the Microsoft Windows platform. 'AfterMidnight' allows operators to load and execute malware on a target machine, disguised as a self-persisting dynamic-link library (unique to Microsoft) and executes 'Gremlins —small payloads which run hidden on computers, subverting the functionality of software as well as surveying the target and exfiltration of data. A payload named 'AlphaGremlin' allows operators to schedule customized tasks to be executed on the machine. Once installed, 'AfterMidnight' uses an HTTPS listening port to check for any scheduled events.

'Assassin' is a similar type of malware to 'AfterMidnight'—an automated implant that provides a simple collection platform on remote computers running the Microsoft Windows operating system. The tool purportedly allows operators to perform specific tasks on an infected computer, periodically sending intercepted information to listening posts. It is made up of four subsystems: 'Implant', 'Builder', 'Command and Control', and 'Listening Post'. The 'Implant' provides the core logic and functionality of the tool on a target computer. The way it is set up determines much of how the tool will behave on the target computer. The 'Builder' arranges the Implant and 'Deployment Executables' before deployment, while the 'Command and Control' subsystem acts as an interface between the operator and the 'Listening Post'. The Listening Post allows the 'Implant' to communicate with the subsystem through a web server.[112]

'CherryBlossom' uses wireless devices to access users' Internet activity and provides a means of monitoring the Internet activity of targets while performing software exploits on them. It is focused on compromising wireless networking devices, such as wireless routers and access points, to do so. Such Wi-Fi devices are commonly used as part of the Internet infrastructure in private homes, public spaces, and small and medium-sized enterprises. They are, therefore, ideal for MITM attacks, as they can easily monitor, control, and manipulate the Internet traffic of connected users. By altering the data stream between the user and Internet services, the infected device can inject malicious content into the stream to exploit vulnerabilities in applications or the operating system on the computer of the targeted user.

'Pandemic' is a persistent implant for Microsoft Windows machines that shares files (programs) with remote users in a local network. Pandemic targets remote users by replacing application code with a trojanized version, if the program is retrieved from the infected machine. To obfuscate its activity, the original file on the server remains unchanged; it is only modified or replaced while in transit from the pandemic file server before being executed on the computer of the remote user. The implant allows the replacement of up to 20 programs with a maximum size of 800 megabytes for a selected list of remote targets. As the name suggests, a single computer on a local network with shared drives that is infected with the Pandemic implant will act like a "patient zero" in the spread of a disease. It will infect remote computers if the user executes programs stored on the pandemic file server. It appears to be technically feasible that remote computers that provide file shares can themselves become new Pandemic file servers on the local network to reach new targets.[113]

Another type of CIA malware is known as 'Scribbles', designed to track when documents are leaked by whistleblowers or "Foreign Intelligence Officers". Scribbles is designed to allow the embedding of 'web beacon' tags into documents that are likely to be stolen. Web beacons typically go unnoticed. A tiny file is loaded as part of a webpage. Once this file is accessed, it records unique information about the target (such as the IP address) and sends it back to the creator of the beacon. The CIA is therefore able to see when sensitive documents are accessed by third parties, including by potential whistleblowers.

The tool generates a random watermark for each document, inserts that watermark into the document, saves all such processed documents in an output directory, and creates a log file that identifies the watermarks inserted into each document. Scribbles can watermark multiple documents in one batch and is designed to watermark several groups of documents. It was successfully tested on Microsoft Office versions 1997-2016 and documents that are not locked forms, encrypted, or password protected.[114]

Hive is a multi-platform malware suite that provides "customizable implants" for Windows, Solaris, MikroTik (used in Internet routers), Linux platforms, and AVTech Network Video Recorders (used for CCTV recording). Such implants allow the CIA to communicate specific commands and communicate via HTTPS with the webserver of a cover domain. Each cover domain is connected to an IP address at a commercial VPS provider. This forwards all incoming traffic to 'Blot' servers. The redirected traffic is examined to see if it contains a valid beacon. If it does, it is sent to a tool handler (known as Honeycomb), where the CIA can initiate other actions on the target computer.

To hide the presence of such malware, public HTTPS interfaces (a protocol for secure communication over a computer network within an encrypted connection) utilize unsuspicious-looking cover domains (meaning those targeted would be unaware of the CIA's interference). A 'self-delete' function is described in documentation accompanying Hive, revealing that the implant destroys itself if it is not signaled for a predetermined amount of time.

In March 2017, *WikiLeaks published hundreds of files which it claimed show that the CIA went to great lengths to disguise its own hacking attacks while pointing the finger at Russia, China, North Korea, and Iran. The files gave insight into the CIA's Marble software, which can forensically disguise viruses, trojans, and hacking attacks.* The source code suggests Marble has test examples in Arabic, Chinese, Farsi, Korean, and Russian, which permit a forensic attribution by pretending that the spoken language of the malware creator was not American English but another language. That could lead forensic investigators to wrongly conclude that CIA hacks were carried out by Russia, China, Iran, North Korea, Arabic-speaking terror groups, or potentially any other source (one must assume that other governments have a similar capability).

In 2017, WikiLeaks published thousands of documents claiming to reveal top CIA hacking secrets, including the agency's ability to infiltrate encrypted apps, break into smart TVs and phones, and program self-driving cars. *It also claims the CIA can bypass the encryption of WhatsApp, Signal, Telegram, Wiebo, Confide, and Cloakman by hacking the smartphones the applications run on.* The Agency was also apparently looking at hacking the vehicle control systems used in modern cars and trucks.[115] It is safe to assume that anything a hacker can or wants to do anywhere in the world, can be done, or already has been done, by the CIA, NSA, DIA, or other members of the US intelligence community.

Prism

As part of the data provided by Edward Snowden in 2013, the world learned that the NSA had obtained direct access to the systems of Apple, Facebook, Google, and other US Internet giants, part of a previously undisclosed program called Prism, which allowed USG officials to collect individual search histories, the content of e-mails, file transfers, and live chats, among other things. The NSA's Power Point presentation was obtained by *The Guardian* from Snowden—classified as top secret with no distribution to foreign allies—which was apparently used to train intelligence operatives on the capabilities of the program and claimed to have collection capabilities directly from the servers of major US ISPs. This, along with a host of other revelations from Snowden at the time, captured the world's attention as few other stories had during the Era of Virtual Terrorism.

The NSA access was enabled by changes to US surveillance law introduced under President Bush and renewed under President Obama. Prism facilitates extensive, in-depth surveillance on live communications and stored information, and the law allows for the targeting of any customers of participating firms who live outside the US or those Americans whose communications include individuals outside the US. It also opened the possibility of communications made entirely within the US being collected without warrants, which was against the law.

Disclosure of the Prism program followed the near simultaneous revelation of a top-secret court order compelling telecom provider Verizon to turn over to the USG the telephone records of millions of US customers. The participation of the Internet companies in Prism added to the vigorous debate in the media, ignited by the Verizon revelation, about the scale of surveillance by intelligence services. Unlike the collection of call records, Prism surveillance could include the content of communications (not just the metadata).

Some of the world's largest Internet brands were believed to have been part of the information-sharing program since its introduction in 2007. Microsoft, which had been running an advertising campaign at the time with the slogan "Your privacy is our priority," was the first, with collection beginning in December 2007. It was followed by Yahoo in 2008; Google, Facebook, and PalTalk in 2009; YouTube in 2010; Skype and AOL in 2011; and Apple, in 2012. At the time, it was revealed to the world, the program was continuing to expand, with other providers due to come online. Collectively, the companies covered the vast majority of online e-mail, search, video, and communications networks around the world.

The Prism program allowed the NSA—the world's largest surveillance organization—to obtain targeted communications without having to request them from the service providers and without having to obtain individual court orders. Under the program, the NSA was able to reach directly into the servers of the participating companies and obtain stored communications, as well as perform real-time collection on targeted users. Based on Prism, where the NSA previously needed individual legal authorizations and confirmation that all parties were outside the US in order to eavesdrop on them, it only needed 'reasonable suspicion' that one of the parties was outside the country at the time the records were collected by the NSA to be in compliance with the law. The Prism program allowed the agency to directly and unilaterally seize communications off the companies' servers.[116] It raised profound questions about the limits of government power, compliance with the law, and whether individual and privacy rights actually matter in the US, when they can be superseded by concerns about national security.

Domestic Spying

The USG's propensity for spying on its citizens is well documented. All governments do that, but the US deserves special mention not only because of its capabilities, but because of its laws, which are supposed to strictly guide what can and cannot be done to US citizens, in and outside of the US. During his final year in office, President Obama's administration significantly expanded efforts to search NSA intercepts for information about Americans, distributing thousands of intelligence reports across government with the unredacted names of US residents during the midst of a divisive 2016 presidential election.

The data, made available in May 2017 by the Office of the DNI (ODNI), provided the clearest evidence about how information "accidentally" collected by the NSA overseas about Americans was subsequently searched and disseminated after President Obama loosened privacy protections to make such sharing easier in 2011, in the name of national security. The revelations were particularly sensitive, since the NSA is legally forbidden from directly spying on Americans, and its authority to conduct warrantless searches on foreigners is subject to renewal.

In all, government officials conducted 30,355 searches in 2016, seeking information about Americans in NSA intercept metadata, which included telephone numbers and e-mail addresses. The activity amounted to a 27 percent increase over the prior year and more than triple the 9,500 such searches that occurred in 2013, the first year such data was kept. In 2016, the government also scoured the actual contents of NSA intercepted calls and e-mails for 5,288 Americans, an increase of 13 percent over the prior year and a massive spike from the 198 names searched in 2013. The searches ultimately resulted in 3,134 NSA intelligence reports with unredacted US names being distributed across the government that year and another 3,354 reports in 2015. About half the time, US identities were unredacted in the original reports, while, in the other half, they were unmasked after the fact by special request of Obama administration officials.

Among those whose names were unmasked in 2016 or early 2017 were campaign or transition associates of President Trump, as well as members of Congress and their staffers. The data kept by the ODNI lacked some information from one of the largest consumers of NSA intelligence, the FBI. The numbers are likely much higher when the FBI's activity is added. An April 2017, release of a previously classified Foreign Intelligence Surveillance Court (FISC) document[117] revealed that the NSA had a "potentially very large and broad" collection of data on US persons that was never intended under the law.

The NSA is allowed to spy on foreign powers without a court warrant under Section 702 of the Foreign Surveillance

Intelligence Act (FISA) but is forbidden to target Americans. For years, the NSA was required to follow strict rules to protect the accidental intercepts of Americans from being consumed by other government agencies. The rules required a process known as minimization, where the identity of an intercepted American is redacted or masked with generic references like "American No. 1". The intelligence community fought hard over the last decade (beginning under President George W. Bush) to gain greater access to NSA intercepts of Americans overseas, citing the growing challenges of stopping lone wolf terrorists, state-sponsored hackers, and foreign threats. Obama obliged with a series of orders that began in 2011, moves that were approved by the FISC.

In 2017, the power to unmask an American's name—once considered a rare event in the intelligence and civil liberty communities—resided with about 20 NSA officials. The FBI also has the ability to unmask Americans' names collected under FISA to other intelligence professionals and policymakers, though it has not provided data on its frequency. The justification for requesting such unmasking can be as simple as claiming "the identity of the US person is necessary to understand foreign intelligence information or assess its importance", according to a once-classified document that the Obama administration submitted in October 2011 for approval by the FISC. That memo laid out specifically how and when the NSA could unmask an American's identity. Intelligence officials try to assuage concerns by saying that FISA Section 702 activities are really focused only on foreign powers and stopping national security threats.

However, the NSA 'accidentally' collects information on Americans and then shares it after the fact. The FBI, for instance, regularly queries the NSA database; the declassified court document said, "there is no requirement that the matter be a serious one nor that it have any relation to national security". The reality is that the USG operates an invasive surveillance program whose impact on Americans is substantial. A federal judge in Washington ruled in 2013, and again in 2015, that the NSA collection of data on Americans violates the 4th Amendment of the Constitution. The FISA court, meanwhile, continues to support the intelligence community's continued use of the data.[118]

<u>North Korea</u>

In 2014, former president Obama had grown so frustrated by North Korean intransigence over its missile and nuclear weapons programs that he ordered the Pentagon to enhance the US's cyberwarfare campaign against North Korea. The goal was to sabotage any test launches within seconds. Soon, a large number of the North's military rockets began to explode, veer off course, disintegrate in midair and plunge into the sea. A 2017 examination of the Pentagon's disruption effort found that the US still does not have the ability to effectively counter North Korean nuclear and missile programs. President Trump has signaled his preference to respond aggressively against the North Korean threat. He could order the escalation of the Pentagon's cyber and electronic warfare effort but that carries no guarantees.

The decision to intensify the cyber and electronic strikes came after Obama had concluded that the $300 billion spent since the Eisenhower era on traditional antimissile systems, often compared to hitting "a bullet with a bullet", had failed the core purpose of protecting the continental US. Flight tests of interceptors based in Alaska and California had an overall failure rate of 56 percent, under near-perfect conditions. Privately, many experts have warned the system would fare worse in real combat. So the Obama administration searched for a better way to destroy missiles. It reached for techniques the Pentagon had long been experimenting with under the rubric of "left of launch", because the attacks begin before the missiles ever reach the launchpad or just as they lift off. For years, the Pentagon's most senior officers and officials have publicly advocated these kinds of sophisticated attacks in little-noticed testimony to Congress and at defense conferences.

The approach taken in targeting the North Korean missiles has distinct echoes of the American- and Israeli-led sabotage of Iran's nuclear program, the most sophisticated known use of a cyberweapon meant to cripple a nuclear threat. But even that use of the "Stuxnet" worm in Iran quickly experienced an important limitation—it was effective for several years, until the Iranians figured it out and imposed counter measures. Iran posed a relatively easy target: an underground nuclear enrichment plant that could be attacked repeatedly. In North Korea, the target is much more challenging, since missiles are fired from multiple launch sites around the country and moved about on mobile launchers in an elaborate shell game meant to deceive adversaries. To strike them, timing is critical.

In the last year of his presidency, Obama often noted publicly that the North was learning from every nuclear and missile test—even the failures—and getting closer to its goal. In private, aides noticed he was increasingly disturbed by North Korea's progress. Once the US uses cyberweapons against nuclear launch systems—even in a threatening state like North Korea—Russia and China may feel free to do the same, targeting fields of American missiles. Some strategists argue that all nuclear systems should be off limits for cyberattack. Otherwise, if a nuclear power thought it could secretly disable an adversary's atomic controls, it might be more tempted to take the risk of launching a pre-emptive attack. Advocates of the sophisticated effort to remotely manipulate data inside North Korea's missile systems argue that the US has no real alternative because the effort to stop the North from learning the secrets of making nuclear weapons has already failed. The only hope now is stopping the country from developing an intercontinental missile, and demonstrating that destructive threat to other nations.[119]

A New Form of World War

In 1914, Sir Arthur Conan Doyle, creator of the fictional detective Sherlock Holmes, published a short story entitled "Danger!" just 18 months before the outbreak of World War I. In it, he presented a fictional war in which an imaginary country fights and defeats Britain. What made that possible was the submarine, which at the time had only recently become a practical weapon. Global leaders paid little attention to the book. The German U-boat subsequently became one of the most dangerous weapons used in World War II.

In the future, technology and warfare will combine to include a global cast of characters fighting at sea, on land, in the air, and in two new places of conflict: cyberspace and outer space. Warship captains will battle through a modern-day Pearl Harbor, fighter pilots duel with stealthy drones, teenage hackers battle in digital playgrounds, previous war veterans will be forced to fight as low-tech insurgents, Silicon Valley billionaires will mobilize for cyberwar, and serial killers will carry out their own vendettas online. Victory will depend on who can best blend the lessons of the past with the weapons of the future.[120]

We are already witnessing the emergence of an array of technology that was only recently in the realm of science fiction. The emergence of weapons that will likely shape tomorrow's wars range from cyberwarfare to drones and from AI to virtual reality to Virtual Terrorism. And, as was the case in Doyle's ignored warning to Britain, the US (and by definition, the rest of the world's countries) will not be prepared.

Based on China's approach to cyber and military strategy, it seems unlikely that trade, diplomacy, and common interests between the US and China will necessarily avert a real conflict. Part of the reason is China's "Assassin's Mace" program, which is designed to fight a technologically superior adversary. The program includes cyberwarfare, space warfare, and other systems that could disable the fighting ability of the US military. Many experts refer to the Chinese breach of the OPM as America's "Cyber Pearl Harbor", but the breach is nothing compared to what a real military cyberattack would look like. Such an attack would very quickly move a war beyond borders and into the homelands of rival nations in ways never seen before.[121]

In 2015, China published its first official military guidelines under Xi Jinping, officially shifting its focus toward "winning informationized local wars". Under the new strategy, the space and cyber domains are thought of as the 'commanding heights of strategic competition'.[122] IT will play a larger role in all aspects of military operations for all elements of the PLA's combat-related activities. The new guidelines focus on the central objective of "winning" informationized local wars, indicating that high technology will become the basic form of warfare in the 21st century.[123] In some ways, it already has.

In 2017, Russia's military admitted for the first time the scale of its information warfare effort, saying it was significantly expanded after the end of the original Cold War. During the Cold War both the USSR and the West poured significant resources into propaganda to influence public opinion globally and sell their competing ideologies. The same is true today, and both sides' "information troops" are much more effective and stronger than the former counter-propaganda section used to be. But Russian "information warfare" occupies a wider sphere than the current Western focus on cyberwarriors and hackers. *Their aim is to control information in whatever form it takes, with one purpose being to undermine the notion of objective truth and reporting. In the 21st century, a victory in information warfare can be much more important than victory in a classical military conflict. Although bloodless, the impact can be overwhelming and can paralyze all of an enemy state's power structures.*[124]

All of the "big three" nations in the cyberwarfare arena have formidable capabilities and tools at their disposal. Each has a unique platform from which to launch cyberattacks, alternative approaches to achieving their objectives, and different means of countering cyberthreats, which they may not wish to make publicly known so as to maintain an edge on their adversaries. As advanced as each nation is in their own cyber tradecraft, it is important to remember that the Virtual Terrorism they collectively practice remains in an embryonic state. The Internet era is not yet even three decades old. Given how far cyberwarfare has already advanced—particularly in the past ten years—it is hard to imagine what the landscape will look like ten or twenty years from now. That is a truly chilling prospect and the stakes could not be higher.

When the Cyber Era and Governments Collide

Global politics have been in a state of metamorphosis since the beginning of the 21st century, the result of the rise of extreme political parties, the War on Terror, the birth of instant communication, globalization, and a general propensity in favor of the upending of the status quo. The birth of the cyber era meshes quite well with this age of political disruption and transformation, for it is propelling the speed and depth of that change and the world would appear to be ripe for it.

While the cyber arena and geopolitics have many characteristics that separate them—such as borders, anonymity, and the rule of law—it is these very things that are also making them more similar. For example, states have borders in the physical world but, in the cyber world, nations are able to project their power without borders. The same anonymity that is afforded hackers in the Dark Web makes government actions indistinguishable from individuals or non-state groups, since attribution may never be known for certain. And since there is no rule of law in cyber space, any actor can benefit from its absence.

The cyber era also puts all cyber-enabled countries on a more equal footing. Those countries which are more advanced technologically and have more financial, intelligence, and military resources will naturally be more adept at projecting their power in cyberspace. That said, smaller and less advanced countries with fewer resources are also able to get on a more level playing field and punch well above their weight in the cyber arena. Iran and North Korea are two good examples. That is having a profound impact on the virtual geopolitical landscape and will continue to effect if, how, and when nations battle each other in cyberspace, with unpredictable outcomes.

The linkage between change in the cyber and political spheres can only become stronger as each continues to impact the other. Because the cyber era is in an embryonic stage of development, and since it has already clearly influenced, and been influenced by, global politics, it is difficult to envision a future in which their fortunes are not intertwined and do not collide. No one can predict just how this intrinsic marriage will evolve but it is safe to assume that they will continue to impact each other's evolution for a long time to come.

4. The Private Sector

When American Superconductor began doing business with China, the company made sure its data systems were locked tight. It used strong encryption and had a solid system for cybersecurity. When, in 2011, it tested its software on Chinese company Sinovel's turbines, although the system had been programmed to shut down after the test, the blades kept spinning. Sinovel had successfully broken its encryption. It turned out that the breach took place through one of its employees—an Austrian named Dejan Karabasevic, who would later spend a year in jail for his crime. The Chinese offered him women, an apartment, and money. All it took for the company to lose its key product to China was for Karabasevic to say "yes".[125]

In 2014, the USG sent 97,000 incident reports and 12,000 actionable alerts to US businesses, warning about cyberattacks. It was estimated at the time that US businesses received alerts on more than 250 threats every day. Even with that, incidents of cybertheft were increasing about 25 percent each year. In spite of all the alerts, all the antivirus software, and all the money and resources spent trying to combat cyberattacks, the reality is that there is no such thing as complete security; rather, the objective is to achieve a degree of comfort, so that decision makers, employees, and shareholders can feel as though everything that can be done is being done to avoid and manage cyberattacks.

According to a comprehensive survey[126] of 3,000 companies in the US, UK, and Germany in 2017, less than half were prepared to address cybercrime in terms of strategy, resourcing, technology, and process. The report found 53 percent of the companies were ill-prepared to deal with an attack, and just 30 percent were rated "expert" in their overall cyber readiness. The survey's producers estimated that cybercrime cost the global economy more than $450 billion in 2016, with in excess of 2 billion personal records stolen and more than 100 million Americans having had their medical records stolen.[127]

Many cyberattacks against corporations go unreported and the number of attacks on corporates is much higher than what makes headlines, according to a 2015 report by Lieberman Software Corporation, which surveyed almost 150 IT professionals. Some 51 percent of respondents believed their corporate networks were continuously targeted by hackers. In addition, 71 percent of the IT professionals believed their company would be targeted by advanced cyberattacks within the next six months. The upshot is that companies may be losing more money than they are admitting, with 87 percent of the respondents saying that large financial hacks are happening more often than reported.[128]

Cybersecurity has moved beyond the idea that attacks can be prevented and more toward achieving cyber resilience. The difference between cybersecurity and cyber resilience is an understanding that no system will ever be completely secure. This has become the new starting point when addressing threats in cyberspace and is based on the idea that traditional cyber defenses are simply inadequate to address the threat landscape that already exists. *Cyber resilience is all about being able to function while simultaneously fending off and reacting to cyberattacks.*

Part of the objective is to educate staff so as to not accidentally compromise company networks. Some companies send e-mails to their staff designed to look like phishing attacks and keep track of how many employees fall for it. Phishing attacks are becoming a common tool in the hacker arsenal, mainly because they bypass a company's security protocol and are directed at employees. The attacks often take the form of spoof e-mails, with infected files attached. If the target opens the file, it infects his computer. What is surprising is that many of these phishing attacks actually work. One would think that Internet users would have some orientation toward what may look suspicious and what may not but most people are not very sophisticated adversaries for hackers. Just as most infrastructure and soft targets were not built with security in mind, the Internet was not, either.[129]

High Stakes

One of the best known and highest stakes cyberattacks ever made against a business occurred in 2012, courtesy of Iran. A previously unknown hacker group called the Cutting Sword of Justice took responsibility for carrying out an extremely destructive attack on oil and gas giant Saudi Aramco. The attack occurred on the eve of one of the holiest nights on the Islamic calendar—Lailat al-Qadr—when Aramco's 50,000 employees were at home celebrating. At stake was the country's 260 billion gallons of oil, valued at the time at more than $8 trillion (14 times the market capitalization of Apple).

An unknown insider with access to the company inserted an infected USB thumb drive into a single PC connected to the company's computer network. Within minutes, the drive's viral payload, known as Shamoon, spread quickly across the company's 30,000 corporate computers. Though its goal was apparently to disrupt oil and gas production at the company's facilities, the existence of some antivirus protection meant the virus 'only' destroyed corporate data. Shamoon erased 75 percent of the company's computers' hard drives, destroying documents, spread sheets, e-mails, and files, and replacing all of it with an image of a burning American flag.

The attack predated a number of other successful attacks by the Iranian government against private sector entities, including a series of DDoS disruptions in 2013, targeting the US financial services industry, which affected Bank of America, Chase, Citigroup, and Wells Fargo. Some of the banks were hit with a sustained flood of traffic that peaked at 70 GB per second—as if one billion people had simultaneously phoned one of the banks, hung up, and immediately dialed back one second later. In order for a call or visit to the bank's website to get connected, one billion people would have been connected before you.[130] The ticket for entry to this game is not difficult to obtain—almost at will in some cases—and the stakes are extremely high.

Cyber Agreements without Teeth

Cyberattacks are often carried out from countries that have no extradition treaties with other countries and are directed toward businesses that are not allowed to launch counterattacks and whose CEOs are petrified of making news of the attacks public for fear of lawsuits and the wrath of angry investors. It is a crime with a high profit margin and relatively little risk. Even businesses that sell allegedly stolen products remain able to continue to sell those products freely in most countries. Although some laws exist to prevent it, there is no meaningful enforcement mechanism in place to combat it.

Many nations are guilty of routinely stealing other nations' intellectual property and engaging in cyberespionage. China has been particularly brazen in its exploits, which are well documented. As previously mentioned, in 2015, former President Barack Obama announced a deal with President Xi Jinping to end cyberattacks meant for economic gain but the very next day Chinese cyberattacks on US businesses continued as usual. The Chinese economy has become so reliant on the theft to power its growth that it cannot simply switch it off, even if it wanted to.

Despite all the noise around Chinese economic theft, there is an air of quiet tolerance among Western businesses—a kind of blind acquiescence and grudging acceptance that it is the price that must be paid in order to do business with the most populous country and second largest economy in the world. Compounding this, of course, is that *neither the US nor any other country has a meaningful strategy or policy framework for addressing cyberattacks because there can be none, based on the current state of affairs.*

As an example, the US firm American Superconductor had its software stolen in China, prompting the company to fire 600 of its nearly 900 employees there and costing the company more than a billion dollars. Sinovel, the company partly owned by the Chinese regime that allegedly stole it, now exports wind turbines that run on American Superconductor's technology. The Chinese were even able to sell one of the turbines to the state of Massachusetts, which paid for it with federal stimulus funds. The case is a clear example of what a cyber agreement with China needs but lacks—sanctions that actually discourage *theft*.

When American Superconductor began doing business with China, the company made sure its data systems were locked tight. It used strong encryption and had a solid system for cybersecurity. When, in 2011, it tested its software on Sinovel's turbines, although the system had been programmed to shut down after the test, the blades kept spinning because its Chinese corporate partner had successfully broken American Superconductor's encryption. It turned out that the breach took place through one of its employees—an Austrian named Dejan Karabasevic, who would later spend a year in jail for his crime. The Chinese offered him women, an apartment, and money. All it took for the company to lose its key product to China was for Karabasevic to say "yes".

The CCP has reduced its cyberattacks against the US since the agreement was signed, although many of its hacker units remain active. In June 2016, cybersecurity company FireEye reported that, since mid-2014, it had seen a notable decline in China-based groups' overall intrusion activity against entities in the US and 25 other countries. The CCP's revised program on state-sponsored cyberattacks has two points of focus: to expand the reach of Chinese factories and to steal intellectual property from competitors directly.

It builds on existing programs for economic theft the CCP already had in place, which run parallel to its cybertheft operations. These include its Torch program for high-tech commercial industries, its 973 Program for research, and its 211 program for using universities. All of these programs leverage foreign collaboration and technologies to cover key gaps and use methods that include encouraging skilled experts to return to China or to have them serve in place, providing information gained from Western employers. This is being combined with selectively pushing foreign companies out of China if their own domestic products are at a level where they can compete with each other in global markets. The companies they allow to remain in China are those they can still learn from.[131]

Obama signed an executive order giving him the ability to sanction companies that commit economic theft and the threat of sanctions was believed to be one of the incentives used to arrive at the cyber agreement but *sanctions were not mentioned directly in the agreement. In essence, the cyber agreement gave China a platform for dialogue with the US on the subject while continuing to pretend it is not part of the problem nor having it pay a price for cybertheft.* The problem of economic theft seems complicated on the surface but, when you boil it down, it is really simple: *governments will use any means they have to steal intellectual property and grab market share. To address the problem, every nation needs to broaden its view of economic theft beyond cybersecurity, implement laws with enforcement and sanctions teeth, and be willing to hold other nations accountable for their actions.* [132] Clearly, that is easier said than done.

May I Please Give You My Encryption Keys?

The CCP's National Security Law from 2015 addresses nearly every facet of Chinese society. Part of it is aimed at foreign companies and proclaims that all information systems in China must be "secure and controllable". Under it, *every company operating in China is required to give Chinese authorities their source code, encryption keys, and backdoor access to their computer networks in China.* In other words, businesses must now simply hand Chinese agents the lifeblood of their companies and products, while also giving the CCP a free pass to spy on their networks. *The Chinese government has arranged that, in order to do business in China, the information that Chinese agents once had to steal through cyberattacks are now automatically provided for the 'privilege' of doing business there.* Incredibly, even the largest, best known, and most influential foreign companies that operate in China are doing just that.

IBM became the first major US tech company to agree to the new rules. At one of IBM's Chinese facilities, agents with the Chinese Ministry of Industry and IT were invited into a secure room where IBM allowed them to look at some of their source code. It was not clear which IBM products they opened up for review nor how long the Chinese agents were allowed to review it. While the agents were not allowed to take the code out of the room, it is unclear what, if any, security precautions were taken by IBM to ensure the agents were not recording the process with hidden cameras.

IBM began delivering its technical knowledge to Chinese companies that had clearly stated their objective of replacing

IBM's markets in China. The company passed information about how to build its high-end servers and the software that runs the servers to Beijing-based Teamsun, which proudly declared its strategy to 'absorb and then innovate', enabling it to eliminate the capability gap between Chinese and American companies and create products that could replace those sold by companies in the US.[133]

That was not the first time IBM had done something similar. In 2014, IBM sold its x86 server division to Chinese computer company Lenovo. The $2.1 billion sale included the x86 BladeCenter HT servers used in some critical US Navy systems, including its Aegis Combat System, which controlled the Navy's ballistic missile and air defense systems. When a business with products used in critical government and military networks reveals its code to another government, it becomes a national security issue.

The US Navy was subsequently forced to identify and purchase new servers, concerned that Chinese government agents could remotely access the systems by compromising routine maintenance. A vulnerability on Lenovo computers was subsequently discovered, which took advantage of the Lenovo System Update, leaving the door open for hackers. The servers were used by Navy assets, including its guided missile cruiser and destroyer fleets, and ballistic missile and anti-air defenses.[134]

In 2015, Hewlett-Packard (HP) sold more than half of its networking and server operations to China, whose restrictions on foreign technology vendors pushed its banks, military, and major companies to stop buying foreign technology. HP gave up control of its then $4.5 billion business to remain in the Chinese market, selling 51 percent of its networking and server operations in the country to an arm of Beijing's Tsinghua University.[135] Presumably, the reason HP was being allowed to remain was because the Chinese government had not yet acquired what it perceived to be all of HP's intellectual and material capital. Once that has been accomplished, HP will presumably be asked or told to leave, either directly or via passage of a new law, with which it will be found to be non-compliant.

China's first Cybersecurity Law, enacted in 2017, increases costs for multinationals while leaving them vulnerable to industrial espionage and ultimately giving some Chinese companies an unfair advantage. Aspects of the measure have been widely welcomed as a milestone in much needed data privacy but it could also have the effect of helping Beijing steal trade secrets or intellectual property from foreign companies. The law is both extremely vague and exceptionally wide in scope, potentially putting companies at risk of regulatory enforcement that is not related to cybersecurity.

The law is part of a drive by Beijing to shield Chinese data from the eyes of foreign governments. Under it, companies must introduce data protection measures—a novelty for many Chinese businesses—and data relating to the country's citizens or national security must be held on *Chinese* servers. Companies must submit to a review by regulators before transferring large amounts of personal data abroad. "Critical" companies—which designation encompasses sensitive entities such as power companies or banks but also any company holding data that, if breached, could "harm people's livelihoods"—must store all data collected in China within the country. These companies, and any services bought by them, must go through a "national security review" to ensure they and their data systems are "secure and controllable". A proposed supplementary law on encryption allows the government to demand "decryption support" in the interests of national security, meaning the government can force companies to decode encrypted data.

Among its key provisions are:

- Government departments and companies gathering private information must protect digital data (for example, through encryption);

- Collecting "citizens' personal information" without permission is a criminal offense.

- All companies must undertake a security assessment before moving data out of China if it contains the personal information of more than half a million users or data "likely to affect national security or social public interests";

- "Critical infrastructure" companies must store "personal information and other important data" collected in China inside the country; and

- "Important network products and services" must undergo a "national security review" before being sold in China.

The measure allows Beijing to request computer program source code (usually known only by the software developer) and national security reviews may also permit China to delve even further into companies' intellectual property. Fast-food delivery companies could be considered critical infrastructure, Shanghai regulators ruled during a pilot run for the law, because they hold information about millions of users. Multinational corporations will be hardest hit, as the data localization measures prevent them from pooling client data in cloud storage databases across the world, creating data fragmentation and adding significantly to data storage costs.[136]

A Target-rich Environment

The private sector is vulnerable to Virtual Terrorism in so many ways but is often unaware of its own vulnerabilities. For example, most businesses are unaware that *since 2002 nearly all photocopiers have internal hard drives that store every document that is either copied or scanned.* Since many of these devices are either leased or sold, the data they contain is available for anyone who is so inclined and who is capable of downloading its contents.

Unbeknownst to most printer users, many color printers add small dots to each page printed, which serve as identifiers. While barely visible to the naked eye, these "microdots" form a coded design, reveal the exact date and time that pages are printed, and encode a serial number for the printer. Based on their positions, when plotted against a grid, the dots denote specific hours, minutes, dates, and numbers, which can be decoded to learn where a document came from and whether it could be a forgery. For example, many banknotes around the world feature a unique five-point pattern called the Eurion constellation. In an effort to avoid counterfeiting, many photocopiers and scanners are programmed not to produce copies of banknotes when this pattern is recognized. Intelligence agencies (and some companies) have logs listing each time a document is printed and by whom.[137]

In 2010, CBS News visited a New Jersey warehouse that had 6,000 used photocopiers for sale, all loaded with corporate and government secrets. Reporters and researchers purchased four of the copiers and used widely available data recovery tools to uncover tens of thousands of documents, including 95 pages of paystubs (with names, addresses, and Social Security numbers), $40,000 in copied checks, and 300 pages of individual medical records.[138]

Hackers have also gained access to networked copiers to monitor what is being copied in real time. Some office printers have been remotely hacked to gain access to Wi-Fi networks and administrator passwords. An embedded firmware attack discovered in 2011 proved that millions of HP printers could receive instructions remotely to send them into overdrive and literally catch fire. Other common office equipment can also easily be hacked, such as videoconferencing systems, many of which have no security protocols at all. One enterprising hacker was easily able to gain access to more than 500,000 conference rooms all over the world.

Heating, ventilation, and air-conditioning systems in newer buildings are going online and are being integrated with a plethora of alarms, security card readers, elevators, parking gates, and other building systems. All are centrally controlled and can, of course, be hacked. Target stores learned the hard way how vulnerable it was as a result of the interlinkages of its online systems. The company had outsourced its heating and cooling management to a Pennsylvania-based vendor (Fazio Mechanical Services), which directly interfaced with Target's supplier and contract management system. *When a Fazio employee opened a phishing e-mail with a malware-infected attachment, he infected his company and, because it was linked to Target, the result was a breach of the credit card details of 110 million US customers.* Apart from all the other associated costs of the breach, in 2015, Target agreed to pay the victims $10 million.

In 2011, the US Chamber of Commerce was attacked through a newly installed Internet-enabled thermostat in Washington, DC. The installation created a back door to its corporate network. Chamber officials discovered that the thermostat had been secretly communicating with an Internet address in China. The hackers made a mistake when instructing a Chamber printer used by executives and, instead of sending themselves documents, the printer ended up spontaneously printing pages with Chinese characters—another indication of the origin of the hacking. They were ultimately successful in obtaining highly sensitive information related to financial and budgetary matters, as well as trade policy issues in Asia.[139]

An Embarrassment of Breaches

As brazen as China has become in practicing its unique form of cybertheft, the volume, variety, and scope of private sector cyberattacks more generally is truly impressive, unfortunately. Whether the result of being deliberately targeted or due to employee carelessness, as the following examples from 2016 exemplify, cybertheft has become a daily event and fact of life throughout the private sector. March was a particularly costly month that year.

January: The University of Central Florida announced a data breach that affected approximately 63,000 current and former students, faculty, and staff. Unknown cybercriminals compromised the university's computer system and stole a variety of information, including Social Security numbers, first and last names, and student and employee identification information.

March: 700 current and former Snapchat employees had their personal information stolen when hackers used a phishing scam to trick an employee into e-mailing them private data. Posing as Snapchat chief executive Evan Spiegel, the attackers simply requested—and received—sensitive employee information, including names, Social Security numbers, and wage/payroll data.

March: 21st Century Oncology revealed via a statement on its website that 2.2 million patients may have had personal information stolen when the company's system was breached in October 2015. The breach was discovered in November 2015 but the FBI discouraged the company from making a public announcement until March, as the investigation was ongoing. Hackers had access to patient names, Social Security numbers, doctor names, diagnosis and treatment information, and insurance information.

March: A data breach was reported by Premier Healthcare after a laptop computer was stolen from the billing department of its Bloomington, Indiana headquarters. The laptop was protected by a password but it was not encrypted and contained sensitive data pertaining to more than 200,000 patients. Most victims had their names, dates of birth, and other basic information compromised but 1,769 also may have had their Social Security numbers or financial information taken as well.

March: Verizon Enterprise Solutions was hit by hackers who stole the information of about 1.5 million customers. The data was found for sale in an underground cybercrime forum. Verizon acknowledged the breach, saying it had identified the security flaw.

March: A data breach at Systema Software was not the result of hackers but an internal error during a system upgrade in which data storage was set up improperly and made publicly available on the Internet. A white-hat hacker found the information online and reported it but, by that point, customer information had been exposed for 75 days. Affected customers included the Kansas State Self Insurance Fund, the CSAC Express Insurance Authority, American All-Risk Loss Administrators/Risico, Millers Mutual Group, Crosswalk Claims Management, and Salt Lake County.

March: Current and former employees of Tidewater Community College had their personal information stolen in a tax season phishing scam. An employee in the school's finance department received a request from a fake College e-mail address requesting all employee W-2 information. Not realizing that the e-mail was fake, the individual responded with sensitive information, including names, earnings, and Social Security numbers. At least sixteen College employees subsequently reported false tax returns filed under their Social Security numbers.

May: Hold Security discovered more than 270 million of its customers' e-mail user names and passwords were given away for free in the Russian criminal underground. Hold identified about 57 million Mail.ru accounts, 40 million Yahoo accounts, 33 million Hotmail accounts, and 24 million Gmail addresses in the breach. The breach included hundreds of thousands of German and Chinese e-mail providers, along with username and password combinations that belonged to employees of major banking, manufacturing, and retail companies.

May: In January 2016, Wendy's began investigating a potential data breach after receiving reports of unusual activity involving payment cards at some of its restaurant locations. The company believed that malware infiltrated one particular point of sale system at fewer than 300 of approximately of its 5,500 franchised North American restaurants, starting in the fall of 2015. Some breached locations were still leaking customer card data in April. In June, Wendy's announced that the data breach was worse than it originally thought.

May: In 2012, 117 million e-mail and password combinations were stolen by hackers from LinkedIn. That information then became publicly available in May 2016. LinkedIn acted quickly to invalidate passwords of all LinkedIn accounts that were created prior to the breach and had not been reset.

August: Newkirk Products announced a data breach that may have affected up to 3.3 million people. Unknown hackers were able to gain access to a server that contained sensitive member information, including names, mailing addresses, dates of birth, and details about health insurance plans.

August: The company that owns the MICROS point-of-sale system, used in more than 330,000 cash registers around the world, became victim of a data breach. A large Russian cybercrime group was likely to blame, having placed malware on company computers and on the MICROS customer support portal to steal usernames and passwords. The hackers were probably able to plant malware in the MICROS point-of-sale systems and could have been responsible for major data breaches at retailers around the country.

September: In 2012, Dropbox helped a small amount of users secure their accounts after some usernames were stolen. At the end of August, 2016, it was revealed that more than 68 million Dropbox users had their usernames and passwords compromised in that initial breach. All Dropbox users who had not reset their passwords since 2012 were prompted by the company to do so.

September: In what may be the most expansive data breach of all time, Yahoo announced that a hacker had stolen information from as many as 500 million accounts, in late 2014. The thief, believed to be working on behalf of Russia, stole e-mail addresses, passwords, full user names, dates of birth, telephone numbers, and in some cases, security questions and answers.

October: More than 43 million Weebly users were notified about a data breach that happened in February but was only discovered in October. Stolen data included usernames, passwords, e-mail addresses, and IP information. Hackers were not able to log directly into customer websites because passwords were protected by bcrypt hashing.

October: The National Payment Corporation of India (NPCI) was notified by international banks (primarily in the US and China) that some of its customers' debit cards were being used illegally. Experts believe the breach began with a malware attack that originated at an automated teller machine (ATM). The NPCI said that 3.2 million debit cards across 19 Indian banks were compromised.

November: An incorrect security setting on the mobile version of Cisco's "Professional Careers" website created a privacy hole that exposed the personal information of job seekers. Discovered by an independent researcher, the security vulnerability made sensitive data available between August and September 2015, and again from July to August 2016.

That data included names, addresses, e-mails, phone numbers, usernames, passwords, answers to security questions, resumes, cover letters, and voluntary information such as gender, race, veteran status, and disability.

November: Adult FriendFinder was targeted by hackers for the second time in two years. This time, the number of accounts compromised was immense—approximately 412 million users had personal information stolen and published in online criminal marketplaces. The breached data included e-mail addresses, passwords, VIP member status, browser information, the last IP address used to log in, and purchases.

December: Less than three months after announcing its original data breach, Yahoo announced that it had discovered another breach from 2013 that may have compromised the personal information of *one billion Yahoo accounts*, making it the largest data breach in history by far. At the time of the breach announcement, Yahoo did not have much additional information to share with the public, as it remained unclear who was responsible, how they got into the system, and what they stole.[140]

As these examples amply demonstrate, any business—large or small, global or domestic, and well-known or not—can fall victim to cyberattacks. That so many large, global, and well-known firms become victims speaks volumes about just how vulnerable all businesses are. No firm should be under the illusion that it is exempt from being made a target.

Hackers Love Hollywood

As noted in Chapter Two, in 2017, the group of hackers that leaked the fifth season of "Orange is the New Black" secured access to some three dozen other shows and movies. The Dark Overlord provided cybersecurity blog DataBreaches.net with a long list of movies and television shows it claimed to have stolen from Larson Studios, a Hollywood-based audio post-production company. In addition to "Orange Is the New Black," it also listed a number of high-profile shows from the big US broadcast networks, including ABC's "The Catch", NBC's "Celebrity Apprentice", CBS's "NCIS Los Angeles" Fox's "New Girl", IFC's "Portlandia", FX's

"It's Always Sunny in Philadelphia", "Breakthrough" from NatGeo, E!'s "The Arrangement", "Bunk'd" from the Disney Channel, and Netflix's "Bill Nye Saves the World."

It is unknown whether The Dark Overlord was successful in extorting money from any of the studios and networks. The hackers had previously unsuccessfully tried to solicit extortion money from Larson Studios, as well as Netflix, in order to not release "Orange Is the New Black". It is believed they used the release of the entire season as a way to pressure others to pay up,[141] but Netflix refused. Anyone who subscribed to Netflix would get to see the new season as part of the subscription anyway.

Later in the year, hackers also demanded a pirate-like ransom from Disney prior to the formal release of its *Pirates of the Caribbean: Dead Men Tell No Tales*, the fifth installment in the highly profitable franchise. Hackers threatened to release the film in segments until the ransom was paid via Bitcoin. Disney also did not pay, judging that it would become a victim of other forms of 'piracy' after the film was released in any event. It seems Hollywood already had a tacit agreement in place not to pay ransom.

Security for third-party vendors has been a problem for Hollywood for many years. It was only in 2017 that it became a mainstream issue for the entertainment industry. The big Hollywood studios have put a lot of effort into improving their security following the Sony hack in 2014, in which hackers likely associated with North Korea breached the company's networks and released more than 170,000 e-mails as well as 30,000 internal documents—many of which later were published on Wikileaks—in retaliation for the company's release of the film *The Interview*, which had mocked North Korean leader Kim Jong Un. The studios have raised the bar significantly in the last several years but they continue to work with a large network of third-party vendors which are increasingly spread all across the globe.

Visual effects, subtitles, color grading, audio post-production and many other specialized tasks are routinely outsourced to other companies. Some of them are sizable players in their own right, but others have a dozen or fewer employees.

Studios may audit the security of these vendors, but even the best audit only provides a snapshot at a given point in time and certainly does not guarantee that an employee at a vendor will not fall for a phishing scam the following week. It is like a game of chess with no kings. [142] This is a problem with any organization that uses third-party vendors and will remain a point of vulnerability for them, just as it will remain an opportunity for virtual terrorists.

Hearts Really can be Broken

In 2016, hedge fund Muddy Waters released a report claiming that Minnesota-based St. Jude Medical's implantable radio-frequency-enabled pacemakers and defibrillator devices contained severe security flaws which, if hacked, could endanger the lives of patients using the devices. The transmitters record and receive radio frequency traffic from the embedded medical devices before sending this information to physicians through the Merlin.net Patient Care Network. Once inside, attackers can modify the programming of these devices (leading to battery depletion), tamper with set heart pacing, or introduce shocks.

At the time, the company vigorously denied the report, claiming it was merely an attempt by the fund to drive down its share price. St. Jude Medical's lawsuit against Muddy Waters maintained that the fund had created a short-selling scheme that involved shorting the firm's stock at the time the report was released, estimating that share prices would be affected for at least two years. At the same time, MedSec, a research and security solution provider to the healthcare industry, was hired by the fund as a consultant, earning fees and becoming entitled to a percentage of the fund's investments.

This led to a complicated legal battle that resulted in St. Jude releasing a patch to fix the vulnerabilities, stating it would "complement the company's existing measures and further reduce the extremely low cybersecurity risks" while admitting that "all medical devices using remote monitoring are exposed to the risk of a potential cybersecurity attack". Muddy Waters believed the patches did not address many of the larger cyber issues associated with some medical devices, including the existence of a universal code that could allow hackers to control the implants. The FDA subsequently determined that the health benefits to patients from continued use of these devices outweighed the cybersecurity risks but agreed to monitor the situation.[143]

Dragged Kicking and Screaming into the Digital Era

When, in 2016, a group of more than 150 filmmakers and photojournalists called on Canon, Nikon, and other well-known camera manufacturers to add encryption features to their products, the campaign exposed a sore spot for the camera industry, since cameras do not have built-in encryption to protect their contents. The absence of security measures underscores a deeper struggle for the traditional camera industry, of course, which has wrestled for years to adapt its products to the Digital Era.

Japan's biggest camera makers—including Canon, Nikon, Olympus, and Sony—all declined to provide details about what security measures they were studying following the calls to add encryption features to their products. Canon said it did not consider market demand for security measures to be high (which is correct, given the general ignorance of consumers to the risk). Other companies point to security measures that are already built into image storing devices, although such safeguards are of little use if cameras are stolen or confiscated. Experts believe it would be a challenge to implement encryption features without compromising convenience, cost, and user experience. This would be the case especially for professional photographers who work under stress in combat zones and struggle to meet deadlines.

Critics say the lack of attention given to security measures by the most established camera manufacturers is testimony that the industry is hesitant to address the disruption caused by the rise of online platforms such as Instagram and smartphone photography. New industry players may fill the void for consumers who want the sophisticated imaging of top-quality photography along with solid security measures and the convenience of compact smartphones. In 2017, Silicon Valley company Light launched the L16, designed to replace a professional digital single-reflex camera with a compact $1,700 device that fits in the palm of a hand and can create pictures of up to 52 megapixels by computationally merging images from the camera's 16 lenses. The camera uses the Android operating system, which comes with inbuilt encryption.[144] As is often the case, some conventional and stodgy industries, companies, and products must be dragged kicking and screaming into the Digital Era.

Legalized Selling of Personal Data

In 2017, the US Congress voted to allow ISPs to sell the browsing habits of their customers to advertisers so as to deliver personal ads online. Critics charged that the move fundamentally undermined consumer privacy in the US and overturned Obama-era rules designed to give individuals more control over their personal data. Drawn up by the FCC, those rules were scheduled to take effect by the end of 2017 and would have forced ISPs to gain individuals' consent before selling their data to advertisers and others. *ISPs such as Comcast, Verizon, and AT&T became free to track all browsing behavior—including web visits, clicks, searches, app downloads, and video streams—and sell it to advertisers without consent.* This represents a huge treasure trove of personal data, including health concerns, shopping habits, and pornography preferences.

Not all ISPs want to harvest their users' data. At the time President Trump and the Congress implemented the new law, some of the smaller players—including Sonic, Cruzio Internet, and Etheric Networks—wrote to the US Congress opposing the repeal of the FCC's privacy rules, unsuccessfully. Most Americans, particularly those in rural areas, have very little choice of broadband provider, with approximately 80 percent having just one or two options where they live; even if they wanted to change providers, they could not, which is unfortunate.

AT&T had previously considered using personal data to inject personalized advertising into its browsing experience, offering customers the ability to opt out (for $744 per year) but the program was terminated just before the FCC introduced the new privacy rules. Verizon attempted to insert undetectable "supercookies" into all of its mobile customers' traffic, which allowed the company to track all their browsing behavior—even if a web user was browsing in incognito mode or clearing their cookies and history. The company was sued by the FCC for not obtaining customer permission to track them.

Do consumers have any options? A VPN redirects Internet traffic to disguise where a computer, phone, or other device is when it makes contact with websites. It also encrypts the information sent across the Internet so that it is unreadable to anyone who wants to intercept that traffic—including ISPs (VPNs are widely used in China to work around the government's draconian restrictions on Internet usage). In 2015, the free VPN service Hola was revealed to be selling its users' idle bandwidth to paying customers, including possible botnets. Unfortunately, VPNs typically slow down Internet speed and prevent users from benefitting from some web services, such as Netflix (which wants to prevent consumers from accessing content not licensed in their home countries).

The Tor browser protects users by bouncing communications around a distributed network of relays run by volunteers all around the world, preventing someone from monitoring your Internet connection and learning what sites you visit. It also prevents the sites you visit from discovering your physical location, while enabling you to access sites that may be blocked. Tor can be used on most operating systems without needing to install any software, can run off a USB flash drive, and comes with a pre-configured web browser to protect your anonymity.[145] Tor can be challenging to set up, can lead to slower average Internet speeds, and needs regular updates to ensure the connection is secure.[146] Savvy technophiles can choose from a range of options to bypass traditional Internet options.

Can Public-Private Partnerships Actually Work?

Although both the private and public sectors are sources of cyberattacks, as well as victims, neither can effectively tackle the problem alone. A partnership between them stands the best chance of achieving enhanced success in countering cyberattacks. There have been numerous attempts to do so, including holding cyber 'summits', summoning C-suite meetings between leaders of business and government, and passing legislation designed to begin to do something meaningful. Most of these efforts, while not having been 'wasted', have not resulted in the desired outcome, whether the result of a failure to devote sufficient resources to the problem, a lack of resolve on either or both sides, or simply a failure to execute. Clearly, something more needs to be done in this area and there is a long way to go.

To illustrate just how far, the Computer Fraud and Abuse Act (CFAA) was enacted by US Congress in *1986* as an amendment to existing computer fraud law that had been included in the Comprehensive Crime Control Act of 1984. It was written to clarify and increase the scope of the previous version, while limiting federal jurisdiction to cases with a compelling federal interest (i.e. where computers of the federal government or financial institutions were involved, or where there was interstate crime). In addition to clarifying a number of the provisions in the original Act, the CFAA also criminalized additional computer-related acts. Provisions of the Act addressed the distribution of malicious code and DDos attacks. Congress also included in the CFAA a provision criminalizing trafficking in passwords and similar items.

The Act had been amended a number of times—in 1989, 1994, 1996, in 2001 (by the Patriot Act), 2002, and in 2008 by the Identity Theft Enforcement and Restitution Act. In 2015, President Obama proposed expanding the CFAA and the Racketeer Influenced and Corrupt Organizations Act in the *Modernizing Law Enforcement Authorities to Combat Cyber Crime* proposal, which would have made many regular Internet activities illegal.[147] However, like so many other pieces of proposed legislation designed to try to limit activity on the Internet, that proposal was never approved by Congress.

In March 2017, legislation was floated in the US House of Representatives that would give companies attacked by hackers free rein to penetrate those hackers' networks, as long as they agree not to destroy anything while they are there. The proposed Active Cyber Defense Certainty Act (with the excellent acronym, ACDC) would have allowed companies under attack to break into their attackers' networks either to stop an attack or to gather intelligence about the attackers' identity to share with law enforcement. In other words, *it would have legalized retaliation* but would not have protected companies from prosecution if they destroy any data in the process, cause injury to someone, or otherwise endanger public health or safety (the bill draft also expressly forbad vigilantism).

USG officials have typically warned against allowing companies to "hack back" out of fear they would accidentally harm innocent bystanders or, in the case of nation-state-backed hackers, force the government into an unwanted or unexpected diplomatic or military conflict. US lawmakers and executive branch officials frequently complain, however, that, in the case of highly resourced nation-state-backed hacking groups, industry is being forced into a fight it cannot win, and government is not doing nearly as much as it could to protect the private sector from cyberattacks. In a sense, the bill would have given businesses and individuals legal leeway to defend themselves online, just as they could during a physical assault. [148]

Most cyber scholars are wary of allowing private companies to move beyond their own networks in combating cyberattacks, but others support the idea of governments "deputizing" certain companies that are well vetted to take on some cyber investigations and retaliatory cyber strikes. "Active defense" measures begin with sharing information about adversaries, luring them with misinformation, and hunting down information about hackers on the Dark Web. They extend, in rare circumstances, to going on "rescue missions" to retrieve or destroy stolen data inside an intruder's networks or locking an attacker's network until stolen information is returned, just as the hackers themselves do (also known as "white hat ransomware"). Supporters of active defense note that the risk of harming innocents is a risk worth taking, and that innocents are hurt all the time by hackers, who are by their nature often indiscriminate.

Some active defense measures include "seeding" a network with beacons that, if stolen by a hacker, will send back information about the hacker's computer, using technical measures to disconnect botnets that computer hackers use to launch attacks that overwhelm a website, and cooperating with governments to combat foreign adversaries through indictments and sanctions. Clearly, governments need to issue public guidance describing what active cyber defense measures are allowed by current laws, which will give companies more latitude to aggressively defend themselves without fearing prosecution.

The CFAA, now more than 30 years old, is definitely outdated and insufficiently detailed to be truly useful in the 21st century. In 2016, the US Justice Department released a set of principles (drafted in 2014) to guide prosecutors considering bringing charges under the law. It included a number of factors prosecutors must consider in order to ensure that charges are brought only in cases that serve a substantial federal interest, including:

- The sensitivity of the affected computer system or the information transmitted by or stored on it, and the likelihood and extent of harm associated with damage or unauthorized access to the computer system or related disclosure and use of information;

- The degree to which damage or access to a computer system or the information transmitted by or stored on it raises concerns pertaining to national security, critical infrastructure, public health and safety, market integrity, international relations, or other considerations having a broad or significant impact on national or economic interests;

- The extent to which the activity was connected with a larger criminal endeavor or posed a risk of bodily harm or a threat to national security;

- The impact of the crime and prosecution on the victim or other third parties;

- Whether the criminal conduct is based upon exceeding authorized access consistent with several policy considerations, including whether the defendant knowingly violated restrictions on his or her authority to obtain or alter information stored on a computer, and not merely that the defendant subsequently misused information or services that was authorized to obtain from a computer at the time he or she obtained it;

- The deterrent value of an investigation or prosecution, including whether the need for deterrence is increased because the activity involves a new or expanding area of criminal activity, a recidivist defendant, use of a novel or sophisticated technique, or abuse of a position of trust or otherwise sensitive level of access, or because the conduct is particularly egregious or malicious;

- The nature of the impact that the criminal conduct has on a particular district or community; or

- Whether any other jurisdiction is likely to prosecute the criminal conduct effectively, if the matter is declined for federal prosecution.[149]

This is a very comprehensive listing of variables that could prompt federal prosecution. There is great benefit to living in a country that prides itself on law and order and that strives to be better than the criminals it pursues by not becoming like them while pursuing them. That said, *in the Era of Virtual Terrorism, there is an argument to be made that individuals, businesses, and governments do not have the luxury of playing the game of combatting Virtual Terrorism any differently than the virtual terrorists they pursue who perpetrate it.*

The concern is that adhering to a strict letter of the law could become a distinct disadvantage. While those who believe in playing the game that way have the benefit of 'moral clarity' and being able to look themselves in the mirror, they will never ever win the long game. The old adage, "an eye for an eye", has particular appeal in this instance. Can governments which ordinarily strictly adhere to the rule of law identify a common 'middle ground' that would enable them to fight fire with fire in the virtual world? That is the challenge.

A Reluctant USG

In April 2014, the US Senate introduced a bill that sought to incentivize private sector sharing of cybersecurity data by providing liability protection against lawsuits. Like previous bills addressing cybersecurity that came before the US Congress, it was also not adopted. There was sharp disagreement among legislators about whether the protection of corporations from liability would properly incentivize the private sector to adopt cybersecurity measures. Some Senators felt that offering "safe harbors" against liability for damages to third parties caused by breaches of cybersecurity in exchange for company compliance with government cybersecurity frameworks and laws would not lead companies to develop dynamic, effective cybersecurity measures. Instead, such an approach may have the opposite effect, they worried—giving companies unprecedented liability protections based on cybersecurity standards that they themselves have developed could increase the likelihood that the American taxpayers will one day find themselves on the hook for corporate bailouts of unknown scope following a cyber disaster.

In the face of strong private sector opposition, the USG has largely resorted to cajoling the private sector to implement cybersecurity measures and has eschewed mandatory regulation. Rather than continue to attempt to push through legislation that a skeptical Congress has rejected many times over, the federal government has decided to take a number of preliminary steps to encourage the private sector to adopt more stringent cybersecurity measures.

In 2013, it identified a number of possible incentives that could be used to entice the private sector to adopt cybersecurity best practices, including cybersecurity insurance, federal grants and legal protections for companies that invest additional money in cybersecurity efforts. The government also offered 16 critical infrastructure sectors guidance about how to shield themselves from cyberattacks, but did not mandate compliance with its recommendations.

The US General Services Administration, in conjunction with the US Department of Defense (DoD), recommended that private sector entities be required to comply with "baseline" cybersecurity principles at all levels of the supply chain as a condition of being awarded contracts with the federal government. The recommendation was unfortunately never adopted. Several pieces of legislation have been proposed in Congress to either sanction private sector entities that fail to adopt 'reasonable' data security practices or to grant the Federal Trade Commission (FTC) authorization to craft cybersecurity regulations for the private sector. These bills also did not become law.

Private Sector Hesitancy

The private sector has its own hurdles to overcome on the road to envisioning public-private partnerships (PPPs) to fight Virtual Terrorism. Despite the risks associated with not tackling cyber risk head on, the private sector has been generally reluctant to adopt strong cybersecurity measures, which is driven by a combination of principles and practical concerns. There are a number of reasons for hesitancy with regard to adopting government mandated private sector cybersecurity standards. First, significant segments of the private sector consider proposed requirements to introduce cybersecurity measures to be merely an additional form of government regulation. The Business Software Alliance has opposed placing "undue regulatory burdens on industry," and the US Chamber of Commerce has objected to "legislation establishing regulatory-based cybersecurity standards". The Heritage Foundation rejected the same bill because it would "create a cumbersome regulatory process".

These commentators reflect a desire to adhere to the laissez-faire and libertarian principles that private enterprise has a right to be left alone by the government, and that the private sector is capable of independently determining how much and what kind of cybersecurity it needs. But the truth is that the private sector has failed spectacularly to secure cyberspace (just as governments have), and it may be 'mission impossible' in any event. A plethora of businesses appear to be willing to take their chances. If they end up being targeted, there is precious little they may realistically be able to do

124

either to thwart an attack or pursue the perpetrators—so they may be inclined to ask, what is the point?

Since corporations are considered rational actors, one might well expect that they would voluntarily take measures to protect their trade secrets and profits. CEOs tend to focus on short-term costs and benefits, at times to the detriment of longer-term impact. They may argue that the consequences of stolen trade secrets often take years to unfold, given that competitors need time to use the information they gain to build and market their own products, and they may ask, "why worry about that today"? This mode of thinking is compounded by many decision makers' inexperience with technology, which may prevent them from truly grasping the enormity of the problem. Just as firms tend to underinvest in pollution controls because some costs of their emissions are borne by those who are downwind, they also tend to underinvest in cyber defenses because some costs of intrusions are externalized onto others.

Second, other opponents of government cybersecurity regulations claim that government mandates will actually hamper cybersecurity and other innovations in the private sector. In 2012, the US Chamber of Commerce called on Senate Republicans to filibuster a bill that would have established cybersecurity standards for private sector critical infrastructure, on the grounds that the bill could actually "hamper companies trying to defend against cyber intrusions". Their argument is that establishing clear standards for companies would impede their flexibility by forcing them to introduce cumbersome or inefficient cybersecurity measures. While this may be true, many corporations have not filled the void on their own.

Third, private sector representatives have suggested that cybersecurity regulations would impose substantial costs, which the private sector would be incapable of meeting profitably. A company may indeed need to spend many millions of dollars in order to develop effective cybersecurity systems. Given that tens of thousands of strains of malware are created daily, it would take substantial sums of money to stay ahead of the curve. Fourth, many businesses consider it unfair and inappropriate for the government to impose on private industries security requirements that businesses consider a public sector responsibility. Such requirements are viewed as 'unfunded mandates'.

Some corporate leaders believe that the provision of cybersecurity is the job of the government—if the government requires others to do part of the job by adding security measures above and beyond those they already independently introduce, corporations should then be compensated for the resulting costs. Such claims are difficult to justify when one considers the size of many private sector corporations' budgets. For example, Target, which was the object of a major breach in 2013, had a $1.6 million cybersecurity system in place at the time, with revenues of $72 billion, making its investment in cybersecurity roughly 0.0002 percent of its revenue.

Having that system did not prevent its high profile cyberattack. One law office that provides corporate counsel estimated that Target's potential total costs at the time of the breach could exceed $1 billion. Another source estimated that the cost of Target's failure could top $18 billion once lost revenues due to negative publicity were factored in. This is an important point—*indirect costs resulting from cyberattacks may far exceed direct costs and can be exceedingly difficult to ascertain with any degree of accuracy.*

In addition, the private sector has expressed concern that regulations mandating that corporations report cybersecurity breaches to the federal government, and share news of cyberthreats with their industry peers, would result in damaging publicity or lead to lawsuits alleging liability for damages to private citizens as a result of cyber breaches.

Security Implications

There are several reasons why there is no way to decouple the cybersecurity of the private and public sectors— particularly in any country where there is an active defense industry. Using the US as an example, the government awards hundreds of billions of dollars of contracts to private entities each year—much of which goes to defense contractors. Inadequate cybersecurity at private firms potentially allows adversarial governments and nongovernmental actors to acquire information that could greatly harm US security.

As noted earlier, in 2014, the USG announced charges against five members of the PLA's Shanghai cyberunit, alleging that the hackers infiltrated the computer networks of several American corporations. Among these were Allegheny Technologies, which provided materials and components to a diverse group of clients, including defense contractors, and Alcoa, which manufactures a range of materials used in defense. In the past, General Dynamics, Boeing, Lockheed Martin, Raytheon, and Northrop Grumman have all fallen victim to hackers.

The private sector is responsible for supplying and maintaining much of the technology (including IT) used by the government. The computers and software used by the DoD and other federal agencies are themselves designed, manufactured, and often serviced by the private sector. Prior to the 1990s, the Pentagon used in-house programmers to design secure software tailored to the military's needs. However, the military has since increasingly shifted to off-the-shelf commercial software as a means of cutting costs and satisfying Congress, which has naturally been influenced by private sector lobbying. *These technologies are vulnerable not only because they are produced in the private sector, but also because the private sector often sources its equipment and components overseas.*

The private sector is also responsible for the maintenance of much of the US's critical infrastructure, including energy, telecommunications, transportation, health services, and banking and finance. Without the private sector's willing adoption of stronger cybersecurity measures, these critical services remain vulnerable to kinetic cyberattacks. In short, the difference between the public and private sectors is much smaller than is often assumed in public discourse. *There can be no reliable cybersecurity in the public realm unless there is also heightened cybersecurity in the private realm.* The security chain is only as strong as its weakest link, and the private sector's link is simultaneously poorly forged and critically important to US defense and security.

The private sector, especially those firms that manufacture defense hardware such as submarines and aircraft carriers, as well as those that provide software to the government, would be much more attentive to cybersecurity needs if private corporations were to be disqualified from receiving government contracts if they are not in full compliance with government cybersecurity standards. It is astonishing that this is not already the case. Given how vulnerable and dependent Congress is to defense industry and other lobbyists, there appears to be little chance this may change in the future.[150]

Movement in the Right Direction

That said, the USG took strong action, in 2015, to move the needle in the direction of being in a better position to partner with the private sector via the creation of the Cyberthreat Intelligence Integration Center (CTIIC), under the tutelage of the ODNI. Its mission is to better understand foreign cyberthreats to US national interests, integrate information from the defense, intelligence, and law enforcement communities, facilitate information-sharing, and support interagency planning to craft more holistic approaches against cyber adversaries. The CTIIC engages with other cyber centers and the primary producers of intelligence to generate maximally meaningful analysis of threat activity. The Center's work acts as a building block for event and trend analysis to build situational awareness—identifying knowledge gaps— and support interagency efforts to develop options to degrade or mitigate adversarial threat. The CTIIC identifies ways to facilitate critical decision points and creates repeatable threat actor-agnostic frameworks that balance risks and potential benefits early in the decision-making process.[151] That can only benefit both the public and private sectors.

Any robust PPP in the cyber arena must be radical if it is to be effective. Companies must feel comfortable disclosing information with the government and vice versa. Only by creating a confidential reporting mechanism, coupled with limiting financial liability, will corporations be willing to openly report cyber incidents. One way to encourage that would be to adopt a regulatory regime similar to that imposed on financial institutions following the passage of the US Patriot

Act in 2001. By shielding suspicious activity reports under legislation associated with that Act from discovery in civil litigation, and by limiting the financial liability of a corporation that reports suspicious activity, information sharing dramatically increased between financial institutions and government regulators. Such a model should be replicable to spur information sharing involving cyber incidents.

Another idea is to expand the powers of the FISC to allow companies to petition for a government response to cyber offenses committed against their interests. Presently, the FISC is responsible for issuing warrants for domestic surveillance of suspected foreign operatives in the US. If an American corporation in the aerospace industry is hacked and the responsible party is deemed to be an agent of a sovereign nation, there are few legal options for the company. Under an expanded FISC, the aggrieved corporation could petition a government body for redress. That body would make a special appeal for emergency action, and if the expanded FISC agreed that action was necessary, the government would be permitted to take action against the sovereign nation with impunity. Another variant of this idea would be to create a stand-alone cyber court to provide judicial oversight of the response, rather than adding cyber jurisdiction to the FISC. It will clearly take unorthodox solutions to remove the disincentives currently inhibiting cyber PPPs.[152]

Fortunately, there is growing awareness in the C-suite of the importance of tackling the problem head on, and a growing number of corporate boards are requiring regular updates from Chief Information Security Officers (CISOs) and CIOs about their relative states of readiness. To enhance that process, business leaders should consider adopting the following steps:

Understand the challenge: Create ongoing monitoring methods and identify resolutions to reporting challenges that allow executives to see well ahead of the curve.

Establish accountability: Company management should request quarterly reports on the organization's most pressing cyberthreats, to ensure that executives develop and track metrics which enable them to quantify the impact of any intrusion. It should also appoint a designated cyber leader and a team of individuals inside the organization that who will report to him or her.

Coordinate efforts: Assure that cybersecurity is well-managed, not only in company headquarters but all along the supply and value chain.

Communicate: Cybersecurity officers should maintain regular communication with others who are responsible for cybersecurity within their company and with industry associations and government contacts to ensure they are in sync with evolving best practices.[153]

The only way real progress is going to be made in the cyberwar against virtual terrorists is through the combined efforts of the public and private sectors. The private sector needs to do a much better job of enhancing its awareness and devoting the resources necessary to have real impact in combatting the problem. Understanding the challenge, establishing internal accountability, coordinating efforts, and effectively communicating in and outside the firm is the pathway forward on that front.

A Wake-up Call for Investors

The WannaCry cyberattack that infected hundreds of thousands of computers across 150 countries in 2017 was a wake-up call for businesses and governments regarding robust online defense, as well as being a warning to investors that shareholders risk heavy losses if companies suffer a cyberattack that leads to a consumer backlash and/or fines from regulators. While many corporate boardrooms have gotten the message, many investors are lagging behind. Apart from simply invading an organization's internal computer systems, hackers can also easily target a company via "social engineering"—going after executives individually. They build a profile of an executive using press reports or social media, then tailor an e-mail to the executive that appears to be from a friend or colleague but contains malware.

Companies have begun to realize there are human as well as technological vulnerabilities, but investors must grapple with 'if' or 'how' companies are successfully mitigating technological and human vulnerabilities. The EU has introduced rules to be implemented in 2018—the General Data Protection Regulation (to be explored further in Chapter 15)—that could affect the share prices of companies with weak cyber defenses. In the UK, the most a company can be fined for breaching the existing Data Protection Act is £500,000. Under the new EU rules, fines could reach €20m (or 4 percent) of a company's global annual turnover and are specifically designed to force companies to become more cyber resilient or face the consequences. Some of the more recent entrants into online technology (such as retailers) have not adopted the deeper levels of security that some banks have, which is clearly a risk that will have a greater impact on national economies. The legislation is an effort to flag and do something about this risk.

It is difficult to assess the risks accurately as an outsider, however, which is, and will remain, the primary challenge for investors inclined to perform cyber due diligence. In an attempt to increase the information available to investors, the UN-backed Principles of Responsible Investment group, which represents almost 1,400 investors managing $62 trillion of assets, in 2016 created a committee to assess cybersecurity risks in retail, financial services and healthcare. The objective was to obtain information from 50 listed companies about their plans in the event of a data breach. Investors want to know that boards have a clear understanding of any impact to the company from data loss or disruption.[154] It is a small step, but an important one, in what will surely prove to be a long road in the direction of private sector transparency and cybersecurity.

5. Cybercrime

Cybercriminals know how to get what they want. They need a constant stream of new e-mail accounts in order to send spam and conduct phishing attacks, and since they need to insert CAPTCHAs to prove that users are not robots or bots, which can slow them down, they have created software systems that automatically take the CAPTCHA images they have been shown and provide it to random strangers to enter the required phrase. To crowdsource the problem, the cybercriminals have simply created dozens of free porn sites and told visitors to enter a CAPTCHA phrase to prove they were over 18 years of age. The riddle the horny random strangers were solving was actually the CAPTCHA phrase the criminals needed to create their e-mail accounts—cut, pasted, and switched in real time.[155]

Sophisticated, Informed, Efficient, and Forward-Thinking

Cybercriminals have long understood that they can act much more effectively together than they can individually. They utilize a great variety of tools to engage with one another while evading detection. Criminal communities in general provide a place for actors to collaborate by sharing tips and successful methods that help them defeat security measures, but cybercriminal communities also allow for a division of labor and economies of scale that feed their unique ecosystem. Indeed, many cybercrimes depend on the actions of a cast of characters working in concert, including malware developers, cryptor writers, spammers, botnet masters, payment card specialists, and cashiers, among others. If cybercriminals were required to carry out their schemes on an individual basis, it would take them many years to develop the necessary cross-domain expertise.

In a cybercrime community, members specialize according to their comparative interests and talents, allowing them to reach higher levels of proficiency in each link of the cybercrime chain. They are then able to share this knowledge with other

132

community members (whether for free or for pay), which raises the overall level of activity, expertise, and efficiency in the system. As a result, the barrier of entry for new participants is lower, since they can merely purchase the goods and services they need, as opposed to spending significant time and money building capacity themselves.

The traditional meeting place for cybercriminals is the online messaging board (or web forum), which is the beating heart of the cybercrime economy. Members meet, recruit additional support, buy technical tools (i.e. malware), and sell their illicit goods and services through these online forums. As is the case with street gangs, cybercrime communities have rules (both explicit and implicit), an organizer (administrator), enforcers (moderators), unique jargon, and barriers to entry. Once acceptance to the "club" is gained, members have access to the institutional knowledge and resources afforded by the forum and its members, which can be substantial.

Cybercriminals evaluate communication platforms based on the encryption protocol used, where encryption keys are stored, the jurisdiction in which the services' servers are located, whether they can be accessed by law enforcement agencies, and the privacy policy of the service, among others. Such platforms have differing anonymity and encryption capabilities that make them less or more attractive to cybercriminals. They naturally prefer services that are simple and intuitive to use. The communication platforms may be promoted heavily, or even exclusively, to speakers of a particular language; sometimes the platform becomes a predominant method of communication for criminals and civilians alike.

The range of Internet-enabled instant communication services widely available for use by anyone has certainly made cybercriminals' job easier. Among the top messaging services commonly used by them are Skype, Telegram, ICQ, Jabber (XMPP), Pretty Good Privacy, AOL Instant Messenger, WeChat, QQ, What's App, and Kik. Cybercriminals, of course, tend to prefer services with encryption and anonymity protections built-in, with Jabber, Telegram, and WhatsApp among the top picks.

Russian-speaking cybercriminals are well-known for their prowess and are universally considered the most innovative and sophisticated actors in the cybercrime ecosystem. For this reason, actors from other language communities often emulate Russian cybercriminals in an attempt to raise their own levels of capability. Regardless of their language, skills, location, or affiliation, cybercriminal groups tend to share a strong desire to reap the benefits of cross-community collaboration, information sharing, and mentorship, which fosters consistent access to reliable means of communication.

Since a cybercriminal's livelihood may depend on his or her ability to communicate with peers while evading third-party detection, the decision to utilize one communication tool over others is not taken lightly and is often influenced by numerous contextual social, cultural, and geopolitical factors.[156] In short, cybercriminals are sophisticated, informed, efficient, and forward-thinking, which makes hunting them down all the more difficult.

Ransomware as a Service

Ransomware (otherwise known as crimeware, scareware, or rogue antivirus) is malicious computer code that plays on a user's fear of virus infection. Cybercriminals have discovered that ransomware is the most effective way to make money in the shortest amount of time. The advent of new tools that wrap victims' data with tough encryption technology, hard-to-trace digital currency (like Bitcoin), and online sites that offer to do the data ransoming in return for a piece of the action, have made this method of cybertheft easy and therefore attractive. The skills that used to be required to be a cybercriminal no longer apply; ransomware has allowed people who are not computer experts to become computer thieves. In 2013, investigators were pursuing approximately 16 variants of ransomware that were predominantly being used on victims in Eastern Europe. By 2017, there were dozens of types of ransomware, all supported by an underground industry.

The WannaCry attacks of 2017 were a powerful escalation of earlier, smaller examples of ransomware in action. Hackers exploited a vulnerability in Microsoft servers that was first discovered by the NSA and then leaked online by a group of hackers. One day after the attack, several Bitcoin accounts associated with the ransomware had received the equivalent of $33,000 (according to a firm that tracks online financial transactions involving virtual currencies). As the ransom was $300 per computer, it meant that only 110 people had paid the ransom during the first 24-hour period. What might have been a haul of tens of millions of dollars (if every person with an infected computer had paid) turned out to be a pittance by comparison, which implied that a different approach would yield a greater payout in the future.

In 2012, the idea of paying a criminal on the Internet was very much a foreign concept. Technicians and security experts could find ways to unlock computers without paying a ransom and, at that time, security experts estimated that less than 3 percent of victims paid. In 2017, that figure was more like 50 percent (in general), even with antivirus software and backup capability among a broader spectrum of computer users. Bitcoin had given cybercriminals an easy and anonymous way to receive their profits, which is much harder to track than credit cards or wire transfers.

"Ransomware as a service" (a play on the Silicon Valley jargon "software as a service") describes the delivery of software over the Internet. Now anyone can visit a web page, generate a ransomware file with the click of a mouse, encrypt someone's systems, and demand a ransom to restore access to the files. If the victim pays, the ransomware provider takes a cut of the payment. *Ransomware criminals also have customer service lines that victims can call to get help paying a ransom, with live chat options.*

Nearly half of ransomware attacks begin by persuading an employee to click on an e-mail, but sometimes the methods used by cybercriminals are more complex. As noted previously, a watering hole attack infects a website with ransomware code when users visit the site, and that code is downloaded onto their computers. The other half of attacks tend to target victims with "brute force" methods: hackers scan an organization for software vulnerabilities, weak passwords, or other unlocked digital doors and ransomware; the attackers then try to encrypt as many files as possible.

Hackers often move from file to file, manually encrypting hundreds of systems so that they can demand the highest Bitcoin ransoms. Ransomware attackers are not above playing martyr, either. In one instance, the attackers tried to convince their victim that paying a "contribution" (a ransom) would benefit sick children around the world. Threat actors are now playing with peoples' emotions, trying to put a pretty face on criminal activity.[157] There would appear to be no limit to the degree of vulnerability and a desire to trust among the general populace, as scammers from Nigeria and Eastern Europe learned many years ago.

A Multi-Trillion Dollar Business

If you happen to be a cyberthief, one of the great things about running your business is that there is virtually no overhead. Doing business online, with no physical presence, is an extremely efficient business model. As a result, although no one can know the exact amount, it has been estimated that cybercrime generates trillions of dollars of profit per year, and by 2021, it will be a $6 trillion business[158]. Cybertheft long ago stopped being the domain of teenagers with nothing better to do, operating from their parents' basements. Cybercrime syndicates, such as the Russian Business Network, Innovative Marketing, ShadowCrew, and Superzonda were created to meet the broad range of opportunities generated by next-generation crime. While in the 'early days' of cybercrime up to 80 percent of cyberthiefs were independent freelancers, according the to the RAND Corporation, *up to 80 percent of hackers now work as part of organized crime syndicates.*[159]

Like any well-run business, cybercrime syndicates reject top-heavy organizational structures, preferring a lean, real-time oriented, on-demand approach to doing business. Many cybercriminals appear to value proper work-life balance (who could blame them? Cybercrime is hard work, after all). They may gather en masse for an 'engagement', then dissipate until reconvening for another session. These online crime swarms often coalesce based on criminal sub-specialty. One group of actors with deep technical skills may hack into a corporate data system and pass the baton to a group of data brokers who distribute stolen personal information to produce fake documents. Those executing the financial fraud then forward funds to a 'mule' network, to ensure that all criminal parties are properly paid for their services.

All work is obviously carried out remotely, obviating the need to ever meet in person. Work is compartmentalized to ensure that lower-level participants never learn the true identities of others in their network, helping to ensure anonymity and security for the various players along the way. Underground online hacking forums and other communication channels serve as the primary introduction, recruitment, and assembly points that enable these groups to work on specific projects. As is the case with other 'businesses', there is a rationality to how cybercriminals operate, utilizing proven tactics to maintain competitive advantage and avoid potential sources of business interruption.

One group of cyberthieves responsible for hacking JetBlue, 7-Eleven, JCPenney, and the Nasdaq stock exchange created a system of 'trip wires' to provide an early-warning system to notify them if news of their exploits had become public. They created a series of Google alerts with carefully selected keywords covering their targeted victims to learn when any news was released of their exploits, at which time they could quickly extricate themselves before they could be tracked by police or intelligence agencies. *Hackers have become the new Mafia and are contributing to the ever-increasing industrialization and professionalization of cybercrime.*

Of all the business innovation techniques utilized by cybercriminals, none has been as widely adopted as crowdsourcing, which began as a legitimate tool to leverage the wisdom of crowds to solve complex business challenges. Some of their techniques are intended to give them an advantage over police. In the US, mobile apps such as Buzzed, Checkpoint Wingman, and DUI Dodger allow those who have had too much to drink to crowdsource the location of DUI checkpoints. Cybercriminals have taken this concept and put it on steroids. "Crime sourcing" can be defined as taking all or part of a criminal act and outsourcing it to a crowd of witting or unwitting individuals. *By aggressively adopting crowdsourcing techniques, cybercriminals are able to build*

137

largely anonymous criminal networks that can self-organize and assemble with amazing rapidity.

In 2013, cybercriminal bosses in Russia and Ukraine unleashed more than 100 money mules on a hospital in Washington State they had hacked, resulting in the theft of more than $1 million from the hospital's payroll system. It was laundered through 96 accounts in a few days. Some of the mules were working from home as "regional account receivable representatives", unaware of who they were working for or where the money came from.

Cybercriminals need a constant stream of new e-mail accounts in order to send spam and conduct phishing attacks, and since the need to insert CAPTCHAs to prove that the user is not a robot or bot can slow them down, they have created a software system that automatically takes the CAPTCHA image they have been shown and provides it to random strangers to enter the required phrase. And why would these random strangers do this? To gain access to pornography, of course! To crowdsource the issue, the cybercriminals simply created dozens of free porn sites and told visitors to enter a CAPTCHA phrase to prove they were over 18 years of age. The riddle the horny random strangers were solving was actually the CAPTCHA phrase the criminals needed to create their e-mail accounts—cut, pasted, and switched in real time. Everyone won—the strangers got their porn in exchange for unwittingly crowdsourcing participation in a phishing scam that handsomely rewarded the cybercriminals.

The Dark Side of Crowdfunding

When, in 2013, Apple first announced the introduction of Touch ID fingerprint recognition scanning for its iPhone 5S, it was challenging cybercriminals as never before to crack the code on its much-admired security feature. It did not take long for that to occur—just one day. Using elements of both crowdfunding and 'gamification' (the application of game-design elements and game principles in non-game contexts[160]) , hackers set up a website called "IsTouchIDHackedYet.com" and offered a bounty of $20,000 (contributed by fellow hackers). The prize went to Starbug of Germany's Chaos

Computer Club (CCC), who cleverly discovered how to subvert Apple's security. He took a high-resolution 2400-DPI photograph of the fingerprint oils left behind on the TouchID screen by the device's owner, imported the image to Photoshop, and printed the image on film using a thick toner setting. He then smeared white glue onto the pattern. When dry, it could be held over the sensor to unlock the phone. An "A+" for ingenuity—an extremely low-tech solution to an extremely high-tech challenge.

Another, more serious, crowdfunding enterprise was created in 2014, called the "Assassination Market", which selected eight USG officials who were targeted for assassination by a cyber anarchist called Kuwabatake Sanjuro. Of the eight selected, former Federal Reserve Bank Chairman Ben Bernanke received the largest number of votes. Donations to carry out the assassination were made via encrypted and untraceable online currencies. Sanjuro crowdfunded $75,000, payable to anyone who killed him (fortunately, that did not happen).

As shocking as that amount of money may seem for an online-funded assassination, thieves around the world crowdsourced an outlandish robbery in 27 countries simultaneously. It occurred in 2013 when coders, engineers, and a research and development team in Eastern Europe broke into the network of two credit card processing companies in India and the United Arab Emirates. The hackers stole prepaid MasterCard and Visa debit card numbers and then hacked the processor's internal computer systems to remove all withdrawal limits on the cards they had stolen. They successfully stole hundreds of debit cards, each capable of withdrawing unlimited funds from the global ATM network.

The hackers then sent encrypted messages via the digital underground to crime associates in more than two dozen countries. Those receiving the stolen data used their own professional-grade credit card printers to print the debit cards and encode the card numbers on the magnetic strips on the backside of the cards. The cards were then distributed to hundreds of teams of criminals around the world, who went on a synchronized withdrawal spree, hitting as many ATMs as possible.

In the space of 10 hours, they completed 36,000 ATM transactions and successfully withdrew and walked away with $45 million. Since the hackers had already hijacked the banks' computers, they could watch exactly how much money was withdrawn, and thus how much each of their accomplices was due for his or her 'service fee'. Although some of the group were eventually tracked down by police, the masterminds of the plot were never identified or caught. *Modern cybercriminals deploy the very latest business practices and are essentially free to profit at will, limited only by the degree of their creativity and finesse.* Between 2013 and 2015, cybercriminals are estimated to have earned at least $500 million (tax-free) dollars.

A Cornucopia of Illegality

Cybercrime is a mammoth business, encompassing every conceivable part of the global economy. So many people are involved, in so many corners of the world, that there is literally nothing that *cannot* be done in the name of online criminal activity. *If it can be thought of, it has been done, and if it has not yet been thought of, it will be, posing an insurmountable challenge for governments, intelligence agencies, and law enforcement.* What follows is a sampling.

Counterfeit Currency: Although widely available online, counterfeit currency varies by currency type, quality, and the amount that can be purchased. Tor hidden sites such as Guttenberg Print, Cheap Euros, and WHMX Counterfeit offer high quality notes for 24 cents on the dollar. Vendors promise that all notes will pass pen and UV light tests.

Drugs: Illicit and prescription drugs of every type are available in the digital underground, up to bulk dealer-to-dealer-sized sales. Not only is the 'standard fare' available — such as cocaine, ecstasy, heroin and marijuana — but even more exotic drugs such as Scopolamine, a powdered 'zombification' drug that, when blown in someone's face, leaves him or her coherent but with no free will. Once ingested, it allows burglars, robbers, and rapists to have complete control over their victims within minutes, and completely wipes them of any memory of what happened while they were drugged.

Stolen Electronics/Luxury Goods: Dark Web sites such as Tor Electronics, CardedStore, and Buttery Bootlegging offer factory-new brand-name electronics and luxury goods at a steep discount. All of the items have been stolen, diverted from factories, or have mysteriously disappeared from delivery trucks.

Credit/Debit Cards: Cybercriminals buy and sell credit and debit cards from every bank and country in the world. All of the financial data stolen via malware, hacking, and credit card skimmers ends up for sale on the Dark Web. Once stolen, cybercriminals make online purchases, or can encode data on new counterfeit cards they use to go shopping or large dollar merchandise that can quickly be resold for quick cash. The US is the largest victim of such theft, accounting for approximately half of all fraudulent card activity globally as of 2016.

Identity Theft: Personal information such as birth dates, places of work, bank account numbers, bank routing numbers, driver's license numbers, mothers' maiden names, e-mail addresses, Social Security numbers, and other data are commonly used to steal money, create phony forms of identification, take out credit cards, get jobs, and even find a place to live. It is estimated that at least 20 percent of US citizens will become victims of identity theft in their lifetimes. It is estimated that tax fraud from identity theft will cost the US Internal Revenue System (IRS) as much as $21 billion by the year 2020.

Weapons, Ammunition, and Explosives: Handguns, machine pistols (with silencers), assault rifles, Uzis, and AK-47s are all available for purchase, with no background check. So is C-4 explosive, using shielded packaging, designed to look like other products. Firearms are broken into their component parts and shipped separately. Weapons merchants even arrange 'dead drops' where they hide their wares in pre-defined places that can be picked up at will by the buyer. After payment is received, buyers are sent GPS coordinates and descriptions of where the items are hidden.

Child Sex Abuse Imagery: Nothing in the Era of Virtual Terrorism could be more grotesque than the sale of child sex abuse imagery, and yet, the Dark Web is a sanctuary for the merchants of child pornography. One site is a veritable YouTube of self-produced videotaped child sexual abuse; it provides links sorted by a child's age and gender. E-books are for sale with titles such as "Producing Kiddie Porn for Dummies". Many sites allow pedophiles to communicate to share images and fantasies. Across the Dark Web pedophiles teach one another how to evade law enforcement and discuss encryption and anonymity techniques to avoid detection online. Live child rape is also unfortunately on the menu.

Human and Organ Trafficking: Numerous websites facilitate the trafficking of adults and children. Almost 70 percent of survivors of child trafficking said they were advertised online at some point during their ordeal. Immigrants and other at-risk populations are also frequent victims. The sale of body parts on the black online market is regrettably vibrant, the result of grave robbing and targeting by traffickers of the living poor. The World Health Organization estimates that illicitly obtained organs are sold hourly through these online marketplaces.

An Amazon for Cybercriminals and Terrorists

Cybercrime is an increasingly complex multinational enterprise, involving not only direct sales to individual buyers but also bulk sales between suppliers. At the top of the food chain are the highly experienced, well-financed and resourced, and totally anonymous kingpins, but beneath them are those that are less skilled and less well-resourced, who need a place to go to obtain the goods and services that enable them to do what they do. The Dark Web has become a Turkish bazaar of forbidden fruits with product storefronts complete with online shopping carts, checkout management systems, coupon codes, payment processing, technical support and live customer service chats. They do not accept credit cards, however, (only Bitcoin) which has undoubtedly contributed to the tremendous growth in the value of Bitcoin, which had risen from a starting price of $85 in July 2013 to an astounding $3,000 by June of 2017[161] (largely as a result of its overwhelming use by cybercriminals and others lurking in the Dark Web).

The IS is believed to be the world's richest terror group. While it has previously generated the majority of its funds through oil fields seized in northern Iraq and Syria, it has become increasingly reliant on other ways to secure its operational financing. Donations from (primarily) wealthy Middle Eastern sympathizers greatly helped the IS when it was first established, but since global governments have been actively tracking and seeking to block its funding efforts through banking channels, donations have become harder to receive. The group now uses cryptocurrencies such as Bitcoins as an anonymous and untraceable way to transfer money.

Virtual currency is an electronic cryptocurrency used to purchase both virtual and actual goods and services. It is not contractually backed by assets or legal currency laws, it is not controlled by a central authority, and it is not a tangible good. Bitcoins can be sent to or received by anyone with an Internet connection. Cryptocurrencies can, of course, themselves become the target of cyberthieves. In July 2017, $32 million was stolen from Bitcoin rival Ether by hackers.

The first step in trading this type of currency is to set up a virtual wallet where Bitcoins and their transaction histories are stored. The wallet houses a file of secure digital keys used to access a Bitcoin address and sign transactions. They are traded by sharing a wallet's anonymous private identification number with a merchant or peer. Wallets are a way to store the digital documentation of the Bitcoin value and grant access to users to spend them. There are many kinds of virtual wallets, the most popular among them being desktop wallets, Internet-based wallets, and mobile wallets.

Desktop Bitcoin wallets: Desktop wallets offer the most security and anonymity. This type of wallet is a software program that is downloaded onto a user's computer. Desktop wallets process user transactions, allow users to create new addresses, and store the user's private key.

Internet-based Bitcoin wallets: Internet-based wallets store a user's private key online via a main computer or server that is connected to the Internet. Such wallets allow for more flexibility as they connect to a user's desktop wallet and mobile device wallet. However, Internet-based wallets have greater risks than desktop wallets, since they hold user keys, leaving users vulnerable to any complications resulting from service provision, such as hacking, technical problems, or regulatory issues.

Mobile-based Bitcoin wallets: Mobile wallets work via smartphones. Users must download an app to access their virtual currencies. These apps are simple vehicles that can be used on your smartphone. They only use a subset of the block chain and rely on other networks to ensure all the correct information is there for the transaction to take place.

Like most forms of technology, fraudsters, criminals, and terrorist groups have found ways to exploit Bitcoins for nefarious purposes. Due to its anonymity and untraceability, Bitcoins are used for criminal activities such as laundering money, buying and selling illegal goods and services, and transferring money to support criminal or terror activities. Since Bitcoins are untraceable by governments, they cannot be stopped by regulatory screening processes, and Bitcoins can access any country to send money instantly.

Dark wallets offer Bitcoin users more protection in relation to privacy and identity, which are consistent with Dark Web criminality, such as murder, child pornography, drug and weapon sales, and terror group financing. It is not surprising that the IS would use cryptocurrencies as a way to receive funds, but doing so raises challenges vis-à-vis how to turn Bitcoins into physical currency in the states in which it operates. Many IS-controlled territories do not have the technology to extract high amounts of Bitcoins for cash, and, of course, doing so removes the benefit of anonymity. Bitcoin ATMs work just like bank ATMs, allowing Bitcoins to be exchanged for cash without the need for a cashier. When a Bitcoin ATM is not available, users can sell them online; however, this type of sale often requires users to verify their identity.[162]

It is estimated that half of all Bitcoin sales are related to the Dark Web. There are a variety of criminal software tool kits for sale on the Dark Web, including:

- Bugat: Priced at $1,000, Bugat's specialty is spoofing bank account and wire transfer requests. In 2010, it was used to produce a phishing e-mail campaign that sent tens of millions of LinkedIn members an 'update your account' message, which installed malware on their Web browsers, awaiting the next time they logged on to their bank accounts.

- Zeus Builder: Ranging from $5,000-$7,000, Zeus's functions range from capturing user keystrokes to stealing encryption certificates required for online banking. Microsoft has estimated that Zeus has infected more than 13 million computers and stolen more than $100 million globally.

- SpyEye: At a very affordable $500 and intended to compete with Zeus, its inventors included an antivirus module to detect Zeus's presence on infected computers, remove it, and repair the entry point to ensure that SpyEye remained the only malware that could operate on that computer.

Like their more legal competitors, software tool kits sold on the Dark Web continually update their products and have purchase options that enable users to 'subscribe and save'. Some kits are even available on a rental basis and come with free updates and technical support. Depending on the tool kits, users may select the manner by which malware can attack a targeted computer, such as by embedding a Trojan in a document, concealing it on a website, or placing it on a USB drive. One preferred kit, Blackshades, has become the tool of choice for stalkers because it allows its users to remotely turn on a computer's camera and microphone without giving the target any idea it is being used (such as a by triggering a green light to go on). Blackshades was so good that the Syrian government used it to spy on political activists in the country.[163]

Testing Boundaries

Cybercriminals' focus on child pornography is particularly disturbing and worthy of special attention because of the questions it raises and challenges it poses. Few other areas where cybercriminals roam test the boundaries of morality and legality as does child pornography. In 2016, the FBI was authorized to operate 23 child-porn websites on the Tor network in order to collect data on malware users. For 13 days that year, the FBI took over operations of Tor-hidden site Playpen, which the agency described as "the largest remaining known child pornography hidden service in the world". The FBI used malware (which the Bureau calls "network investigative techniques", or NIT) to infect more than 4,000 computers globally. Interestingly, membership on Playpen rose by a third while being operated by the FBI, and its performance improved beyond its original capability. The Bureau denied making improvements to the site.[164]

Prior to the operation, the site had approximately some 150,000 users. The FBI's command of the Playpen site enabled the agency to infect more than 8,000 users' computers with malware and hack them. Notably, the site was said to be more efficient and even experienced a boost in audience numbers with the FBI in charge of its content. A total of 870 arrests were made in connection with the case, uncovering a pedophile ring that ran through Europe and the Americas, following a two-year investigation.

The FBI revealed that in the US more than 350 arrests were made. Other arrests and law enforcement actions were carried out in countries around the world, including Chile, Israel, Malaysia, Peru, Turkey, and Ukraine. Europe accounted for the major share of arrests and convictions, with 368 suspects being charged. The website's founder was handed a 30-year jail sentence. More than 300 children who had suffered sexual abuse at the hands of Playpen members were identified or rescued.

The Bureau said it had uncovered the site almost immediately after it had been launched but lacked information to trace the location or identity of the site's owner, as it was rooted in the

Deep Web and was only accessible through Tor, which grants anonymity to its users. The FBI was criticized and taken to court for using techniques that brushed up against the Fourth Amendment of the US Constitution—the part of the US Bill of Rights that prohibits unreasonable searches and seizures and requires any warrant to be judicially sanctioned and supported by probable cause.

Another issue is that. by deploying the NIT over the Internet, any computer in any jurisdiction (i.e. outside the US) may be subject to the FBI action, which would make it outside the purview of US law. A federal judge refused to consider that action[165], but some Internet privacy experts found the FBI's handling of the case highly questionable and contrary to privacy laws, noting that the Bureau's warrant did not specify any particular person to search or seize, nor did it identify specific users of the website. In response, the head of the European Cybercrime Centre said at the time that *19th century legal principles would not be effective in fighting cybercrime.*[166] Of course, he is right about that, but 'the law' is stuck in the 20th century at the present time, before the Cyber Era came into being (legal aspects of Virtual Terrorism will be explored in detail in Chapter 16).

<u>A Perpetual Game of Catchup</u>

Just as the global legal regime attempts to ramp up its fight against cybercriminals on the Dark Web, that Web is getting progressively darker, posing ever greater identification and enforcement challenges. In the first study of its kind to map Tor, in 2016, researchers at King's College London found that 57 percent of the sites designed for Tor (known as .onion sites) facilitate exclusively criminal activity. To collect the data, researchers at the College developed a "crawler bot" that scraped Tor to identify sites that can only be viewed using a Tor browser. It found 5,205 live websites and managed to classify the content of 2,723 of those. After categorizing the content, the researchers found 1,547 of the sites contained illicit and illegal material. While a plethora of 'predictable' sites, ranging from drugs and weapons to illegal pornography, were found, there was, surprisingly, a near absence of Islamic extremist sites on Tor. Apparently, militants and extremists do not find Tor's hidden services infrastructure particularly useful, which may be a blessing.[167]

Soon, anyone will be able to create their own corner of the Internet that is not just anonymous and untraceable but entirely undiscoverable without an invite. While the majority of people who run Tor software use it to browse the web anonymously and circumvent censorship in countries such as China and Iran, Tor also maintains code that allows anyone to host an anonymous website or server, which forms the basis for the Dark Web. New code being developed is designed to strengthen its encryption while simultaneously enabling administrators to create entirely secret sites that can only be discovered by those with knowledge of a long string of complicated characters, which may well serve as the basis for a new generation of encryption applications.

Tor's network is comprised of volunteers' computers that serve as "nodes", bouncing traffic around the globe. Anyone can position their computer as a specific node, one of thousands of hidden service directories that route visitors to hidden services. For that routing system to work, all hidden services must declare their existence to those directories. Based on a study released at the annual hacker Defcon conference in 2016, it was noted that more than 100 of the 3,000+ hidden service directories were secretly crawling every site whose address they came across, in order to scan the Dark Web for previously undiscovered sites.

In theory, the only people who should know about a given hidden service are the people who are told about it by the service provider. However, the next generation of hidden services will use a clever method to protect the secrecy of those addresses. Instead of declaring their .onion address to hidden service directories, they will, instead, derive a unique cryptographic key from that address and give that key to Tor's hidden service directories. Any Tor user looking for a certain hidden service can perform that same derivation to check the key and route themselves to the correct darknet site. But the hidden service directory cannot derive the .onion address from the key, preventing snoops from discovering any secret Dark Web address.

The result will be Dark Web sites with new, stealthier applications. A small group of collaborators could, for instance, host files on a computer known to only to them. No one else could ever find that computer, much less access it. You could host a hidden service on your own computer, creating a way to untraceably connect to it from anywhere in the world while keeping its existence secret from snoops. Tor already offers a method to make hidden services inaccessible to all but certain Tor browsers, but that involves finicky changes to a browser's configuration files. The new system will make that level of secrecy far more accessible to the average user, and that has potentially profound implications for cybercriminals and the law enforcement and intelligence organizations that hunt them down.

Tor has even grander plans to create more tools that allow untraceable, private communication, like Ricochet and the Tor-based filesharing application Onionshare. Those apps automatically create Tor hidden services on their users' computers for private communications, so preventing anyone from discovering those private Tor instances will make similar apps easier to build and more secure.

Tor's hidden services have come under increasing scrutiny since law enforcement purges in 2013 and 2014 took dozens of Dark Web sites offline. Security researchers at Carnegie Mellon worked with the FBI to "mark" Tor's hidden services traffic with a unique piece of data that could be recognized by both the node that hidden services first connected to (which knows the services' IP address) and the address tracked by the hidden service directory (which knows its .onion address.) By combining the data between those two computers, the authorities had enough information to pin down the locations of servers running the illegal sites and seize them. However, Tor fixed the flaw that allowed those attacks within days of its discovery.

Even if a similar vulnerability were found in the future, the new hidden service directory system would, in theory, mean that the most secret hidden services would remain safe; law enforcement would not be able to use the attack on any site whose address it did not already know, though those with widely publicized addresses might still remain vulnerable.

149

That potential to foil law enforcement raises questions about whether undiscoverable hidden services will become a magnet for the worst parts of the Dark Web, including markets for stolen data, hacking tools, and child pornography. Tor's creator argues that strong privacy tools offer a societal tradeoff, and asks whether making socially deleterious uses of the Internet insecure means all Internet users must also be made insecure. Is humanity better off with privacy than without it? The advent of the Dark Web raises that question to an entirely new dimension.[168]

There are so many philosophical questions raised by the rise of the Dark Web and cybercrime that it is hard to determine where to begin to address them. By definition, many of these questions have no single answer. Can a platform be developed that improves anonymity, authentication, and availability, but does not incentivize illiberal and illegal behavior at the same time? How can Tor hidden services be modified to induce more self-identifying service providers such as Facebook to jump in while pushing more criminals out? Which Dark Web systems should be considered fair game for law enforcement and intelligence agencies and which should be left alone? We are only at the beginning of a serious debate about the "cryptopolitik".[169]

The Search for Solutions

Intelligence agencies and law enforcement around the world are busy trying to get a handle on, and stay a step ahead of, cybercriminals. Progress is being made, even as the Dark Web continues to get darker, but much more remains to be done. Among the basic steps that still need to be taken are:

- Improving public education systems for all potential Internet users about the threat posed by cybercrime, including means of detecting potential cyberattackers and methods of protection;

- Fostering incentives for the development of products less likely to be the subject of attack;

- Creating producer liability for software and other Internet applications;

- Establishing an efficient online self-reporting system for cybercrime victims to enable widespread gathering and analysis of cybercrime statistics;

- Crafting an international treaty to promote global cooperation on the detection, investigation, and prosecution of cybercrime;

- Intensifying research into cyberattackers' psychological profiles, motives, and behavior; and

- Establishing virtual task forces to promote better international coordination between interregional law enforcement and governmental security agencies.[170]

Some more ambitious objectives include active targeting of underground forums to disrupt the circulation of the most powerful cybercrime tools, disrupting the infrastructure of malicious code writers and specialist web hosts through the active identification of developer groups and a joint action of law enforcement, and dismantling so-called "bullet proof" hosting companies.

More must be done to harness the intelligence of network and information security stakeholders, not only to provide a more accurate and comprehensive assessment of cyber criminality, but also to ensure that responses are effective and timely. Active partnerships with ISPs, Internet security organizations, and online financial service providers are important, but so is more centralized coordination at regional and interregional levels to streamline and strengthen the fight against cybercrime. The establishment of virtual task forces to target Internet-facilitated organized crime should be pursued in conjunction with giving law enforcement authorities the flexibility they need to include a variety of stakeholders (including militaries, the private sector, academia, user groups, and NGOs) in order to take the battle directly to the Dark Web and its users.[171]

6. Terrorist Groups

> Sarah Hervouët, a 23-year-old convert to Islam who was planning an attack in the southeastern French commune of Cogolin, had been communicating with Rachid Kassim, the IS's European virtual planner, via Telegram. Acting on his orders, Hervouët wrote her will, along with farewell letters to relatives, and made a video proclaiming her allegiance to the IS. She lost her appetite for the operation that Kassim envisioned for her—a "suicide-by-police" attack—so Kassim connected her with two other women preparing to carry out an attack in Paris instead. Though the women failed to carry out the dramatic attack that Kassim had hoped for, the case demonstrates the speed and agility with which virtual planners can operate. Kassim not only convinced four women to carry out violent attacks in the IS's name, but also rapidly adapted his plans to the preferences of his operatives and merged two deadly projects together to increase the likelihood of success. [172]

In the context of conventional terrorism, citizens of many parts of the world have become accustomed to thinking of 'terrorists' as Muslim or Islamic extremists, a unidimensional approach to the subject that fails to capture the sheer diversity of terrorist and extremist groups. It has been widely estimated that a very small percentage of the world's Muslims subscribe to the views of Islamic extremists, and it is no doubt the case that a small percentage of members of any racial, ethnic, or religious group believe in or adopt the measures taken by extremist elements among their ranks. There are, of course, exceptions to this rule, such as Palestine, which has twice voted to have Hamas (which is regarded as a terrorist organization by numerous countries and international organizations) lead its government. It should be remembered that one person's terrorist is another person's freedom fighter.

A core focus of this chapter is the IS, simply because it is the leading terrorist group in the world and also because it is the most successful in a variety of respects—in terms of its ability to attract members from every corner of the globe, to raise funds, to complete attacks, and as a force to be reckoned with in the virtual world. As is noted below, governments and others can learn a lot from the IS's approach to cyberwarfare. Other terrorist groups are creative, adaptive, and resourceful, but none comes close to the level of sophistication and achievement of the IS.

According to a 2017 Pew study[173], Muslims will double their share of the population in the US by 2050 and surpass Christianity as the world's dominant religion by the end of the century. Based on demographic trends, Pew projects that the world's Muslim population will grow by 70 percent between 2015 and 2060, compared with an overall population growth of 32 percent. That far exceeds the projected growth of the second- and third-fastest growing religions, Christianity and Hinduism, respectively.

Muslims have higher fertility rates than Christians and members of other religions. The projected birth rate of Muslim women from 2015 to 2020 is 2.9 babies per woman, compared to a non-Muslim fertility rate of 2.2.[174] The world is predicted to have 9.7 billion people in 2050[175]. If so, then 2.8 billion of them are likely to be Muslim.[176] *If just one tenth of one percent of that population adheres to the ideology of the IS (an admittedly conservative estimate), then by 2050 some 2.8 million Muslims around the world could become virtual jihadists.*

Virtual Jihad

Cyberspace is the ideal platform for terrorists because, unlike conventional warfare, barriers to entry into cyberspace are much lower—the price of entry is an Internet connection. The surreptitious use of the Internet to advance terrorist group objectives has created a new brand of Holy War—"Virtual Jihad"—which gains thousands of new adherents each day. For terrorist organizations, a clear benefit of cyberspace is its ability to readily radicalize individuals from a distance and at any time, utilizing the Internet and superior social media intelligence (SOCMINT) to gain attention and remain relevant globally.

Cyberspace offers potential jihadists the opportunity to receive instruction and training on topics ranging from data mining to psychological warfare. As already noted, the use of the Dark Web and encryption programs allow terrorist groups to effectively communicate in secret. The first issue of AQ in the Arabian Peninsula's quarterly online magazine *Inspire*, in 2010, highlighted Asrar al-Mujahideen (also known as "Mujahideen Secrets"), which represented the first Islamic computer program for secure exchange of information on the Internet, boasting five of the best encryption algorithms and data compression tools available at the time. Since the program's debut, *Inspire* magazine has offered a tutorial in each issue about how to properly encrypt communications, as well as providing recommendations regarding the ideal encryption tool to use.

The software's second installment—"Mujahideen Secrets 2"—was released in January of 2008 and revised twice as of 2012. Issued by the Global Islamic Media Front and offered for free on the password-protected site Ekhlaas.org, MS2 was distributed with the express intent of supporting the mujahideen (holy war fighters) in general and AQ in Iraq in particular. It proved useful for less tech-savvy jihadists who required instructions about how to properly deploy mujahideen on the battlefield. The advent of encryption software has also coincided with the rise of jihadist technical specialists who research emerging trends in the fields of information, communication, and electronics, as well as produce software for use with mobile devices.

Although terrorist organizations have been adept at utilizing the Internet to spread propaganda and provide instructions for attacks, their ability to launch offensive attacks via computer networks has been limited. Cyberattacks attributed to terrorists have largely consisted of unsophisticated tactics such as e-mail bombings of ideological foes, DDoS attacks, or defacing of websites. Even when such attacks have been successfully deployed, the damage inflicted has been limited, largely because global intelligence agencies actively monitor their websites, conduct analyses to determine potential terrorist plots, and render some of the domains inaccessible to the public.[177]

A Virtual Caliphate

Long after the current collection of terrorist groups have ceased to be a major threat from a physical perspective, they will remain omnipresent in cyberspace, promoting a virtual caliphate from their safe haven behind computer keyboards around the world. Islamic extremists are natural candidates to transition to the virtual world because it offers them automatic citizenship beyond the nation-state. Decades of violent conflict, border disputes, and shifting refugee populations have left millions of Muslims without a clear national identity —a virtual caliphate offers refuge, free from terrestrial constraints, which can be accessed from anywhere in the world.

Since the IS was founded, its leaders have deftly and continually rewritten the narrative by which they could claim that the group's desired caliphate exists, where it is located, and who its adherents are. Unconstrained by the absence of a definitive Quranic guideline for what constitutes a caliphate, the IS created its own self-promoting doctrine. The group expanded its caliphate narrative to include a wide range of options for participation: membership included everyone from the passive observer reading a blog or curiously following a Twitter feed, to the keyboard jihadist editing Rumiyah or hacking a website, to the real-world operators attacking a nightclub or running down holiday celebrants with a delivery truck. The IS has successfully exploited the sociopolitical environment and young adults' obsession with technology to establish a growing community of devotees in the ungoverned territory of cyberspace, ensuring its ability to continue to coordinate and inspire violence well into the future.

This notion of a virtual caliphate clashes with traditional notions of statehood and governance but it is not the first attempt that has been made to create a virtual state. In 2014, Estonia took the unprecedented step of offering any person in the world a chance to become an Estonian 'e-resident', in an attempt to create a 'digital nation' for global citizens by offering to provide government-issued digital identification to anyone in the world, and enable non-Estonians access to Estonian services such as company formation, banking, payment processing, and taxation. *Doing so would allow Estonia to continue operating as a state even if its physical territory were ever seized.* By harnessing the millions of people who form its social network, the IS has expanded its community of e-citizens to promulgate its radical ideology and direct attacks across the globe.

The IS has also capitalized on the world's evolving propensity to integrate online activities with real world activities. Social media has had an incredible multiplying effect on radical messaging, and the IS has had great success publishing online, which has resonated particularly well with disenfranchised Muslims and youths, inspiring some to act on inspiration and guidance received online. The IS has exploited their search for meaningful identity by promising to restore their dignity and might so that they may find personal fulfillment and purpose.

The virtual world is in some ways more compelling than the real world, because storylines can be artfully crafted to be maximally appealing, while omitting anything that may be perceived of as negative. A promise is much easier to make online, as is the vision of fulfilling aspirations (as Chapter 7 will describe, the IS has created virtual messaging that is wildly at odds with the reality of life as an IS fighter on the ground). Cyberspace has enabled the IS to turn tactical defeats on the battlefield into glorious martyrdom operations that highlight the bravery and commitment of its fighters. The loss of territory and the deaths of key leaders have served to feed propaganda efforts that are used to prove the resiliency of the caliphate.

In the face of the force-multiplying impact of the IS's adaptive narrative, even concerted efforts by Muslim clerics have largely failed to undermine IS's caliphate narrative. While the vast majority of the world's estimated 1.6 billion Muslims are not IS supporters (perhaps just a fraction of one percent, although no one can say for certain), the group's ability to engage virtually with large swaths of this population drives varying degrees of participation in the virtual caliphate, including non-supporters, passive observers, benign fans, "keyboard jihadists", and real-world actors. This diverse range of participants helps to ensure that the notion of a virtual caliphate will endure long after the current crop of IS leaders are gone. The IS is finding its own salvation via the Internet, particularly since it has already passed the peak of its real-world power.[178]

The Reinvention of Media-Savvy

The volume of media output produced by the IS far exceeds most estimates, which had until 2016 been conservative. Disseminating an estimated average of 38 unique propaganda events per day from all corners of its 'caliphate', its media campaign is exceptionally sophisticated, both in terms of quantity and quality. While there is broad consistency in the overall IS narrative, it changes on a daily basis, according to priorities on-the-ground. *Composed of six non-discrete components—mercy, belonging, brutality, victimhood, war, and utopia—the messaging associated with the caliphate brand is constantly shifting.*

The themes of mercy, belonging, and brutality are dwarfed by the latter three narratives in terms of prominence. This is a marked shift from the group's previous propaganda norm and is indicative of changes in tactical outreach. More than half of all the propaganda was focused on depicting civilian life in IS territories. While the specter of extreme violence was ever-present, the preponderant focus on the caliphate's "utopia" demonstrates the priorities of the group's media strategists. Economic activity, social events, abundant wildlife, unwavering law and order, and pro-active, pristine 'religious' fervor form the foundations of IS's civilian appeal. In this way, the group seeks to attract supporters based on ideological and political appeal.

Apart from civilian life, the propagandists go to great lengths to portray IS's military, depicting it in various 'victorious' offensives. On the few occasions when its defensive war is documented, the group also seeks to perpetuate an aura of supremacy and momentum. A large proportion of military-themed events is devoted to showing IS's war of attrition, with mortars and rockets being fired towards an unseen enemy. The locations from which many of these reports emerge, as well as the aftermath of such strikes, is rarely, if ever, documented, leading to the conclusion that such low-risk attacks are falsely choreographed to perpetuate a sense of the IS constantly being 'on the offensive'.

Fostering international infamy has gradually become secondary to intimidating its population, however, in order to discourage rebellion and dissent. *The quantity, quality, and variation of IS propaganda far outweighs that of any attempts by state or non-state actors to challenge the group in cyberspace.* The global desire to find a panacea counternarrative to undermine the IS brand is misplaced, for there is no such thing. Those engaged in the information war on the caliphate must do as the IS has done and prioritize quantity, quality, variation, adaptability, and differentiation. Most importantly, though, it must be based upon an alternative (not counter) narrative.[179]

In 2011, the USG created the Center for Strategic Counterterrorism Communications (CSCC), to coordinate, orient, and inform government-wide foreign communication activities targeted against terrorism and violent extremism. The Center was intended to function like a war room in a political campaign by conducting opposition research and launching attack ads. It used the IS's own horrific video footage to subvert the idea that recruits were heading to Syria for some worthy cause, and, instead, sent a message that the IS was exactly the opposite. Critics at the US State Department and White House saw the use of graphic images as a disturbing embrace of the adversary's playbook. The CSCC's defenders could never determine whether it had accomplished its main objective of discouraging would-be militants from traveling to Syria.

The USG continues to search for a messaging strategy that might resonate with aggrieved Muslims and stem the spread of Islamist militancy. Previous US efforts have ranged from covert CIA propaganda programs to a Walt Disney-produced film. Their ineffectiveness has hindered attempts to rebalance US counterterrorism policy, leaving the government heavily dependent on armed drones, commando teams, and other instruments of lethal force.

During President Obama's second term, his administration decided to stop taunting the IS. The State Department launched a new entity—the Information Coordination Cell (ICC)—which enlisted US embassies, military leaders, and regional allies in a global messaging campaign to discredit groups such as the IS. The ICC's approach was designed to be more factual and testimonial, intending to highlight IS hypocrisy, emphasize the accounts of its defectors, and document its losses on the battlefield, without recirculating its gruesome images or matching its snide tone. In short, the idea was to let the facts speak for themselves.

The ICC was a major departure and significant advance from the earliest efforts made by the USG to change hearts and minds. Among them were videos commissioned in 2002 by a former Madison Avenue advertising executive appointed to a new public diplomacy post one month after 9/11. His $15 million "Shared Values" campaign profiled Muslims living contentedly in the US, including a baker in Ohio and a fire department medic in Brooklyn. Some in the State Department derisively labeled it the "Happy Muslim" campaign. It was quickly shelved, but in 2005, President George W. Bush appointed his longtime communications adviser, Karen Hughes, to be the new head of public diplomacy. She created a unit named the Digital Outreach Team to defend US policies in online chat rooms that seethed with hostility toward the US. She also persuaded Disney to produce a feel-good "Portraits of America" film that was shown in airports and US embassies.

But the IS has redefined media-savvy. Its media wing employs a virtual production line, turning battle footage captured on GoPro cameras into polished propaganda films that are disseminated by an army of followers. Researchers also point to "the backfire effect" which occurs when one party tries to disabuse another with a strongly held belief to change his or her thinking, which often only results in making their belief even stronger. The USG's approach to battling IS in the cyber media space underscores the difficulty of experimentation in government, where there can be zero tolerance for risk and little willingness to let a program naturally evolve.[180] It also did not help that the State Department's anti-terrorism cyber initiatives were, from the start, severely under-funded—just a fraction of the cyber funding afforded to the CIA and DoD.

At the beginning of the Trump administration, attempts to win the hearts and minds of the disenfranchised, vulnerable youth, or individuals who simply hate the West were largely put on the back burner in favor of the quest for annihilation. In the words of Secretary of Defense James Mattis: "We have shifted from attrition tactics to annihilation tactics. Our intention is that the foreign fighters do not survive the fight to return home to North Africa, to Europe, to America, to Asia, or to Africa. We're not going to allow them to do so. We're going to stop them there and take apart the caliphate. We're going to shatter their sense of invincibility there in the physical caliphate. That's only one phase of this. Then we have the virtual caliphate—we have got to dry up their recruiting and fundraising. The way we intend to do it is to humiliate them, to divorce them from any nation giving them protection, and humiliate their message of hatred and violence."[181] He also admitted that, ultimately, this would be a long fight and a battle of ideas. Once the 'physical' fight has largely ended, it will be all about the cyberwar.

The Art of Virtual Planning

The IS has been fighting that war since its inception, having created a "virtual planner" model for managing physical attacks via its "lone wolf" soldiers, wherein operatives who are part of its external operations division coordinate attacks online with supporters across the globe (which means they are not strictly 'lone wolves' but, instead, act individually with 'guidance'). Most of these supporters have never met any of the IS operatives they are conspiring with, and most of the group's most prominent virtual planners appear to be based in Iraq and Syria, to have access to the IS's top leadership.

Since all that is required to be a virtual planner is an Internet connection and good encryption, they could theoretically operate from anywhere, although being geographically dispersed carries heightened risk of detection in some nations. It is presumed that at least some of the virtual planners continue to operate from Iraq and Syria, in spite of how degraded many of the group's operational theaters there have become in recent years.

The virtual planner model has revolutionized jihadist external operations. IS has taken advantage of recent advances in online communications and encryption to engineer a process by which the group's top operatives can directly guide lone attackers, playing a central role in the conceptualization, target selection, timing, and execution of future attacks. Virtual planners offer operatives the same services once provided by strictly physical networks: seamlessly executing the group's guiding strategy and maximizing the impact and propaganda value of attacks waged in its name, while avoiding many of the risks typically associated with physically training operatives—such as the risk of being tailed or the chance an operative might get caught re-entering his or her home country.

Virtual planners have been integrated into the group's geographical command structure and function much like theater commanders but in the cyber realm. The IS's virtual planners are also assigned areas of responsibility according to their nationality and linguistic skills and tasked with actively recruiting and handling attackers from these areas. The decision to assign virtual planners to geographic areas with which they are familiar allows them to rely on contacts involved in a given domicile.

For example, in April 2015, Australian police disrupted a cell plotting an attack on Anzac Day, a day of remembrance for armed forces from Australia and New Zealand. The leaders of the cell were in regular contact with the IS's Australian virtual planner, Neil Prakash, who reportedly helped formulate the plot. He and the plotters had links to Melbourne's al-Furqan center, an Islamic center viewed by local police as a hub for militancy. After departing for the IS's 'caliphate', Prakash allegedly encouraged some young militants to also make their *hijra* there, while directing others to stay behind and carry out the attacks.

At times the IS's theater commanders function interchangeably as virtual planners, as was the case for Bahrun Naim, one of the group's top Indonesian militants. In September 2016, Indonesian police disrupted a cell in Batam coordinating with him to launch a rocket attack on Marina Bay in Singapore. The Batam cell had been measuring elevation points and the distance from those hills to their target in Singapore, while Naim had planned to deploy technicians thereafter to make explosives and prepare for the attack.

The IS's virtual planner model is an outgrowth of an approach to encourage attacks by lone wolf actors by Anwar al-Awlaki —the American-born propagandist for AQ in the Arabian Peninsula (AQAP), before he was killed by a US drone strike in 2011—who became notorious for using the Internet to call for lone wolf attacks. The IS's virtual planners are casting a wider recruitment net than Awlaki, who, as a result of his superb oratorical skills, was able to establish remote intimacy with people halfway across the world. The advancement of Internet-based communication and explosion of social media have enabled the planner to have greater reach to a larger audience than ever before.

By building an "intimate" relationship with a potential attacker, the virtual planner provides encouragement and validation, addressing the individual's doubts and hesitations while generating confidence and a strong desire to carry out an attack. Virtual planners can replicate the same social pressures that exist with in-person cells. Individuals can simply wander into searchable online networks, rather than having to be identified with and socialized by in-person networks that must act covertly. Unlike with physical networks, the virtual planner model does not risk the capture or punishment of the network's key operatives.

Individuals inspired by the IS can directly reach out to virtual planners for guidance and assistance in carrying out attacks. Junaid Hussain, a former British hacker turned terrorist, illustrates how virtual planners can coach domestic militants. The operative Junead Khan had been on British counterterrorism authorities' radar since 2014. Khan had originally planned to travel to the caliphate, but in early 2015 he changed his mind and began to focus on carrying out a domestic attack, using his job as a deliveryman to scope out US military bases in the UK. In July 2015, Khan exchanged several messages with Junaid Hussain over Surespot, discussing the logistics of various possible plans of attack. Hussain sent Khan a bomb-making manual and instructed him to make and use explosives against police who arrived on the scene of his attack. Though Khan was arrested before he could strike, the case illustrates how virtual planners can provide all the services that used to be characteristic of only physical cells.

In addition to recruitment and operational guidance, virtual planners can bring disparate individuals and cells together to form larger attack networks. In September 2016, French authorities arrested a group of female terrorists who had carried out the failed plot to set off a car bomb near Paris's Notre Dame Cathedral. Before the attempted attack, none of the women had had any type of relationship with one another. They were brought together by IS's European virtual planner, Rachid Kassim. In connecting the women, Kassim merged two different lines of terrorist effort in two different parts of France based on one operative's reluctance to carry out a particular kind of operation.

Sarah Hervouët, a 23-year-old convert to Islam who was planning an attack in the southeastern French commune of Cogolin, had been communicating with Kassim via Telegram. Acting on his orders, Hervouët wrote her will, along with farewell letters to relatives, and made a video proclaiming her allegiance to IS. She lost her appetite for the operation that Kassim envisioned for her—a "suicide-by-police" attack— so Kassim connected her with two other women preparing to carry out an attack in Paris instead. Though the women failed to carry out the dramatic attack that Kassim had hoped for, the case demonstrates the speed and agility with which virtual planners can operate. Kassim not only convinced four women to carry out violent attacks in the IS's name, he also rapidly adapted his plans to the preferences of his operatives, and merged two deadly projects together to increase the likelihood of success.

The IS's virtual planners allow the group to effectively seize ownership over what would previously have been considered lone wolf attacks. By creating a bridge between potential militants and the organization, virtual planners empower lone actors to fulfill the IS's objectives while requiring minimal resources from the organization. Virtual planners transform these individuals into ambassadors for the IS's global brand, becoming soldiers who can advance its strategic aims. Virtual planners help maximize the psychological and reputational impact of violence committed in the IS's name, further enticing other potential devotees to join its cause.

The success of the virtual planner model underscores jihadist groups' ongoing process of organizational learning but has its own disadvantages, such as the inability to provide in-person training or be optimally nimble during an attack to modify plans as circumstances may change. Cells directed by virtual planners are also at greater risk of being detected by SIGINT, despite advances in end-to-end encryption. Nonetheless, the virtual planner approach is a low-cost, high-reward strategy with enormous destructive potential, especially as the IS and other terrorist groups continue to develop and refine the model. Adaptations to jihadists' modes of operation have continually outpaced states' ability to effectively counter them, and will likely continue to do so.[182]

Hacking IS

In 2015, the locations of 98 IS recruiters were leaked by a hacker organization known as GhostSec. A query of its IP addresses showed that roughly half of them were located in the former Soviet Bloc—with many in Slovenia, the Czech Republic, Lithuania, Bulgaria, and Armenia—but the majority were in Russia. It could not be confirmed which addresses were the actual locations of the recruiters and which were IS members routing their connections through different locations. However, GhostSec provided images showing that several IS websites were routing their connections through a California-based tech firm. This suggested that many of the more tech-savvy members of the IS were operating off-site in the former Soviet Bloc.

The information highlighted the deepening ties between the IS and terrorist organizations in Russia's North Caucasus region. Perusal of some of the IS recruitment websites gave credence to this theory. One of the larger Russian language terrorist websites was filled with recruitment information, profiles on terrorists, and general news about terrorist activities around the world. The large concentration of IS recruiters in Russia and Eastern Europe was consistent with the strong focus the group had put on recruiting fighters from

Russia. At the time, the Russian foreign ministry said approximately 2,200 Russian nationals were fighting for the IS and other terrorist groups in Syria and Iraq.[183] The Western media has been very much focused on the flow of jihadists from the Middle East and other parts of the Muslim world, leaving the impression among many in the West that the flow of jihadis to Iraq and Syria was a more 'regional' problem than it really is. To be clear, it is global in scope.

In 2016, a hacker who had become well-known for hacking and humiliating IS recruiters—WauchulaGhost, part of the hacker collective Anonymous—leaked hundreds of IP addresses and thousands of phone numbers from contact lists of alleged IS online recruiters. The leak contained 682 IP addresses, which included the locations of the accounts used by the recruiters and 10,400 phone numbers that WauchulaGhost found stored across 20 of the accounts. The phone numbers appeared to be from the recruiters' personal phone books. All the phone number lists were in Arabic, except for one that was in Russian.

The accounts were located in many countries throughout the world, with 219 in Saudi Arabia, 170 in Iraq, 50 in Turkey, and 10 in Palestine. Many others were in the West, including 40 in the US, 11 in the UK, 9 in Russia, and 7 in Germany. The goal of the operation was to gain control of the accounts of the virtual recruiters the IS used to recruit and spread its propaganda. WauchulaGhost and other hackers seized control of Twitter accounts used by IS recruiters and then used the accounts to humiliate the IS and generate distrust and paranoia among its ranks.[184] In 2017, WachulaGhost flooded IS Twitter accounts with gay imagery and messages, claiming it took him less than one minute to do so. This is evidence of how some hackers have a social conscience and will risk their own safety to pursue their own moral compass.

A tacit alliance has developed between numerous Western states and several Anonymous affiliates based on a shared interest in combating militant Islamist groups. The goal of Anonymous is to pressure Twitter into removing more accounts linked to Islamic extremism. Twitter has taken action against many accounts, but social media more generally remains uncertain about how to proceed. Do they double down or stop getting involved, and what might the implication be of doing anything? The examples serve to emphasize the importance of communication and coordination among and between civilian activists, governments, and businesses, as each plays a role in confronting security challenges tied to religious extremism.

Anonymous, and groups like it, could succeed where some government initiatives have not. There is certainly an argument to be made that the Western governments should provide greater support for any entity already combating the IS and should even consider paying them to do so. While increased pressure would probably push the IS deeper into the Dark Web, enabling tech-savvy civilians to attack the IS's web presence may help minimize the impact of the group's social media and web presence. A "cyber-militia" could help to address many of the new technological challenges faced in today's cyber conflicts.

Alternatively, Anonymous support could prove detrimental to state efforts to combat the IS, since government investigators may actually prefer that the accounts remain visible. Removing virtual trails to suspected militants could hinder investigators' ability to gather intelligence, map out communication networks, and track down operational cells. By being in a position to monitor accounts, intelligence practitioners can glean information about potential threats and improve existing counterterrorism efforts.

Policymakers must evaluate the trade-offs between limiting propaganda and coordination versus hindering intelligence collection. Anonymous interventions may also generate unintended negative consequences, as has been the case in some previous operations. Anonymous affiliates have been mistaken in identifying suspects in a number of criminal cases, and there is no accountability in place when things go wrong. Without specific coordination with investigators and the intelligence community, an Anonymous activist might disrupt an ongoing operation or spark retaliatory actions by the IS.

Policymakers must also be mindful of how increased civilian participation could introduce new challenges in the fight against the IS. The involvement of social media in efforts to combat violent extremism complicates policymaker decision-making, and direct civilian participation in combat operations has raised important questions about the legality and desirability of involving non-state actors in violent conflict. While the participation of Anonymous, and other groups like it, could very well provide an additional tool in the battle against the IS and violent extremism, the effects of its participation are, and will remain, unclear, and possibly different in each instance.[185]

Cyber Vigilantism

Like most other governments, the USG still lacks clear regulations governing content hosted on US servers. For groups such as the IS, this has become a point of exploitation, and the irony is that there is a growing propensity to use US servers to host IS websites and forums. Investigators in the US have been overwhelmed by the sheer volume of online activity from the IS. The DHS admitted in 2015 to having trouble differentiating those supporters focused only on promoting pro-IS rhetoric (which may be protected speech) versus detecting those prepared to engage in violence on the group's behalf. Cyber vigilantes are helping to pick up the slack.

Extremist websites are surprisingly easy to locate and access, and experts believe there are thousands in existence. Some websites look completely benign, appearing to be classified ads or online directories, but with one click, a secret door opens to the actual home page. The sites invoke the call of jihad, contain bomb-making advice, or may even offer webinars for those who want to hear and interact with clerics and group leaders. Cyber vigilantism by private citizens is a response to their frustration with the number of extremist sites in operation and what they believe is the inability of a given government to take them down.

While the idea of private citizens engaging the enemy on the Internet either helps or hinders the fight against terrorism, it occurs every day, and the actors are increasingly savvy and effective. There is no typical extremist "hacktivist"; they are men, women, young, old, ex-military, businessmen, lawyers, housewives, and techies. They live in big cities or small towns and their reasons for engaging and methods of infiltration vary. Some have come out of the shadows but most use pseudonyms and are colorful characters, often as intriguing as their work.

Cyber vigilantes patrol popular websites for jihadist postings, flagging them and working through established procedures with the site owners to have the videos removed. One site claims to have had more than 15,000 videos removed and identified dedicated "channels" maintained by groups such as the Taliban. Usually, the service provider complies with the removal requests because providing services to known terrorists violates existing laws. Emerging threat and scam mail vigilantes are a newer phenomenon and may be unintentionally helping the fight against terror.

"Scam baiting" targets illicit e-mail fundraising schemes by sending bogus replies, tracking IP addresses of the sender (reporting these to authorities), defacing websites, and reporting the e-mail as spam to ISPs. The scam communication (legally known as "419 advance-fee fraud") may relay news of an inheritance or a lottery win, tell a tragic story about a child, or bring news of a hot new investment scheme, and asks for bank account information and wiring instructions. These scams are a rising concern in the counter-terrorism realm with respect to fundraising. While the scams tend to be targeted toward innocent, gullible Westerners, most are launched from Nigeria (which yielded the "Christmas Day Bomber" Umar Farouk Abdulmutallab and is an established source of manpower for AQAP and Boko Haram) or from other places with active terrorist linkages and networks.

Some of the cyber vigilantes have unique skills and deploy techniques not seen before and not easily replicated. Like their competitors in the Dark Web, they can bring down most any website in the world, instantly. Their goal may not be to permanently bring down an extremist website but rather to randomly disrupt it or take the site off line for a set period of time. The disruption results in anger and frustration because the Internet may be terrorists' virtual lifeline to the world. One such cyber vigilante, Jester, initiates DDos attacks against extremist websites using a single, low-spec computer with low bandwidth. A concern is what happens when someone like Jester may change his allegiance or turn his skills to non-terrorist targets.

Shannen Rossmiller is a lawyer and mother of three from Montana who taught herself Arabic and began engaging in chat rooms on jihad websites in 2003. She spent years creating her personas. Posing as an AQ sympathizer, she ensnared several Americans who had become radicalized. One would-be terrorist was convicted and is spending 30 years in jail for offering to blow up US pipelines. Her most notable case is that of an Army National Guard specialist who was preparing to deploy and is now serving a life sentence for treason, aiding the enemy, and attempted espionage.

In 2008, Bill Warner, a private investigator and self-proclaimed cyber crusader, shut down three extremist websites hosted by a Tampa, Florida ISP. One site contained graphic images and video related to attacks on US troops in Iraq and Afghanistan, along with propaganda such as inflated casualty counts. The site had 19 million hits in 10 months. Cyber vigilante Aaron Wiseburd is the creative force behind "Internet Haganah", a repository of extremist site information. Wiseburd gathers and stores intelligence on the site, which is accessible to anyone, and states he has dismantled thousands of extremist sites on his own.

Cyber vigilantes generally operate without government oversight or the red tape or legal restrictions that inhibit government action, allowing them to infiltrate IS recruitment networks and launch attacks on terrorist websites without the need to worry about political fallout or public scrutiny. GhostSec was started by a group of highly skilled hackers following the attacks on the Paris office of satirical newspaper Charlie Hebdo, in 2015. In the months that followed, GhostSec claimed to have taken out nearly 60,000 IS social media accounts that were being used for recruitment or to send threats and shut down approximately 100 IS websites used for recruitment, spreading propaganda, and planning attacks. It also quietly monitored many terrorist websites, including those hidden in the Dark Web.

Individuals and organizations like GhostSec work in a gray area. Hackers typically frown on cooperating with governments, and governments rarely trust hacker groups that conceal their identities, but GhostSec works closely with another hacker group known as CtrlSec (Control Section) and also collects intelligence from the hacker collective Anonymous. Although Anonymous would not approve, it also works with elements of the USG, given that many IS websites are hosted on privately held servers based in the US. However, GhostSec avoids attacking these sites, as doing so would be seen as attacking US infrastructure.

Government agents naturally know about the sites and monitor them. Cyber vigilantes may therefore unwittingly interfere with the information gathering process, existing counter-terrorism cyber operations, or psychological operations. Open source analysts, theologians, social scientists, psychologists, and professors also visit extremist sites to glean information on shifting ideology, social trends, and subtle changes in behavior. If the sites are taken offline, their ability to contribute to knowledge about cyberterrorism is clearly negatively impacted. The most influential changes in this battlefield are occurring at the micro-level—page by page, e-mail by e-mail, and attack by attack.[186] The cyber vigilante plays an increasingly important role in the Virtual Terrorism ecosystem, and what GhostSec and other similar groups are doing has already set a precedent for future efforts to fight terrorism.

Coordination, Flexibility, Adaptability

Virtual jihad has not only gained prominence and credibility as a wholly legitimate alternative to traditional conceptions of jihad but has also progressively outpaced physical jihad. *While physical jihad continues to hold aspirational appeal to a great many actors, virtual jihad has supplanted traditional notions of jihad for a new generation of adherents who are either unwilling or unable to engage in physical violence themselves.* The rise of the virtual jihadist has assumed an important (perhaps irreplaceable) role in rejuvenating the concept of jihad and facilitating the dissemination of its "counterculture" narrative to new audiences. The well-known maxim "the medium is the message" helps explain how the promotion of virtual jihad has fundamentally recast the ideology of jihadism to maintain its relevance in the virtual era.[187]

The removal of content on the Internet has a limited effect, since it is easy to set up alternative sites, and has forced the IS and other terrorist organizations to adapt and become better at evading detection and creating new forms of hidden communication. Virtual jihadists have the advantage of being able to piggyback off Western laws and individual free speech protection; formally criminalizing the dissemination of radical content can result in violations of the right to freedom of expression. An online posting crosses a legal line if it can be proven that the statements made are intended to incite terrorism and that a causal link can be established between such statements and the imminence and likelihood of the actual act being committed.

In any effective form of communication, there are a number of recurring elements that need to be taken into account: the target group, the message, the messenger, and the channel used to communicate the message. Particularly when dealing with terrorist organizations, which are themselves adept at effective communication, a one-size-fits-all counternarrative formula cannot work. Terrorist groups have a plethora of moving parts, from sympathizers, followers, and active facilitators, to active believers (who take the lead in debates), religious leaders, foreign fighters, former fighters, and recruiters, among others. Targeting 'the group' theoretically implies targeting the various sub-groups as well and results in the potential need to craft separate campaigns addressed at each of them. This also implies customizing each campaign by such variables as language, age, sex, group type, website. and social media platform, which is a Herculean task. The inability or inadequacy of government efforts to master the art of effectively countering terrorist narratives is of course one of the reasons why radicalization continues to grow.[188]

As a result of the Internet, there is virtually no Muslim (or non-Muslim for that matter) anywhere in the world who does not have access to jihadist propaganda if he or she desires it, which is available at will and in abundant supply. In order to defeat the IS in cyberspace, the US and other Western governments must overhaul their strategy, which clearly has not worked. What is needed is an entirely new strategic approach that emphasizes coordination, flexibility, and adaptability. A useful first step would be for governments to emphasize coordination and information sharing—not only *among* government agencies, but also *between* them, international partners, and NGOs engaged in the global effort to fight extremism. There is too little cooperation among these organizations, which has led to a tremendous duplication of effort, repetition of mistakes, and an ongoing need to create new strategies.

The US should also create nimble "cyber cells"—specialized, flexible, and adaptable units capable of carrying out online surveillance and information operations. These could operate under the direction of the Global Engagement Center (GEC, an interagency organization housed at the State Department), which was created in 2016 to coordinate the US counterextremism messaging efforts. The GEC is well suited to the information sharing that these cells would need, and the Center has already shown a willingness to innovate. Since 2016 the GEC has used public data from social media sites to find users interested in jihadist causes and has targeted them with anti-extremism YouTube ads.

Understanding the IS's propaganda messaging and creating counter messaging to undermine them is fully within reach of US analysts. US cyber cells dedicated to fighting online propaganda should be able to expand current counter messaging to reach all those interested in jihad, despite what their public social media profile data may indicate. Just as policymakers accept the risk of occasional misfires in kinetic warfare, they should allow cyber cells the freedom to operate without excessive restraint.

There are some basic, relatively easily implementable tactics that can be deployed on the Internet to challenge the IS at its own game. As its websites and social media accounts have been taken down, the IS and its supporters have had to develop ways to transfer their network of followers from one account to the next. The most popular method is to simply add a number to their Twitter username and then increase that number each time they are shut down and open a new account. By knowing which Telegram channel or Twitter account IS supporters follow, governments can attempt to create the account before the IS does, replacing extremist content with their own.

Since many IS followers listen to the group's Kalifah News to learn of new passwords, cyber cell analysts could create its own versions of the Khilafah News Telegram channel, knowing that IS supporters would migrate there once Telegram shuts down the latest News site. The same technique can be used to disrupt the group's YouTube channels and other social media platforms. Fake accounts would utilize the names and logos of actual IS-affiliated groups, and recruits would view their content, believing them to be real.

Another potential weakness is the IS's use of Twitter hashtags. In 2014, the group famously hijacked World Cup hashtags in English and Arabic, posting propaganda with the hashtag #WorldCup2014 and thereby shocking social media users with images of graphic violence. The IS has also called upon its supporters to use special hashtags when searching for new propaganda. Anti-IS messages could be posted using the group's own hashtags, putting alternative narratives into the same social media conversation. The US has already begun to take tentative steps in this direction, with government analysts taking over #IS, #IslamicState, and other popular IS hashtags. Such efforts could be vastly expanded, given a clearer understanding of the group's marketing techniques, and armed with personnel who have native fluency in the IS's preferred languages. Adopting a new cyber strategy along these lines would enable the US and its allies to create viable, proactive alternatives to IS messaging while reaching target audiences and potential recruits.[189]

As noted, at times the greatest impediment to making more progress in combatting virtual jihad is the West's own laws. Existing law can limit what governments can and cannot do to prevent cyberattacks. The USG's strategic communications and information operations remain hindered by the US Information and Education Exchange Act of 1948, which dictates that information about the US and its policies intended for foreign audiences "shall not be disseminated within the US, its territories, or possessions". This effectively creates a wall between domestic and foreign audiences by limiting the information that the US can legally make available to counter extremists in cyberspace, for fear of potential blow-back on American citizens. It also limits the ability of the USG to legally respond to extremism in cyberspace by mounting its own information and propaganda campaigns. Unless governments find the means to more effectively counter the cyber activities of jihadist groups and degrade their cyber capabilities, the force multiplier effect of cyber utilization will loom as an even greater problem for governments in the future.[190]

7. Social Media

When Facebook purchased Instagram for $1 billion in 2012, a lot of people thought Mark Zuckerberg was crazy. $1 billion? For a relatively new company that made little money and had just 13 employees? Just three months later, Facebook announced that it would sell the names, images, and photographs of Instagram users to advertisers. According to its updated Tops, Instagram said that parents who had uploaded photographs of their minor children had implicitly consented to the use of the images in advertisements. As a result of its ToS change, 16 billion photographs became Instagram's intellectual property.[191] Zuckerberg was not crazy; he was sly like a fox.

Invasion of the Data Snatchers

In the US, *social networks are considered to be public spaces and any information shared there is covered under the so-called 'third-party doctrine', which means that users have no reasonable expectation of privacy regarding the data their service providers collect about them.* This exception to the Fourth Amendment of the US Constitution's prohibition on unreasonable search and seizure means that *any data you post online in any format (regardless of privacy settings), or any data collected by the third parties with whom you may have an agreed-upon business relationship, is not considered private.* As a result, any data that 'leaks' to places you did not explicitly authorize cannot be clawed back, and there is usually nothing you can do about it.

Data 'leakage' is, as a result, routine in a variety of contexts and has become a big business. More than 80 percent of divorce attorneys admit to searching social media sites for evidence that can be used against their client's spouses, for example. All the data shared on social media, all cell phone call records, and all GPS locational data records become fair game in divorce proceedings. The profile you may have created on a dating website when you were still single is perfectly admissible in a divorce trial. If a husband complains

175

that his wife was inattentive, and an unfit mother, all the time she spent playing games online that happened to coincide with the exact timing of her child's soccer practice or ballet class becomes a virtual weapon.

A survey conducted by Microsoft of 2,500 recruiting professionals in four major developed countries[192] found that 70 percent of human resource professionals had rejected job candidates based on information uncovered in online searches. Some employers now demand social media passwords for prospective employees as a condition of being hired. They may even demand the same of current employees. City and state job applicants across the US have been required to produce social media passwords as a condition of employment. While a few states (such as California) have banned the practice, there is no federal law banning it, and the practice remains legal in 80 percent of the US.

College athletes at schools such as the University of Oklahoma and the University of North Carolina have been required to provide their social media passwords to their coaches as a condition of being 'allowed' to play sports. Some of these athletes have been required to install monitoring software on their personal computers and phones to track their activity in real time, to ensure that athletic departments are protected against potentially damaging posts made by student athletes.

The DHS began using social media sites to observe the daily life of immigrant applicants in 2010. *US federal agents can access social data via subpoenas, national security letters, and other administrative orders delivered to ISPs, who, under the third-party doctrine exception to the Fourth Amendment, do not even need to notify the subject of the request.* As a result of advances in technology, the cost of participating in the 'surveillance economy' has dropped precipitously. There is no longer a need for teams of agents to follow someone around anymore; one study has estimated that by using proxy surveillance technologies, the USG now spends an average of just $574 per taxpayer to track each US citizen. A survey by the International Association of Police Chiefs of more than 500 law enforcement organizations revealed that 86 percent of police departments now routinely include social media searches as part of their criminal investigations.

Data Overload

Every digital process—whether a sensor, GPS device, mobile phone, medical lab test, credit card transaction, hotel door lock, car engine, or social media exchange—produces data. We are drowning in it. In 2010, Eric Schmidt of Google said that the world produced as much information in two days as we did from the dawn of civilization until 2003.[193] In 2014, it was estimated that each day the world creates 2.5 quintillion bytes of data, so much that *90 percent of the data in the world at that time was created in the previous two years.*[194] As of 2016, *we produced as much information in 10 minutes as did the first 10,000 generations of human beings.* These mind-boggling statistics illustrate that we have a rather large problem, because there is no way humanly possible to monitor and protect all of that data. The more data, the more data breaches.

Facebook admitted in 2011 (when it had 'just' 500 million users) that more than 600,000 of its accounts were compromised every single *day*. Each of those security breaches could have been used for identity theft, criminal impersonation, tax fraud, health insurance scams, or a plethora of other possible criminal offenses. Consider the information that most of us willingly provide to Facebook and other social media platforms—our name, birth date, place where we live, when and where we travel, photographs of our children, and so on. Since 75 percent of people typically use the same password for multiple Internet sites, and 30 percent use the same log-in information for all of their online activities, it is easy to see why this is a problem. As shocking as these statistics are, imagine the potential impact of having a single account hacked if you happen to be one of them.

The list of social media companies that have been hacked is impressive (not in a good way) and includes Google, Yahoo, LinkedIn, Twitter, and Snapchat. Transnational organized criminal groups are believed to be responsible for up to 85 percent of these breaches, which means it is not generally being done by a vengeful former lover, but, rather, by people who intend to steal from you and harm you. Whether social media and Internet companies are good stewards of our data or not, the sad fact is that _any_ data we entrust to them can be leaked to criminals, terrorists, or others.

Of course, it is not just these groups that are responsible, and this is not a new problem. In 2010, Google reported that the Chinese government hacked the firm in search of the Gmail accounts of activists in the Asia, Europe, and the US who had raised concerns about its human rights practices. During the hack, China also apparently took the opportunity to target Google's trade secrets and source code. It was later revealed that China's PLA took the source code, which gave the CCP ongoing access to Google's global password management system, giving the Chinese the ability to monitor at least a portion of Gmail's 900+ million users.

Unseen Risks

It is estimated that at least 40 percent of social media users have been exposed to at least one form of malware, and more than 20 percent have had their social networking or e-mail account compromised or taken over by a third-party without permission. One way this is increasingly being done is by using 'breaking news' to dupe people into clicking on a virus-laden link. Some of the examples used are when a celebrity is apparently nude or found in a compromising position, when natural disasters strike, or when the latest 'shocking' news story has occurred.

One of the better-known pieces of social media malware, known as "Koobface", targeted Facebook users with the eye-catching headline "OMG –I just saw this naked video of you". Now, if they were to stop and think about it, most people would realize that this is very unlikely to be true, but, human nature being what it is, many people click on the link. Once infected, Koobface forces a computer to take part in DDoS attacks against third parties and hijacks Internet search returns and clicks to take the user to untrusted websites. Designed by a hacking group in St. Petersburg, the Russian government has refused to extradite the group to face trial.

Social media attack tools have become so streamlined and automated that someone who is not a 'master hacker' can get in on the act. Firesheep is a simple Firefox browser plug-in that anyone can download to take over others' Facebook sessions and hijack their accounts. So, for example, if, like millions of people do during the day, you happen to check your Facebook account at your local Starbucks while in the process sharing its network with 30 other people, and if one of them happened to be running Firesheep, the hacker could use the plug-in to log in as you on your own Facebook account. Known as "sidejacking", this happens all the time.

Hackers also target social media sites through online games and third-party apps which grant them access to bank accounts and other sensitive personal information. The 17-year-old son of Lisa Lockwood, of Baltimore, Maryland, provided the wrong information to the wrong Facebook gaming app. It offered the teen extra gaming points in exchange for filling out an account application that required his Social Security number. Criminals used the number to complete seven car loan applications on his behalf. Lisa only learned about it when a local car dealer called her to inquire about her son's application.

Facebook has unfortunately also become a favorite target of pedophiles and stalkers, and it is an extremely target rich environment. Some child molesters target single mothers with young daughters or sons by trawling their online profiles and searching for references to their children. Their goal is to work their way into the home, often using a false pretense and/or name, in an effort to begin a relationship with the child's mother. Once invited into the home and having developed a level of comfort, the pedophile will find a way to be alone with the daughter or son.

Cyber stalkers send unwanted e-mails, tweets, and text messages, or spread rumors online. They easily obtain detailed information about their victims, such as home address and phone number. Sometimes this information is used to meet or confront the victim in person. In one case, in Sydney, Australia, a hacker meticulously studied the profile of his 18-year-old victim before contacting her. Using her self-declared love of animals, he created a fake profile and claimed he was a human resources (HR) recruiter for local animal rescue group. After communicating for a short while and gaining her trust, he asked if she would be interested in a job opening at the shelter. She agreed to meet him for an interview. He offered to drive her to the shelter, supposedly located in a secluded area outside Sydney. She agreed. It was there that he strangled and murdered her. A terrible story, it demonstrates how easily someone can be lulled into trusting another person she has never met, via social media, and what can happen as a result.

Sometimes the data we willingly post on social media sites are being used in unexpected ways and appear in unexpected places. Bobbi Duncan, a 22-year-old lesbian student at the University of Texas at Austin, came from a strict Christian family and had kept her sexual orientation a secret from her parents. She joined a number of student groups on campus, including the Queer Chorus, to meet other gay and lesbian students. Upon joining the Chorus, its president welcomed Bobbi by adding her to the group's Facebook discussion page, which he did without her permission (since there was no Facebook setting at the time to prevent a third-party from adding you to a group). When he did so, Facebook sent an automatic notification to her entire list of friends (including her father), notifying them that she had joined the Chorus. Two days later, Bobbi was disowned by her parents. In another example, Paul Bristol flew from Trinidad to England to stab his ex-girlfriend to death after seeing a post of a photograph with her new boyfriend on Facebook.

Social media profiles also make us vulnerable to hate crimes, in which bigots, racists, and homophobes target individuals based on race, religion, creed, color, sexual orientation, or gender. Online data allows criminals to identify victims based on their own specific biases. The volume of hate crimes involving media in the US pales by comparison to other countries. In Russia for example, thousands of attacks are made by neo-Nazi youth, and one UK documentary highlighted more than 1,500 kidnappings of young gay men by bands of self-proclaimed vigilantes. The attackers fear no retribution from complicit police, so they post their attacks on social media ad nauseam to further humiliate their victims.

Revenge Porn and Sexually Explicit Content

We should presume that anything we put on social media is or will become completely public, since there is no such thing as 'private' data in the world of social media. As a result, we are made vulnerable by those we do not know, as well as by those that we do. Anyone can be betrayed by someone he/she previously trusted but no longer does. The scope of the problem is immense, particularly with respect to pornography and sexually explicit contact among hook-ups, lovers, spouses, and ex-hook-ups, lovers, and spouses. With an estimated two-thirds of college-aged students engaging in 'sexting' (sharing sexually explicit SMS photographs via their phones), the scope for a problem continues to grow rapidly.

Websites such as MyEx.com encourage jilted lovers to share photographs of their exes online. Another popular site— IsAnyoneUp.com—is a data repository for anyone to submit naked photographs of their exes or enemies and is visited by more than 250,000 people daily. Listed next to each photograph are links to the victim's social media accounts, including his or her full name and home town. The site's creator was even thoughtful enough to make this information fully indexed and retrievable via Google, so that an innocent search by a third-party looking for that person would stumble upon the photographs and social media links. To add final insult to injury, each nude photo is accompanied by comments that allow anyone to comment on it and say anything.[195]

The phenomenon has become so popular it has a name —revenge porn. In 2017 the first comprehensive research on revenge porn shed light on the scale of victimization across Australia, and its devastating impact. A survey of nearly 4,300 people, led by RMIT University and Monash University, found that far more people than researchers expected—both men and women—had sexual or nude images taken or distributed without their consent, or otherwise used against them. As is the case with other elements of Virtual Terrorism, image-based abuse has emerged so rapidly as an issue that existing laws and policies are struggling to catch up.

In the survey, 20 percent of respondents had images or videos of a nude or sexual nature taken without their consent, 11 percent had them shared, and 9 percent had received threats that images of them would be shared. Men and women were equally likely to be victims, but the rate was higher among younger people: one in three teenagers aged 16 to 19 and one in four aged 20 to 29 reported at least one form of image victimization. Marginalized groups, such as indigenous and gay, lesbian, and bisexual Australians, and those with a disability, were especially vulnerable. The online survey of 4,274 people aged 16 to 49 only captured those who had discovered their images had been distributed, mostly on social media. Though victims were equally likely to be male or female, the majority (54 percent) reported that the perpetrator was male. Women (39 percent) were more likely than men (30 percent) to be victimized by an intimate partner or former partner.

Previous findings had shown that images were used as a means of abuse for a range of reasons, including control, intimidation, sexual gratification, monetary gain, and social status building. Revenge porn typically makes one think of a jilted ex-lover or public shaming, but there is a broader range of damage that is often done. Many victims report experiencing it as a form of sexual violation or sexual violence. For many victims, the discovery that their images had been made public constituted a violation of their sexual autonomy and dignity, which had significant and long-term implications and impacts.

Some 80 percent of those who had been targeted by threats to distribute an image reported experiencing high levels of psychological distress that researchers found to be consistent with a moderate to severe depression and/or anxiety disorder. Overall, victims of any image-based abuse were almost twice as likely as non-victims to report experiencing high levels of psychological distress. The report resulting from the study recommended making image-based abuse a crime under federal telecommunications law. Only the states of Victoria and South Australia have specific laws against the distribution of intimate or invasive images without consent, although the survey found overwhelming support for such a measure, with 80 percent of respondents agreeing that it should be considered a crime. The researchers also noted the responsibility of social media platforms and ISPs for taking action to prevent image-based abuse and supporting victims through the creation of safe spaces online.[196]

In January 2017, Facebook had to assess nearly 54,000 potential cases of revenge pornography and "sextortion" for *the month*, disabling more than 14,000 accounts related to this type of sexual abuse, with 33 of the cases reviewed involving children. The company relies on users to report most abusive content, meaning the real scale of the problem is probably much greater. Facebook is using "image-matching" software to stop explicit content from being placed on the site, but Facebook is largely dependent on its users to report offenders, and it is admittedly difficult to draw a line between acceptable and unacceptable sexual content. It and other social media platforms have a real problem on their hands. A company spokesperson said the site received millions of reports each *week* about revenge porn.

At that time, moderators alerted senior managers to 51,300 potential cases of revenge porn, which it defines as attempts to use intimate imagery to shame, humiliate, or gain revenge against an individual. The company escalated 2,450 cases of potential sextortion, which it defines as attempts to extort money, or other imagery, from an individual. This led to a total of 14,130 accounts being disabled, with 16 cases having been pursued by Facebook's internal investigations teams at the time.

Facebook has introduced two "hotkeys" for moderators to help them quickly identify potential cases of sextortion and revenge porn, which it refers to as "non-consensual intimate imagery". The firm allows "moderate displays of sexuality, open-mouthed kissing, clothed simulated sex and pixelated sexual activity" involving adults, and uses sub-categories ranging from "arousal", "handy-work", and "mouth work" to "penetration", "fetish", and "groping". Facebook determines whether to allow or ban remarks based on the level of detail they contain.

Facebook previously permitted sexually explicit wording to be posted on its site and removes them if they are reported, but

183

says that not all disagreeable or disturbing content violates its community standards, and that it gives users the ability to customize and control what they see by unfollowing, blocking, or hiding posts, people, pages, and applications they do not wish to see. In short, it allows general expressions of desire but not sexually explicit detail. Facebook is continually updating certain policies in response to criticism that it has been too slow to delete some sexually graphic content, while simultaneously being too strict about other material. Ironically, in 2016, Facebook was condemned for removing the Pulitzer-prize-winning "Napalm girl" photograph from the Vietnam war because it showed a naked child, but after it was challenged for censorship, it relented.

Facebook allows nudity when it is depicted as "art"—such as paintings, sculptures, and drawings—but does not allow digitally created nudity or sexual activity. The line that has been drawn is also difficult to enforce because it is hard to differentiate between handmade art and digitally made depictions. Facebook moderators had been warned to delete images of Giambologna's 16th-century statue, the Kidnapping of the Sabine Women, in the Loggia dei Lanzi in Florence, if they were reported. They were also told to delete, if reported, images of the Rape of Europa—paintings that depict the mythological story of the abduction of Europa by Zeus.

Facebook has also developed detailed policies around "sexual solicitation" on the site. Providing contact information is allowed, and solicitation using acronyms is permissible, but if the post includes any extra information—such as mentioning sexual acts in a non-medical, scientific, or educational context—then the post should be deleted if it is flagged. Facebook plans to make it simpler to report problems, making it easier and faster for its reviewers to determine which posts violate its standards and how to contact law enforcement if someone needs help.[197]

Why Not Invite a Burglar to your Home?

A surprisingly large percentage of social media users are in the bad habit of posting their vacation plans on social media, or where they are at any particular moment, or how they are enjoying their 'week away' on their fabulous holiday. Why not just invite a burglar to your home? *Criminals no longer wait to see if your newspaper delivery has built up on your front doorstep before they target you for a burglary. Today, either they, or the data brokers they may use, scrape information from your social media for 'lead generation'.*

To highlight the threat, a group of Dutch computer developers created a website entitled PleaseRobMe.com where they aggregated locational data from tweets and Foursquare check-ins to create a searchable database. They were able to check by postal code to see who was away and for how long. This is not a hypothetical threat; burglars are indeed monitoring social media. Way back in 2010 (which seems like ancient history in our swiftly moving cyber world), a group of local criminals in Nashua, New Hampshire used Facebook to determine when their future victims were away from their homes. They succeeded in completing more than 50 home burglaries and stealing more than $200,000 in property. According to a 2011 study of convicted UK burglars, 78 percent of them admitted monitoring social media, and Google's Street View, to research property before committing the theft.

Another way they target their future victims is via locational data in files posted online—the silently implanted metadata in photographs, videos, and status updates shared by mobile devices, which reveal the date, time, and GPS coordinates where photos and videos were taken, as well as the serial number of the phone or camera. The metadata is easily accessible by anyone who knows how to download a simple browser plug-in to access them. With any one of hundreds of free tools, your photos and videos can be made to appear on a Google Map that allows anyone to zoom in on the precise location where the picture was taken.

Photographs posted for sale on eBay or Craigslist undoubtedly have embedded metadata that contains the exact location of your home, where the photo was presumably taken. A couple from New Albany, Indiana decided to sell their plasma TV and stereo system and posted some photos online. Shortly thereafter, they happened to mention on Facebook that they would be attending a concert in nearby Louisville that Saturday night. The couple were robbed of their

TV, two laptops, a digital camera, and some other items. *It is enough to make you want to stop using social media, electronic sale, and dating sites, and perhaps even your smartphone, entirely.*

Fake Profiles

Nearly 90 percent of consumers say that online reviews influence their buying decisions, and 70 percent trust the reviews they read online as much as they would a recommendation from a friend, according to Nielsen. They appear to be misguided. An investigation by the New York State attorney general found that 25 percent of the reviews on Yelp are completely bogus and found that one firm had written more than 1,500 fake reviews on Yelp and Google Places. Even worse, in 2014, a US federal appeals court ruled that it was *legal* for Yelp to manipulate its ratings based on which companies advertised on the site. Reviews on Amazon, eBay, TripAdvisor, and other sites can also easily be faked. Many of those 5-star ratings, it turns out, may have been written by the very businesses themselves. Anyone who has found the reality of a hotel or restaurant to be different from what was reviewed will understand this completely.

According to Facebook's 2014 annual report, up to 11 percent of its accounts are fake, meaning more than 140 million accounts at that time. Would you like to have 5,000 followers on Twitter? No problem. They can be bought for as little as $5. How about 100,000 'fans' on Facebook for just $1,500? For those with even more money to spend, you can have one million new friends on Instagram for $3,700. All of this is for sale on sites such as Swenzy, Fiverr, and Craigslist. Depending on where these 'businesses' pay their human capital to do the work, this will either be done by actual people (such as in Bangladesh and India) or by computer bots (in countries such as Romania, Russia and the Ukraine). Stung by criticism of this practice, social media companies have cracked down, with celebrities such as Rihanna, Shakira, and Lady Gaga each losing tens of thousands of 'fans' in the process.[198]

In 2017, footage emerged of a giant "click farm" that used more than 10,000 mobile phones to provide product ratings and phony "likes" on social media sites. Companies reportedly pay thousands of dollars in order to get more "likes" for their apps by using such services. The covert clip from China showed rows of "like-making" phones all wired to other devices in a factory. Thousands more phones in the same building all had the same purpose.[199]

The IS has also gotten into the fake account business. In 2015, Anonymous was able to trace the location of IS's "CyberCaliphate" (its own hacking collective) to a single IP address in Kuwait, gaining insight into how the group operates. It apparently ran about 10 Twitter accounts, each with different names, posting each day, every 10 minutes. The IS accounts were typically in place for eight hours each day before they were suspended by Twitter. After approximately 10 suspensions, they disappear for a few weeks, only to re-emerge. When the accounts re-emerged, they used a different name but kept the CyberCaliphate banner, which was also traced to the same IP address in Kuwait.

The IS and Social Media

A significant reason why the IS grew from a disparate group of jihadists to a global force to be reckoned with was its mastery of messaging through the use of social media. The IS became skilled at integrating dichotomies to broaden its appeal; for example, by portraying itself as both "ruthless killers" while also being "just like everyone else". Its cutting-edge approach to creating well-choreographed state-of-the-art videos combined with sophisticated messaging makes the West's response look sophomoric and lame by comparison.

The IS first targeted potential recruits in the Muslim world by emphasizing its anti-establishment and conservative credentials, which had instant appeal with young men who were poor, disenfranchised, and angry. The steady flow of gruesome decapitation videos drew fighters from across the Muslim world. The IS used brutality and fear as a form of seduction, appealing to a sense of individualism while glamorizing death and martyrdom. For young men living on the margins of society, with no job and little or nothing to lose, joining the IS gave their lives meaning and enabled them to fight their perceived oppressors.

The organization gradually shifted both the focus of its targeted recruits and its messaging in order to draw in a larger pool of devotees. Its videos changed focus, from the 'unfamiliar', individualism, and anonymity toward themes that were more instantly alluring to a broader range of people and with a more personal flare. For example, one round of videos showed IS members enjoying themselves at a swimming pool, gathered around a fancy car, eating delicious looking food, and portraying themselves as hedonists. This was odd, as it stood in dramatic contrast to the group's original portrayal of itself as highly conservative and anti-materialistic. New recruits were likely to be grossly disappointed when they learned that joining the IS did not, in fact, translate into sipping champagne by the pool. A number of stories emerged of recruits finding the IS distasteful and wanting to escape, only to be held prisoner, tortured, or killed.

The mystery surrounding who the IS actually 'is' was also used by the organization to enhance its perceived appeal. Joining a mysterious organization and not knowing the members' identities was undoubtedly also part of the attraction for some of the recruits—a chance to be different and do something unusual with unknown people in an unknown place. Part of the IS's ability to project an aura of power, at least at its outset, was undoubtedly associated with so many unknowns.

The dual appeal of individualism while being part of a larger group gave the IS the ability to manipulate peer pressure, especially among younger recruits, as an incentive to become part of 'the cause'. As more people from a more diverse range of countries joined the ranks of the IS, the group's 'cheerleaders' increased exponentially. The western media (unwittingly) greatly assisted the IS's cause by dutifully broadcasting its videos, generating some new devotees. This is part of what accounts for so many of the young westerners who sought to join the organization.[200]

The IS not only uses the same social media sites non-terrorists do to recruit people, it uses some of the same

Internet services to guard its own sites against cyberattacks, and attempts to hide at least some of its locations. According to information provided by GhostSec, in 2015, nearly 40 pro-IS websites were using the services of a Silicon Valley company called CloudFlare, a content delivery network that provides services to speed up websites and render them virtually immune to DDoS and other forms of cyberattacks. Of the 40 sites, 34 were used to spread propaganda, 4 were terrorist forums, and 2 offered technical services.[201]

As part of its #OpISIS campaign, Anonymous claimed to have taken 20,000 IS Twitter accounts offline, while GhostSec claimed to have taken down 149 terrorist websites and 6,000 YouTube videos, and flagged close to 101,000 Twitter accounts.[202] Anonymous claimed, in 2015, that the CyberCaliphate fakes most of its cyberattacks—at times releasing public information and claiming they stole it by hacking, and at other times taking credit for cyberattacks carried out by groups of hackers they had no connection to. The IS has taken credit for hundreds of claimed hacks but most turned out to be public information looked up on Google. Perhaps its least impressive 'hack' was publishing every location of McDonald's in England. Another time, the IS copied and pasted the names and phone numbers of US members of Congress (which are available on the US House of Representatives website) and claimed to have obtained the information by hacking US congressional servers.[203] There is no honor among hackers, it seems.

Sock Puppetry

Sock puppetry is a reference to a children's toy puppet, created when a hand is inserted into a sock to bring the sock to life. In the cyber world, organized crime groups do the same thing by combining computer scripting, Internet automation, and social networks to create hundreds of thousands of fake online citizens. Simply by using readily available online directories, these groups pick a first and last name, choose a date of birth, and enable the bot to sign up for a free e-mail account. By then scraping online photo sites, they choose age-appropriate images and create new accounts. The puppets then send out friend requests, re-post others' postings, and randomly 'like' things online. Soon enough, they have created an army of sock puppets to do whatever it is the criminals would like them to do—whether generating phishing attacks, creating online reviews, tricking users into downloading malware, or committing financial fraud.

Deception is not just the domain of thieves, of course. It has been widely reported that the USG extensively uses sock puppets as part of its psychological operations (psyops) to monitor Internet forums. So when "Abdul" says "death to the infidels", the Pentagon or CIA has a virtual "Hassan" ready to respond with a verse from the Quran extolling peace, mercy, and understanding. In 2011, the US Central Command awarded $2.8 million to a California company to create fake online personas for the purpose of manipulating online conversations and spreading pro-American points of view on social media. Each fake persona was contractually required to have a plausible personal history. The military's goal was to create an online persona management dashboard that would allow each of its service personnel to control 10 separate identities to degrade the enemy's narrative. Operating in a large number of languages, it was part of a $200 million operation called "Operation Earnest Voice", first developed during the Iraq War. According to Freedom House, at least 22 governments manipulate social media for propaganda purposes.[204]

The USG also ventured into the online gaming domain. The US Intelligence Advanced Research Projects Activity's (IARPA's) "Project Reynard" was the its initial effort to fight terrorism through online gaming environments. IARPA's objective is to have a reliable means of quantifying the way characters act in these games so that they can draw reasonable conclusions about the people who control the avatars. In essence, the program, which started in 2009 and is believed to have ended in 2012, wanted to know what guild you join on World of Warcraft, the shops you frequented in Second Life, and the characters you chatted with revealed about your nationality, your economic status, and your inclination towards real world violence. Armed with enough data, virtual clues may be able to reliably identify groups with terrorist associations.[205] The only way to hope to make meaningful progress against virtual terrorists is to play their game their way.

The Battle Against the IS on Social Media

Terrorist groups operate around the clock, tweeting every second and, in the process, gaining new followers on an ongoing basis. To get a sense of the enormity of the challenge of monitoring and taking down bad players on social media, consider these 2016 statistics Internet Live stats, which documented Internet traffic on these platforms *per second*:

- Twitter: 7352 tweets

- Instagram: 741 photos uploaded

- Skype: 2,271 calls made

- YouTube: 131,082 videos viewed

- Spam: 253,123 e-mails sent[206]

A 2016 study from George Washington University[207] found that there were about 2,000 Twitter accounts supporting the IS that were active *each day*, and that Twitter and Facebook were the two main platforms used by IS supporters to spread its propaganda. By analyzing a list of English-speaking IS adherents, the study found that the number of readily discoverable English-speaking IS supporters on Twitter was relatively small, usually fewer than 1,000 accounts. Extending the discovery process using advanced social network analysis produced a network of fewer than 3,000 accounts at any given time. IS English language social networks are extremely insular, meaning users mostly follow and interact with each other.

The number of users in the network who were based in Iraq and Syria appears to have declined over time, partly because of suspension activity, but also because of operational security concerns within the IS, and the deaths of some prominent Syria-based network participants. The average number of Twitter followers any given IS supporter could expect was 300 to 400 (with the average follower counts being periodically reduced by aggressive waves of suspensions). Over time, individual users who repeatedly created new accounts after being suspended suffered devastating reductions in their follower counts. Network and individual declines persisted even when suspension pressure eased, suggesting that suspensions diminish activity in ways that extend beyond the simple removal of accounts. The amount of pro-IS content available on Twitter was also limited by suspensions, since all of a user's tweets were typically deleted when his or her account was suspended.

IS supporters have deployed several countermeasures in an effort to offset the negative effects of suspensions, including the use of applications and simple hacking techniques to quickly create new accounts for users who had been suspended, as well as elaborate tactics to rebuild follower networks. IS supporters had explored the use of other social media platforms as a supplement to Twitter but felt that a robust presence on Twitter and Facebook was integral to their recruitment and propaganda efforts, so they continued returning to those platforms despite challenges. Suspensions typically had a significant detrimental effect on repeat offenders, shrinking both the size of their networks and the pace of their activity. Each time an IS account gets suspended, the user needs to create a new account. Over time these accounts suffered devastating reductions in their follower counts.[208]

Onboarding Social Media Firms in the Fight

Social media companies are paying attention to the challenge of online support for terrorism and are doing something about it. Social media sites have for years used software such as Microsoft's PhotoDNA to automatically identify still images they wish to remove, but there has been no comparable tool for video. As is the case with Facebook, they are therefore forced to rely primarily on their users to report videos that might violate the companies' policies against posting terrorist propaganda. In 2017, Facebook announced its intention to add an additional 3,000 reviewers to help better monitor video posted to the site, which highlights the magnitude of the problem. Clearly, there is not yet a magic algorithm to identify terrorist rhetoric and recruitment efforts on the Internet.

That may change. A researcher behind PhotoDNA is developing software called eGLYPH, which applies PhotoDNA's basic principles to identify video promoting terrorism, even if the clips have been edited, copied, or otherwise altered. Large video files create a real problem for search tools because, depending on the quality, they might consist of dozens of different images per second. Software analyzing individual images in video files would be impractical because of the computer processing power required, but eGLYPH's algorithm, which analyzes video, image, and audio files and creates a unique signature (called a "hash"), can be used to identify either an entire video or specific scenes within a video. The software can compare hashes of new video clips posted online against signatures in a database of content known to promote terrorism. If a match is found, that new content could be taken down automatically or flagged for review.

One of the software's advantages is that it quickly creates a signature for a video without using too much computing power, because it analyzes changes between frames rather than the entire image in each frame, removing as much of the redundancy in the data as possible and extracting the signature from what is left. eGLYPH's partner is the Counter Extremism Project (CEP), which has built up a vast repository of hashed images, audio files, and video that contains the worst of the worst content. eGLYPH compares the signatures it generates with those stored in the CEP's considerable database.

The CEP offered free access of its database to social media platforms, but Facebook, Twitter and YouTube all declined, having announced, in 2016, plans to develop their own shared database of hashed terrorism videos. Each of the large social media companies say they plan create their own database of signatures identifying videos and images depicting the most extreme and egregious terrorist images and videos they have removed from their services. The companies have not revealed details about their plans to hash new videos posted to their platforms, or how they will compare those signatures (called "fingerprints") to hashed videos stored in their databases. Each company will decide independently whether to remove flagged videos from its site and apps, based on each company's content posting policies.

One reason for the companies' fragmented approach to purging videos that support or incite terrorism is the absence of a universal definition of what constitutes "terrorist" or "extremist" content. Microsoft's policy is to remove from its Azure Cloud hosting and other services any content that is produced by or in support of organizations on the Consolidated United Nations Security Council Sanctions List. Facebook is more content to continue to rely on user reporting but is developing AI algorithms that can analyze video posts for content that violates it standards. The tremendous volume of posts it receives each day presents a challenge. In 2016, Facebook users worldwide watched 100 million hours of video *daily*. Another challenge is creating an algorithm that can accurately identify content that should be taken down without falsely flagging images and video that comply with Facebook's rules.

YouTube's guidelines prohibit video intended to "recruit for terrorist organizations, incite violence, celebrate terrorist attacks, or otherwise promote acts of terrorism", but it does allow users to post videos "intended to document events connected to terrorist acts or news reporting on terrorist activities" as long as those clips include "sufficient context and intent". Such a thin line creates a predicament for any software designed to automatically find prohibited footage, which might explain why YouTube also continues to rely on its users to flag inappropriate content.

Three recent lawsuits filed against the major social media companies are 'helping' social media firms see the light. The lawsuits cover the June 2016 Pulse Nightclub attack and the November 2015 Paris and December 2015 San Bernadino mass shootings. The suits allege that Facebook, Google, and Twitter "knowingly and recklessly" provided the IS with the ability to use their platforms as "a tool for spreading extremist propaganda, raising funds and attracting new recruits". The suits cite specific instances of attackers using social media before and even during the attacks, and maintains that social media firms have not been strenuous enough in monitoring and removing content posted by terrorist groups. In response, Facebook said its Community Standards make clear that there is no place on Facebook for groups that engage in terrorist activity or for content that expresses support for such activity, and that it takes swift action to remove such content when it is reported. That is certainly an argument in favor of ramping up their game.

The technology being developed will not prevent the IS or its supporters from live-streaming video of an attack or propaganda speech on services such as Facebook Live or Twitter's Periscope. Such video would have no matching signature in a database, and any attempt to flag a new video would require an algorithm that defines "terrorism" so it knows what to look for. Algorithms that might automatically identify faces of well-known IS members in video work reasonably well but are not nearly accurate or fast enough to keep up with massive amounts of video streamed online. The good news is that, although they are late to the party, the social media companies have gotten the message that they must do more to combat the problem.[209]

Transcending the IS Media Halo

Based on a study done by Quilliam Foundation in 2015[210], the volume of output produced by the IS far exceeds most estimates. The study estimated that the IS disseminated an average of 38 unique propaganda events per day from all corners of the IS caliphate, in an exceptionally sophisticated information operation campaign of extremely high quality. While there is broad consistency in the IS narrative, it changes on a daily basis, depending on the requirements of on-the-ground priorities. Its narrative is constantly shifting, based on the previously referenced six distinct topics of mercy, belonging, brutality, victimhood, war, and utopia.

The quantity, quality, and variation of IS propaganda in just one month far outweighs the quantity, quality, and variation of all attempts (state or non-state) to challenge the group. The global desire to find a panacea counter-narrative to undermine the IS brand is misplaced, for there is no such thing. *To be effective, the information war against the IS must* borrow from the group's own media strategy and prioritize quantity, quality, variation, adaptability, and differentiation, but based upon an alternative rather than a counter narrative. Those involved in the information operations campaign must have a robust comprehension of what they are actually countering in order to be effective. The ideals portrayed by this vast operation can only be challenged by a scaled up, progressive and energetic set of counter-propaganda campaigns from state and non-state actors that understand the need for narrative and audience variation.[211]

If the West really wants to destroy the IS's deceptive "media halo" it should foster its own forms of crowdsourced messages—for example, broadcasting the stories of refugees, told in their own words, that would strongly undermine the narrative that is so crucial to the IS's identity. The group depicts itself as a veritable Eden, a place where placid lakes literally teem with fish and well-fed children are always smiling. *What if the West gave refugees the digital tools and Internet access necessary to produce content that not only rebuts those depictions but also conveys the daily horrors of living in a society where violence and repression is the only constant? To do so, their security and that of their families must be guaranteed. As the law stands now, they are more likely to end up in prison than on YouTube.* Of course, determining which returnees are truly no longer threats will be challenging, but deradicalization programs in Europe have yielded data that can help build appropriate psychological assessment tools.[212] Surely, if refugees with direct experience of living under the IS, former IS prisoners, or former IS fighters are willing to tell their stories, the West should be willing to find a way to accommodate them. Their words will be far stronger than anything Western governments can dream up.

Making Social Media Safer

The task of making social media safer from virtual terrorists is a very tall order indeed, because in the Internet they have the safe space they need to breed. It has taken more than a decade for the social media goliaths to become as attuned to the plethora of security risks that exist for them and their users. Now that many of them are starting to devote the resources necessary to really tackle the problem, one of the principle ingredients needed to make a difference is the passage of time. That said, there is clearly a growing need for enhancements to social network platforms so that users can more meaningfully manage their profiles and connecting tools. There is an acute need for convergence and integration of social networks into the larger virtual world, for data integration from different networks to have some security protocol commonalities, and for specific standards to be developed and implemented across social media.

Many social networks still need standard programming interfaces to enable users to import and export their profiling information using standardized tools. Facebook and Google have applied new technologies that allow user data portability among social websites, representing a new source of competition among social networking services. More of that needs to occur. Ultimately, the sector should graduate to a single sign-in functionality so that identifications can be used across social media websites, in conjunction with greatly enhanced security protocols to prevent hacks, fraud, and abuse. Social media platforms should build awareness regarding security precautions and information disclosure, so that users are encouraged to take more care and become more conscious about revealing their personal information in their profiles. Ideally, the platforms would embark on broadly-based educational campaigns and governments would do the same.

But before any of this is done, *it is incumbent upon social media users to do their part to take some basic precautions to protect themselves and take the question of security more seriously. They are the first and last firewall, for it is they who decide what sites to go to and which links to click on.* As noted above, most social media users remain unconcerned about the importance of avoiding unnecessary personal information disclosure. Many users who are aware of the many threats that lurk on the Internet choose inappropriate privacy settings and manage privacy preference improperly. There is also, in general, too few appropriate authentication mechanisms to address the variety of security and privacy issues that exist.

In 2017, Google outlined four steps it is taking to fight the spread of extremist material on YouTube:

1. Devoting more engineering resources to develop additional AI software that can be trained to identify and remove extremist content.

2. Expanding the number of independent experts in YouTube's Trusted Flagger program. Google will add 50 expert non-government organizations to the 63 organizations that are already part of the program and support them with additional grants (the Trusted Flagger reports are accurate 90+ percent of the time).

3. Taking a tougher stance against videos that do not clearly violate YouTube's rules. For example, a video that has inflammatory religious or supremacist content will not be monetized, recommended, or even eligible for users to make comments on. The aim is to provide these videos with less engagement so they are harder to find.

4. YouTube is working with Jigsaw—a company behind "The Redirect Method"—which uses ad targeting to send potential IS recruits to anti-terrorist videos in an effort to change their mind about joining extremist organizations. In system trials, potential recruits clicked through on the ads at an unusually high rate and watched more than half a million minutes of video content that debunked terrorist recruiting messages.

The measures build upon Google's previous efforts to fight extremist content on its platform.[213] For social media users, the following commonsense precautions should be taken to safeguard personal information and security:

- Download the latest antivirus software, and _update it daily_.

- Always have strong passwords that have _at least one capital letter and one special character_ (the more the better).

- Change your passwords regularly (preferably monthly).

- Limit the amount of personal information to that which is required.

- Do not trust other online users.

- Do not answer questions from unknown users or companies.

- Read privacy policies.

- Become more aware of e-mails and links from unknown users.[214]

- *Take advantage of two-factor authentication whenever possible* (which confirms a user's identity by utilizing a combination of two different components, typically the account password and a confirmation code), which is sent to the user via text message or e-mail.

If more people would take these simple precautions, it would go a long way toward making it more difficult for virtual terrorists to do what they do best. Unfortunately, most people tend not to focus on such issues until they become victims.

A World Without Social Norms

One of the things that makes the virtual world in general, and social media in particular, so compelling for so many groups of people is that, whatever 'rules' or social norms may exist in the real world, they do not exist in the virtual world. That makes it an ideal platform for spreading propaganda and 'alternative' world views. Such is the appeal of online games, where anyone can be unabashed about his or her intentions, objectives, and methods of manipulation. One game may promise world annihilation while another may enable the player to imagine bringing peace to the Middle East. Such multiplayer online role-playing games have great ability to influence conventional ways of players' thinking about the world.

In the online gaming world, users embody their achievements as a player that is part of a larger community that recognizes and rewards an individual's power and competence. These games contain either overt or subtle (hidden) ideological objectives that can be manipulated by their creators, and in the virtual world it is difficult to tell who is actually behind anything. Relationships develop between real people and the avatars they interact with, even though they will likely never meet. This is a great advantage for game creators, and a great disadvantage for players who may be gullible or impressionable.

An important element of any social network is its sense of shared values, which can lead to 'tribal' formation in areas as diverse as religion, fetishes, and radicalism. In the virtual world, groups with disparate 'interests' can live together without ever knowing who each other is. Connectivity is the linchpin that allows digital tribes to form, remain in place, and grow. That can be a wonderful thing vis-à-vis moral values and charity work, but not such a great thing in terms of illegality and radicalization. Hiding behind screen names and avatars, social network and online game players become willing to engage in things they may not otherwise be inclined to do, and discuss things they may not otherwise be inclined to discuss.[215]

Virtual terrorists seize upon the anonymity in this borderless world, preying upon people's worst fears and greatest aspirations in what they know is a safe space. In part, it is the ability to manipulate peoples' emotions and exact a psychological toll in the process which motivates virtual terrorists. In the next chapter we explore how this is done and some of its implications.

8. <u>Psychological Impact</u>

Cybercriminals do not only seek to take advantage of negative human tendencies, they also seek to manipulate individuals' desire to help others. These campaigns are often targeted at customer service departments, with the attackers betting that an employee's desire to lend a hand and make others happy will encourage him or her to divulge or accept more information than they should. As an example, after a woman disclosed on social media that she was a Muslim, a hacker accessed her Amazon account, and, with just her name, e-mail address, and an incorrect mailing address, was able to verify the account via online chat with customer support. Through a series of calculated questions, the scammer obtained his target's correct personal information, gained access to her credit card data, and made a purchase via her Amazon account. The customer support representative was only doing his job, but the hacker knew just how to use his helpfulness against Amazon and the victim.[216]

How many times have political pundits, the media, or the government been just plain wrong about if or when a terrorist attack will occur, who is behind an attack, or what terrorists' motives are? The short answer is too often, pointing not only to how limited accurate information can be, but also how often we completely misinterpret the information that is at our disposal. While accurate information can indeed be limited with respect to Virtual Terrorism, we are also guilty, collectively, of making some false assumptions about virtual terrorists, based on our own experience and biases.

Our leaders typically label terrorists and/or their acts more broadly as 'cowardly', but this label is actually not an appropriate term to describe them, for "cowards lack courage, and are fearful or timid".[217] Does that sound like an accurate description of what a terrorist is to you? The term is used so frequently because it gives those of us who are not terrorists a sense of moral superiority, and therefore makes us feel at least a little better when acts of terrorism occur. But using that term also serves to illustrate just how powerless we are to do much about random acts of terrorism—particularly those that remain undetectable—no matter how many billions of dollars or countless resources we throw at the problem.

A core feature of terrorism, which gives it such potency (apart from the act itself), is the exploitation of peoples' emotions in the process—the fear of becoming a victim, fear of losing a loved one or friend, the uncertainty about what the future holds, and a sense of loss of control. *The perception of the threat posed by terrorism versus the actual danger it represents is disproportionate, but when fear and emotions are involved, that does not matter. This 'fear factor', combined with emotional manipulation, give terrorism a powerful secondary punch often far greater than the act of terrorism itself.*

It also changes the way we think. If it were not for terrorism, most of us would not think quite so hard or as much about which airline we should fly outside our home country, or whether there is a security protocol at an office building or movie theater (and whether there should be). Many of us would also not lose as much sleep or need to have conversations with our children explaining why the latest terrorist attack they just saw on television has happened, and why they should not worry because it is not going to happen to them. It is a shame we cannot honestly tell them they are unlikely to be a victim of Virtual Terrorism at some point in the course of their lives because we know they probably will become one.

How Threats of Terrorism Influence Individuals

Much of the research that has been conducted about the psychological impact of conventional terrorist attacks has focused on the immediate increase in psychiatric symptoms and disorders and the relatively quick 'normalization' of psychopathology in the weeks, months, and years following an attack. Such conclusions may mask the underlying sense of fear and worry that many people have about terrorism threats, or future terrorist attacks, however. Lingering fear varies across time and context, affecting people in a variety of ways, and although these symptoms do not necessarily reach the level of a psychiatric disorder and require treatment, they may can significantly influence daily activities such as decisions about employment, who to socialize with, whether to use public transportation such as buses and trains, and whether to venture into public and crowded places. That is an unfortunate reality for many of us.

Yet, most people arguably respond to threats of future terrorism in a rational and constructive manner, particularly given how long we have all been living with it, how frequently we hear about it, and how often we see it on television. Compelling research has shown that whether an individual's response is primarily fear versus anger may have a significant impact on their behavior. In the context of anger, people tend to exhibit greater subsequent levels of optimism and preference for confrontation, whereas those who respond with fear tend to exhibit greater longer-term pessimism and a preference for using conciliatory measures to de-escalate conflict. Other research has highlighted the paradox of how terrorism fears can negatively affect some people and societies while at the same time serving as the central force in strengthening resilience and fostering post-traumatic growth.

A Government's Best Friend or Worst Nightmare

The idea that exposure to terrorism threats, and the psychological reactions that ensue, affects political engagement, trust in government policy making, and governments' ability to generate public support for its policies, is not new. The evidence indicates that people place larger degrees of trust in their government's ability to keep them safe from future acts of terrorism following large-scale terrorist attacks. For example, American citizens' trust in the USG increased markedly following the 9/11 attacks, but that degree of trust has, of course, fluctuated over time.

Some scholars have argued that, when high levels of emotionality are activated through threat alerts (i.e. being in a state of 'orange alert' literally for years, as the US was following 9/11), it impacts how people engage their respective political systems. *Fear, in comparison to anger, has been associated with a greater degree of perceived risk, as well as preferences for more precautionary, conciliatory measures to reduce external threats. Anger may actually lead people to*

203

experience a greater locus of control over their environment, whereas fear is associated with less perceived control.

The emotional dynamics are complex, as they are influenced by other factors, such as political ideology. In the US, for example, research suggests that individuals identifying themselves as Democrats may, when primed with high levels of emotion in the context of terrorism, be more skeptical towards policies aimed at improving a sense of security, while Republicans are perceived as the ones making such policies. Cultural differences in support of governmental policies also emerge as a function of emotional reactions. Societies where there are high levels of baseline trust in the government may respond differently to terror threats than societies where there is a lower level of trust.

The 2011 Norwegian terror attacks by Anders Behring Breivik, fueled by his far-right militant ideology and Islamophobia, killed 77 people in a premeditated terror attack. Researchers from Norway found that increased support for the government in the aftermath of this attack did not arise as a result of public fear; rather, high levels of existing institutional trust appear to have buffered the government against the negative effects of fear and the elevated terror threat level that followed the attack. In "high-trust" societies, this trust, rather than fear, may have very different impacts than what is common in "low-trust" societies. An enhanced sense of national 'togetherness' and strengthened interpersonal and institutional trust have a predictable outcome. But ongoing threats and fear can modify a well-established culture over time. In countries where there is protracted conflict—such as in Syria—fear is arguably a powerful motivating force for individuals to pursue personal safety and security in spite of what the government and combatants may or may not be doing and regardless of which side of the conflict they may support.

Using fear and the emotions of the public to achieve political objectives is hardly a new strategy. During the Cold War era, US Senator Joseph McCarthy used the threat of communism to inject fear into the political process, manipulating public and political views regarding who could be trusted and who were secretly communist spies. President George W. Bush's now infamous declaration of the War on Terrorism helped remind the public of the persistent threat of terrorism, which was central to the success of his re-election campaign. Since then, the sense of insecurity related to the potential threats we face have contributed to the development of a massive and integrated security infrastructure to keep us safe from these admittedly ambiguous threats. Some have even argued that we have become a "securitized" culture, with other national priorities taking a back seat to complex and ever expanding national security priorities and initiatives.

What is important to understand, however, is the array of factors that have contributed to this evolution. Increasing our awareness and understanding of the significant impact emotional processes have on individuals and societies in decision-making can be crucially important in determining how terrorism threats and warnings are constructed and disseminated. Fostering a sense of control and agency within these messages by presenting basic steps for preparedness and focus can reduce unwarranted fear.[218] There is plenty of fear that is entirely warranted, however.

Emotional Manipulation

Conventional terrorists can maintain a background of fear that lingers well beyond a physical act of terror. Psychology professionals point to an actual element of psycho-physiological *arousal* that contributes to the enduring impact of terrorism because of terrorists' ability to create a sense of dread or fearfulness. However, this sense of long-term fear and dread may be more limited in scope with conventional terrorism because most people understand that, statistically speaking, they are themselves unlikely to personally become a victim of conventional forms of terrorism.[219] *Fear and dread are magnified many times with Virtual Terrorism, however, because the more someone knows about it, the more they come to realize that they either have already become a victim or probably will be at some point in the future.*

Until about the turn of the century citizens' sense of security was a derivative of safe streets and borders, but in today's world a person can live in a safe nation and still feel high anxiety for his or her safety online. This can impact one's psyche weeks or months after a cyberattack has taken place.

Some studies have found that two weeks after learning about identity theft, victims experienced irritability, anger, fear, anxiety and frustration, sleep deprivation, nervousness, loss of appetite, weight changes, and headaches. Twenty-six weeks later, emotional responses turned to severe distress and desperation, mistrust and paranoia, nervousness, gastrointestinal problems, and headaches. Qualitative research has also suggested that fear of cyber identity theft stokes fear of financial losses, damage to reputation, and loss of online privacy. These results are not really different from the psychological trauma an ordinary burglary or non-violent home invasion may cause.

As one of our most powerful motivators, fear is arguably the most commonly manipulated emotion. Whether in the form of a fake e-mail saying that your online bank account has been compromised and requires a password change, an urgent bank security notice, or a call to action allegedly sent by a known 'friend', these scams leverage a specific threat directed at a given target, designed to strongly encourage him or her to act quickly in order to avoid or rectify a dangerous or painful situation. Such scams presume the target will be obedient, given that the 'order' its creators are sending is supposed to be from an authoritative source.

We are, of course, taught from a young age to obey authority, and in spite of the realities of the world we live in, many people do just that, knowing that there is some risk involved in doing so. It is not only individuals who fall for such schemes, however. Toy maker giant Mattel paid almost $3,000,000 to a cybercriminal who disguised himself as the company's CEO in an e-mail to a finance executive, with instructions to approve a payment to a vendor in China. Fortunately, Chinese authorities were able to help the company recover the funds.

Among the other human emotions cyberscammers appeal to is, of course, greed, which is why too many people continue to fall for those silly "419 Nigerian scams", which earned its name from cybercriminals claiming to be a Nigerian official or agency promising a handsome reward in return for sending them a small sum of money. The price of entry is the bank account information required to receive the reward. In fairness, it is not just Nigerians who practice such scams—they merely perfected it. People all over the world have fallen for this, because they are greedy. They do not stop to think that if something sounds too good to true—especially on the Internet—it almost certainly is.

Cybercriminals not only seek to take advantage of negative human tendencies, they also seek to manipulate individuals' desire to help others. These campaigns are often targeted at customer service departments, with the attackers betting that an employee's desire to lend a hand and make others happy will encourage them to divulge or accept more information than they should. As an example, after a woman disclosed on social media that she was a Muslim, a hacker accessed her Amazon account, and with just her name, e-mail address and an incorrect mailing address was able to verify the account via online chat with customer support. Through a series of calculated questions, the scammer obtained his target's correct personal information, gained access to her credit card data, and made a purchase via her Amazon account. The customer support representative was only doing his job, but the hacker knew just how to use his helpfulness against Amazon and the victim.[220]

Fueling Hate

Terrorist groups sometimes call on their adherents to do things that they believe would have an impact on enemy states in unanticipated ways. A 2016 report from AQ called for its operatives to instigate terrorist attacks by fueling hatred and racial tension among groups in the US, listing populations such as "oppressed blacks", immigrants, foreigners, communists, and white supremacists. The report said terrorists can manipulate these groups by inciting feelings of hatred in them and in their opponents, stating that they would do the rest. The document was an updated version of an AQ terrorist guide and was spread on the Internet by previously unidentified AQ affiliated social media accounts. It detailed tactics and strategies for terrorists to take advantage of crisis scenarios and natural disasters as targets of opportunity for increased effectiveness of attacks.

One section taught adherents how to make bombs from common items found in stores. Aside from the document's focus on conventional terrorist attacks, it had several sections dedicated to highly unconventional tactics focused on spreading disinformation and creating disruption. One section called for terrorists to intentionally cause traffic jams, noting that traffic congestion costs the US $160 billion per year. Another section called on terrorists to tarnish the reputation of large companies by creating front advocacy or scientific organizations that could publish fake reports to prove that the products these companies created were harmful to people's health or the environment. Other sections were even more bizarre, such as the call to cause horror by placing a huge snake in a person's food or water, planting harmful species of trees, or intentionally planting trees over sewage lines so their roots would break the pipes.[221]

Whether the intent was to think of new ways to stay relevant as a terrorist organization in an otherwise competitive landscape (with the IS having established itself as the pre-eminent terrorist group in the world by that time) or simply as a means of keeping its enemies guessing what could possibly be coming next, the fact that AQ would seek to incite hatred in the US is evidence of an overt psychological component to its war against the West. No doubt it had limited impact while it lasted, but the US was more divided along race, class, and gender lines in 2017 than it had been in half a century, and AQ sought to foment a psychological war to supplement its physical and cyber wars against the US.

Psychological Well-being and Confidence

Using experimental video clip manipulations, three studies were conducted between 2013 and 2016 wherein 552 subjects were exposed to simulated lethal and non-lethal episodes of cyberterrorism. The studies' findings proved that exposure to cyberterrorism is not benign and shares many traits with that of conventional terrorism, such as stress, anxiety, insecurity, a heightened perception of risk, a reevaluation of confidence in public institutions, and support for forceful government policies. In the cyber realm, this translates into support for such policies as Internet surveillance, government regulation of the Internet, and a forceful military response to cyberterrorism (including conventional and kinetic retaliation).

The results show that cyberterrorism, even though generally non-lethal, impacts civilian populations in several ways, by aggravating anxiety and personal insecurity, exacerbating perceptions of threat and personal insecurity, and (particularly for those with high levels of threat perception) a willingness to support strong government policies. These policies split along two lines and included foreign policy (cyber and/or military responses to cyberattacks) and domestic policy (a tolerance of government surveillance and control of the Internet). As threat perception increases, individuals tend to take increasingly stringent political views. *As is the case with conventional terrorism, cyberterrorism hardens political attitudes as individuals become willing to exchange civil liberties and privacy for security, supporting government surveillance, greater regulation of the Internet, and forceful military reactions in response to cyberattacks.*

The results indicate that the perception of a threat (rather than an actual attack) is sufficient to cause emotional distress in individuals, so governments need to recognize that they cannot reduce fears of cyberterrorism and its pervasive effects solely by eliminating cyberattacks (that will in all likelihood only grow more frequent and/or severe with time). Rather, policymakers must think about ways to enhance resilience akin to the way they have sought to do so in the context of conventional forms of terrorism and other forms of disaster. To the extent that individuals feel they can communicate their concerns to their government, and the authorities are perceived to be able to do something about it (i.e. citizens have a sense of political efficacy), then threat perceptions may be reduced.

Compliance with cybersecurity measures depends upon how accurately the public assesses the risk of cyberattacks, and how successfully governments and private agencies communicate cyber risks and the precautions individuals must take to protect themselves.[222] Therein lies the challenge— Virtual Terrorism will only grow in scope, frequency, and severity with time. Can authorities convince the general public that they are ahead of the curve and have the ability to stay that way for the long-term? With each passing week and month, this becomes more difficult because fewer people believe that governments actually have the power to forever stay ahead of virtual terrorists.

Assessing the Psychological Effects in the Lab

One of the ways Virtual Terrorism transcends physical terrorism is by targeting peoples' minds, from the decision-making apparatus of CEOs and politicians to an adversary's global image to the average man or woman on the street. North Korea's hacking of Sony was probably not intended to force the company into bankruptcy but rather to embarrass it, which it certainly did. When 10 members of the US navy were captured by Iran in 2016 and videotaped with all of them forced to kneel and one of them crying, that was an effort to humiliate the US. When politicians have their e-mails leaked, it is an effort to undermine them,[223] and when individuals hesitate to make decisions (or make different decisions) as a result of cyberterrorism-inspired fear, that is a victory for virtual terrorists.

To evaluate the psychological effects of cyberterrorism, Israeli researchers conducted a series of laboratory experiments to simulate cyberattacks on individuals.[224] The experimental attacks simulated those that hacktivist and non-state actors perpetrate, and whose goal is to disrupt the lives of individuals and establish a platform for their grievances. Both kinetic and cyberattacks use short lived, spectacular attacks to strengthen the morale of their compatriots while placing their political cause firmly on the world's front pages and discomfiting their enemies by underscoring their weaknesses.

The manipulations chosen for the study were designed to simulate the way ordinary citizens may experience a cyberattack as individuals, rather than mass casualty attacks, as the most efficient means of generating personal discomfort or anxiety. The manipulation had the sole purpose of generating the recognition among respondents that their private online identity was no longer private. By using video chats, a threatening logo, and a text message via their phones, the researchers sent the participant a clear message that they were not alone. To simulate intrusiveness and breach of privacy they conducted the experiment through a lab computer and the participants' private cell phones. The text message to the participants' cell phones cemented the feeling among them that *they* were the target of the cyberattack—not the lab computer. Before and during the manipulation, subjects provided a saliva sample to measure cortisol, a hormone associated with stress.

To test the impact of simulated cyberattacks, they designed fully controlled, randomized experiments and began with a battery of questions asking participants to describe their computer savviness and usage, probe political attitudes, and describe their overall psychological well-being. After providing the saliva sample, respondents continued the survey and saw a pop-up screen with a message from Anonymous, which only the research assistant could unlock. If questioned about whether it was part of the experiment, the assistant was instructed to reassure the subjects that she knew nothing and that the subjects should ignore it and continue the study.

After a few additional questions, a Skype-like split video screen popped up where subjects could see themselves live, and see and hear a suspicious looking person typing. After 5 survey questions, they received an Anonymous phone text message which stated that their personal data had been hacked. If a respondent became uncomfortable, the assistant again suggested that the participant continue. Control group respondents completed the very same questions, but without the cyberthreat component.

At the completion of the survey, all respondents provided a second saliva sample, again reported their overall psychological well-being, and completed a battery of questions on cyberthreats and policies. There was an average decrease of about 7 percent in the cortisol level of the control group, while the treatment group experienced an average rise of a 16 percent in cortisol, a clear indication that the cyberattack caused stress and anxiety. These findings were further supported by data that show that individuals subjected to cyberterrorism are agitated and significantly more likely to fear imminent cyberattacks. When subjects were asked to what extent cyberattacks on Israel undermined their sense of personal security, those who had experienced simulated cyberterrorism reported a significantly greater sense of personal insecurity. The data confirms a positive relationship between non-violent cyberterror (i.e. simulated attacks on computers and cell phones), stress, dread, and personal insecurity.

These findings suggest that future cyber research should take into account not only the number of casualties and physical damage caused by cyberterrorism attacks but also the way in which individuals are likely to be psychologically impaired following such an attack. Although it is also an intuitive conclusion, the research confirms empirically that cyberattacks that steal identities, data, or money, disclose confidential information, or threaten individuals with random, personal harm cause significant fear, stress, and anxiety that can impinge upon the rational decision-making of individuals.

Beyond stress response, there is also evidence that the psychological and physiological reactions following exposure to threatening events such as political violence affect the immune system negatively and cause inflammation in the body in a way that can lead to significant radicalization of political attitudes and behavior. The effects of such attacks are presumed to be much greater when they take place outside a lab setting and when a person is the actual owner of the computer or phone that is attacked.

Psychological distress also shapes attitudes and political decision-making. Exposure to kinetic terrorism leads to psychological insecurity that induces militant attitudes and violent and non-conciliatory political responses. Perceived threats, fear, and anxiety are the single best predictor of militarism. Traumatic events can undermine a person's basic assumptions about the world, triggering enhanced perceptions of the world as a threatening place, and a correspondingly strong desire to reduce the perceived threat through an enhanced propensity toward militancy. Chronic exposure to war and terrorism not only harm personal well-being but also contribute to an ongoing cycle of violence, as affected citizens harden their political viewpoints in an attempt to cope with stress.[225]

The Impact of Cyberbullying

Among the most vulnerable of any population are its youngest members. What forms the foundation of many of their lives in the Era of Virtual Terrorism are smartphones and social media, which are a most unfortunate gateway into cyberbullying, which has the ability to far surpass more conventional means of bullying in terms of brutality and impact. The recent focus on cyberbullying has in part been driven by the connection between it and adolescent suicides, which is a troubling phenomenon. Cyberbullying subjects its targets to a barrage of degrading, threatening, and/or sexually explicit messages and images using web sites, instant messaging, blogs, chat rooms, cell phones, e-mail, and personal online profiles that is very difficult to supervise or detect. Targets of cyberbullying often experience intense anger, a sense of powerlessness, sadness, fear, loss of confidence, disassociation, a general sense of uneasiness, trauma, and aggressiveness.

The effects of cyberbullying have been predominantly explored by researchers in terms of adolescent mental health, examining the relationship between involvement with cyberbullying and adolescents' tendency to internalize issues (such as by the development of negative affective disorders, loneliness, anxiety, depression, suicidal ideation, and somatic symptoms). Research has proven a significant relationship between one's involvement in cyberbullying and affective disorders, with a significant relationship between cybervictimization and depression among adolescents and college students. In one study, 93 percent of cyber victims reported negative effects, with the majority reporting feelings of sadness, hopelessness, and powerlessness.

Many cyber victims fear for their safety, in large part because they do not know who their attackers are. According to one study, half of the victims did not know the identity of their perpetrators, which means they could even be a 'friend', co-worker, or family member. Other studies have found that different forms of cyberbullying may elicit different emotional reactions—being bullied online may evoke a different emotional reaction than being bullied via a cell phone, and that photos and video images were the most harmful to adolescents. Cybervictimization can also disrupt adolescents' relationships, with parents and peers in particular.

There have been relatively few studies examining the effect of cyberbullying on adolescents' physical health but, of those, a significant relationship was found between cyberbullying and psychosomatic difficulties. One such study of American adolescents found that those youths who were both victims and perpetrators of cyberbullying experienced more severe forms of physical health concerns (for example, difficulty sleeping, headache, poor appetite, and skin problems). Adolescents' grade level moderated these negative effects, with high school students who were both perpetrators and victims of cyberbullying reporting the highest levels of anxiety, depression, and the most number of physical health problems.[226]

Not a Victimless Act

The fear, anxiety, and mental suffering that cyberterrorism can bring belies the notion that it is a victimless act. It is clear that psychological suffering often follows in the wake of cyberterrorism. Individuals tend to experience the distress and anxiety that come with the disruption of daily services when they cannot ensure their privacy, access their bank accounts, fill prescriptions in a timely manner, travel as necessary, maintain communications, or run their computers with a degree of confidence. Such effects may be particularly severe among vulnerable groups, such as the poor and elderly, but ordinary citizens may be no less affected.

On January 21, 2014, South Koreans awoke to find that thieves had stolen the credit card numbers, names, and addresses of 40 percent of the entire population. The immediate result was widespread panic, system crashes, massive lawsuits, and a run on banks to cancel credit cards. The culprit was a Korean but the effect upon the citizenry was no different than if it had originated from an individual or group outside the country. Such attacks contribute to an amorphous fear that comes with assault by unknown, malevolent agents whose agenda is neither clear nor predictable. Cyberterrorism stokes anxieties about loss of control and unpredictability that might be as inescapable as those accompanying war and kinetic terrorism.

By rendering or threatening to render a population mindless with terror, cyberterrorists can deprive governments of something they need to govern—a population capable of making rational choices. However, there is no need that a population be "mindless with terror" in order to undermine its rational decision-making capability. If by terrorism the issue is terrorization, then *Virtual Terrorism is not as much about acts of terror as it is acts that violate the principle of noncombatant immunity*. Virtual Terrorism can undermine morale, public trust, and governability, which may be even more dangerous than conventional forms of terrorism. It is accomplished by attacking the foundations of everyday life.[227]

Fake News

Fake news has assumed an important role in playing with people's minds and has contributed greatly to the generation of angst, confusion, and fear among people who, until recently, did not have to wonder whether what they were hearing on the news was fantasy or reality. Fake news has so dominated the airwaves that people could be forgiven for questioning whether anything they hear on the news is fact or fiction. When we have difficulty determining what to believe, we begin to question basic aspects of our lives and societies, which is part of what those who create fake news are counting on.

In a 2016 study by Stanford University, researchers made an alarming discovery: across the US many students could not tell the difference between a reported news article, a persuasive opinion piece, and a corporate ad. This absence of media literacy makes young people, in particular, vulnerable to getting duped by fake news. To strengthen your ability to tell real news from fake news, consider the following criteria:

The source: Real news contains the byline of an actual journalist reporting for a trustworthy and established outlet, while fake news (including "sponsored content" and traditional corporate ads) generally does not.

<u>The claim</u>: Real news includes multiple sources (particularly when discussing a controversial claim) while fake news may include fake sources, false links, or "alternative facts" that can be disproven upon further research.

<u>Publication date</u>: Do not trust anonymous sources or stories that cite other news outlets and compare the story being told with various outlets. Fake "Breaking news" should raise an eyebrow, particularly if it happens to be about celebrities or gossip.

<u>Language</u>: When outlets use "we are receiving reports" or "we are seeking confirmation", it is probably well worth ignoring.[228]

<u>Emotions</u>: Fake news is designed to elicit strong emotions. If you read a news item that makes you angry, double-check the claims by comparing it to the news on any major media outlet and decide for yourself if the item is real news or fake news.[229]

Many governments produce fake news as part of their disinformation campaigns. Russia, in particular, has proven adept at both creating and refuting fake news. In part as a result of the many fake news allegations lodged against it, in 2017, the Russian government launched an official fake news tracker of unfavorable Western news reports towards Russia, discrediting them as inaccurate. The Russian Ministry of Foreign affairs launched a page on its official website featuring reporting from such publications as *The New York Times*, Bloomberg, NBC, and Britain's *Daily Telegraph*. While some of the reporting listed was based on unnamed sources, the Ministry did not make public the criteria it used to deem a report fake.[230]

To better understand how fake news can be effectively produced, there is no better place to turn than a government, and Russia again serves as a useful example. What follows is a description of how Russia produces fake news through a Create, Push, Share, Discuss, and Challenge campaign:

<u>Create</u>: Russia uses its state sponsored media outlets and associated conspiratorial websites to *create* propaganda

across political, social, financial, and calamitous message themes. This content, much of which is fake news or manipulated truths, provides information tailored for specific portions of an electorate it seeks to influence. Russia's own hacking and theft of secrets provides plenty of material for delivery via its state sponsored media outlets and covert personas. This information fuels not only its state sponsored outlets but arms the click-bait content development of profiteers and political parties who further amplify Russia's narratives amongst Western voters.

Push: Unlike some other means of fake news dissemination, Russia synchronizes the *push* of its propaganda across multiple outlets and personas. Using sock puppets and automated bots appearing to be stationed around the world, Russia simultaneously amplifies narratives so as to grab mainstream media attention. Other social media bots push false and misleading stories for profit or politics, but their patterns lack the synchronization and repeated delivery of pro-Russian content, and usually follow rather than lead in the dissemination of Russian conspiracies.

Share: Like-minded supporters, aggregators (gray accounts), and covert personas (black accounts) *share* coordinated pushes of Russian propaganda with key nodes on a one-to-one or one-to-many basis. This coordinated sharing seeks to further amplify and cement influential content and themes among a targeted set of voters. Their sharing often involves content appealing to either the left or right side of the political spectrum, as well as many anti-government or social issues. This widespread targeting often varies from profiteers and political propagandists that seek a high rate of consumption across a narrow set of themes, designed for an even narrower target audience.

Discuss: Russian overt supporters and cover elements *discuss* Russian themes over an enduring period, driving the preferred messaging deep into their target audience. This collaborative discussion amongst unwitting Americans makes seemingly improbable false information more believable. By comparison, bots and campaigns from profiteers, satirists, and political propagandists more frequently appear as "fire-and-forget" messaging operations.

217

Challenge: Heated social media debates during election season are commonplace, but Russian influence operations directly *challenge* their adversaries for unnaturally long periods, and at peculiar intervals. Russian covert personas heckle and push chosen themes against political opponents, media personalities, and subject matter experts to erode target audience support for Russian adversaries and their political positions. These challenges sometimes provide the Kremlin with the added benefit of diminishing Russian opponent social media use (other social media influence efforts may not go to such lengths).

Russian cyber-enabled influence operations demonstrate never before seen synchronization of "active measures". Content created by chosen outlets promotes the release of compromising material that will generate manipulated truths and falsehoods from conspiratorial websites promoting Russian foreign policy positions and Kremlin preferred candidates or attacking Russian opponents. Hackers, hecklers, and honeypots rapidly extend these information campaigns among foreign audiences. The full spectrum synchronization, scale, repetition, and speed of Russia's cyber-enabled information operations may even outperform the IS's successful terrorism propaganda campaigns or any other electoral campaign seen as of 2017.

This scope and scale of operation cannot be conducted in a vacuum, however. There are a host of real world actors that assist Russian influence operations in cyber space:

Useful Idiots: Meddling in the US and European elections has been accentuated by Russian cultivation and exploitation of Useful Idiots, a Soviet Era term referring to unwitting American politicians, political groups, and government representatives who further amplify Russian influence amongst Western populaces by utilizing Russian *kompromat* (compromising materials about a politician or other public figure used to create negative publicity, for blackmail purposes, or to ensure loyalty).

Fellow Travelers: Russia has at times curried the favor of Fellow Travelers, another Soviet term referring to individuals ideologically sympathetic to Russia's anti-EU, anti-NATO, and anti-immigration ideology. A cast of alternative right characters across Europe and the US openly push Russia's agenda, both on-the-ground and online, accelerating the spread of Russia's cyber-enabled influence operations.

Agent Provocateurs: Agent Provocateurs are Russian agents or manipulated political supporters who entice others to commit illegal, surreptitious acts to discredit opponent political groups and power falsehoods in cyberspace. The Kremlin has the ability to foment, amplify, and (through covert social media accounts) encourage Americans to undertake actions, either knowingly or unknowingly, as Agent Provocateurs.

Each of these actors assists Russia's online fake news efforts to divide Western electorates across political, social, and ethnic lines while maintaining a degree of plausible deniability with regard to Kremlin interventions. Russia's fake news campaign in Crimea and its alleged links to a fake news attempted coup in Montenegro in 2016[231] demonstrate the blend of real world and cyber influence it can use to win over target audiences. The promotion of gray media outlets and overt Russian supporters in Eastern Europe were essential to Russia's alleged influence in the US presidential election and its ability to sustain plausible deniability.[232]

Following news that a number of countries in the Middle East broke diplomatic relations with Qatar in 2017 over their allegations of its support for terrorism in the region, US investigators were reported to have discovered that Russian hackers breached Qatar's state news agency and planted a fake news report that contributed to the crisis. Intelligence gathered by US intelligence agencies indicated that Russian hackers were behind a cyber intrusion reported by the Qatari government. The alleged involvement of Russian hackers intensified concerns by US intelligence agencies that Russia continued to deploy some of the same cyberhacking measures on US allies that intelligence agencies believe it used to meddle in the 2016 US presidential elections.

The Russian objective appeared to be to cause rifts between the US and its allies. The Kremlin's spokesman dismissed what he called fake news, noting that CNN, which was the source of the report, used unnamed sources, and alleging that the report had no connection with reality. The Qatari government had said that a news report on its Qatar News Agency attributed false remarks to the nation's ruler that appeared friendly to Iran and Israel and questioned whether President Donald Trump would last in office.[233] So what is fact and what is fiction? You be the judge.

Psychological Warfare

As is the case with conventional terrorism, *part of what gives Virtual Terrorism such potency is its ability to elicit extreme anxiety and fear among its victims and those who worry they may become victims. The anxiety and fear may be completely disproportionate to the actual risk of becoming a victim; this is part of what makes Virtual Terrorism so frightening.* The net result of acts of Virtual Terrorism (such as uncertainty and a climate of fear) may be even more powerful than the acts themselves. It also, as noted earlier, fits into a psychological narrative of generating subliminal arousal to events associated with violence, since *the media in many societies have desensitized populations' predisposition to abhor violence and, instead, people crave it because of a constant barrage of violence on television, in movies, and online.*

"Terror" as a clinical term refers to a psychological state of dread or fearfulness associated with an abnormally high level of psycho-physiological arousal; central to virtual terrorists' objectives are the generation of short-term anxiety and fear. Again, one of the distinctions to be made between conventional forms of terrorism and Virtual Terrorism is that *conventional acts of terrorism achieve more of their objectives among a populace that is directly impacted by such acts, while Virtual Terrorism can achieve at least an equal degree of its objectives by creating fear of the unknown* and the recognition among the global population of a higher likelihood of becoming a victim at some point in time.[234]

Virtual terrorists have the advantage in that they can rely on a constant barrage of attacks at any time, directed at anyone. Stress blurs the boundary between reality and fantasy, but regardless of how significant a threat we may realize Virtual Terrorism to be, there is no need to blow it out of proportion. It is a fact of life, and everyone must live with it. It is important to stay grounded in reality by seeking out reliable sources of news and information, minimizing the ingestion of fake news, and avoiding a rush to judgment without being able to verify information. Overreacting in an emotional way impedes clear and logical thinking.

While it is difficult enough for adults to comprehend the world of Virtual Terrorism it is, of course, doubly difficult for children, who are bombarded by images and information they see through the media and on social media. Children may generalize the 'fantasy' world they see via online games and social media with the real world, making it difficult to distinguish between the two. Answering their questions and monitoring their reactions to what they see and experience can be important to helping them understand what is real and what is not. Parents can also help by avoiding stereotyping people by religion or country of origin, to avoid the development of prejudicial viewpoints, which can only exacerbate the problem.[235]

Whether you are a teenager, parent, in business, a government official, or are just trying to make sense of the world, *the Era of Virtual Terrorism has made it increasingly difficult to get from point A to point B without having to think or worry about whether someone is watching, whether you might be in danger, or whether someone half a world away is about to take control of your life. Such concerns are not simply a phenomenon of the Internet era, they are directly related to the advent of the Era of Virtual Terrorism, which is so new and relatively unexplored by mental health professionals that the cumulative toll it takes on us all is largely unknown.*

As has been demonstrated in this chapter, what research has been done is pointing in the direction of harmful and potentially devastating psychological impacts, which could endure well past an act of Virtual Terrorism. Having your personal information stolen, your identity manipulated, or being held for mental ransom by unknown parties is a chilling prospect for many people, every bit as anxiety producing or frightening as if they had been personally attacked. Virtual Terrorism has a chilling face, and it can invade and consume anyone's home, business, or mind at any time.

9. Infrastructure

In the US neither the utility industry, North American Energy Reliability Corporation, Federal Energy Regulatory Commission (FERC), nor the Nuclear Regulatory Commission (NRC) have required hardware mitigation to be implemented to prevent Stuxnet or Aurora-type attacks from occurring. The traditional mindset is that all industries rely on the grid, so the grid is presumed to have a high level of cyber protection. However, Aurora uses electric substations as the vehicle for launching attacks against any generator, AC motor, or transformer connected to a substation. Consequently, *it is the grid that can be the source of the attack.* Depending on the equipment, the damage from an Aurora attack can take months to repair or replace—assuming the equipment can be manufactured, transportation is available for delivery, and trained staff are available to install it.[236]

Infrastructure

Part of what makes infrastructure generally vulnerable to Virtual Terrorism is the fact that so much of it is dependent upon software and so many of its systems are interconnected. Much of the world's critical infrastructure utilizes supervisory control and data acquisition (SCADA) systems, which automatically monitor and adjust switching, manufacturing, and other process control activities based on digitized feedback data gathered by sensors. These tend to be specialized, older computer systems that control physical pieces of equipment that do everything from route trains along their tracks to distribute power throughout a country. SCADA systems have increasingly become connected to the Internet but were not designed with cybersecurity in mind.

This is a big problem that has been widely written about but becomes more of a threat each year. A study done in 2014 concluded that *almost 70 percent of critical infrastructure companies across multiple sectors in the US had suffered at least one security breach that led to the loss of confidential information or the disruption of operations during the preceding 12 months.* Virtual terrorists could do tremendous damage if they wanted to, ranging from taking control of water treatment facilities to shutting down power generation plants to causing havoc with air traffic control systems—and *all of these systems are extremely vulnerable to attack.*

Despite the fact that cyberattacks occur with greater frequency and intensity around the world, many either go unreported or are under-reported, leaving the public with a false sense of security about the threat they pose and the lives and property they impact. While governments, businesses, and individuals are all being targeted on an exponential basis, *infrastructure is becoming a target of choice among individual and state-sponsored cyberattackers who recognize the value of disrupting what were previously thought of as impenetrable security systems. This has served to demonstrate just how vulnerable cities, states, and countries have become.*

The Threat is Real

In December 2015, a presumed Russian cyberattacker successfully seized control of the Prykarpattyaoblenergo Control Center (PCC) in the Ivano-Frankivsk region of Western Ukraine, leaving 230,000 without power for up to 6 hours. This marked the first publicly recognized time that a cyberweapon was successfully used against a nation's power grid. The attackers were skilled strategists who carefully planned their assault over many months, first doing reconnaissance to study the networks and siphon operator credentials, then launching a synchronized assault in a well-choreographed dance. The control systems in Ukraine were surprisingly more secure than some in the US, since they were well-segmented from the control center business networks with robust firewalls,[237] emphasizing just how vulnerable power systems are globally.

The PCC operated a SCADA system, which allows for remote controlling and monitoring of industrial processes. The attackers overwrote firmware on critical devices at 16 substations, leaving them unresponsive to any remote commands from operators,[238] effectively leaving plant operators blind. Given the degree of sophistication of the intrusion, the attackers could have rendered the system permanently inoperable; that they did not led some in Ukraine to speculate that the attack was a message from Russia not to pursue pending power plant nationalization legislation, since some of those plants were owned by a powerful Russian oligarch with close ties to Vladimir Putin.

The Ukraine example was hardly the first cyberattack on a SCADA system. Perhaps the best known previous example occurred in 2003, though at the time it was publicly attributed to a downed power line rather than a cyberattack. The northeastern US blackout that year caused 11 deaths and an estimated $6 billion in economic damages, having disrupted power over a wide area for at least two days. Never before (or since, for that matter) had a 'downed power line' apparently resulted in such a devastating impact (some cyber professionals maintain that it was a cyberattack, which makes a lot more sense). Subsequent to that attack, SCADA attacks occurred in the UK, Italy, and Malta, among others.[239] Cyberattacks against SCADA systems doubled in 2014 to more than 160,000.

In recent years, numerous forms of malware targeting SCADA systems have been identified, including Stuxnet, Havex, and BlackEnergy3.[240] What these three forms of malware have in common is their ability to sneak through Industrial Control Systems (ICS) undetected by exploiting the weakest link in the cyber defense network (people) and posing as a legitimate e-mail or by finding a back door in the SCADA system[241]. The power sector has already demonstrated itself to be particularly vulnerable and must dedicate substantially more resources to closing back doors and training employees to avoid clicking on malicious files.

The US energy grid connects more than 5,800 power plants with more than 450,000 miles of transmission lines—the ultimate soft target. Yet some 70 percent of the grid's key components are more than 25 years old, and most of them use older SCADA technologies that are readily hackable. An investigation by the US House Energy and Commerce Committee revealed that more than a dozen US utility companies reported daily, constant, or frequent attempted cyberattacks, ranging from phishing to malware infection to unfriendly probes. One utility reported that it had been the target of more than 10,000 attempted cyberattacks each *month*. The US has more than 57,000 ICS connected to the Internet. In 2015, the DHS responded to 295 hacking incidents related to industrial controls, up from 245 in 2014.

Iranian hackers infiltrated a small New York state dam in 2013. Although they did not take control of the dam's ICS, they did probe the dam's defenses. The classified breach occurred amid a wave of Iranian hacks on US banks three years after Israel and the US released the Stuxnet virus on Iran's nuclear weapons infrastructure. According to the NSA, China and up to two other countries would be able to shut down portions of critical US infrastructure with a cyberattack (although left unsaid, the other countries would undoubtedly be Russia and Iran). The IS has also begun to explore cyberattacks on critical infrastructure.[242]

Hackers are having a field day. At the CCC Conference, an annual gathering of hackers held in Germany, analysts have demonstrated how to get full control of industrial infrastructure in the chemical, oil, gas, and energy industries. Hackers then shared this information with each other and created fully searchable public databases of known exploits that can be used to commandeer critical infrastructure. One well-known hacker database, Shodan, provides helpful tips on how to exploit everything from power plants to wind turbines and is searchable by country, company, or device. Since it is hosted on multiple servers across the world, Shodan cannot be easily shut down. Moreover, in many countries it is not illegal to publish such vulnerabilities (even though it clearly should be).

Examples of other instances when SCADA systems have been breached abound, some of which did not involve sinister dark forces or governments, as far back as the 1990s. Another earlier example occurred in Maroochy Shire, in Queensland, Australia, in 2001, when a hacker gained control of a sewage treatment plant's ICS and caused millions of liters of raw sewage to spill out into local parks, rivers, and the grounds of the Hyatt Regency hotel.

Cybercriminals have also gotten in on the act, as a means of extorting money from utilities and governments. A number of incidents were reported in Brazil between 2005 and 2007, when numerous cyberattacks were carried out in Rio de Janeiro and in the state of Espirito Santo, when nearly 3 million people were left in the dark because the local electricity provider had failed to meet the extortion demands of the hackers. The city of Vitoria, home of one of the world's largest iron ore producers, had numerous plants forced offline, costing the company almost $7 million.[243]

Given the relative ease with which hackers can find a single system vulnerability, and the impossibility of plugging every conceivable security hole, cybersecurity professionals are in essence playing an endless game of cat and mouse, whereby a would-be attacker attempts to enter a system while security professionals attempt to defend a computer system from attack by applying continuous patches. The adversary then quickly moves to exploit the latest discovered vulnerability. That is why many computer security programs produce patches numerous times per day—even for home computers. [244]

Systemic Vulnerabilities

Cyberattackers tend to view an infrastructure facility and its ICS in a holistic way, identifying physical vulnerabilities of the controllers and processes with options for exploiting its vulnerabilities via digital manipulations. Traditional cyberattacks focus on the Windows operating system using zero-day (previously unknown) vulnerabilities or other IT flaws to capture valuable data or cause a DDoS (loss of data) attack. Targeted ICS attacks such as Stuxnet and Aurora exploit system design features, with the IT system being typically focused on Advanced Persistent Threats (APT) and traditional insider threats. Many ICS devices, including new ones, remain insecure because many legacy ICS cannot implement the latest security technologies. Even so, these devices tend not to be replaced because they still function, and many infrastructure owners do not want to pay to upgrade their systems until the system no longer works, exacerbating the cyberthreats.

While the majority of the equipment that comprises a SCADA system resides in the control center network behind firewalls, localized SCADA communication equipment directly connected to the ICS can be as vulnerable as the ICS themselves. A digital attack or intrusion on these localized communication systems can have a greater effect on the overall system and allow the attacker access to all ICS connected to them. This gives the attacker the ability to operate all ICS, creating broader systemic impact.

Modern industrial systems operate with standard ICS produced by only a few vendors (about half are US-based) with similar architectures, training, and even the same default passwords. The control system designs generally lack the cybersecurity requirements and engineering (hardware and software) to be able to protect against the many failure modes related to attacks by hackers. Since the same ICS are used across multiple industries, a compromise of the ICS features in systems in one facility or industry can affect all facilities or industries that utilize the same systems and devices.

The BlackEnergy malware referenced above was designed to attack the human-machine interface (HMI) of several major ICS vendors, allowing root access to HMIs used in multiple industries around the world. BlackEnergy was used in the 2015 Ukrainian hack and has infected many US electric grids since late 2014. *All of the cyberattack mechanisms used in Ukraine can also be deployed against the US electric grid, so it is unclear why the US DOE, DHS, and the North American Electric Reliability Corporation (NERC) have chosen to explicitly play down this threat to the US electric grid.*

From the attacker's perspective, exploiting features rather than bugs has a significant advantage, as they cannot be expeditiously repaired by a vendor releasing a patch. The Stuxnet attack bypassed automated safety systems and prevented manual safety systems from being initiated. Aurora used the safety systems to produce the targeted attack. ICS with some protection against cyberattacks have been released, but the installation and upgrade cycle is long, and it cannot be guaranteed to be effective in new attack scenarios. Cyberthreats can damage equipment and simultaneously attack multiple locations, leading to extended long-term outages, with the need to replace or repair long-lead time equipment.

Most ICS cybersecurity guidance and training is given to end-users and ICS vendors. By contrast, very little guidance is available to others (such as system integrators) who are often used to implement new designs and upgrade older legacy designs. This becomes an important issue with older legacy systems where the original vendor is no longer supporting its products and is therefore unaware of how its systems are being reconfigured. There have been many ICS cyber incidents that have occurred because of insiders creating or "exploiting" cyber vulnerabilities without being aware of it. Three examples that resulted in significant impacts were the 2007 Plant Hatch nuclear plant shutdown, the 2008 Florida outage, and the 2010 San Bruno, California natural gas pipeline rupture. Stuxnet was also a case where the system integrator is thought to have unintentionally inserted the malicious malware.

In July 2017, *the DHS and FBI jointly issued an urgent report stating that, since May of that year, hackers had been penetrating the computer networks of companies that operate nuclear power stations, other energy facilities, and manufacturing plants in the US and other countries.* Among the companies targeted was the Wolf Creek Nuclear Operating Corporation, which runs a nuclear power plant near Burlington, Kansas. The hackers appeared determined to map out computer networks for future attacks, the report concluded, but investigators had not been able to analyze the malicious "payload" of the hackers' code, which would have provided more detail into what their objective was.

In the US, nuclear facilities are required to report cyberattacks that relate to their safety, security, or operations. None of the 99 nuclear plants in the US had reported that the security of their operations had been affected by the attacks, but in most cases, the attacks targeted people—industrial control engineers who have direct access to systems that, if damaged, could lead to an explosion, fire, or a spill of dangerous material. The report indicated that an "advanced persistent threat" actor was responsible, which points to government-backed hackers. The hackers' techniques mimicked those of the organization known as "Energetic Bear", a Russian group believed to have been responsible for attacks on the US energy sector since at least 2012.

Hackers wrote highly targeted e-mail messages containing fake résumés for control engineering jobs and sent them to the senior industrial control engineers who maintain broad access to critical ICSs. The résumés were Microsoft Word documents laced with malicious code. Once the recipients clicked on those documents, attackers could steal their credentials and infect other machines on a network. In some cases, the hackers also compromised legitimate websites that they knew their victims frequented (watering hole attacks). In others, they deployed MITM attacks in which they redirected their victims' Internet traffic through their own machines.[245]

A Particularly Menacing Piece of Malware

Hackers allied with the Russian government have devised a cyberweapon that has the potential to be the most disruptive yet against electric systems. *The malware, believed to have been used in the Ukraine power grid hacks, has been dubbed CrashOverride, and is the first malware framework ever designed and deployed to attack electric grids. With modifications, it could be deployed against US electric transmission and distribution systems with devastating impact.* CrashOverride is the fourth ever piece of ICS-tailored malware (after STUXNET, BLACKENERGY 2, and HAVEX) used against targets, and the second ever to be designed and deployed for disrupting physical industrial processes. What makes CrashOverride particularly alarming is that it is part of a larger framework, designed like a Swiss Army knife that can be flipped open to extract the tool needed or to be added to achieve different effects. Theoretically, the malware can be modified to attack different types of ICS, such as water and gas.

CrashOverride manipulates the settings on electric power control systems, scans for critical components that operate circuit breakers, and opens them, which stops the flow of electricity. It continues to keep them open even if a grid operator tries to close them, creating a sustained power outage. The malware also has a "wiper" component that erases the software on the computer system that controls the circuit breakers, forcing the grid operator to revert to manual operations, which requires literally going to one or more substations to restore power. With this malware, the attacker can target multiple locations with a "time bomb" functionality and set the malware to trigger simultaneously. That could create outages in different areas at the same time.[246]

CrashOverride is not unique to any particular vendor or configuration, but leverages knowledge of grid operations and network communications to cause impact. It can be immediately re-purposed, and with a small amount of tailoring could be effective anywhere in the world. The malware could be leveraged at multiple sites simultaneously, but would probably result in outages for hours or days rather than weeks or months. The functionality of the CrashOverride framework serves no espionage purpose; the only real feature of the malware is to lead to electric outages.[247]

Anatomy of an Attack

On December 17, 2016, remote terminal units (RTUs) used to monitor and control circuit breakers in the Pivnichna (North) electrical substation in Ukraine went offline unexpectedly. The 330-kV transmission substation serves Kiev's power distribution system. The RTUs' failure resulted in power losses in the northern right bank section of Kiev, but, a few minutes later, the power was restored. Ukrenergo's engineers were perplexed by the potential cause of the incident, which was eerily similar to the attack that occurred one-year prior, almost to the day. Ukrenergo's engineers wondered whether the event was another cyberattack, since the incident occurred amid a flurry of 6,500 cyberattacks over two months.

Just as many professionals employ "best practices", so do elite hackers, otherwise referred to as the "cyber kill chain". There were primary similarities and differences between the attacks:

Similarity: BlackEnergy malware and KillDisk (a data deletion program) were used in both attacks. Hackers' direct interaction with the ICS caused the blackouts.

Difference: In 2015, hackers attacked multiple distribution substations (seven 110 kV and twenty-three 35 kV) while, in 2016, hackers attacked a single transmission substation.

Similarity: In both incidents, hackers targeted substation RTUs.

Difference: In 2015, hackers used malicious firmware to permanently disable the RTUs after opening breakers and then used KillDisk to damage operators' terminals, which prevented remote repair of the RTUs. In 2016, the hackers merely deactivated the RTUs, which made restoration easier (hence the short down time of just a few minutes).

Based on the facts associated with both breaches, it is believed that multiple groups were involved in the 2016 attack. The presumed narrative is that hackers would have first identified employees who hold key positions within and knowledge about Ukrenergo, such as system administrators and engineers. Hackers also would have identified target victims; detailed information could have been gathered about them online (from social media sites). Hackers would have gathered information such as devices, operating systems, and business applications used throughout Ukrenergo, which can be gleaned, for example, by looking at employee LinkedIn job descriptions and skill sets. Particularly valuable would be IT credentials, account details, weak passwords, and organizational processes and procedures. Hackers could have found some of this accidentally published online or cracked it with relative ease.

Hackers could have started learning about their ultimate targets by using the Shodan search engine to find Ukrenergo infrastructure exposed to the public Internet. Detailed information on the RTUs and ICS targeted in the 2015 attack was readily available online. In 2015, hackers weaponized Microsoft Word files with malicious macros. Hackers probably customized attacks toward targeted victims, such as recipients of spear phishing e-mails. Next, the hackers would have gained access to Ukrenergo's network, using clever coding techniques to obfuscate methods and evade signature-based attack detection. They would have also used macros to detect security technologies in Ukrenergo's

232

environment, including intrusion prevention systems and sandboxes. The 2015 incident began with a spear phishing e-mail and the hackers gained access using native functionality in Microsoft Word to download BlackEnergy 3.

The tools used in the 2015 and 2016 attacks would undoubtedly have been similar, with BlackEnergy malware having been downloaded to a victim's computer via spear-phishing, the hackers would have been "called back" to the hackers' remote command and control (C2) infrastructure. The C2 infrastructure would have allowed hackers to extract data from Ukrenergo's network, download additional tools onto its network, and issue commands remotely to its compromised systems. With C2 established, hackers most likely would have created multiple back doors into Ukrenergo's network to allow ongoing access. The hackers would then have begun to harvest administrator credentials for Ukrenergo's IT infrastructure. In the 2015 attack, hackers installed additional BlackEnergy plugins. This would have allowed hackers to map Ukrenergo's internal networks and move laterally across systems and subnets.

Failure to catch hackers early in an intrusion can be costly. According to a 2016 report,[248] hackers remained on victim networks in 2015 a median of 146 days prior to discovery. No one immediately noticed the hackers' network presence in the 2015 or 2016 Ukraine attacks. In the 2015 attack, hackers spent months exploring IT environments, eventually finding and accessing the virtual private network, which lacked two-factor authentication and, along with a misconfigured firewall, allowed hackers entry into, and ongoing access to, the ICS and SCADA system network. The hackers remained on Ukrenergo's network for months, gathering system logs, monitoring network traffic, and studying the behavior of system administrators. In both incidents, hackers skillfully hid their network presence. Investigators said the 2016 hackers "lived off the land", a technique whereby intruders use the same credentials and tools as system administrators to avoid detection.

Researchers investigating the 2016 attack have alluded to an ominous trend, suggesting it was merely "training". In early January 2017, as investigators were piecing together the

2016 incident, Russian cybersecurity firm Kaspersky Lab ICS-CERT reported a then-ongoing "targeted attack" against 500 organizations in 50 countries. Kaspersky wrote that the worst affected were companies in the smelting, electric power generation and transmission, construction, and engineering industries. Most of the organizations attacked were vendors of industrial automation solutions and system support contractors. In other words, *the attack targeted organizations that design, build, and support industrial solutions for critical infrastructure.* Kaspersky said the spear phishing campaign began in August 2016. As of mid-2016, 33 percent of 1,552 publicly disclosed ICS vulnerabilities had no available security patch.[249]

Electromagnetic Pulse

In 1962, the US military exploded a nuclear weapon high above an atoll in the Pacific Ocean to evaluate the impacts of nuclear explosions in space. The 1.4 megaton warhead exploded 240 miles above the earth. What surprised scientists at the time was the magnitude of the impact of the resulting electromagnetic pulse (EMP), which was powerful enough to affect the electric grid in Hawaii, blowing out streetlights and resulting in telephone outages and radio blackouts. Today, *EMP against critical infrastructure (and in particular, the power grid) is one of the greatest threats to any country.* One curious facet of an EMP event is that people do not feel it pass through their bodies. The EMP would pass unnoticed through us, even as it fries the smartphones in our pockets, knocks out our telecommunications system, and renders our cars and computers without the ability to function, while it takes out the power grid.

Given its interdependencies and interlinkages, a single missile with a warhead (that need not be very large) has the potential to take out the entire US power grid, destroy its electronics networks, and create an existential crisis like nothing the world has ever witnessed. According to a 2008 report by the Commission to Assess the Threat to the United States from Electromagnetic Pulse Attack,[250] "a single EMP attack may seriously degrade or shut down a large part of the electric power grid in the geographic area of EMP exposure, effective instantaneously. There is also the possibility of functional collapse of grids (beyond those that are) exposed, as electrical effects propagate from one region to another. Should significant parts of the electric power infrastructure be lost for any substantial period of time, the consequences are likely to be catastrophic, and many people may ultimately die for lack of the basic elements necessary to sustain life in dense urban and suburban communities".

There are three components associated with a nuclear EMP:[251]

- The *E1* pulse is brief, intense, and very quick (traveling at over 90 percent of the speed of light), and can take out computers and telecommunications equipment as a result of its ability to exceed voltage limitations.

- The *E2* element is intermediate in duration, lasting from a microsecond to a second after the initiation of the EMP, and is similar in its effects to lightning (as such, the grid is generally shielded against E2).

- By contrast, the *E3* pulse is much slower, a result of the nuclear explosion affecting the earth's magnetic field, and is very similar to the effects of an intense solar storm. The E3 effect of a nuclear blast or severe solar storm would be to create massive currents on power lines, which could then destroy electrical transformers and potentially impact power plants as well.

While the US military has been strengthening its anti-EMP capabilities since the 1960s, *there has been no coordination of any attempt to strengthen civilian infrastructure*, and the USG's response has been regrettably tepid, even though *two Congressional Commissions (in 2004 and 2008) raised the alarm. They found that the EMP threat poses a significant and existential threat to the US. Legislation to address the issue never seems to make it out of committee, regulators produce weak standards (no doubt a byproduct of the power industry's lobbying on Capitol Hill), and nothing happens.*

One reason for inaction has been because key information on the EMP threat and how to counter it was highly classified during the Cold War (until the EMP Commission was able to make its reports public in 2008), so the US public and even many government officials are still not aware of the issues. *From the USG's perspective, it is as if an event such as 9/11 never happened or never could happen to the nation's power grid. The FERC has directed the NERC to develop plans against an electromagnetic storm, but the result has been astonishingly lackluster. The FERC has to ask NERC to draft regulations, standards, and procedures along the lines that the Commission specifies, but the power industry controls the NERC. This essentially allows the NERC to privatize the rewards and socialize the risks to the US taxpayer.*

The Russia Factor

One of the Soviet Union's greatest fears was that the US had an EMP attack in its military doctrine, and they prepared for it. On January 25, 1995, a Norwegian meteorological rocket was launched to study the Aurora Borealis. The Russians thought it was an incoming missile and went on high alert, actually bringing their 'nuclear briefcase' to then-President Boris Yeltsin, while their intercontinental ballistic missiles were placed on high alert to prepare for a nuclear strike. Why were they so worried about a single missile? They thought it was an EMP missile intending to paralyze the country's military forces to enable a surprise attack. As absurd as that sounds today, the event occurred one week after the Soviet Union had lost the battle of Grozny (in the Chechen Republic). Soviet leaders apparently thought that, if the roles had been reversed and the US military had suffered a defeat in the Cold War, doing so would deliver a 'coup de grâce' against the US, so they naturally thought US leaders would think the same way. *Today, the risk exists, but on a much broader potential scale, given that 9 nations now possess nuclear weapons.*

In 2004, the USG was visited by a delegation of Russian generals, including two of its top EMP experts, who said that the Soviet Union had developed a 'Super EMP' weapon, and that, during the post-Cold War brain drain, some of its scientists went to North Korea. They, along with South Korean military intelligence, believed that North Korea could develop a super EMP weapon of its own. *The Western press has characterized North Korea's nuclear tests as relatively small (at one-to-three kilotons), but that is exactly what a super EMP would look like—low yield, but designed to maximize the production of gamma rays which, if detonated above the earth's atmosphere, would interact with the geomagnetic field to produce the EMP effect.* It is worth adding that although *Iran is not typically thought of in EMP terms, in 2013 Iran launched satellites that could carry a light weight Super EMP weapon.*

A super nuke would inject 200,000 volts into the grid in a nanosecond, but this can be protected against with a scaled-up surge arrestor, which would need to be faster than lightning surge arrestors (that are too slow). An E1 pulse goes right through before it can be shut down, so a faster and more robust surge arrestor would be needed to deal with E1 and E3 effects. Any counter measure to EMP and its resulting surges must be designed to account for the highly interconnected nature of the power grid. Although so much attention has been paid to the security of power lines (which would indeed act to magnify the strength of an EMP), power plants are themselves also extremely vulnerable.

There is a very serious mismatch between a for-profit power industry which aggressively lobbies the US Congress and American national security. It is clear, since the problem has been around since the 1950s, that *the US does not have the political will to address this issue with the resources and gravity it deserves. In truth, most of the people who could do something about the problem appear to prefer not to even talk about it.*[252] Of course, that does not mean that it will simply disappear as a problem. As is the case with so many other things, it will undoubtedly take an EMP attack to focus legislators' minds.

The Evolving Landscape

In the US, the utility industry, NERC, the FERC, and the NRC have not required hardware mitigation to be implemented to prevent Stuxnet or Aurora-type attacks from occurring. The traditional mindset is that all industries rely on the grid, so the grid is presumed to have a high level of cyber protection. However, Aurora uses electric substations as the vehicle for launching attacks against any generator, AC motor, or transformer connected to a substation. Consequently, *it is the grid that can be the source of the attack.* Depending on the equipment, the damage from an Aurora attack can take months to repair or replace, assuming the equipment can be manufactured, transportation is available for delivery, and trained staff are available to install it. It would appear to be a matter of time until something similar happens in the US.

Many of the same control systems used in the electric industry are used in other industries. The vulnerabilities in general are the same, especially if they are based on the design features of the control systems. Both Stuxnet and Aurora affected a wide swath of industries and government entities in addition to the electric industry. Closely aligned to an electric utility is electrified rail, where operations depend on electric substations and AC equipment in electrified locomotives. Diesel-electric locomotives have their own vulnerability to Aurora. In the refining industry, pumps and compressors are critical infrastructure and their failure can shut down the entire refinery for days or weeks.

The burgeoning natural gas industry, which is providing some measure of energy independence to the US for the first time since the late 1960s, is vulnerable to Aurora because of the critical use of compressors. Pumps, motors, and compressors in the water and wastewater utilities are vulnerable as well. ICS honeypots (systems that look like real systems but are actually "test systems" used to identify who is attempting to attack them) are being attacked by Chinese, Russian, Iranian, North Korea, and other hacking groups. *The chemicals, food, and pharmaceuticals industries are also vulnerable, to greater or lesser degrees. Far less well-known for vulnerabilities are the users of rotating machinery, building automation systems, boiler control systems, and distributed control systems.*

ICS cyber incidents have impacted electric grids, power plants, nuclear plants, hydro facilities, pipelines, chemical plants, oil and gas facilities, manufacturing, and transportation around the world. Impacts have ranged from trivial to significant environmental releases, equipment damage, and widespread electric outages leading to injuries and deaths. While the risk is different depending on the industry and the application, the equipment is often the same.[253] It seems clear that many vulnerable industries may not recognize their own vulnerabilities and are not in a position to do much about a cyberattack if and when it occurs.

Not Even Close to Ready

A 2014 survey[254] of critical infrastructure security preparedness among 600 global IT and IT security executives in 13 countries was conducted among individuals who were familiar with security and well-known standards and regulations regarding the protection of information assets and critical infrastructure. Among the key findings was that just 17 percent of the companies had most of their IT security program activities deployed, 50 percent of respondents said their IT security activities had not yet been defined or deployed, and only 28 percent believed that security was one of the top five strategic priorities across the enterprise.

This was particularly surprising since 67 percent of respondents said their companies had experienced at least one security compromise that had led to the loss of confidential information or disruption to operations over the previous 12 months. According to 34 percent of respondents, their companies do not get real-time alerts, threat analysis, or threat prioritization intelligence that could be used to stop or minimize the impact of a cyberattack. Despite recognition of the threats facing their companies, the majority of respondents believed they were not effective at managing security risks, they did not have state-of-the art technologies to minimize risk to SCADA, nor did they have sufficient resources to achieve compliance to existing regulations. Also, very few believed regulations and standards had decreased the risk of attacks.

Most companies in the research said they were stuck in the early or middle stage of maturity, meaning their IT security programs had not been defined or deployed, or were in the process of being deployed. Most organizations fell short in terms of security governance, with the majority saying important security governance activities were only partially implemented, or not at all. More than half (57 percent) of respondents did not have fully implemented training and awareness programs about security requirements, and 54 percent of C-level executives were not often or had *never* been briefed or made fully aware of corporate security initiatives.

Just 16 percent of the IT professionals were fully aware of the vulnerabilities that exist in their systems. The root cause of most of their breaches was most likely to be a negligent employee (noted 47 percent), with negligent insiders being recognized as the biggest single security threat. Nearly one-third of respondents said that more than a quarter of their network components were outside their control. All of this is evidence that critical infrastructure companies are not prepared to deal with a plethora of attacks against IT and ICS.

Many enterprises see implementation of new security measures or upgrades as a source of potential disruption to their existing operational systems. Further complicating their security posture, most companies do not receive actionable intelligence on APT, insider attacks, or any other alerts to contain or repel cyberthreats. As a result, they must rely on reactive tactics, which by definition means the damage is often already done and remediation usually consists of an endless cycle of upgrades, patches, and maintenance. What these firms need to develop is *a forward leaning security strategy that aligns security requirements with business strategies and long-term objectives.*

A comprehensive, proactive strategy can eliminate many threats while remaining non-disruptive. Security systems must be agile enough to address the security requirements of a wide array of systems, and be deployable with minimal effort. User credentials should be strictly enforced to shore-up existing network segmentation and security. Common security measures still present too many targets to external hackers and malicious code. Masking the number and types of targets can greatly reduce the number of incidents and hacking attempts. Employee and partner use of their own smart devices introduces yet another attack surface for hackers and an entry point for malicious code. Encrypting wireless data eliminates a vast number of potential vulnerabilities.[255]

Focusing on Cyber Resiliency

Very few private sector firms can truly say they are cyber resilient. It is a very long road. Implementing sufficient IT counter-measures takes time, sucks up resources, and cuts into profit. Not factored into many organizations' thinking process on this subject is how to put a price on Virtual Terrorism or the inevitable loss of reputation that goes along with it when cyberattacks become public (which can of course be significant). If corporate executes were thinking more along these lines, perhaps more companies would be taking the risk more seriously. One advantage individuals have is that they tend to upgrade their computers and other electronics every 3-5 years—more frequently than companies tend to upgrade theirs (which is every couple of decades in the case of control systems).

So, what can be done, apart from raising awareness to the problem, devoting more resources, and making actions to counter Virtual Terrorism compulsory instead of voluntary? Creating a more holistic approach to the problem, becoming proactive (instead of reactive) in thinking about how to address the problem, implementing routine cybersecurity audits, and creating teams of individuals dedicated solely to the problem inside companies is a good place to start. Budgets therefore need to be adjusted to devote more resources to addressing the problem across the board. Security and privacy risk mapping, benchmarking, and scenario planning should become a standard component of a cyber risk management protocol.

Clearly, businesses, governments, and individuals must devote greater resources to becoming more cyber resilient, which means they must devote more resources toward anticipating and protecting against attacks. Governments and businesses need to also engage in more PPPs in order to adequately address the issue. In 2013, President Obama issued Executive Order 13636 (ICIC) which, among other things, called for the establishment of a voluntary risk-based cybersecurity framework between the private and public sectors.

The ICIC was intended to enhance the security and resilience of America's critical infrastructure by encouraging efficiency, innovation, and economic prosperity. It was an attempt to set industry standards and best practices to help organizations manage cybersecurity risks. This framework allows for all USG agencies, regardless of their size or cybersecurity capability, to apply the best possible risk management practices in improving the security of critical infrastructure. The primary importance of the framework is that it allows for all those who voluntarily participate to adequately communicate and understand the risks, which is vital to achieving a functioning national and international cybersecurity network.

Some 16 infrastructure sectors have been deemed 'critical' by the USG, are obvious targets for Virtual Terrorism, and are now regulated under the NCSF—including financial services, telecommunications, and food production and distribution. Both the NCSF and ICIC were intended to be guidelines, rather than a mandate for corporate behavior — and herein lies a problem which is familiar to government attempts to address man-made risk more generally. As is the case with the COP21 guidelines, *there is no law requiring compliance, nor any penalties for a failure to comply*. The same may be said about the fight against terrorism. Both governments and companies are generally hesitant to implement strict security protocols to protect themselves without having experienced an attack.

The EU finalized similar measures in 2016 as a critical first step in defending against cyberattack. The Network and Information Security Directive (the "NIS" Directive) is the first piece of EU-wide legislation on cybersecurity, designed to bring cybersecurity capabilities to the same level of development across all EU Member States while ensuring that exchanges of information and cooperation are efficient at the cross-border level. It forces member states to adopt more rigid cybersecurity standards, and creates an avenue for all of its Member States—and the operators of essential services such as energy, transportation, and healthcare sectors—to communicate.[256] Other nations are in the process of acting accordingly, however no nation allocates sufficient resources to adequately respond to the increasing threat of a cyberattacks against critical infrastructure, nor does any nation have a truly comprehensive plan to prevent or meaningfully react to the outcome of such attacks.

The enormity of the challenge in determining the nature of the threat and monitoring vulnerability at the government level can be summarized by a *2015* report from the USG Accountability Office, which noted that *most federal agencies overseeing the security of America's critical infrastructure still lack formal methods for determining whether those essential networks are protected from hackers*, and that *of the 15 critical infrastructure industries examined—including banking, finance energy and telecommunications—12 of them were overseen by agencies that did not have proper cybersecurity metrics.* These sector-specific agencies had not developed metrics to measure and report on the effectiveness of all of their cyber risk mitigation activities, or their sectors' basic cybersecurity posture.

Although in 2016 the DHS then issued a report downplaying future cyberattacks against the US power grid, just a few months after issuing the report, it joined forces with the FBI to commence a program warning utilities around the US of the dangers of future cyberattacks. A US Senate Committee on Homeland Security and Governmental Affairs hearing also discussed cybersecurity of the power sector and identified the most pressing concern as the need to create post-attack plans to assist affected populations. Governments around the world have plans in place to deal with the consequences of natural disasters, yet none have disaster relief plans for a downed power grid. Clearly, this must change. Local and state governments must work together with their national counterparts to produce and quickly implement plans to address the future attacks which are coming.[257]

In 2017, the US Department of Energy said in its Quadrennial Energy Review that America's electricity system "faced imminent danger" from cyberattacks, which were growing more frequent and sophisticated, and that a widespread power outage caused by a cyberattack could undermine "critical defense infrastructure" as well as much of the economy, and place at risk the health and safety of millions of citizens. The report added that the total amount of investment required to modernize the US electricity grid ranged between $350 billion and $500 billion.[258] Governments, corporations and individuals are really only starting to understand what

Virtual Terrorism is, and what its potential impact can be. If we fail to turn the tide against Virtual Terrorism quickly, it will soon be impacting us all in ways we had never imagined.[259]

DARPA to the Rescue

DARPA is working with a private sector firm to forge alternative communication networks that would come into use in case of a cyberattack on the US electrical power grid. Although the aim is to ensure safe connectivity among all civilian entities that depend on the power grid, the program is particularly focused on securing defense networks and operational combat activities. Entitled Rapid Attack Detection, Isolation and Characterization Systems (RADICS), the program consists of a variety of technical capabilities, including an ability to recognize or provide early warning of impending attacks, map conventional and ICS networks, and ad hoc network formation and analysis of control systems.

DARPA is interested, specifically, in early warning of impending attacks, situation awareness, network isolation, and threat characterization in response to a widespread and persistent cyberattack on the power grid and its dependent systems. The goal of the new protective technology is to detect and disconnect unauthorized internal and external users from local networks within minutes, and create a robust, hybrid network of data links secured by multiple layers of encryption and user authentication. The systems rely on advances in network traffic control and analysis to establish and maintain emergency communications. It also quickly isolates the attacked system and moves to an alternative Secure Emergency Network (SEN).

The purpose for the program is to provide a technology that quickly isolates both the enterprise IP network and the power infrastructure networks to disrupt malicious cyberattacks. The SEN can take the form of wireless Internet technology and radio communications or satellite systems to ensure the grid continues to function if under attack. The coordination that is essential to critical operational traffic necessary to restart and then facilitate the stable operation of the power grid is managed by the SEN. It is an indirect network control that can support a seamless switch-over and transport of critical communication. The SEN is designed to function essentially as a wireless network without an infrastructure that ensures end-to-end communication between power grid nodes to provide transport of critical real-time communication within the affected area.

Once activated, the private sector firm's technology detects and disconnects unauthorized internal and external users from local networks within minutes. It is designed to create a robust, hybrid network of data links secured by multiple layers of encryption and user authentication. Coordination of a SEN needs to be completed according to a sequential process, enabling relevant portions of the grid to connect with one another so a secure network can stand up. Threat analysis is a key element of the initiative because the RADICS effort seeks to anticipate and thwart both current and future attacks. The project is a 3-phase, 4-year program that ends in 2020. The first two phases are focused on research and development of technologies while the last phase is focused on technology transition. Potential recipients of technology transition include electric grid operators, DoD systems and the DHS.[260]

The Frightening Prospect of 'Smart' Cities

Each year FEMA asks each US state to rank how prepared it is for various forms of disaster. In a report released in 2015, cybersecurity was ranked the weakest aspect for the fourth straight year, and it is taking its toll. San Diego, for example, is hit by an average of 60,000 cyberattacks per *day*. New York City faces about 80 million cyberthreats per *year*, ranging from phishing attacks to attacks meant to overwhelm websites. Hackers can tamper with traffic control systems, smart street lighting, city management systems that control work orders or other facilities, public transportation, cameras, smart grids, wireless sensors that control waste and water management or mobile and cloud networks.[261]

A Smart City uses technology to automate and improve city services, and in the Smart City of the future, everything will be connected and automated. While this is not yet a reality, many cities around the world are committing significant funds to become 'smarter'. Saudi Arabia is investing US $70 billion into smarter cities, in Dubai 1000 government services are in the process of going smart, and Barcelona is already ranked as the world's smartest city. According to some estimates, by 2020, the potential market for smart cities could be more than $1 trillion.

In Smart Cities, city services deploy new technologies to automate as much as possible in an effort to make cities run more efficiently. Among the city services that would be automated in Smart Cities are smart traffic control (in which traffic lights and signals adapt based on volume and ongoing traffic conditions), smart parking (where citizens can use a parking application to find available parking slots, and review pricing, including pricing changes based on time of day and availability), smart street lighting (by being managed centrally, street lights can adapt to weather conditions, report problems, or be automated by time of day), smart public transportation, smart energy management, smart water management, smart waste management and even smart security (wherein traffic and surveillance cameras, gunshot detection sensors, and other security devices provide real-time information on what is happening and where). Sounds utopian, right? From a cybersecurity perspective, it sounds like a real potential nightmare. *Cities are (unsurprisingly) already implementing new technologies without first testing cybersecurity.*

To put the potential for problems in perspective, consider these two examples in California that occurred because of 'software glitches'. In 2012, a traffic jam on Interstate 80 occurred when the Placer County court accidentally summoned 1,200 people to jury duty on the same morning. And in 2013, San Francisco's Bay Area Rapid Transit was shut down due to a technical problem involving track switching, which began shortly after midnight, affected 19 trains and up to 1,000 passengers who were trapped on board. If these two 'minor' examples are anything to go by, a city-wide 'software glitch' could easily become disastrous.

In 2003, a blackout affected an estimated 10 million people in Ontario (Canada) and 45 million people in eight US states. Its primary cause was a software bug in the alarm system at a control room of the FirstEnergy Corporation, located remotely in Ohio. The absence of alarms left operators unaware of the need to redistribute power after overloaded transmission lines hit unpruned foliage. This triggered a software bug known as a race condition in the control software, part of General Electric Energy's Unix-based XA/21 energy management system. Once triggered, the bug stalled FirstEnergy's control room alarm system for more than an hour. System operators were unaware of the malfunction, which deprived them of both audio and visual alerts.

What would have been a manageable local blackout cascaded into widespread distress across the electric grid. The impact included 508 generating units at 265 power plants that were shut down, water systems in several cities that lost pressure, and at least 10 deaths. New York City received 3,000 fire calls, its 311 information hotline received more than 75,000 calls, mobile networks were overloaded and disrupted, and hundreds of flights were cancelled. New York State was responsible for billions of dollars in associated costs.

Apart from halting the march toward Smart Cities (which of course will not happen), there are some basic precautions cities can take to reduce the risk of being attacked:

- Ensure proper encryption, authentication, and authorization is in place, and that systems can be easily updated.

- Require all vendors to provide all security documentation. Make sure Service Level Agreements include on-time patching of vulnerabilities and 24/7 response in case of incidents.

- Fix security issues as soon as they are discovered (do not wait).

- Create specific city CERTs that address cybersecurity incidents, vulnerability reporting and patching, coordination, and information sharing.

- Implement and make known to city workers secondary services and procedures in case of cyberattacks, and define formal communication channels.

- Implement fail safe and manual overrides on all system services.

- Restrict access to public data by requesting registration and approval to use it (track and monitor access and usage).

- Regularly run penetration tests on all city systems and networks.

- Create threat models and scenario testing for any conceivable event.[262]

A program called Securing Smart Cities released guidelines in 2015 for Smart City technology adoption, which included using strong encryption, designing systems that have strong protection against tampering, and ensuring systems can only be accessed by people authorized to use them. New York City's government created a Cyber Interagency Working Group with 90 members from 50 public and private organizations, including government offices, banks, ISPs, and local, state and federal law enforcement. It also wrote guidelines to address how it would inform the public, restore systems and coordinate across agencies in the event of a city-wide attack.

In Michigan, a 50-person "cyber civilian corps" trains for emergencies as an IT version of a volunteer fire department. The group is working with other states to help develop similar response plans. To simulate the domino effect of a cyberattack on other city services, 10 states practice their response plans using Alphaville, a "cyber village" that includes a school, city hall, library, power grid and more than 10 virtual machines that users can customize to simulate their own networks.[263] As Smart Cities become a reality, current 'dumb' cities will need to become smarter about cybersecurity, but many of them will inevitably learn the hard way what must be done to foster greater cyber resiliency.

And that is *the* core issue where Virtual Terrorism collides with infrastructure: can any country (or city or state) afford to wait until a cyberattack or EMP is successful to seriously address the problem, devote sufficient resources or act proactively? The short answer is of course 'no', but that does not mean that much is likely to change in the near or even medium-term. Regrettably, potential problems tend not to become a priority until they 'have to' become a priority, which, in the case of infrastructure, is a serious—and potentially catastrophic—mistake.

Countries around the world should develop a separate, secure, Internet-like infrastructure to serve their critical infrastructure. A "smart grid consortium" is currently being explored by the US DOE by conducting research on ways to build a new, more secure national electricity infrastructure. *The US Congress routinely creates economic incentives for corporations to pursue beneficial activities. It should create monetary incentives for companies to strengthen cybersecurity, and become more aligned with government and industry standards.* The Congress should enhance cybersecurity legislation and enforce cybersecurity regulations already in place. Going forward, perhaps a set percentage of spending on future infrastructure investment will automatically include a minimum amount of set spending for cybersecurity measures. This can only happen with enhanced PPPs—one more thing to be put on the laundry list of things that should be done to try to get ahead and stay ahead of the infrastructure cybersecurity curve.[264]

10. <u>Financial Services and Telecommunications</u>

Using mobile phone malware, hackers can install a 'rootkit' on your phone that gives them control over all features of the device, including the touch screen and number pad. Rootkits hide normal computer processes from a user's view and give hackers administrative ("root") access to any device. Cyber criminals know the toll-free numbers of financial institutions all over the world. If your phone number is infected with malware, once you dial your bank's customer service number, the rootkit detects that one of its targeted institutions is being phoned, and it intercepts and reroutes the call. Your call is then silently and invisibly rerouted to a call center operated by international organized crime. Given the broad use of foreign call centers by financial institutions, few people would today question a foreign accent on the other end of the phone. Once you are connected, you are typically asked for your account number, mother's maiden name, password, and other sensitive security information. Next you would be told that their computers have just gone down and they request you to call back another time.[265]

<u>Financial Services</u>

<u>Mimicking as an Art Form</u>

In late 2013, an ATM in Kiev started dispensing cash at seemingly random times of the day, even though no one had apparently inserted a card or touched a button. Bank cameras showed that the piles of money had been swept up by customers who appeared lucky enough to be passing by just at the right moment. An investigation later revealed that the bank's internal computers, used by employees who processed daily transfers and conducted bookkeeping, had been penetrated by malware that allowed cybercriminals to record their every move. The malware lurked in place for months, sending video feeds and images to a criminal group (including Chinese, Europeans, and Russians) about how the bank conducted its daily business. The group then impersonated bank officers and transferred millions of dollars from banks in Japan, the Netherlands, Russia, Switzerland, and the US into dummy accounts set up in other countries.

The scope of this attack on more than 100 banks and other financial institutions in 30 nations made it one of the largest bank thefts ever at the time, conducted without the usual signs of robbery. Investigators uncovered evidence of $300 million in theft but believe the total amount stolen could easily have been triple that. An accurate projection was difficult to verify because the thefts were limited to $10 million per transaction, and some banks were hit multiple times. No bank came forward and acknowledged the theft, which is a common problem. The silence around the investigation appeared motivated in part by the reluctance of banks to concede that their systems were so easily penetrated, and in part by the perception by investigators that the attacks appeared to be continuing. *This prompted legislators around the world to suggest passage of laws that would require public disclosure of any breach that compromised personal or financial information.*

By mimicking a bank's procedures, hackers directed the banks' computers to steal money in a variety of ways, such as transferring money into hackers' fraudulent bank accounts, using e-payment systems to send money to fraudulent accounts overseas, and directing ATMs to dispense money at set times and locations. How a fraud of this scale could have proceeded for nearly two years without banks, regulators, or law enforcement catching on may lie in the hackers' savvy and technique.

In many ways, this hack began like many others. The cybercriminals sent their victims infected e-mails (such as a news clip or message that appeared to come from a colleague) as bait. When the bank employees clicked on the e-mail, they inadvertently downloaded malicious code that allowed the hackers to crawl across a bank's network until they found employees who administered the cash transfer systems or remotely connected ATMs. They then installed a RAT that could capture video and screenshots of the employees' computers in order to be able to mimic their activities. In doing so, everything would appear to be a normal.

The cyberattackers took great pains to learn each bank's system, while they set up fake accounts at banks in China and the US that could serve as the destination for future transfers. When the time came to cash in on their activities—a period of time investigators believed ranged from between two to four months—the hackers pursued multiple routes. In some cases, they used online banking systems to transfer money to their accounts, while in others they ordered the banks' ATMs to dispense cash to terminals where one of their associates would be waiting.

The largest sums were stolen by hacking into banks' accounting systems and briefly manipulating account balances. Using the access gained by impersonating the banking officers, the hackers would inflate a balance, and the amount above the original balance would then be transferred outside the bank. The actual account holder would not suspect a problem, since the balance did not appear to have been altered. Investigators learned that many banks only checked accounts twice per day, enabling thieves to do their work uninterrupted. Not surprisingly, the hackers' success rate was impressive. One bank lost $7.3 million through ATM withdrawals alone. Another lost $10 million from the exploitation of its accounting system.[266]

Watching Me Watching You

Of all the industries that are the subject of daily attack by virtual terrorists, financial services have devoted the most private sector monetary and HR to becoming more cyber resilient, because the money at issue and stakes at hand are staggering. Likewise, virtual terrorists have devoted a substantial amount of their time and effort to create new ways of stealing and scamming from banks and their customers, and they are really giving banks a run for their money. They use software that is so sophisticated that they can keep track of how much money has been stolen from each bank account in each bank, and *monitor it in real time*.

When each customer logs on to his or her breached account, the hackers will use an algorithm so that the money they have stolen appears to have been added back into the account— the account holder never knows that any money has actually been stolen. *Purchases made by cybercriminals with a stolen credit or debit card are automatically struck from the 'recent transactions' list on online statements before they appear on a customer's screen. Even the PDF copies of banking and credit card transactions sent to a customer's printer are modified before they come up on the screen.*

It is not just cybercriminals who are watching, either. Using the Bloomberg terminals that are the lifeblood of the financial services industry, *professional stock traders used to be monitored by reporters from Bloomberg*, who had been granted administrative access that allowed them to monitor their clients' activities. This came to light when a Bloomberg journalist called Goldman Sachs to inquire whether a partner still worked there, noting that he had not logged into his terminal for several days. This casual observation set off alarm bells, and Goldman went public with the story in 2013.[267] It was later revealed that Bloomberg's 2,400 reporters were able to see the histories of user log-in information on the company's terminals, as well as the various search functions they used, such as for commodities and equities. What was supposed to be proprietary information was not so secret—it was common knowledge in the Bloomberg newsroom how to use the terminals to 'break' news.

Rootkits

Remember the days when you called your local bank, spoke to your personal banker and could rely on him or her for help with a high degree of confidence that what you asked to be done would in fact be done? Those days are largely gone— not because there are no personal bankers around—but rather, because of smartphones. Using mobile phone malware, hackers can install a 'rootkit' on your phone that gives them control over all features of the device, including the touch screen and number pad. Rootkits hide normal computer processes from a user's view and give hackers administrative ("root") access to any device.

Cyber criminals know the toll-free numbers of financial institutions all over the world. If your phone number is infected with malware, once you dial your bank's customer service number, the rootkit detects that one of its targeted institutions is being phoned, and it intercepts and reroutes the call. Your call is then silently and invisibly rerouted to a call center operated by international organized crime. Given the broad use of foreign call centers by financial institutions, few people would question a foreign accent on the other end of the phone. Once you are connected, you are typically asked for your account number, mother's maiden name, password, and other sensitive security information. Next you would be told that their computers have just gone down and they request you to call back another time.

Apart, perhaps, from the number of questions such a caller is asked to answer (which should have seemed excessive), there is nothing in that conversation that would necessarily prompt a caller to become suspicious, particularly someone who is not attuned to Virtual Terrorism. However, by the time the few seconds have passed between when you were asked the questions and when you answered them, cyber criminals would have your personal and banking details, and would no doubt be using them to swiftly remove funds from your account, and quite likely to seize control of any credit cards associated with your account. This is possible because the screens we have become accustomed to relying on (and may in fact be addicted to) can sometimes show us an approximation of reality, rather than the real thing.[268] Virtual terrorists take advantage of this.

Supply Chain Vulnerability

In 2016, it was reported that the UK's banks were not revealing the full extent of their cyberattacks to regulators, for fear of punishment or bad publicity. One large global financial institution reportedly experienced *more than two billion such events each month*, ranging from an employee receiving a malicious e-mail to user or system-generated alerts of attacks or glitches. That bank's cybersecurity defenses filter that number down to 200,000 before a human team cuts the number down to 200 "real" events per month.

Under UK law, banks are not obliged to reveal every instance as cyberattacks, but rather any event that could have a 'material impact' (whatever that means). In the US, forced disclosure makes reporting more consistent. The failure to report more serious incidents, even when they are unsuccessful, deprives regulators of information that could help prevent further attacks. While reporting all low-level attacks such as e-mail phishing attempts would clearly overload authorities with unnecessary information, some banks do not share data on more harmful intrusions because of concerns about regulatory action or damage to their brand.

The SWIFT messaging network, with more than 11,000 user organizations, was attacked at least three times in 2016, but the real number is a mystery since many banks chose not to report breaches. The lesson of the SWIFT attacks is that the global banking system is heavily interconnected (just like power grids) and dependent on the trust and security of its members, so more information sharing is vital. In spite of the billions of dollars spent each year by the big banks on cybersecurity, supply chain vulnerabilities are a real obstacle to making meaningful progress.[269]

An examination of SWIFT's culture and practices showed that it was ill-prepared for some of the toughest challenges of the cyberattack era. Security standards for banks using the SWIFT network were determined by an *eight-gigabyte-sized handbook*, but it was rarely read (or enforced) at the time, which left the system vulnerable and was a contributing factor in how cyberthieves (presumed to be from North Korea) hacked into Bangladesh's computer systems in 2016, stealing its SWIFT access codes and sending fraudulent messages across SWIFT's network.

Bangladesh joined the SWIFT network in 1995 and over the next two decades some risky practices by Bangladesh's central bank went undetected. Incredibly, *the central bank failed to change its SWIFT passwords between late 2015 and early February 2016, and was also not deploying two-factor authentication on the system it used to access SWIFT.* The hackers used malicious software to remotely monitor routine activity at the central bank for weeks before they struck. The hackers had sent the New York Federal Reserve Bank fake payment orders requesting nearly $1 billion. The Fed paid out $101 million, of which $20 million was recovered after a banker in Sri Lanka spotted a typographical error. The Fed rejected some orders for formatting errors and others because the requests were picked up by a sanctions screen. The Fed subsequently stopped making payments based on the strength of SWIFT messages alone and adopted a policy of double-confirming orders from Bangladesh by phone.

It was widely reported that the cyberthieves were successful in stealing $81 million from Bangladesh's central bank, and that the funds were subsequently routed through a variety of countries, most which was never recovered. SWIFT first called the attack "an internal operational issue", but when SWIFT learned that hackers were using software that disabled customers' ability to print out logs of their messages, *it issued a software patch but left it up to customers to implement the upgrade.*

In 2016, SWIFT revealed that it was investigating 26 attempted cyberattacks on its bank customers. After repeatedly urging them to follow voluntary guidelines, SWIFT eventually rolled out a series of mandatory security measures, introduced a new system to help users identify and block suspicious payments, and it is now requiring customers to attest annually to their own security protocols. SWIFT also warned banks that they will be reported to regulators if they fail to comply, it tripled the size of its security team and hired a new CISO. [270] It is astonishing that, for a financial system as large as SWIFT, these basic measures were only implemented *after* numerous attacks on the SWIFT system and is evidence of the depth and complexity of the challenge of establishing even basic cybersecurity measures that apply on a global user basis.

The type of malware used in cyberattacks against banks in 31 countries stopped short of being a full-fledged AI-driven piece of software, but while it was in the system, it tried to copy the actions of the network in order to blend in so that it could learn the behaviors of employees on the network and remain undetected for as long as possible. For several years, Taiwan and South Korea had been proven testing grounds for some of the more advanced groups in China. While they had high-speed Internet and widespread Internet penetration, these countries did not tend to have much cybersecurity infrastructure in place. The attackers had a pattern: test something, make improvements, and return six weeks later to test again before launching attacks against their real targets.[271]

The large banks are attractive targets for virtual terrorists, but 53 percent of cybercrime perpetrated against financial institutions in the past five years has been against firms making more than $1 billion annually; the average target company size has decreased 28 percent since 2012. Financial institutions with less than $35 million in revenue are being targeted by cyberhackers most aggressively because they tend to be more vulnerable. Such banks and credit unions accounted for 81 percent of hacking and malware breaches at financial institutions in 2016, compared with 54 percent the year before. Among the top (self-imposed) threats are using unencrypted data, deploying new technology without adequate security, use of third-party vendors, and unsecured mobile banking.[272]

<u>North Korea: Punching Well Above its Weight</u>

When hackers associated with North Korea tried to break into Polish banks in 2016, they left a trail of information about their apparent intentions to steal money from more than 100 organizations around the world. A list of IP addresses showed that the hacking targets included institutions such as the World Bank, European Central Bank and large American banks. The 'hit list' was found embedded in the code of the attack on the Polish banks, and underlined how sophisticated the capabilities of North Korean hackers have become.

The list of targets is part of a growing body of evidence demonstrating how North Korea is using its cyberattack abilities to generate cash with progressively bolder methods. Investigators of the Polish hacks established firm links with the Bangladesh heist and the 2014 attack on Sony Pictures. North Korea's hacking network is immense, encompassing a group of 1,700 hackers aided by more than 5,000 trainers, supervisors, and others in supporting roles, South Korean officials estimate.

The Polish attack began around October that year, when the hackers planted a virus on the website of the Polish financial regulator, then waited for banks to inadvertently download it when they visited the site. The perpetrators then used a watering-hole attack to go after the banks; in this case, the watering hole was the financial regulator's website. When the visitors on the list landed on the page, they were redirected to software that would attempt to download malware. While Polish banks were the most numerous targets, the second-largest number was in the US, but the central banks of Russia, Venezuela, Mexico, Chile, and the Czech Republic were also on the list. The only targets associated with China were branches of the Bank of China in Hong Kong and the US.

Cyberthieves who attempted to steal $170 million from an Indian bank in 2016 used methods that strongly resemble those of the Bangladesh heist. The attack on India's Union Bank began when an employee opened an attachment on an e-mail that appeared to have come from India's central bank, which activated a piece of malware that allowed the hackers to steal Union Bank's access codes for SWIFT. The hackers then used those codes to send authentic-looking instructions to a Union Bank account at Citigroup in New York, which handles processing of wire transfers and clears the bank's dollar transactions. The instructions ordered the $170 million to be sent to accounts in Thailand, Cambodia, Australia, Hong Kong, and Taiwan. The money was then sent to several shell companies associated with Asian (and in particular Chinese) organized crime syndicates.

The Bank recovered the money sent to Thailand, Cambodia, and Australia— more than half of the total—within 24 hours. It got a court order in Hong Kong to retrieve the rest of the funds, and got the remainder of its money back within days. In both the Bangladesh and Indian cases the malware reached the target banks via e-mails addressed to employees and took control of SWIFT functions at the originating bank. Both hacks also disabled computer systems that create automatic logs of the transactions.[273]

In 2011, investigators in South Korea found that a South Korean bank had been hit by malware when an infected computer used by a maintenance company employee was briefly hooked into the bank's server network. The investigators were impressed by how the North Korean hackers had been so constantly on alert, apparently for hours or days on end, waiting for the short window during which the infected computer was connected to the bank's servers so that they could activate the virus.

Because of North Korea's poor infrastructure, the hackers typically work abroad and are constantly monitored by minders for possible breaches in allegiance to the government. Being a North Korean hacker is clearly tough work, so its government tries to incentivize the country's army of overseas hackers—as long as they meet their government-set targets, they are not only allowed to live abroad but are often afforded the added perk of running illegal gambling sites online, generating profits they can share with their supervisors.[274] What could be more fun than that?

Fighting Back

The average "dwell time" for a typical cyberattack—the time a cyber infiltrator has undetected access to a compromised network—ranges from 80[275] to 170[276] days. The key to defending financial market infrastructure is to detect incursions earlier, and radically curtail dwell time. Currently, a financial institution's typical information security group is overwhelmed by attacks as well as false alerts and struggles to triage the flood of incidents on a daily basis. Increasing the focus and accuracy of alerts to be relevant and targeted is clearly a priority.

A rapidly growing marketplace of cyber tools and services has emerged to empower organizations to reduce the "noise" inherent in cybersecurity monitoring. Third-party cyberthreat intelligence services offer streaming feeds on suspicious and malicious actors by providing a continually updated list of threat-associated IP addresses. Software solution offerings have also emerged to improve the ability of organizations to detect unusual behavior on their own networks. This is increasingly possible through the application of sophisticated data analytics to disassociate "normal" network behavior from anomalies or genuine problems. Data analytics-based network anomaly detection systems must be big and fast in order to add value.

Security analytics—a new class of big data cyber monitoring solutions—applies rapid data analytics to identify network behavioral anomalies soon after they occur. These solutions spawn alerts to information security staff so they can shutdown incursions quickly, reducing dwell time. These big data platforms also typically integrate and leverage cyberthreat intelligence feeds, enhancing statistical anomaly detection with alerts on known rogue actors. Such advanced approaches to big data analytics flip the advantage to institutions, delivering a mechanism for pinpointing hidden anomalies in machine-to-machine interchanges. Doing so enables financial institutions to identify and address credible threats efficiently, accurately, and in a timely manner. Such tools put a powerful weapon in the hands of financial institutions to guard against a rapidly mutating cyber landscape of persistent global threats.[277]

Apart from the exploding landscape of cybersecurity experts and service providers available to help bolster cyber resiliency in the world's financial services sector, many national legislators have come to understand the gravity of the threat, and are acting. In part in response to the Bangladesh theft, the world's largest economies have pledged to jointly fight cyberattacks on the global banking system. In 2017, G20 finance chiefs agreed to fight attacks regardless of their origin and promised cross-border cooperation to maintain financial stability. The group committed to promote resilience of financial services and institutions in G20 jurisdictions against malicious use of information and communication technologies (including from countries outside the G20); however, it stopped short of making specific reference to enhanced security requirements for financial services. The EU was considering testing banks' defenses against cyberattacks.[278] This is clearly a step in the right direction, but still short of where governments and the banking industry need to be to give virtual terrorists a real run for their money.

Telecommunications

Smartphones aren't Actually so Smart

'Smart' phones are notoriously easy to hack because the software is simple to subvert and device protection is generally immature and insufficient. As a result, cyber thieves now use the same ability that law enforcement and intelligence agencies use to keep tabs and snoop on people. *There are a plethora of viruses and Trojans specifically designed to give hackers access to your cell phone's camera and microphone, recording any sounds even when you are not on the phone. Mobile phone malware can be used to track your location in real time. Your video camera can be turned on remotely, without triggering the 'record' light, so you will have no idea it is even running. <u>Literally anything you do on your cell phone</u>—e-mails, calls, texts, photographs, the address book, passwords, and social media activity—<u>can all be intercepted, hacked, and forwarded to criminal enterprises —virtually at will</u>.*

There is so much information readily accessible on the Internet (whether via programs for sale or via YouTube) that almost anyone can hack a phone. It is sometimes as easy as sending a text message to your target. Since mobile communications are 'the future', the sector has become a primary focus of virtual terrorists. As of 2014, McAfee had identified nearly 4 million distinct pieces of mobile phone malware, and according to a study by Apple, *99 percent of all mobile malware is targeted against Google's Android mobile operating system*. Given that 85 percent of smartphone handsets around the world as of 2014 run on Android (an open source mobile operating system developed by Google), and that one *billion* additional Android mobile devices will be shipped by the end of 2017, the scale of the problem is almost unimaginable. *The open source nature of Android's operating system is one of its biggest selling points, but the ability to customize its free software comes with a rather large liability—the absence of security. The lack of regular updates and 'bug' fixes to the phones' operating system is the real source of the problem.*

Those annoying apps that come pre-loaded on to mobile phones are not only of generally dubious value, their poorly thought out implementation is a major source of the security threat on Android devices. In addition, phone manufacturers and carriers are forced to customize installation of Android to work on individual phone models, which is an expensive and time-consuming process that results in far fewer updates per device. What is worse, this customization process (which is often itself using insecure software) leads to up to 60 percent of the security threats in the Android ecosystem.

By comparison, Apple controls its entire hardware and software ecosystem, ensuring that its iPhone iOS software works more seamlessly, and prevents carriers from altering its operating system. *As of 2013, 82 percent of Apple's 800 million mobile devices were using its most up-to-date version of its mobile operating system. Just 4 percent of Android users could say the same. If Android users would simply upgrade to the latest version of Android software, it is estimated that up to 77 percent of security threats could be largely eliminated.* It is in large part the failure of Google and its partners to make security updates widely available to its user base that givers cybercriminals the time they need to find holes in the Android operating system.

Mind the Apps

Many of those apps you have on your phone are a problem because they increasingly contain malware hosted by what you would presume is a reputable app site, but *by 2013, more than 42,000 apps in Google's online store had already been found to contain spyware and information-stealing Trojan programs.* The malware in these apps specifically targets the data on your phone, particularly financial information. Only days after the original Android Market app store launched, cyber criminals had uploaded fake banking apps from major financial institutions around the world. The apps were completely realistic looking and tens of thousands of people were duped into downloading them. When they failed to work, angry customers called their banks only to learn that the banks did not yet even have an app to download.

Malware is even more rampant in third-party app stores. While there is at least limited algorithmic security screening in the official Android Market, there is often none at all in these other sites. And since there are, by definition, no security reviews for these third-party sites, the apps (and malware) they contain can have virtually unlimited shelf lives, providing lifetime 'annuities' to the cybercriminals who produce and use them. Although Apple's iOS ecosystem is tightly regulated, some users find the control of the apps too restrictive, so they do something really dumb—they 'jailbreak' their devices using specialized software to hack their own phones and gain administrative access over their iPhone's features. As of 2016, nearly 10 million iPhones had been jailbroken and they have jeopardized their phones' otherwise excellent security by downloading third-party apps, opening their phones to the same tainted security environment that the Android phones operate under. The vast majority of people who do this probably have no idea what a security threat they present to themselves in the process.

Ever wonder why so many of your apps claim to need 'access' to your contacts? The simple reason is that the majority of them are a convenient way for cyberthieves to steal your data, learn your location, install keystroke loggers, and capture your financial information. The permissions granted to these apps, especially in the Android ecosystem, mean that your data is at risk. As is the case with other ToS, we mindlessly approve them and in essence grant them 'permission' to steal from us.

Three quarters of all cell phone malware exploits loopholes in mobile payment systems by sending fraudulent 'premium' SMS messages, each one generating $10 in instant profit. When multiplied by hundreds of thousands, the money generated is enormous. In one case, scammers were able to post fake versions of hugely popular games such as Angry Birds into an app store. Each time a user would open it, the app would send three premium SMS messages without the user's knowledge, generating $7.50 per message.

Hijacked mobile phones are increasingly being used to send spam e-mail messages as they join botnet networks, a collection of enslaved malware-infected computers that work in unison to produce massive amounts of spam or take part in DDoS attacks, without the knowledge of the device's owner. Millions of mobile phones have been commandeered, creating 'zombie' networks that are ready to be unleashed against any target at any time.

Legitimate apps can also put users at risk. Shortly after Facebook's failed attempt to purchase Snapchat in 2013, it was revealed that Snapchat had a security flaw that exposed millions of iPhone users to DDoS attacks. The vulnerability meant that hackers could target a specific phone by sending a thousand Snapchat messages in just 5 seconds, thereby crashing the phone and making it unavailable for use until a hard reboot of the device was performed. Hackers were also able to compromise nearly 5 million Snapchat user accounts and published a database of user names and phone numbers on a hacker website. It was also subsequently revealed that nude photographs that were 'supposed' to self-destruct in seconds did not and remained accessible on the recipient's device as well as Snapchat's servers. As a result, tens of thousands of Snapchat photographs are thought to have appeared on the Internet and to have been reposted on Instagram or revenge-porn sites. Some of them were then used for purposes of extortion or other criminal offenses. Those Snap users certainly got more than they bargained for.

In 2017, Snapchat introduced a map feature that lets users track other people's location in real time, raising concerns among safety and privacy advocates. Snap Maps plots users and their snaps onto a map so friends and other Snapchatters can see where they are and what they are doing. The Maps also incorporate "actionmojis", a new type of personalized avatar that Snapchat automatically creates by analyzing a user's location, time of day, or speed of travel. When they first use the feature, users can select whether they want to make their location visible to all of their friends, a select group of connections, or to no one at all. The feature raised concerns among safety experts who feared it could be used to stalk or bully others.[279]

Wearables Aren't Just Fashionable, They're Hackable

Telecom companies have been a net beneficiary of the fashion craze associated with wearable devices, such as Fitbits and Apple Watches. All that data is ultimately transmitted over their servers, which means it is of potential value to virtual terrorists. In 2016, scientists from the Stevens Institute of Technology and Binghamton University combined data from embedded sensors in wearable technologies (such as smartwatches and fitness trackers) with a computer algorithm to try to crack private PINs and passwords. They discovered that the algorithm had an 80 percent accuracy rate on the first try and more than 90 percent accuracy after three tries. If a group of academics with limited resources can achieve that type or result, just imagine what virtual terrorists could do.

Hackers can reproduce the trajectories of a user's hand, then recover secret key entries to ATM cash machines, electronic door locks, and keypad-controlled enterprise servers. With extensive experimentation, the research team was able to record millimeter-level information of fine-grained hand movements from accelerometers, gyroscopes, and magnetometers inside the wearable technologies, regardless of a hand's pose. Those measurements led to distance and direction estimations between consecutive keystrokes, which the team's "Backward PIN-sequence Inference Algorithm" used to break codes with alarming accuracy—without context clues about the keypad. Theirs was the first technique that revealed personal PINs by exploiting information from wearable devices without the need for contextual information. Although wearable devices track health and medical activities, their size and computing power does not allow for robust security measures, which makes the data within them more vulnerable to attack than other types of smart devices.[280]

Please—*Don't* Take Your Work Home

It is estimated that approximately 90 percent of employees today access work-related information on their mobile phones, and some 40 percent of them do so without the permission of their companies (although in many financial institutions it is forbidden to either take company electronic devices home or bring employee devices into the office). This means that more and more corporate information is at risk, especially given how creative and capable cybercriminals have become.

For just a few hundred dollars, a cybercriminal can set up a femtocell—a wireless network extender to help cell phone users improve their reception in areas with poor network service. Femtocells are in essence mini-mobile phone towers that can easily be hacked to trick your phone to believe it is a legitimate service provider. *Upon accepting a femtocell's invitation, all the information you would regularly send through your ISP is routed through the femtocell, and voila, the cyberthieves have access to all the information that flows through your phone.*

Femtocells are particularly useful for industrial espionage, as hackers need only set one up outside the perimeter gates of an otherwise secure facility. It can pick up data emitted by hundreds of cell phones in a business. Other prime targets include airports, conferences, and other locations where a lot of business people may congregate[281] (that would include coffee shops in Palo Alto and around the White House).

Just Showing Off for His Mates

DDoS attacks remain a serious threat to telecommunication providers around the world, with telecom websites in 70 countries having been attacked in 2016. The most affected country by far was China, with South Korea and the US also among the leaders. The telecommunications sector was hit about twice as hard as the financial services sector. Each DDoS attack can reduce network capacity, degrade performance, increase traffic exchange costs, disrupt service availability, and bring down Internet access if ISPs are affected. DDoS attacks can also be a cover for a deeper, more damaging secondary attack, or a route into a key enterprise subscriber or large-scale ransomware attack.

DDoS attacks are also evolving, with 2015 witnessing attackers amplifying the power of DDoS attacks by turning them into Distributed reflection Denial of Service (DrDoS) attacks, through the use of standard network protocols. Another approach that is becoming more commonplace is the compromise of end-user routers via network-scanning malware and firmware vulnerabilities. Faster mobile data transfer speeds and the growing adoption of 4G are also making smartphone-based botnets more useful for implementing DDoS attacks. The worry is that even inexperienced attackers can organize quite an effective DDoS campaign using such techniques.

To illustrate just how easy it can be to conduct a DDoS attack in the telecom sector (or any sector for that matter), consider the 2015 TalkTalk hack in the UK, perpetrated by a 17-year-old who was "showing off for his mates". He netted around 1.2 million customers' e-mail addresses, names, and phone numbers, as well as many thousands of customer dates of birth and financial information. Forensic investigation revealed that he had used a 'smokescreen' DDoS attack to conceal his primary activities.

The core infrastructure of a telecommunications company is a highly desirable target for cybercriminals, but gaining access is supposed to be extremely difficult. Breaking into the core requires a deep knowledge of GSM architecture, rarely seen except among the most skilled and resourced cybercriminals. Such individuals can generally be found working for advanced, international APT groups, nation-state attackers, and other entities that have a powerful interest in obtaining access to the inner networks of telecommunication companies. This is because compromised network devices are harder to detect by security systems, and they offer more ways to control internal operations than can be achieved through simple server or workstation infiltration. Once inside the core infrastructure, attackers can easily intercept calls and data, and control, track, and impersonate subscribers.

Persistent Vulnerabilities

Despite all the high-profile hacks and embarrassing data in recent years, attackers are still breaching telecom defenses and making off with vast quantities of valuable personal data. In many cases, attackers are exploiting new or under-protected vulnerabilities. To protect a telecom from misconfiguration and network device vulnerability, companies should pay close attention to vulnerabilities in the network services of telecommunication equipment, establish effective vulnerability and configuration management processes, and regularly perform security assessments—including penetration testing for different types of attackers.

Even if critical systems and devices are protected, it is difficult to fully control all possible forms of attack. While insider-assisted attacks are uncommon, the impact of such attacks can be devastating, as they provide a direct route to the most valuable information. Examples of insider attacks in recent years include a rogue telecom employee leaking 70 million prison inmate calls (many breaching attorney-client privilege) and an SMS center support engineer who had intercepted messages containing one-time passwords (OTPs) for the two-step authentication required to login to customer accounts at a popular fintech company. The engineer was subsequently found to be freely offering his services on a popular Dark Web forum.

Cybercriminals generally recruit insiders through two approaches: enticing or coercing individual employees with relevant skills, or trawling around underground message boards looking for an appropriate employee or former employee. Employees of cellular service providers in particular are in demand for fast track access to subscriber and company data or SIM card duplication or illegal reissuing, while staff working for ISPs are needed for network mapping and MITM attacks.

A very successful attack vector for recruiting an insider for malicious intrusion is blackmail. Data breaches, such as the 2015 Ashley Madison leaks, reveal information that attackers can compare with other publicly available information to track down where people work and compromise them accordingly. These leaked databases often contain corporate e-mail addresses, including those of telecommunication companies.

Sometimes attackers avoid highly technical means of exploiting a network and instead simply rely on the trust and naiveté on company employees. In 2015, the TeamHans hacker group penetrated one of Canada's biggest communications groups (Rogers) by repeatedly contacting IT support and impersonating mid-ranking employees, in order to build up enough personal information to gain access to the employees' desktop. The attack provided hackers with access to contracts with corporate customers, sensitive corporate e-mails, corporate employee IDs, documents, and more.

Such 'social engineering' and simple phishing expeditions are both highly successful. In a 2016 study, up to 30 percent of phishing e-mails were opened by telecom employees and 12 percent clicked on malicious attachment, with the entire process taking less than 2 minutes on average for hackers to gain entry into a telecom system. Social engineers and phishers also use multiple methods for increasing the likeness of authenticity in their attacks, enriching their data with leaked profiles, or successfully impersonating employees or contractors.

Cybercriminals have successfully stolen tens of thousands of Euros from dozens of people across Germany after finding a way around systems that text a code to confirm transactions to online banking users. After infecting their victims with banking malware and obtaining their phone numbers, they called content security policy (CSP) support and, impersonating a retail shop, asked for a new SIM card to be activated, thus gaining access to OTPs used for two-factor authentication in online banking.

Telecommunication providers should implement notification services with financial institutions that alert them when a subscriber's SIM card has been changed, or when personal data is modified. Some CSPs have also implemented a threat exchange service to inform financial industry members when a subscriber's phone is likely to have been infected with malware. USBs, modems, and portable Wi-Fi routers remain high-risk assets for subscribers, with multiple vulnerabilities in their firmware and user interfaces. This includes vulnerabilities in web interfaces designed to help consumers configure their devices. These can be modified to trick a user into visiting a specially crafted page.

The threat landscape shows that vulnerabilities exist on many levels (hardware, software, and human), and that attacks can come from many directions at the same time. Telecom providers need to start regarding security as a process that encompasses threat prediction, prevention, detection, response, and investigation. A comprehensive, multi-layered security solution is a key component, but it needs to be complemented by collaboration, employee education, and shared intelligence. Many telecommunications companies already have agreements in place to share network capability and capacity in the case of disruption. Now is a good time to start using it.[282]

Focus on Protection

As this discussion of the financial services and telecommunications sectors clearly shows, even the largest, best known, and wealthiest businesses in the world are subject to many of the same risks that their smaller, lesser-known, and less well-off brethren are. Any organization, regardless of its sector, size, location, reputation, or supposed 'resiliency' is vulnerable to Virtual Terrorism and can be brought to its knees as a result of it. For that reason, the focus really *must* be on establishing a secure environment in which to function. While the challenges are numerous, fortunately, taking some basic precautions at a business and individual level can make a difference. Doing so does not, of course, mean that you or your organization will not be hacked, but it may just reduce the likelihood and/or severity if you are.

People sometimes need to be reminded that actions can have consequences, especially when handling sensitive data online, or when traveling or using a non-secure network. A focus on protecting corporate data and thwarting social engineering efforts is a good place to start. Ensure that senior management are routinely briefed—even weekly—about breaches and the latest threats. Invest heavily in systems to encrypt data, protect networks and endpoints, including IoTs sensors, point of sale terminals, and mobile devices. Audit your networks, retool and continually update security policies, and migrate systems to a more secure provider (this should incorporate mobile devices and wearables). About 40 percent of companies with greater than 1,000 employees have a digital forensics expert on staff, who are critical to investigating security issues. If your firm can afford to hire one, do so.

It is not possible to achieve a high degree of cybersecurity without accepting responsibility for doing so. Here is a checklist of some basic practices, most of which are easy to do and cost effective to achieve:

- Set a PIN with capital letters and special characters.

- Turn on your phone's auto-lock.

- Back up information to cloud services, and store as little as possible on devices.

- Back up information on a secure external hard drive, in case cloud services get hacked or become otherwise inoperable.

- Ignore spam e-mail and avoid downloads that do not come from an approved app marketplace.

- Use two-factor authentication whenever possible.

- Ensure that your devices have remote wiping capabilities installed and turned on. As soon as you realize you may have lost a device, or if it is stolen, wipe it immediately.

- Avoid unsecure Wi-Fi connections.

- Keep Bluetooth out of discovery mode when not in use.

- Encrypt all corporate data using the security software your company provides.

- Connect your smartphone to company networks via VPN connections.[283]

Think carefully before posting your mobile phone number to a public website. Attackers can use software to collect mobile phone numbers from the Internet and then use those numbers to target attacks. Carefully consider what information you want stored on the device, given that any attacker can obtain your stored information if he or she wants to. Do a little research before installing apps and check what permissions each app requires. If the permissions seem beyond what the app should require, do not install it, as it could carry malicious code.

Disable interfaces that are not currently in use, such as Bluetooth, infrared, or Wi-Fi. Attackers can exploit vulnerabilities in software that use these interfaces. *Set Bluetooth-enabled devices to non-discoverable because, when in discoverable mode, Bluetooth-enabled devices are visible to other nearby devices, which may alert an attacker or infected device to target you.* When in non-discoverable mode, Bluetooth-enabled devices are invisible to other unauthenticated devices.

Avoid joining unknown Wi-Fi networks and using public Wi-Fi hotspots. Attackers can create phony Wi-Fi hotspots designed to attack mobile phones and may patrol public Wi-Fi networks for unsecured devices. Also, enable encryption on your home Wi-Fi network. Be sure to delete all information stored in a device prior to discarding it (you would be amazed how many people do not do this). Check the website of the device's manufacturer for information about securely deleting data.

Be careful when using social networking applications and be especially careful when using services that track your location. *Do not "root" or "jailbreak" your devices.* As already noted, third-party device firmware, which is sometimes used to get access to device features that are locked by default, can contain malicious code or intentional security vulnerabilities. Altering the firmware could also prevent the device from receiving future operating system updates, which often contain valuable security updates and other feature upgrades.

Report any lost devices to the manufacturer, ISP provider, and your employer (if appropriate) immediately. Change your account credentials as soon as you can, and if you used your phone or other lost/stolen device to access any remote resources (such as corporate networks or social networking sites) revoke all credentials that were stored on the lost device. This may involve contacting your IT department to revoke issued certificates or logging into websites to change your password.[284] Staying safe can be hard work, but it is worth it. Just consider the amount of work involved in cleaning up the mess that would occur if you did not do so.

11. Bioterrorism

In 2016, the Nuffield (UK) Council of Bioethics warned that 'garage scientists' could unleash dangerous genetically modified organisms into the environment using unregulated technology which is already available online. Chemistry kits which allow genetic editing can already be bought online for under £100. Scientists are concerned that a technique called Clustered, Regularly Interspaced, Short Palindromic Repeat is now so cheap and widely available that amateurs will start experimenting at home or in school labs. The technique works like genetic scissors to cut away DNA code and replace it with new genes. It has been hailed as one the most significant scientific breakthroughs in recent years, but there are fears that in the wrong hands, the procedure could unleash dangerous strains of bacteria or other organisms. Kits to make E.coli resistant to antibiotics are already for sale on the Internet.[285]

The New Weapon of Choice

Biological weapons are very attractive to terrorists because they can be difficult to detect, are cost effective, and can be easy to use. Aerosols of biological agents are invisible, silent, odorless, tasteless, relatively easily dispersed, and they are 600 to 2000 times cheaper than other weapons of mass destruction (WMD). It has been estimated that the cost is about 0.05 percent the cost of a conventional weapon to produce similar numbers of mass casualties with biological weapons per square kilometer. Production is comparatively easy, using common technology available for the production of some antibiotics, vaccines, foods, and beverages, and delivery systems such as spray devices from an airplane, boat, or car are commonly available.

Another appeal of biological agents for terrorists is the natural lead time provided by the organism's incubation period (3 to 7 days for most potential organisms), which would allow terrorists to escape before an investigation by law enforcement or intelligence agencies could even begin. And apart from the use of an endemic infectious agent likely causing initial confusion because of the inability to differentiate a biological warfare attack from a natural epidemic, for some agents, the potential exists for secondary or tertiary transmission by person-to-person transmission or natural vectors. For these reasons, biological weapons have become a new weapon of choice for virtual terrorists, who seek to acquire toxic pathogens or their ingredients online.

The consequences of biological weapons use are many. Civilian populations are completely susceptible to infections caused by these agents, and their potential for mass casualties can quickly overwhelm emergency services and health care systems. Resulting illness is usually difficult to diagnose or treat early, particularly in areas where the disease is rarely seen. Their use tends to have high mortality rates. For instance, one kilogram of anthrax powder has the capability to kill up to 100,000 people, depending on the mechanism of delivery. The agents with potential for biological terrorism include bacterial, fungal, and viral pathogens, and toxins produced by living organisms, such as marine organisms (i.e. shellfish and blue-green algae).[286]

A bioterrorist attack that could wipe out tens of millions of people is becoming increasingly likely because it is easier than ever to create and spread deadly pathogens. Bill Gates, the co-founder of Microsoft, has been sounding the alarm in recent years, warning that an outbreak of a lethal respiratory virus such as smallpox would be more dangerous than even a nuclear attack. He believes that bioterrorism is a much larger risk than a pandemic because advances in biology have made it far easier for a terrorist to recreate smallpox, a highly fatal pathogen for which there is no immunity. He believes that the greatest threat to humanity comes either from a natural epidemic or an intentionally spread bioterrorism event.

The widespread nature of global travel may mean that a future pandemic would be even more deadly than the Spanish Flu outbreak of 1919, which killed up to 100 million people. It could just be that the Ebola and Zika epidemics are a precursor to what may be coming in the decades ahead. With human-to-human respiratory illnesses like measles, the flu, or smallpox, a single person on a bus or plane could create a global health crisis.[287] It could certainly be argued that the world was lucky with the West African Ebola Crisis of 2013-2016, because it demonstrated how behind the curve global institutions and governments were at the outset to contain it and gives these institutions and the world's governments time to do something about it.

The Do-It-Yourself Rage

In 2016, the Nuffield (UK) Council of Bioethics warned that 'garage scientists' could unleash dangerous genetically modified organisms into the environment using unregulated technology which is already available online. Chemistry kits which allow genetic editing can already be bought online for under £100. Scientists are concerned that a technique called Clustered, Regularly Interspaced, Short Palindromic Repeat (CRISPR) is now so cheap and widely available that amateurs will start experimenting at home or in school labs. The technique works like genetic scissors to cut away DNA code and replace it with new genes. It has been hailed as one the most significant scientific breakthroughs in recent years, but there are fears that in the wrong hands, the procedure could unleash dangerous strains of bacteria or other organisms. *Kits to make E.coli resistant to antibiotics are already for sale on the Internet.*

The comparatively low cost and ease of use of the CRISPR system (which is a naturally-occurring defence mechanism used by bacteria) have made it feasible for a greater range of users beyond those who would ordinarily make use of the techniques of molecular biology. Do-it-Yourself biologists, biohackers, and enthusiastic amateurs are already carrying out informal research and making biological products. Genetically altered organisms present a theoretical risk of harm to those handling them, and if they were to escape or were purposely released from laboratories or controlled environments, to other people and natural ecosystems.[288]

Is the Threat of Bioterrorism Attacks Far-Fetched?

Given that neither Ebola, Zika, nor other potential pandemics materialized on a global scale, some legislators, national security experts, and biologists wonder just how real the prospect of a terrorist-induced biological attack is. On one hand, some scenarios about how pandemics would be spread by terrorist groups (by poisoning water supplies, for example) are overblown based on logistical challenges. If it were that easy to do, would it not already have been done? Some experts believe that only a nation-state with substantial technical, logistical, and financial resources would be able to be successful in spreading a pathogen such as Ebola. Then again, if the IS were to obtain samples of Ebola and ten of their members were to purposely infect themselves with it and then board airplanes before they became symptomatic, the logistics seem less far-fetched because they would arrive in their targeted destinations before exhibiting symptoms. It is worth considering, however, that none of the people who spread it around the world from West Africa were a nation-state or known to be a terrorist. Perhaps the next time there is an Ebola outbreak, that is exactly what the IS or other extremist group will do.

There is, of course, historical precedent for states trying to tap viruses for bioterror. During the Cold War, the Soviet Union grew large amounts of microbes for potential use in bioterrorism, attempting to cultivate smallpox, anthrax, tularemia, botulism, and hemorrhagic fevers (including Ebola). Exactly how the country would have deployed the microbes remains an area of speculation. Less speculation has been associated with how the Syrian government deployed bioweapons on its people and enemies, with sarin gas having been used in 2013, and other substances believed to have been used as recently as 2017. The Japanese cult, Aum Shinrikyo, used sarin gas in an attack on the Tokyo subway in 1995 and also looked into Ebola as a potential biological weapon. In 1992, the group sent 40 of its followers ostensibly to help provide assistance during an Ebola outbreak in the Democratic Republic of the Congo, but it was subsequently uncovered that their real purpose was to collect Ebola virus. Fortunately, they were unsuccessful.

The virus could potentially be used for small-scale Ebola attacks in several different ways, each of which would encounter substantial logistical, financial, and biological barriers. Ebola could be weaponized by taking large quantities of the virus and inserting them into small "bomblets" that, once detonated, would spray the virus over a small area, potentially infecting people as it landed on their faces, on cuts, or on hands that they might then touch to their eyes, nose, or mouth. Doing so would be like 100 people simultaneously touching an Ebola-infected person. Ebola would not need to be altered in any way to make such a plot work.

The virus is already so capable of spreading from person to person via contact with bodily fluids that in its natural state it could do serious damage. Any delivery method could in theory work, and an individual who is infected and symptomatic need only get into a public space and infect others by vomiting or bleeding onto others. Genetically modifying the virus to enable it to spread more readily, perhaps through the air, is another option, but that would presumably entail having access to state-of-the-art laboratories. Transforming the Ebola virus from a pathogen that primarily affects the circulatory system to one well suited for the respiratory system would be a major research undertaking.[289]

Now consider what AQ had already done from its headquarters in Afghanistan before being dislodged by US forces in 2001. Between 1999 and 2001, AQ training camps in Afghanistan conducted basic training courses in chemical, biological, and radiological weapons for hundreds of extremists. In 1999, AQ recruited a mid-level Pakistani government biologist with extremist sympathies to develop a biological weapons program. He was provided with a laboratory in Kandahar, Afghanistan.

That same year, AQ started a second, independent, parallel program with extremist group Jemaah Islamiah, in Indonesia. It was the first time Islamist terrorist groups jointly attempted to develop WMD. They jointly developed a lethal anthrax pathogen. Shortly thereafter, a person fitting the description of Mohammed Atta, one of the 9/11 hijackers, applied for a loan to purchase a crop duster in Florida but was refused. Another 9/11 plotter was detained with crop duster manuals in his possession. Using anthrax in that way must be assumed to remain to be an objective of both AQ and the IS.

In 2002, CNN ran an exposé on AQ's experiments with crude toxins and poisons, testing the lethality of cyanide creams, ricin, mustard, sarin, and botulinum. AQ associates infiltrated Turkey, Britain, Spain, Italy, France, Sweden, Germany, and other countries to begin coordinating and planning ricin and cyanide attacks via a loose association of cells. USG knowledge of the extent of the network grew from a handful of terrorists in one country to dozens of extremists in 30 countries. In 2003, British police arrested seven extremists plotting to use ricin poison on the London Underground. The arrests confirmed intelligence reports, producing forensic evidence of planning for crude-poison and toxin attacks.[290]

Fast forward to 2014, when the IS seized control of Muthanna, Iraq—once the home of Saddam Hussein's primary chemical weapons production facility. US troops were supposed to have destroyed weapons there following the 2003 invasion of Iraq, but officials admitted, when the IS conquered the city, that a stockpile of weapons still existed. The following month, the IS launched its first chemical attack on the Kurds in Kobani, Syria, using mustard gas—with an agent known to have been made at Muthanna.

The IS may also have access to weapons containing sarin nerve gas that remained in Syria, as well as mustard agents and nerve agent rockets from Iraq and chemical materials leftover from Libya programs. While it is unclear how effective these agents would be after years of storage, they could still be usable. A laptop belonging to a Tunisian physicist who joined the IS was found to contain a paper on weaponizing bubonic plague bacteria obtained from animals. In 2016, an IS operative was arrested with the intention of spreading bacterial infection using an 'animal testes' bomb. The suspect had plastic bags filled with animal excrement and testes. IS leaders are continually trying to develop terrifying biological weapons—even in their crudest form—to sicken the public.[291]

The IS has money, scientists on the payroll, and an abundance of deadly toxins stockpiled, with the ability to make more. The IS has used mustard and chlorine gases in Iraq and Syria. It would also be fairly simple for IS sympathizers to obtain the materials for chemical and biological attacks in Europe, in particular, as the continent has a lot of these materials and security protocols are generally inadequate. Some chemical weapons, whether gaseous, liquid, or solid, are fairly easy to make. To attack the Kurds, for example, the IS simply repurposed fertilizer. It is one thing to obtain chemicals but quite another to weaponize them. An EU report noted that the IS may have manufactured crude shells containing toxic chemicals. Weaponization can be achieved (admittedly crudely) by putting the substance into shells and firing them. Alternatively, the IS could capture already weaponized chemicals. Some analysts believe that it is probable that the IS has deployed both the weapons it made itself and weapons it has captured.

Suitable pathogens are readily available at academic laboratories, vaccine factories, and pharmaceutical companies—all of which are civilian facilities with questionable levels of security. Even if few such institutions no longer exist in the IS territories, the group could attempt to obtain bacteria from sympathizers in Europe or the US. Remember, though, that biological terrorism can be carried out without weaponization,[292] so the IS need not strike a home run to achieve its objectives. That is what IS members wanted to do in Morocco before they were arrested in 2016.[293]

The Threat is Real

In 2017, Wipro, a multibillion-dollar global IT, consulting, and outsourcing company, received an anonymous e-mail (sent to multiple recipients) threatening a ricin-based chemical weapon attack if the company did not pay a modest amount via Bitcoin. Ricin is a highly toxic, naturally occurring poison found in castor beans that can be deployed in the form of powder, mist, pellet, or it can be dissolved in water. There is no antidote for ricin poisoning. The virtual terrorists claimed to have one kilogram of high-quality ricin and promised to send two grams to the company as proof. The e-mail referred to the carcasses of 22 dogs found along a back road earlier in the year and the individual(s) claimed to have tested their ricin production on the animals.[294]

That 'micro' example is troublesome, and there are others like it, but to understand the true theoretical scope of the risk of bioterror attacks at a macro level, let us examine the potential consequences of a major attack in the agriculture industry, where the pace of digitization has traditionally been slower than in other sectors of the US economy. Imagine a scenario in which computer hackers take control of large areas of farmland and, in one click, destroy a year's harvest by flooding a field with excess water, or leaking sensitive data on soil moisture, or yield, or the nature of the plant germplasm being grown, which could then be held for ransom.

The increased adoption of "precision farming" technology threatens to expose the USG's agriculture sector to hacking and data theft. Entities that are morally opposed to the use of GMOs or pesticides, for example, may deliberately target specific farms that use these products. Beyond digitization, the other big technology innovation in agriculture is gene editing tools such as CRISPR-CAS9, which permits scientists to quickly and precisely alter, delete, and rearrange the DNA of every living organism. The goal is to cure genetic diseases in humans and, in the case of agriculture, develop the next generation of genetically modified crops. Big agriculture companies such as Dow, Monsanto, and Syngenta are investing heavily in CRISPR research to develop genetically modified seeds.

Advances in genome sequencing are allowing scientists to quickly and cheaply generate the DNA sequences of entire organisms and then digitize and store that data for research use. CRISPR makes it inexpensive to intentionally misuse DNA sequencing data and editing software; terrorists could use that information to design bioweapons. *Prior to CRISPR, editing DNA required sophisticated labs, years of experience, a PhD degree, and many thousands of dollars. Today the simple do-it-yourself CRISPR kits could enable virtual terrorists targeting the food supply chain to alter the avian influenza genome and engineer a large bird flu epidemic, similar to the 2009 H1N1 epidemic in Asia that affected not only poultry but also other mammals, including human beings.*

The US agricultural industry is at a heightened risk of cyberattack compared to other industries for a couple of reasons. First, the average age of a US farmer is 58 and rising; many of them have a blind spot when it comes to technology. A 2014 survey by the American Farm Bureau

Federation revealed that an alarming 87 percent of farmers indicated that they had no plans to address the risks associated with cyberthreats. Second, agriculture is rife with legacy pre-Internet technologies with which modern technology must integrate. Legacy devices were designed without consideration of cybersecurity threats and pose a big risk. For example, Monsanto uses satellite imagery to integrate with legacy irrigation systems and automate irrigation decisions. These data, if hacked, could be used to flood entire fields and destroy harvests.

Also, the sheer scale of the agricultural sector makes the logistics of monitoring every piece of farmland virtually impossible unless done with drones and satellites, which have their own vulnerabilities. In 2016, a US permanent resident originally from China was convicted for his role in attempting to steal corn seeds from poorly monitored Monsanto and Du Pont production fields and to give them to a China-based seed company (of which he was an employee). The numbers are not in the agriculture industry's favor, which is emblematic of any number of other industries (such as the medical industry) that are, and will remain, vulnerable to bioterrorism.

Washington has thus far focused its biodefense efforts on a list of known pathogens such as anthrax, smallpox, and Ebola, but the exponential growth of software-based biotechnology has made this approach outdated. In the future, governments could be held for ransom by bioterrorists threatening to unleash a new pest that could destroy millions of acres of farmland, perhaps irreversibly. Non-state actors' use of biological weapons in the agriculture and food sectors includes the 1978 poisoning of Israeli orange groves with mercury by the Arab Revolutionary Army-Palestinian Command, the 1984 salmonella attack on salad bars at Oregon restaurants by the Rajneeshee cult, and the spraying of pesticides on grapevines in two Palestinian villages that destroyed up to 17,000 metric tons of grapes in 1997.[295]

Phishing for DNA

As previously noted, phishing seeks to co-opt user login and other confidential information via data-mining techniques that mimic legitimate organizations' websites or communications.

The biological equivalent of this is mining someone's DNA or other biometric data in order to analyze or manipulate it. Since we are all constantly shedding skin cells and leaving our saliva on every cup, utensil, or cigarette we touch, the only way to ensure that our DNA is not available for collection is to be physically sequestered, interact only with trusted individuals, and securely dispose of any item we have touched, which is, of course, completely unrealistic and a nearly impossible task.

Apart from our homes, cars, and offices, any other place is a potential breeding ground from which to gather biometric data. Hotel rooms are ideal locations for DNA phishing, since bodily fluids, hair, and skin cells are deposited every day by different people—any of which could provide material for analysis. Airline seats and rental cars offer other sources of DNA linked to a particular driver or passenger. Manicurists, hair-stylists, and waiters have easy opportunity to collect samples for future analysis. Vast amounts of data are available from every toilet or used tissue, as well as, potentially, from sewer lines from specific properties, which could be tapped and mined for biological data related to specific individuals (some intelligence agencies have done just that in the past).

Obtaining such data is easier than ever before, with some companies offering to sell microbiomes on the open market. Even if comprehensive precautions were put in place to 'bio-shield' a particular target, their historical DNA data could still be mined. DNA is a stable property and can be isolated from old clothing, papers, and other objects—even after hundreds of years. The DNA of unborn children is also within reach, recovered from baby cells plucked from a mother's blood sample by automated cell sorting.

Biometric data can easily be collected from individuals without their knowledge. Examples include fingerprints, toe prints, facial geometries, retinal scans, and gait analysis (the unique biomechanics of body presentation and movement). Cybercriminals could also phish for genetic code or live cells from biotech companies that would allow them, for example, to clone biologically produced drugs, resulting in biological knock-offs. This could be done by hacking corporate and government databases, bribing technologists to steal samples from bioreactors, or simply by stealing DNA code published in patent applications.

Defending oneself involves a combination of expensive strategies, such as physical sweeps, concentrated contaminating solutions, auditing and confirming the destruction of biological samples, and electronic sensors that are able to detect or thwart remote biometric scanning. Yet, such measures only need fail once for data to be collected. In some cases, the most efficient and economic practice may be the proactive release of genetic data, either under license or open source. *Thousands of individuals in the Public Genome Project have already chosen the latter route, volunteering to share their complete genetic codes and other biometrics with the world. And every time someone sends a sample of their blood to one of the ancestry testing services, they are 'donating' their genetic information to those companies.*

Synthetic Biology

Biological agents could cause workers at a specific plant or country to get ill, die, or otherwise behave erratically at a frequency low enough to be mistaken as a naturally occurring phenomenon. A neurological agent could cause generalized depression or malaise in a population (perhaps even a nation's military), leading to debilitating or demoralizing conditions that might not be noticed until hospitalizations or suicide-rates skyrocket.

It is also possible, as molecular-control mechanisms improve in synthetic biology, that specific agents could be engineered to affect just a single person, such as the leader of a country or company. There are numerous potential economic and political motivations for this. Imagine, for example, if Steve Jobs' cancer was actually an engineered attack by an industrial competitor. Some Venezuelans believe the deceased former president of the country, Hugo Chávez, was deliberately infected with cancer, and many Palestinians believe that Yasser Arafat was killed by a biologically-engineered poison. Agents could also be made more pernicious, affecting low-level neurological functions. Imagine if a nation's president could be made to no longer remember the details of briefings? While such precision is beyond what may be possible today, it is not inconceivable that personalized medicine and targeted molecular therapies could 'advance' toward such use in the future.

As biology emerges as another generalized computing medium, future biological creations may, just like electronic computing, extend their reach into every aspect of our lives, and into every industry, transforming them both to their very core. If our experience with cyberspace is any indication, these developments will unfold unpredictably. The Internet was built for redundancy, not security. Before we enter the age of programmable biology, we must contemplate what we might do differently to avoid the mistakes we made in our development of silicon-based computing. DNA is the common thread that runs through all living things. We have no alternative but to seriously consider how we will protect the world's original operating system.[296]

Six Biological Agents Ripe for Weaponization

Six biological agents are the most suitable for "weaponization": plague, tularemia, botulinum (toxin), the hemorrhagic fevers, anthrax, and smallpox. Three of the six —plague, the hemorrhagic fevers, and smallpox—can be transmitted from person-to-person. The mortality rate of occupationally acquired cases of anthrax in the US is 89 percent. A 1993 report by the US Congressional Office of Technology Assessment estimated that *up to 3 million deaths could follow the aerosolized release of 100 kg of anthrax spores upwind of the Washington, DC area—matching or exceeding the fatality rate of a hydrogen bomb.* The military has a vaccine for anthrax but supplies are naturally limited, production capacity is modest, and sufficient quantities of vaccine for civilian use take years to produce. Depending on the strain, anthrax can respond to ciprofloxacin, doxycycline, or penicillin, but, as is the case with many pathogens, anthrax is capable of developing resistance.

Smallpox, a disease caused by the variola major virus, was declared eradicated from the world as a naturally occurring disease in 1997. Routine vaccinations were discontinued in the US in 1972 and in the rest of the world by 1979. *The vast majority of people around the globe have therefore either never been vaccinated against the disease or have only partial immunity from vaccinations that were administered decades ago.* Historically, the fatality rate from outbreaks of smallpox has been about 30 percent, but it is higher among the unvaccinated. Smallpox vaccine has been out of production for 30 years. There is no proven, effective, specific treatment for smallpox.

TOPOFF

The first sizeable simulation of a national response to a biological attack in the US took place in 2000. Entitled TOPOFF 1, because it involved top officials from all levels of government, the exercise involved a simulated, covert dispersal of an aerosol of plague at the Denver Performing Arts Center that was discovered three days later, when plague was first diagnosed among a wave of flu-like cases that cropped up in the Denver health care system. How TOPOFF 1 played out over the following days is illustrative of some of the systemic response limitations that existed at the time:

- Day 1: A diagnosis of plague was confirmed by a state laboratory and the Centers for Disease Control (CDC).

- Day 2: There was a state-wide shortage of ventilators and antibiotics. Federal antibiotics and other medical supplies arrived later that day, but transporting them from the Denver airport proved to be problematic.

- Day 3: The state borders of Colorado were closed, but the question of feeding the four million inhabitants of the state had not been thoroughly addressed. By the end of that day, overwhelmed by the influx of patients, medical care in Denver was beginning to shut down.

- Day 4: An estimated 3,700 cases of plague resulted in 950 deaths, which is where the simulation was terminated.

By that point in time, disease had already spread to other states and countries, competition between cities for the national pharmaceutical stockpile had already broken out, and it had all the characteristics of an epidemic that was out of control.

The next major simulation, in June 2001, was called Dark Winter and involved a simulated outbreak of smallpox in Oklahoma City. During the 13 days of the exercise the disease spread to 25 states and 15 other countries. The lessons learned from the exercise were that:

1. An attack on the US with biological weapons could threaten vital national security interests;

2. The organizational structures and capabilities at the time were not well suited for managing a biowarfare attack;

3. There was no 'surge' capability in the US healthcare and public health systems, the pharmaceutical industry, or the vaccine manufacturing industry; and

4. Containing the spread of disease presented significant ethical, political, cultural, operational, and legal challenges.

Both simulations were based on the assumption that stores of antibiotics and vaccines at the time would be effective against the biological agent. The depth of systemic inadequacies surprised the exercise sponsors, but not nearly as much has been done to remedy the situation as should have been done in the years that have since passed.

Among the major challenges were revealed in the TOPOFF 1 and Dark Winter exercises were that decision-making was highly inefficient and ineffective, there was a serious lack of coordination of emergency management (due in large part to the absence of predetermined guidelines, which led to chaotic attempts to achieve interagency communication), and there was an obvious lack of priorities and logistics for allocating resources at the federal and local levels. The US (and, by definition, many other countries) were not prepared to respond to a biological attack.[297]

The final TOPOFF exercise (TOPOFF 4) was held in 2007 and involved more than 23,000 participants in simulated "dirty bomb" attacks in the Territory of Guam, Portland (Oregon), Phoenix (Arizona), Australia, Canada and the UK. The scenario simulated widespread casualties and focused on crisis management, information sharing, consular operations, and public messaging. Six years after TOPOFF 1 was completed, major systemic problems persisted:

- Improved coordination, information sharing and real-time planning improved response times, and private sector involvement helped drive realistic decision-making, but decisions and task assigning were not consistently disseminated.

- Department and agencies at all levels at times lacked critical information, and the purpose, definition and consequence of the Homeland Security Advisory System threat levels lacked clarity.

- Decision-makers had trouble interpreting consequence prediction models;

- Unfamiliarity with the process for requesting federal support caused delays;

- Public Information Officers at all levels had difficulty obtaining substantive information on response activities; and

- Departments and Agencies had difficulty communicating the reasoning behind initial protective action recommendations.[298]

Given the looming threat, and inadequacy of the performance of all the TOPOFF simulations, why there are not more readiness exercises annually, and nationally, is a mystery. Whether a function of an absence of legislative priority, a failure to allocate resources, or willful neglect of the problem, failure to continue comprehensive TOPOFF simulations on an ongoing basis until the results are at minimum satisfactory is a dereliction of duty on the part of the USG.

<u>A Tepid Response from the USG</u>

In the wake of the West African Ebola crisis, the US House Committee on Homeland Security's Subcommittee on Emergency Preparedness, Response and Communications convened a hearing, in 2015, to examine US preparedness for a bioterrorist attack. At the time, lawmakers considered the possibility of a bio-attack to be one of the greatest and gravest threats facing the nation, acknowledging that the acquisition of deadly pathogens, and their weaponization and dissemination in aerosol form, would entail fewer technical hurdles than the theft or production of weapons-grade uranium or plutonium and its assembly into an improvised nuclear device.[299]

Also in 2015, the Blue-Ribbon Study Panel on Biodefense issued a National Blueprint for Biodefense, calling for leadership and major reform to optimize efforts to combat the threat of bioterrorism. As if to emphasize the urgency of the threat, that same year, the annual report of the Federal Select Agent Program described 233 potential occupational exposures or releases of select biological agents and toxins outside of the primary barriers of biocontainment in the US. Since 2001, the USG has allocated $6 billion[300] to research the threats, which pales in comparison to the amount spent on cybersecurity, airport screening, or border security.

The funds were, in addition, allocated in a disaggregated manner, in the period following the release of the Blueprint, and not nearly enough has been done to address the threat, especially when considering the impact that bioterrorism and pandemics have had and can have, in terms of lives lost and economic damage done. Between 2015 and 2017, the Zika virus is estimated to have cost the economies of Latin America and the Caribbean $18 billion[301], while the West African Ebola outbreak took more than 11,000 lives and cost more than $32 billion[302] in economic ripple effects.

Remaining reactive rather than proactive on this subject will not end up well. The USG, and all governments capable of doing so, must adopt an "invest now or pay later" economic philosophy, particularly since pandemics do not recognize national borders. Global collaboration, coordination, and a lot more investment will be needed to even begin to adequately address the threat. The fortunes of companies cannot be disconnected from countries or countries from one another. There is a very good chance that the next bioterror attack or pandemic will be much deadlier and costlier than the previous one was.[303]

When the Blueprint was issued, it called for specific actions to be taken within one, three, and five years, by either the White House, a department or agency within the Executive Branch, the Congress, or some combination of these. *Of 46 items the Blueprint recommended for action in the first year following release of the report, partial progress had been made toward only 17 of them and only 2 had been completed as of 2016.* The US Congress had appropriated funding for two programs at recommended levels—the National Animal Health Laboratory Network and the Public Health Emergency Preparedness grant program—but numerous other critical recommendations (such as to instate authoritative White House leadership, establish a meaningful interagency planning body, develop a comprehensive national biodefense strategy, and unify the budget) remained unfulfilled. Among those, the White House rejected the need for a comprehensive strategy that called for the President to develop a National Biodefense Strategy that aligns all federal efforts to establish an effective, unified biodefense enterprise, Congress did not hold joint-committee or joint-chamber hearings, and the DNI did not create a National Intelligence Manager for Biological Threats.

To be effective, each US President should institutionalize leadership of biodefense at the White House, and the siloed biodefense community within the USG should become centralized. The Congress should establish a joint oversight agenda for biodefense, which should be shared among the biodefense committees of jurisdiction and between the chambers. The jurisdictional hurdles that inhibit oversight of homeland security in general and biodefense in particular should be removed. *What is needed is a single, primary DHS oversight committee in the House and Senate to ensure that proper congressional direction can be provided across the DHS, and Executive Branch power can be checked. The USG has a long way to go before it can honestly say it is making meaningful efforts to combat pandemics and the growing threat of bioterrorism.*[304]

The Future Risk of Bioterrorism

The relative ease with which biological weapons can be acquired and disseminated, as well as the resilience of specific pathogens to medical treatments (including vaccines), and ultimately the capacity of these pathogens to cause widespread death and disruption, are all factors which determine the probability of biological weapons use. Multiple pathways exist for those attempting to acquire pathogens that can be used as biological weapons, such as theft from laboratories and culture banks, or via natural sources. Identification of these sources is also becoming easier, as the locations of both outbreaks and laboratory sources for pathogens are freely available on the Internet.

Developing a small-scale bioweapon facility could be achieved at relatively low cost, and even a small-scale facility could allow for large-scale production. Most biological agents have an incubation period, which allows perpetrators to conduct simultaneous deliberate attacks and makes it difficult to differentiate between naturally occurring pandemics and those resulting from biological weapons use.

Although there are many reasons why virtual terrorists may wish to use and deploy biological weapons, there are numerous disincentives for doing so. Finding an effective means of dissemination can be problematic since most biological agents cannot survive at extreme temperatures or levels of humidity and the decontamination process can be straightforward, depending on the pathogen. Even if the difficult task of cultivating resilient deadly pathogens is overcome, producing them in a manner so as to be able to harm large numbers of people is technically difficult. While there is a possibility that pathogens could be synthesized in order to target only specific people—based on chromosomal gender, for example—the technical capacity to do so in the foreseeable future is low, especially outside advanced laboratories under government control.

Laboratories that deal with exotic and dangerous agents exist in more than 20 countries. These facilities are used predominantly for researching virus species, tracing transmission routes, and developing vaccines. It is feasible that such laboratories in countries experiencing upheaval could change their focus to weaponization in a short time frame. Almost all states have the capacity to produce biological toxins that can be used as weapons. This is not a new risk associated with geopolitical upheaval but something that is becoming a more common consideration in analysts' assessment of the potential impact of regime change.

The development of synthetic biological toxins and the diffusion of knowledge and technology which would support their development pose their own associated risks and opportunities. Many types of pathogens, particularly those that thrive in tropical climates, can survive and propagate only in specific environments or conditions. The effects of many biological weapons can be difficult to contain once disseminated and this could dissuade politically motivated terrorists from using them. Certain pathogens could be modified so that they are able to thrive in new environments, or to become more aggressive, selective, or difficult to diagnose and treat. There is a risk that information on the chemical synthesis of viruses could fall into the wrong hands and would-be attackers could use this information to tailor pathogens to their specific interests.

Researchers are in the process of developing compounds capable of quickly neutralizing the effects of some chemical agents used as weapons. The development of new vaccinations and inoculations against deadly pathogens also remains a high priority for many governments. These could be gradually rolled out at a national level in order to protect large populations, or targeted at those working in agencies that would be involved in first response, such as the military, police and fire departments, or health services.

Research is already being conducted on the vulnerabilities of critical infrastructure related to chemical production, in the event that virtual terrorists seek to turn a chemical plant into a WMD. *The threat of cyberattacks targeting chemical or nuclear facilities is an everyday reality. Given that chemical plants are now largely controlled using networked computers, it is possible that cyberattacks similar to Stuxnet could target chemical plants by state or non-state actors, causing critical systems to fail. By hacking into computer networks, an adversary could reprogram an ICS so that it commands the equipment to operate at unsafe speeds or forces valves to open when they should remain closed.*

There are already safety and security measures in place globally which contribute to preventing accidental or intentional leaks of deadly pathogens from laboratories but questions remain over how stringently they are adhered to and how they can be strengthened. Previous incidents indicate that outbreaks of viruses from these laboratories can and do happen. From 2009 to 2014, more than 100 accidents and 'near-misses' at high security laboratories were reported to safety regulators in the UK. Incidents of live anthrax being mistakenly sent between laboratories in both the UK and US also highlight that accidents still happen and can have potentially fatal consequences.

A verification system could diminish the risk of terrorist acquisition of biological agents, given the ever-present possibility of deliberate acts of sabotage or terrorism. A lone actor terrorist or a disgruntled employee with knowledge of the operations of chemical plants or laboratories—having become acquainted with safety and security procedures—could exploit existing vulnerabilities in order to smuggle deadly pathogens out of the facility. Beyond standard measures related to personnel management and access control, there are no reasonable or tested and proven technical solutions available to protect biological materials from insider theft or inappropriate use. Capacity building measures, such as the ability to deploy mobile biological laboratories in high-risk geographies such as Africa, could mitigate the risk in cases of a deliberate outbreak.[305]

It is clear that the risk of bioterrorism will remain high well into the future. There are simply too many potential sources for acquisition of the key ingredients needed to produce biological weapons, and too many individuals who may have reason to want to acquire and use them, for there to be a truly effective deterrent. *The ability to acquire key ingredients via the Internet and to 'hire' individuals with the scientific knowledge to make biological weapons means that bioterrorism is an omnipresent risk.* Given the progress the IS has made in creating such weapons, their attempts to use them to date, and their elusive presence on the Internet, there is, regrettably, every reason to believe that the IS, or other groups or individuals, will eventually be successful in unleashing increasingly destructive bioterrorist attacks in the future.

12. <u>Drones and Robots</u>

In 2017, a small quadcopter drone lifted off from the parking lot of Ben-Gurion University in Beersheba, Israel. It soon trained its built-in camera on its target, a desktop computer's tiny blinking light inside a third-floor office nearby. The light-emitting diode (LED) hard drive indicator that lights up intermittently on computers around the world would generally not arouse the suspicion of anyone working in an office but the LED the drone focused in on was silently emitting an optical stream of the computer's secrets to the camera floating outside—perfect for stealing data unseen, unheard, and unknown. A group of researchers at Ben-Gurion's cybersecurity lab devised a method to defeat the security protection known as an "air gap", the safeguard of separating highly sensitive computer systems from the Internet to quarantine them from hackers. If an attacker can plant malware in a system, secrets can rapidly be extracted from an isolated source. With every blink of its hard drive, an LED indicator can spill sensitive information to any spy with a line of sight to the target computer, whether from a drone outside the window or a telescopic lens from an adjacent roof.[306]

<u>Drones</u>

<u>Flying Robots</u>

A drone is a flying robot that is operated via remote control. Civilian drones, which may be readily purchased in stores all over the world can be weaponized by virtual terrorists relatively easily. Drones have, for years, been a surveillance tool—whether for governments, law enforcement or intelligence agencies, search and rescue missions, or the paparazzi spying on celebrities. They can carry and drop things in pre-defined locations. The tremendous number of Internet-connected devices and lack of robust security built into them points to a bigger threat: *almost any object connected to the Internet and with a camera can be turned into a cyber drone that can watch and listen to people just like a drone can*.

Earlier it was noted that, in 2016, hackers harnessed hundreds of thousands of webcams and other connected devices to flood US-based Internet infrastructure provider Dyn with so much traffic that it could not cope, cutting access to websites including PayPal, Spotify, and Twitter. In the aftermath of the attack, Chinese electronics manufacturer Xiongmai recalled up to 10,000 of its surveillance cameras designed to monitor rooms or shops for personal use because security loopholes had been breached.[307] *A drone can spy on people whether it is invited or not, but usually from a distance. By contrast, a phone, laptop, or webcam is brought into a home or office by the very persons who can be spied upon if their device is turned into a robot via remote control.*

As of 2017, US FAA rules prohibit civilian drones from flying over people, except in limited situations, flying above 400 feet, or flying outside the range of an operator's line of vision. The rules are intended to apply to everyone, with the expectation that drone operators intend to operate within the confines of the law. That is increasingly not the case. Drone hacking toolkits already exist on the Dark Web, and the restrictions have naturally not prevented cybercriminals from doing what they do best. A firm that alerts customers to unexpected drones flying in their vicinities has caught drones flying near office buildings where they could hack into Wi-Fi networks to steal proprietary information, near data centers where they could destroy massive amounts of data by (for example) disrupting cooling systems, and near prisons (presumably to deliver drugs or contraband to prisoners).

Drones are very useful for Wi-Fi-based cybersnooping because they can access networks that would not ordinarily be accessible to an 'earthbound hacker'—say, on the 30th floor of a high-rise building or in an office building with a gated perimeter. A drone can even be programmed to emulate a printer so that documents will be sent to the drone rather than the printer, and drones may also, of course, be hacked. A University of Texas Aerospace and Engineering School professor showed in 2012 how to hack a small drone by spoofing the GPS signal the drone uses to navigate and forced it to land. That prompted a hearing of the US House

Homeland Security Committee. You can imagine how far drones and drone hacking have come since then.

Drones are highly vulnerable to at least two other hacking routes. The first is the command and control link between the drone and its operator, which is not necessarily encrypted and can be either jammed or hijacked by a skilled hacker. The second is the ADS-B system drones and other aircraft use to communicate with each other and avoid collisions. Drones can themselves also be used to spread false ADS-B messages. Imagine the potential impact of a drone flying around near an airport broadcasting false ADS-B messages to ground control and incoming aircraft. Any 'confusion' that may result could become more than just be an annoyance.[308] Any building, event, mode of transportation, or restricted area can become the domain of the drone, and, by definition, also the domain of virtual terrorists.

Air Gaps

Air-gap refers to computers or networks that are not connected directly to the Internet or to any other computers that are connected to the Internet. Air gaps generally are implemented where systems or networks require extra security, such as classified military networks, the payment networks that process credit and debit card transactions for retailers, or ICSs that operate critical infrastructure. A true air gap means the machine or network is *physically* isolated from the Internet and data can only pass to it via a USB flash drive, other removable media, or a FireWire connecting two computers directly. But many companies insist that a network or system is sufficiently air-gapped even if it is only separated from other computers or networks by a software firewall. Such firewalls can be breached, however, if the code has security holes or if the firewalls are configured insecurely.

A number of governments around the world have been siphoning off data from computers for years. Using an NSA hardware implant called the Cottonmouth-I, which comes with a tiny embedded transceiver, the Agency can extract data from targeted systems via radio frequency signals and transmit it to a briefcase-sized relay station up to eight miles away. This, along with the use of attacks via USB flash drives, effectively means that no air-gapped system is beyond the reach of attackers.[309]

If an attacker can plant malware in a system, secrets can be rapidly extracted from an isolated source. A group of researchers at Ben-Gurion's cybersecurity lab devised a method to defeat the security protection of air-gaps. In 2017, a small quadcopter drone lifted off from the parking lot of Ben-Gurion University in Beersheba, Israel. It soon trained its built-in camera on its target, a desktop computer's tiny blinking light inside a third-floor office nearby. The LED hard drive indicator that lights up intermittently on computers around the world would generally not arouse the suspicion of anyone working in an office, but the LED the drone focused in on was silently emitting an optical stream of the computer's secrets to the camera floating outside—perfect for stealing data unseen, unheard, and unknown. With every blink of its hard drive, an LED indicator can spill sensitive information to any spy with a line of sight to the target computer, whether from a drone outside the window or a telescopic lens from an adjacent roof. A small hard drive indicator LED can be controlled at up to 6,000 blinks per second, which allows for data to be transmitted quickly from a very long distance.

Exploiting the computer's hard drive LED indicator has the potential to be a stealthier, higher-bandwidth, and longer-distance form of air-gap-hopping communications. By transmitting data from a computer's hard drive LED with Morse-code-like patterns of on and off signals, researchers found they could move data as fast as 4,000 bits per second, or close to a megabyte every half hour. *That may not sound like much, but it is fast enough to steal an encryption key in seconds.* The recipient could also record those optical messages to decode them later. The malware can even replay its blinks on a loop to ensure that no part of the transmission goes unseen. Drones are an ideal way to breach those air-gaps.[310]

Drone-jacking

Drone-jacking is fast becoming one of the top cybersecurity threats, with hackers increasingly stealing drones (and their cargo) while in flight. Someone looking to drone-jack deliveries could find a location with regular drone traffic, wait for the targets to appear, instruct the drone to land, and steal the drone and its package. In a highly charged situation like a protest or active shooter situation, a police drone would also be a tempting target for someone looking to remain unseen by law enforcement.[311]

A group of researchers from the University of Texas successfully hijacked at civilian drone at the White Sands Missile Range in New Mexico during a test organized by the DHS. The drone was hovering at around 60 feet, locked on to a predetermined position guided by GPS. With a device that costs around $1,000 and a little help from some sophisticated software, the researchers sent a radio signal from a hilltop one kilometer away and fooled the drone into thinking that it was rising straight up instead of flying forward. By deceiving the drone's GPS receiver, they changed its perceived coordinates, and the drone dove straight down, thinking it was returning to its programmed position. If not for a safety pilot intervening before the drone hit the ground, it would have crashed. Having taken place in 2012, it is believed to be the first known instance of a civilian drone being hijacked.

This points to a much larger problem. *GPS, which we all rely on to one degree or another, is mostly unauthenticated and unencrypted. While its open nature has been its biggest strength, it is fast becoming its biggest flaw. The core issue is that we use a lot of GPS infrastructure that is based on a security architecture from the 1970s, roughly equivalent to operating computers without firewalls or basic security checks. Since its signals come from satellites, GPS relies on very weak signals that are extremely vulnerable to spoofing attacks and jamming.*

This weakness has already been exposed in a number of incidents in the past. For example, in 2009, GPS receivers at Newark Airport kept going down intermittently on a daily basis and no one understood why. It turned out that the source of the problem was a driver who had installed an illegal GPS jammer in his truck (which can easily be bought online for $50) so that his employer would not track his movements. In 2001, a boat's television antenna preamplifier rendered inoperable the GPS for the entire harbor town of Moss Landing (near San Francisco) for weeks. These two examples show just how easy it is for anyone to cause major disruption. Neither of the individuals in this instance had nefarious intentions but someone who did could cause major disruption very easily. It is truly surprising these types of incidents do not happen with greater frequency.

In 2009, the DHS began a program called Patriot Watch, a network of sensors that are able to detect, characterize, and locate interference sources, and DARPA has been working on an app that would make Android cell phones able to detect GPS jamming sources. GPS manufacturers clearly need to identify ways to make GPS receivers safer. One solution could be to encourage the production of certified receivers that are equipped with spoofing or jamming detectors. Another alternative is encrypting GPS signals, as military drones do, by using a Selective Availability Anti-Spoofing Module that decrypts GPS signals.[312]

Shooting Down Drones with Cyber Rifles

At the US Military Academy in West Point, New York, the Army Cyber Institute has given the US Army's next generation of leaders a taste of the complexity that cheap commercial technology can bring to modern war. As part of the Army's larger cyber complex, the Institute is an internal think-tank that envisions what the cyberwarfare of the future will look like. As part of the Institute's exercises, a drone pilot may film crawling cadets and an electronic warfare officer aiming a rifle-shaped antenna at a drone that crashes to the ground. "Cyber electromagnetic activities" are defined by an Army field manual as "activities leveraged to seize, retain, and exploit an advantage over adversaries and enemies in both cyberspace and the electromagnetic spectrum, while simultaneously denying and degrading an adversary or enemy the use of the same while protecting the mission command system".

Sometimes that means people sitting at desks working on computers. Other times, it means having an antenna on an airsoft M-4 rifle stock, hooked up to a Raspberry Pi computer, spitting code over Wi-Fi at an unlocked toy quadcopter (a

Parrot AR drone). The specific cyber rifle used in the referenced exercise only works with a certain type of drone. Different drones apparently require different types of rifles to shoot them down the right way. The cyber rifle is an example of what an elegant solution to cheap drones might look like. No need to worry about having the right hacking capabilities; all these gentlemen need is the right rifle.[313] Armed forces around the world are engaging in similar exercises, preparing for a drone-laden future.

Smartphones as Attack Drones

Cyberattacks usually rely on some direct connectivity to a target network in order to launch an attack, but the advent of inexpensive, mass-produced, and wildly popular personal drones has enabled virtual terrorists to access wireless networks inconspicuously via unexpected attack vectors. In 2015, a group of researchers from Singapore demonstrated the feasibility of launching a cyberattack using just a drone and an app running on an Android smartphone. They literally zoomed in on an overlooked weak link that is ubiquitous in every office—the wireless printer. The researchers exploited the common assumption that attackers must be in relatively close physical proximity (i.e. within the local network) to access a printer, and that there was no need to secure or encrypt a printer's wireless access, which usually remains unsecured by default.

Flying a drone equipped with an Android smartphone and a special app, the team had developed enabled remote scanning and access to unencrypted wireless office printers. After identifying an open printer's wireless network, the app established a similar wireless access point on the cell phone residing on a drone hovering within Wi-Fi reception range of the office building. The app tricked the office staff into believing they had sent a print job to the departmental printer, when in reality they had printed a document into the smartphone, so to speak. The smartphone later sent the print job to the cloud via its 3G/4G connectivity and placed it in the attacker's Dropbox. To cover their tracks, the attackers' app could resend the print job back to the printer so that the office staff would be able to collect the printout, albeit without too long a delay, so as not to draw suspicion.

301

To mitigate that vulnerability, the researchers developed a second app they called "Cybersecurity Patrol". Just like the first app, it looked for unsecured printers in the target organization accessible via the drone, but rather than launching an attack, it took photos of the compromised printers and sent them to the organization's CIO. It also sent a print job detailing instructions on how to secure the specific printers that were identified, based on their Service Set Identifiers (SSID). The researchers also demonstrated the feasibility of this attack from *within the building*, by hiding the cell phone inside an autonomous vacuum cleaner and instructing it to continuously and autonomously scan the organization's network for printers with unsecured wireless connections.

An open wireless printer was chosen as the tool for demonstration for two reasons: it was a common weak link and was relatively easy to print specific instructions to secure different brands of printers based on their SSIDs. The same approach can be used for detecting other unsecured wireless connections in an organization.[314] Once again, the attackers in this case were benign, but it does not take too much imagination to consider the consequences should cybercriminals, competitors, or foreign governments wish to simply steal corporate or government secrets at will. It would be rather easy to do.

In another example of remote control hacking, in 2017 a USG-sponsored emergency response team was compelled to issue a warning on a drone that was vulnerable to a rudimentary attack that allowed anyone within range of its Wi-Fi connection to take it out of the sky. The Chinese-made drone was listed at the time as a best seller on Amazon (its price was then $140 but was reduced to $80 following publicity about its vulnerability). The device contained an open access point not protected by any password and a misconfigured file transfer protocol (FTP) server that allowed unauthorized users to read and write to the drone's file system.

One of the attacks the team completed was designed precisely to overwrite sensitive system files in order to gain full root access. The misconfigured FTP access allowed the researchers to overwrite a system file to remove the password for the root user. That gave them complete control of the drone and they shut the power off, preventing the drone owner from controlling it with the system's proprietary smartphone app. Since the drone could take photos and record videos, a malicious hacker could also download the footage without the victim ever knowing. The researchers later bought a different type of drone to verify they could take control and kill it mid-flight, the same as they did before. They did so with complete success.[315]

The IS Loves Drones

The IS has been actively using drones since 2014 to conduct reconnaissance on enemy positions and capture aerial footage of attacks for use in propaganda videos. It has also used drone video feeds to adjust fire from mortars, artillery guns, and rockets against static targets. The group gradually shifted to using drones for offensive purposes as well, either for guided airborne bombs or as vehicles to carry and drop ordnance on enemy targets, which, of course, raises fears that it may attempt to do the same outside of Iraq and Syria, as its safe havens disappear.

The IS drone program's early successes owe much to the chaos, lawlessness, and failed state status of Iraq and Syria. Mosul, in particular, was an ideal place for the IS to conduct drone operations, especially with the small, commercially available drones that the group tends to use. The city offered a close quarters urban combat environment where the battle's front lines could be across the river, across the street, or just in the building next door. Enemy troops were never too far away to be in a position to deploy limited range small drones. Since drone controls use radio frequency emitters, they are easy to identify and track down, which is one reason why IS militants often operated drones from homes or mosques, surrounding themselves with civilians.

Most of the IS's drone attacks have involved lightweight military ordnance such as grenades, rocket warheads, and bomblets from cluster bombs, occasionally modified to improve accuracy. Due to drones' limited carrying capacity, these strikes do not yield the same destructive power that mortar or heavier artillery fire could, but they allow for more precision than mortars or makeshift rocket launchers can provide. The group's attacks rattled Iraqi troops enough that the Iraqi government requested jamming equipment from the US in an effort to prevent drone strikes. As the battle for Mosul dragged on, however, the strikes became less frequent. Even though the drones that the IS uses are widely available on the market, the group found it difficult to replace those it had because of Mosul's perpetual 'siege' environment before it was captured by Iraqi forces in 2017.

It is probably only a matter of time before an IS supporter attempts a drone attack in the West, given the group's influence over grassroots jihadists and the attention its drone operations have received in propaganda and media coverage. In many respects, it is surprising this has not already happened, given how many 'home grown' IS sympathizers there are in the West. Hezbollah, with the help of Iran, has developed the most advanced drone capability of any terrorist group in the world and used drones against Israel and rebels in Syria. Lacking Hezbollah's state-sponsored military drone capability, most aspiring terrorists have to make do with commercially available drones, which will limit the scale and efficacy of prospective attacks.

A grassroots drone attack would probably prove far less deadly than a mass shooting or vehicular attack simply because manufacturing lightweight but deadly drone munitions is so difficult. *Drones would be an ideal way to disperse biological weapons*; however, if a drone attack were conducted in a large crowd, the panic it would generate may well cause more injuries than the device itself. Even though terrorist attacks using drones are likely coming, their physical impact should generally be limited.[316]

Not So Easy in Practice

If the threat of unmanned aircraft from Iraq spraying weapons of mass destruction may sound familiar, it is because that is exactly what former US Secretary of State Colin Powell warned the world about in 2003, at the time using the Iraqi Air Force's dilapidated 1970s era aircraft. Although that did not happen, today the risk of such an event happening is far greater because of drones and remote controlled aircraft. Today, a variety of companies provide a full range of *remote-controlled crop dusters* with payloads of more than 100 pounds (that is a *lot* of potentially deadly biological agents). Spraying drones may seem somewhat exotic but drone makers are busy producing 'budget' octocopter sprayers. Soon there will be more drones than tractors on the average American farm, so how long may it be before such a threat becomes a reality?

Spray drones (with a range of several miles) would be relatively easy for virtual terrorists to obtain. However, it is one thing to have a sprayer drone, but quite another to actually be in a position to use it with toxic chemicals or nuclear materials. That said, any WMD offered online is likely to be a sting operation by the government authorities, so the IS (or other such group) is forced to import the material, then contain it safely, deliver it undetected to its destination, load it without prematurely martyring their team, and successfully take off and deliver the material to its intended target. It is not such an easy thing to do, which is presumably a big part of the reason why it has not yet happened. On the other hand, using toxic materials that do not require importation and might even be purchased locally would improve their chances of success significantly.

Virtual terrorists would need to develop an effective dispersal system that would neither scatter the material so widely it has no effect nor dump it all in one spot. This requires considerable expertise plus someone who knows how to operate a crop-spraying drone. Some spraying practice runs would need to be completed, and while a test with inert material would only have limited value, a live test would be far more useful, but equally difficult. Surveillance of the target area and identification of a suitable launch point before assembling the attack team would also need to occur. All of this would need to be done without attracting the attention of any the world's intelligence agencies or local law enforcement. As previously noted, such an attack would likely end up being more about fear and panic and less about apocalyptic killing and destruction.[317]

Serious Business

To supporters of the IS, the group's success with drone strikes are more than just attacks; they are a legitimization of the IS's "statehood" and an affirmation of its perceived formidability against the world's greatest military powers. Drone strikes are, at the same time, a much-needed boost of morale, as the group's physical dominance of territory is degraded in Iraq and Syria. Apart from that, however, the IS's advance in drone warfare has opened the door for other terrorist groups to do the same.[318]

A long list of militant organizations have acquired drones and attempted to modify them for their own purposes. Hezbollah has repeatedly used drones to probe Israel's air defenses, and the group released video in 2016 that appeared to show a drone dropping Chinese-made bomblets on Syrian rebels. AQ operatives in Pakistan commissioned an avionics engineer to build small attack drones and conducted at least one successful test flight before the program was discovered by police in 2013. Terrorist leaders launched appeals in 2016 for scientists and engineers to travel to Iraq and Syria to work on weapons programs, including drones. At the time, a group of pro-IS technicians used the social media platform Telegram to discuss how common engine parts might be adapted for use in missiles or in military-style attack drones.

At least a few technical experts appear to have responded to the call. When government troops recaptured the Iraqi provincial capital of Ramadi, in 2016, they discovered a small workshop where workers were attempting to manufacture drone parts from scratch. Photographs from inside the facility showed homemade wings and fuselage parts, as well as electronics, camera controllers, and gyro sensors used to control flight. Similar factories built to modify commercial drones were found in liberated parts of Mosul, all pointing to an increasing use of weaponized drones. The IS initially favored small helicopter-like drones with four rotors and sufficient lift to carry a small bomb, usually a mortar shell or similar device with stabilizing fins and a point-detonating fuse built to explode on impact. Subsequent attacks involved fixed-wing drones of uncertain origin.

The IS's lightweight drones are nowhere close to matching the sophistication and lethal power of the Predators and Reapers used by the US military, are generally too small to carry heavy bombs and rockets, and lack the guidance systems used by US pilots to steer missiles toward their targets. However, even a small bomb, such as the three-pound mortar shells typically used by the IS against Iraqi government troops, can have an effective blast radius of up to 45 feet—enough to kill or injure dozens of people if dropped in a crowded area. Despite their limited operational effect on the battlefield, the drones had forced coalition troops to take countermeasures against them, including early-detection systems and electronic jamming, while also requiring that coalition forces spend resources to search for factories and staging areas where the drones are readied for use on the battlefield.

When Iraqi troops captured drone facilities in Mosul, in 2017, they discovered scores of documents detailing an elaborate procurement system for purchasing the aircraft and parts, as well as extensive procedures for altering and testing the equipment. The records addressed the group's efforts to secure, modify, and enhance the range and performance of its drones. When the siege of Mosul began in the fall, IS fighters stepped up their use of small surveillance drones to gather intelligence and showcase their efforts to defend the city, producing mini-documentaries with aerial footage of successful suicide attacks on Iraqi troops. The shift to weaponized drone attacks began late in 2016 and was ramping up dramatically in 2017.[319]

The documents showed the IS's efforts to acquire predictable items like GoPro cameras, memory cards, GPS units, digital video recorders, and spare propeller blades. They also illustrated the group's efforts to secure, modify, and enhance the range and performance of its fleet of drones. To protect the transmission of their drone video feeds, members of the group wanted to acquire encrypted video transmitters and receivers. A long-range radio-controlled relay system was also included on a number of its 'acquisition' lists (to extend the range of its drones), as were various types of servo motors.

While servo motors can be used for a variety of drone-related tasks, they can also be used to facilitate release mechanisms, such as the release of a munition from a drone, a tactic with which the group appeared to have become quite proficient. The inclusion of these types of items demonstrates how, even though the drone material being requested by the IS was something that a sophisticated high schooler could put together, some of these items can be used for more sinister purposes. The documents did not reveal how the IS actually acquired the material found on the lists, but given the specific price information provided on the forms the IS used to order the material, it is possible that the IS was acquiring at least some of the equipment online, or likely through third parties in countries outside the region,[320] including popular online retailers.

Attempting Regulation

As mentioned earlier, in 2016, the FAA finalized the first regulations governing routine commercial use of small drones in the US, which opened the door towards fully integrating drones into the nation's airspace. The rules are an attempt to provide safety regulations for drones weighing less than 55 pounds that are conducting non-hobby-related operations. The rules' provisions were designed to minimize risks to other aircraft, as well as to people and property on the ground, and require pilots to keep an unmanned aircraft within visual line of sight. Operations are allowed during daylight and twilight (if the drone has anti-collision lights). Height and speed restrictions and other operational limits were also addressed, such as prohibiting flights over unprotected people on the ground who are not directly participating in a drone's operation.

The US Transportation Security Administration (TSA) conducts a security background check of all remote pilot applications prior to issuance of a certificate (which means that pilots must first *volunteer* to be 'screened', since the USG has no way of knowing who is actually operating a drone). Operators are responsible for ensuring a drone is safe before flying but *the FAA is not requiring small drones to comply with Agency airworthiness standards or aircraft certification*. Instead, the remote pilot is supposed to perform a preflight visual and operational check of drones to ensure that safety-pertinent systems are functioning properly. This includes checking the communications link between the control station and the drone.

Although the rules do not specifically deal with privacy issues in the use of drones, and the FAA does not regulate how drones gather data on people or property, the FAA 'encourages' all drone pilots to check local and state laws before gathering information through remote sensing technology or photography. The Agency provides all drone users with recommended privacy guidelines as part of the registration process. The FAA also educates all commercial drone pilots about privacy during their pilot certification process and issues 'guidance' to local and state governments on drone privacy issues. The rules are an effort to build on the privacy best practices issued by the National Telecommunications and Information Administration (NTIA), in conjunction with an outreach initiative with privacy advocates and industry.[321]

Is it even possible to ensure that these regulations are adhered to and that drones are operated appropriately and safely? One possibility is via blockchain technology, which are peer-to-peer networks that adhere to specific protocols and are resistant to data modification. Once data is recorded, a block cannot be modified without altering all future blocks with the collusion of everyone else in the block chain. The chain records transactions between two parties in a verifiable and permanent manner.[322] Blockchains may help regularize drone usage by keeping a high-speed, assured ledger of airspace activity and information regarding the drone and its operator, and by distributing it to all appropriate parties.

Augmented by other technologies and software tokens, blockchain could help assemble information and augment avenues for airspace deconfliction in a variety of ways, both intrinsic and external to the drone. For example, a drone's GPS may receive the locations of other drones, either directly from the others or through drone controllers on the ground. It may also receive security validation of its own hardware, software, and provenance.

Radio frequency signal strengths from certain drone models do not differ by a large order of magnitude. An airborne drone may be able to appropriately sense and avoid the location of another drone that is very close by assessing its signal strength. Drones may also receive information using radar by using chemical viewing or other optical and sonic capabilities. Coupled radio direction finding is another way for a drone to measure the direction from which a signal was transmitted, using antenna triangulation or wave timing. It can also analyze signals using cognitive pattern recognition, whereby a receiver notes that there are several local ground control stations which seem to be directing drones to roughly the same place at the same time.[323]

Existing methods of detection can be used to monitor drones and others are in the process of being developed, akin to the development of drones themselves. The 'limited' scope of current regulations governing drones is evidence of the embryonic nature of the drone industry. Local, state, and national governments will continue to struggle with how to regulate and manage drones going forward. At least there has been an attempt made to seriously regulate the drone sector. Doing so comprehensively and effectively will remain a challenge for the foreseeable future.

Robots

Failure to Securely Communicate

We tend to think of robots as computers with arms, legs, or wheels that either help make our lives simpler by performing tasks efficiently and quickly or take jobs away from people. As human-robot interactions evolve, new attack vectors have emerged and threat scenarios continue to expand. There have already been serious incidents involving threats to humans by robots, including a woman being killed by an industrial robot in 2015 in the US, when an industrial robot restarted abruptly. The US Department of Labor maintains a list of robot-related incidents, including several that have resulted in death. What follows are some examples:

- In 2007, a robot cannon killed 9 soldiers and seriously injured 14 others during a shooting exercise, due to a malfunction.

- As of 2015, robotic surgery had been linked to 144 deaths.

- In 2016, a robot security guard at the Stanford Shopping Center in Silicon Valley knocked down a toddler.

- In 2016, a Chinese-made robot had an accident at a Shenzhen tech trade fair, smashing a glass window and injuring someone standing nearby.

While these incidents were accidents, they clearly demonstrate the potential consequences of robot malfunctions. Future incidents could easily be caused by a robot controlled remotely by virtual terrorists, with potential deadly consequences.

A 2017 study[324] found nearly 50 cybersecurity vulnerabilities in robot ecosystem components, many of which were common in home, business, and industrial robots, as well as the control software used by other robots tested. Although the number of robots tested was not a large sample, the fact that dozens of vulnerabilities were uncovered, in such a broad spectrum of robots, is concerning. Most of the robots evaluated were using insecure forms of communications, with mobile and software applications connected to the Internet, Bluetooth, and Wi-Fi without properly securing the communication channel. Although some had weak encryption, most of the others sent data to vendor services or the cloud without *any* protection.

Most of the robots exposed one or more services that can be remotely accessed by computer software, mobile applications, or Internet services. These services included complex and critical functions, such as programming and receiving external commands, as well as simpler functions such as returning basic robot information. Some robot services did not even require a username and password, allowing anyone to remotely access those services. In some cases, where services used authentication, it was possible to bypass the process, allowing access without using a correct password.

Robots can store sensitive information, including encryption keys, user social media, e-mail accounts and vendor service credentials, and send that information to and from mobile applications, Internet services, and computer software—meaning that channel encryption is mandatory to avoid data compromises. Robots also receive remote software updates, so proper encryption is necessary to ensure that these updates are trusted and have not been modified to include malicious software. Most of the robots that were tested did not require sufficient authorization to protect their functionality, including critical functions such as installation of applications in the robots themselves or updating of their operating system software. *This enables cyberattackers to install software without permission and gain full control over the robots.* Most of the robots were also either not using encryption or improperly using it, exposing sensitive data to potential attackers.

Some of the robots with insecure features could not be easily disabled, having features with default passwords that were either difficult to change or those that could not be changed at all. Others were easy to hack because default passwords are usually publicly known or could be easily obtained since many robot models share the same default passwords. Many robots use open source frameworks and libraries. One of the most popular is the Robot Operating System (ROS) 29, used in several robots from multiple vendors. The ROS suffers from many known cybersecurity problems, such as cleartext communication, authentication issues, and weak authorization schemes, all of which make robots insecure. In the robotics community, it is common to share software frameworks, libraries, and operating systems for robot development and programming.

Not all of the robots tested were vulnerable to every one of the cybersecurity issues identified, but each robot had many of the issues, ultimately because many researchers and enthusiasts in the robotics space use the same (or very similar) tools, software, and design practices globally. For example, it is common for robots originally intended as research projects to become commercial products with no additional cybersecurity protections—the security posture of the final product remains the same as the research or prototype robot. This results in poor cybersecurity defenses, since research and prototype robots are often designed and built with few or no protections.

<u>Vulnerability to Cyberattacks</u>

Each robot naturally has different features, and the more features, the more advanced and smarter a robot typically is, but these features can also make robots more vulnerable and attractive to hackers. Certain features are common, intended to improve accessibility, usability, interconnection, and reusability (such as real-time remote control with mobile applications). Unfortunately, many of these features make robots more vulnerable from a cybersecurity perspective, with both critical- and high-risk cybersecurity issues present in many of the features. The following list provides an overview of some possible threats for common robot features:

- <u>Network connectivity</u>: Sensitive robot services are vulnerable to attack from home, corporate, or industrial networks or the Internet.

- <u>External services interaction</u>: Robot owner social networks, application stores, and cloud systems could be exposed, providing access to private user information, usernames, and passwords.

- <u>Remote control applications</u>: Mobile applications or microcomputer boards can be used to send malicious commands. Mobile phones could be an entry point for launching attacks; if a user's phone is hacked, the robot can be hacked also. An attacker could use a hacked robot to launch attacks against the owner's phone.

- <u>Modular extensibility</u>: When a robot allows installation of applications, it can also allow installation of custom malware. Malicious software could cause the robot to execute unwanted actions. Ransomware could also take robots hostage, making them unusable and allowing hackers to extort money to make them usable again.

- Safety features: Human safety protections and collision avoidance/detection mechanisms can be disabled by hacking the robot's control services.

- Firmware: When a robot's firmware integrity is not verified, it is possible to replace the robot's core software and change its behavior in a malicious way by installing malware or ransomware.

- Autonomous robots: A hacked autonomous robot can move around as long as its battery continues to provide power, which allows hackers to control an "insider threat", steal information, or cause harm to nearby objects or people.

- Network advertisement: It is common for robots to advertise their presence on a network using known discovery protocols. Attackers can leverage this to identify a robot in a corporate or industrial network with thousands of computers, and interact with its network services.

- Fast installation/deployment: Since many vendors do not highlight the importance of changing the administrator's password in their documentation, a user may not change it during fast deployment, meaning it can be hacked easily.

- Backups: Configuration files and other information may be backed up on the robot vendor's cloud or the administrator's computer. An unencrypted backup could result in a compromised robot and a leak of sensitive data if obtained by an attacker.

- Connection ports: Physical connectivity ports lacking restriction or protection could allow anyone to connect external devices to the robots and either extract information or insert malware.

- Microphones and cameras: Once a robot has been hacked, microphones and cameras can be used for cyberespionage and surveillance, enabling an attacker to listen to conversations, identify people through face recognition, and record videos.

A hacked robot has many of the same vulnerabilities as computers and can suffer the same consequences. A hacked robot operating inside a home might spy on a family via the robot's microphones and cameras. An attacker could also use a robot's mobility to cause physical damage in or to the house. Compromised robots could even hurt family members and pets with sudden, unexpected movements, since hacked robots can bypass safety protections that limit their movements. Hacked robots could also start fires in a kitchen by tampering with electricity, or they could potentially poison family members and pets by mixing toxic substances with food or drinks, or utilize sharp objects to cause harm.

Robots that are integrated with smart home automation could unlock and open doors and deactivate home alarms. Robots that are not integrated into a smart home could still interact with voice assistants, such as Alexa or Siri, which integrate with home automation and alarm systems. If the robot can talk, or allow an attacker to talk through its speaker, it could tell voice-activated assistants to unlock doors and disable home security. Once robot firmware is hacked, it may be difficult or even impossible to reset the robot to factory defaults and recover data. If the core robot software is hacked, it would be impossible to recover the robot.

Many business robots are customer-facing, so a hacked robot could easily impact one of their most valuable assets. A hacked robot could be made to deliver incorrect orders, share confidential information, or go offline, all of which would negatively impact a business. An attacker could also instruct a robot to physically hurt customers or company employees, and if robots have access to customer information such as personal and credit card data, that data could also be put at risk. Robots could cause destruction of property by starting fires or physically damaging business assets. The potential financial impact for a business is similar to that of a home, but on a larger scale, since business robots are generally much more expensive. A company with several hacked robots could suffer losses, not only to the computers themselves, but in terms of potential liability and other forms of financial loss. Compromised robots could be used to hack other computers or IoT devices on the same network, becoming a platform to attack and/or exploit vulnerabilities in other network devices.

Improving Robot Cybersecurity

Building robots is not an easy task, nor is securing them from cyberattacks, but taking some basic precautions can go a long way toward preventing attacks. It starts with robot manufacturers, who need to do a better job of encrypting their products and advising purchasers that default passwords must be changed upon first usage. Consumers need to be smarter about taking a common sense approach to cybersecurity. What follows are some basic recommendations for doing that:

- Software: Vendors should implement Secure Software Development Life Cycle processes from day one.

- Encryption: Vendors should properly encrypt robot communications and software updates.

- Education: Vendors should invest in cybersecurity education for everyone in their organization, with training not only for engineers and developers, but also for executives and everyone else involved in product decisions.

- Vulnerability Disclosure: Vendors should have a clear communication channel for reporting cybersecurity issues and clearly identify an individual or team to be responsible for handling reports appropriately.

- Security Audits: Vendors should ensure that a complete security assessment is performed on all of the robot's ecosystem components prior to going into production.

- Authentication and Authorization: Vendors should make certain that only authorized users have access to robot services and functionality.

- Factory Restore: Vendors should provide methods for restoring a robot to its factory default state, and ensure that its default configuration is secure.

- Secure the Supply Chain: Vendors should make sure that all of their technology providers implement best practices in cybersecurity.

Many of the cybersecurity issues revealed in the study could have been prevented by implementing well-known cybersecurity practices. Research from the University of Washington, conducted in 2009, found that household robots did not protect users' security and privacy. In the time that has passed since then, robot cybersecurity has gotten worse. Since robot adoption is not yet mainstream, there is still time to improve the technology and make it more secure.[325] That will take sustained effort on the part of robot manufacturers and users, however.

It would also undoubtedly help if governments around the world would pass and implement legislation requiring unique passwords for both drones and robots, as they are produced. Governments and regulators should also update existing laws and regulations on an ongoing basis, rather than once every 5 or 10 years, as is so often the case. As quickly as the drone and robot landscape is evolving, existing regulations quickly become obsolete, and governments fall further and further behind the curve. With stakes as high as they are for governments, businesses, and individuals, we need to build a better mousetrap. As will be explored in Chapter 15, the challenges associated with passing and implementing laws on a global scale that regulate cyberspace are even more daunting.

A Robotic Future

Given perpetual advances in technology, robots are sure to become smarter, faster, and smaller. Dragonfly-sized drones were already being used in the first decade of this century to spy on people, and the US Air Force had already unveiled robotic bumble bees that could not be detected in a hostile environment. Robots already have 'swarm' capabilities and can be programmed to act in unison in collective behavior that mimics the way ants and birds flock together. In 2014, some researchers at Harvard University created the largest robot swarm at that time using 1,024 tiny robots the size of a penny that could find one another and collaborate to assemble themselves into various shaped and designs, like a mechanical flash mob. While there are, of course, nefarious potential connotations to a robotic future, such capability also opens up fantastic possibilities in areas as broad as search and rescue operations, disaster relief, ambulatory services, and oil spill containment.

Autonomous robots already exist and are available for purchase to the general public for anyone who may be tired of vacuuming at home. Such vacuums use algorithms to adapt to unfamiliar environments and avoid obstacles. That is great if you do not happen to fancy vacuuming, but where do we draw the line between how much progress and autonomy is too much? Some defense contractors have already developed drones that can fly into enemy territory, collect intelligence, drop bombs, and defend themselves against attack. In the Korean demilitarized zone, South Korea has deployed border control sniper robots that detect intruders with heat and motion sensors and can automatically fire on targets up to one kilometer away with machine guns and grenade launchers. *What if autonomous drones infected with malware decided for themselves to drop bombs or perform kamikaze missions in a stadium filled with people?*

Lethal autonomous robots take many forms—they can walk, swim, drive, fly, or simply lie in wait. Our ability to outsource kill decisions to machines is fraught with a panoply of ethical, moral, legal, technical and security implications. As robots continue to proliferate, we are more likely to suffer the consequences of Moore's law clashing with Murphy's law. Inaccurate data and software glitches may combine with malware and hardware malfunctions to create an inevitable kill zone where it may be the least desired or expected. All drones and robots are hackable, and it is a question of time until virtual terrorists succeed in turning what would otherwise have been a wondrous technological future into one even more fraught with fear, uncertainty, and peril.

13. <u>Biometrics and Artificial Intelligence</u>

If you want a vision into the future, consider the notion that an AI-based hacker could learn to be you. An AI bot could get into your e-mail, calendar, search history, Facebook page, and music service, learn enough about you to mimic you, and autonomously concoct an e-mail or chat conversation with your boss or your mother. Call it identity theft on steroids. It is one thing to steal your credit card numbers but a much deeper psychological blow when an intruder can threaten to destroy your relationships. A persona-stealing hacker might demand ransom *not* to ruin your marriage, or could seek to impersonate someone important to go after a bigger prize. If an AI bot can mimic a person, chances are it can use that to fool someone into giving up the keys to a system. Such prospects make cybersecurity worries about someone shutting down the electric grid or opening a dam by remote control seem quaint by comparison.[326]

<u>Biometrics</u>

We can be forgiven for thinking that our faces, eyes, voice, and fingerprints are unique elements of our biological makeup and anatomy, and that they belong solely to each of us. That used to be the case. *In the 21st century all of us are, wittingly or unwittingly, sharing large volumes of information about our biological makeup—ranging from fingerprints to retinal scans to voice and facial recognition—with companies, governments, and yes, criminals.* Advances in sensor technology and data processing mean that computers can now perform biometric identification, which is fundamentally altering biometrics and opening the door to new ways of gaining access to our most personal of information.

The days of using a driver's license or passport to identify who we are are gradually being replaced by a biometric revolution. Biometric identification systems use sensors to measure such things as the ridges in our fingerprints, the tone of our voices, and the distance between features in our faces.

All such information is translated into computer code, stored, and can be matched against hundreds of millions of other people, in an instant. The biometrics 'business' is expected to exceed $23 billion by 2019, with more than 500 million biometric sensors expected to be in operation by 2018. As we will see, it is literally a *business*, with a lot of money at stake.[327]

India's Leap into the Future

To give you an idea just how big a business, just what is at stake, and some the existing applications of broadly utilized biometrics schemes, consider the case of India. At a government ration shop in India, a middle-aged woman places her thumb on a fingerprint scanner. A list of the staples she and her family are entitled to for the month under a government ration scheme appears on the shopkeeper's computer. She has no cash or credit card, but she will not need one because, by entering an ID number and presenting her thumb once more, she authorizes payment to the shop that is withdrawn directly from her bank account.

In India, 99 percent of adults are now enrolled in Aadhaar, a government-designed scheme that has amassed the fingerprints and iris scans of more than 1.1 billion people since 2010. With an individual's authorization, any private business or government body can determine whether a person's irises or fingerprints match a unique 12-digit ID number in the government database. India is leading the world in this truly transformational digital innovation, and it is putting all adult Indians on an equal playing field when it comes to accessing money and entitlements.

Before 2010, India had no equivalent of Social Security or other nationally recognized scheme of identification. At the time, less than half of all births were registered and only a small minority of people paid income taxes, while many people who were entitled to government services did not receive them, either because they had not been identified as eligible or because corrupt middlemen had stolen their entitlement. The lists of government beneficiaries were filled with fake names. Corruption was rife, and it was difficult, if not impossible, to get an accurate reading of everything from a census to vote counts.

Linking ration cards to Aadhaar numbers tied biometric data to entitlements and gave the government a much better basis on which to plan budgets and count votes. Instead of an estimated 78 percent of entitlement funds ending up in the wrong hands, now nearly 100 percent ends up in the right hands. By removing false claims from the system, the Indian government estimates that it saved more than $8 billion in just over two years, which far outstrips the estimated $1 billion cost of deploying Aadhaar.

As a result, hundreds of thousands of 'ghost children' were removed from the enrollment lists of schools (their parents or others had found a way to receive state funds by false enrollment). More than 800,000 fictitious voters were subsequently identified in Punjab state. And once the system was fully operational, fake driver's licenses became a thing of the past. Such dramatic improvement in 'leakages' in the system prompted the government to want to use Aadhaar to book train tickets or own a mobile phone.

For a country with no overt privacy laws, this was truly revolutionary, but in India's case, it comes with some problems that would not necessarily occur in many other countries. For example, in order to function, electricity and an Internet link is required, yet many places in India continue to lack both.[328] Still, since Aadhaar was launched, India can now count itself among the very top of the global pyramid of developing countries that have a real handle on who their adult population is and how at least some government money is being spent. There are, of course, still numerous forms of 'leakage' in the system, but it is a far cry from what it was just a few years ago.

The other side of that coin is that, for the first time, the government now has the ability to surveille its adult citizens in an up close and personal fashion. It knows how much money its citizen have, what they buy, when they buy it, where they are, where they plan to go, how they plan to get there, and where they may be planning to go in the future. Of course, there remain ways to evade government surveillance in India, just as in any other country—by not using a phone or by driving a car instead of flying or taking a train—but before

Aadhaar came along, most Indian citizens did not need to think much about such things. Now they do.

Fingerprint and Facial Fraud

India is a clear success story in the use of biometric systems and data on a national scale. Biometric identification systems have since become popular in many places and in many ways around the world. Increasingly, fingerprints and facial scans are used to identify travelers at airport passport control, medical centers use biometric scanners to measure the unique vein patterns in the palm of a patient's hand for identification purposes, and retinal scans are used to gain access to a variety of secure locations.

Hollywood would have us believe that such systems are impossible to hack but we know that is simply not true. Not only can biological markers be gathered without your permission, they can be copied, and biometric databases can, and have, been compromised. In 2011, Israel announced that its entire national biometric database had been stolen, including the names, birth dates, Social Security numbers, names of family members, adoption details, immigration dates, and medical records of 9 million Israelis. The information had been stolen by a contractor and sold to cybercriminals, eventually being posted in full in the digital underground.

Biometric sensors have already been built into the latest smartphone. By 2018, it is estimated that 3.4 billion smartphone users will unlock their phones with their fingerprints, irises, faces, and voices. That is a good thing, as it will greatly diminish the ease with which cybercriminals and others are able to access smart devices, but as has already been noted, it does not prevent someone who is determined to access a smart device from being able to do so. *The darker side of the equation is that it is easy to reset a password, but once your fingerprints are stolen you cannot replace them.* We leave them on everything that we touch; once they are stolen, they are outside your control forever. *The identity theft of the future will be all about stealing irreplaceable, unchangeable biometric data.*

As previously noted, Apple introduced Touch ID with its iPhone 5S in 2013. Other smartphone manufacturers have since done the same. Apple subsequently made its technology available to third-party vendors, allowing a finger to be used in lieu of a numerical log-in to a variety of apps and services. That is great for consumer convenience but opens up a whole new area through which cybercriminals can do what they do best. The fact that the price of fingerprint sensors have dropped precipitously in recent years means that all sorts of devices now use them.

Cybercriminals have spent a considerable amount of time and effort to find ways to crack the sensors, ranging from producing online videos to hacking off fingers of expensive car owners (which gangs in Malaysia have been known to do). A security researcher at Yokohama National University even devised a way to take a photograph of a fingerprint (say, from a glass) and recreate it in a molded gelatin, which turned out to be good enough to fool sensors 80 percent of the time. *Hackers have even used something as simple and readily available as Play-Doh to create molds that can fool up to 90 percent of fingerprint scanners.*

When a heated public debate erupted in Germany, in 2008, over whether biometric means of identification should be widely used, a few of those opposed to the idea had some real fun. The country's then-Interior Minister, Wolfgang Schäuble, was a strong advocate of the idea, so these individuals lifted his fingerprints from a water glass left behind at a public speech and reproduced it 4,000 times. The replica prints were then distributed as an insert to a hacker magazine, along with an article that encouraged readers to use the print to impersonate the Minister, which enabled them to plant his fingerprints at crime scenes. Some folks in China have taken the idea of manipulating fingerprints a step further. As of 2016, Japanese police reported that some doctors in China apparently have a thriving business in biometric surgery, because at least 9 Chinese citizens having been caught attempting identity fraud in Japan by surgically replacing their fingerprints to portray themselves as someone else (many more have undoubtedly not been caught).

Just as fingerprint sensors can be hacked, so too can the face-printing systems increasingly being used to unlock your phone or computer or to gain access to your home or office. Facial recognition technologies now can approach 98 percent accuracy. There are even systems that can match your face to your Facebook profile within 60 seconds as you walk down the street, and then determine your Social Security number 60 seconds later. With some publicly available software, all that is required to achieve such feats is to hold up a photograph of the person you wish to impersonate in front of a scanner. This technique has also worked with iris scanning, allowing hackers to reverse engineer the biometric information stored in a secure database and use it to print a photographic iris good enough to fool most commercial eye scanners.

Behavioral Biometrics

Behavioral biometrics (behaviometrics) measures the ways in which our bodies each perform or behave—traits that can be just as revealing as human fingerprints. Our keyboard typing rhythms, voices, gait, walking patterns, brain waves, and heartbeats can be quantified in ways that provide unique signatures that identify us. Just as anatomical biometrics are being used more frequently for security, identification, and access control, voice biometrics are being used by companies and call centers around the world to uniquely "voice print" customers. Do you recall that recording you hear when you phone a company and they put you on hold, telling you that "your call may be recorded for quality and training purposes"? What they fail to also say is that one of the ways some companies are measuring call satisfaction is by the tone and tenor of your voice and the vocabulary you use during your call.

In an apparent effort to fight fraud (although there could be other purposes, such as linking types of caller characteristics with purchasing habits), companies are producing recorded-voice databases of consumers, generating unique voice prints that can be used in future calls to ensure the person on the line matches the original biometric vocal print taken. If the voices do not match, callers are asked additional verification questions in a process that is completely invisible to the

325

general public. One online education platform uses keystroke recognition to ensure the same student "attends" each virtual class before issuing a certificate of completion.

Some software is designed to run on networks in the background to constantly monitor a user's typing rhythms in order to uncover and block attempts at unauthorized access. Other companies have created tools that note how each mobile phone or tablet user holds his or her phone, at what angle, the way he or she types on the virtual keyboard, and even how he or she swipes and grabs the screen, revealing millisecond pauses between various actions. Any variation from an established "cognitive footprint" will raise the alarm at a bank and block access to an account, for example.

Not long ago, Motorola partnered with a firm to extend human capabilities through virtually invisible wearable electronic radio frequency identification tattoos that can be used for password authentication. A health firm has created a pill that is powered by the acid in your stomach to create a unique 18-bit signal in your body to turn your entire person into an "authentication token". DARPA is developing "active authentication" technology that focuses on a user's cognitive processes, personal habits, and patterns for doing things—a combination which is unique for each of us. Soon enough, virtual terrorists will be hacking the Internet of You.[329]

This raises a host of public policy and privacy-related questions, such as, what are the implications of being able to identify a person typing on a keyboard at any location in the world by virtue of the way he or she is simply typing? That may be a good way to catch a criminal, but it is also an easy way to identify and capture a political opponent. Will knowing that this can be done encourage people to deliberately alter the natural way in which they do what they do? Would you speed up or slow down your keystrokes, or perhaps be less accurate as a typist, if you knew someone was watching you? *An omnipresent and multifaceted surveillance state transcends physical reality and subjects us to a virtual reality that goes well beyond our own consciousness of ourselves*.

Face Time

Facial recognition is not a particularly new phenomenon. In fact, it was first developed in the 1960s by some scientists in the US, in conjunction with a certain intelligence agency. It has come a long way since then. Cameras in billboards in Japan silently scan the facial features of passersby, comparing their facial features in real time with a database of more than 10,000 pre-identified patterns to sort individuals into consumer profile categories, then change the advertisement in real time, based on presumed purchasing preferences. A California biometrics firm enables retailers to scan customer faces in their stores to identify known shoplifters. If one is spotted, e-mails and text messages are sent to all employees with a photo of the suspected thief. A similar system is deployed by Hilton Hotels to scan the faces of its guests, enabling employees to greet visitors by name (and, presumably (though left unsaid) also to be able to identify individuals who are known to be trouble makers or problem guests).

Some restaurants and bars place cameras at their entrances to conduct real time facial recognition analytics that are then sent to apps which allow prospective patrons to pull up live statistics on each establishment in order to determine which places are full of people, the gender mix, and the age of the other patrons. If you do not feel like having a drink with a rowdy, younger crowd on a given evening, no problem—these apps will help you determine which night spot will best cater to your desires. Such apps may also be used to reveal others' height, weight, and ethnicity, which raises legal compliance questions in some countries.

Since Facebook acquired Israeli start-up Face.com, in 2012, the company has performed facial recognition on every photograph you have ever uploaded on Facebook (which you unknowingly agreed to allow Facebook to do by consenting to its ToS, which you never read, like 99.99 percent of the other Facebook users failed to do). The acquisition enabled Facebook to greatly enhance its 'tag suggestions' feature, identifying all the people in the photos you post using biometric algorithms and encouraging you to tag your friends, thereby confirming their biometric identities. *Hundreds of billions of photographs have been uploaded on Facebook since it was founded, making it the largest single repository of biometric data on earth—vastly larger than that of any government.*

Edward Snowden alleged that the NSA had tapped into the servers of the 9 largest Internet companies (including Facebook), giving the US intelligence community access to all that biometric data. He also alleged that the NSA 'consumes' millions of photographs posted online daily and is capable of processing at least 50,000 images per day with facial recognition quality. Police in the UK use facial recognition software to match faces from any crime scene against a database of stored images. When combined with police body cameras, smartphone apps capable of performing fingerprint and facial recognition in the field, and the highest concentration of CCTV cameras anywhere in the world, it is safe the say that the future of law enforcement has already arrived in the UK.

Software called "PittPatt", which was developed in the wake of 9/11 by Carnegie Mellon University (along with funding from DARPA) today makes it possible for police forces to use CCTV to monitor throngs of people everywhere in real time and literally identify every face as it appears on the screen. Police can simply zero in on a given person and instantly see their Social Security number, Facebook profile, credit history, photos from their most recent holiday posted online, and whoever he or she might be dating, through their current dating app. It is one thing to be in the hands of law enforcement, ostensibly for 'public safety' purposes, but what possible purpose could the private sector have for acquiring the same data?

It may come as no surprise to learn that, in 2011, Google acquired PittPatt for use across its range of companies and applications. The most immediate application is with Google Glass, which can provide its users with such information as the name (and particulars) of the person you wish to hit up at a party, or that person's name at work you just happen to have forgotten. Mindful of the potential (and obvious) backlash, Google has, at least for now, banned the use of facial recognition in Google Glass apps, but that has not stopped hackers from accessing Glass devices and creating their own facial recognition apps. One such app is NameTag, which allows users to access a variety of social media applications. Such apps are not unique to Google and can be readily used via the camera on your smartphone. Of course, facial recognition software can be and has been hacked, just as has fingerprint software.

Even with a 98 percent accuracy rate, errors in facial recognition can cause a lot of trouble for someone who happens to be misidentified. What if you are one of those unfortunate people placed on a terrorist watch list, who then have inevitable difficulty getting off it and cannot fly? With 50 million passengers traveling through Chicago's O'Hare airport annually, a two percent error rate means that up to 1 million people potentially stand that fate—and that is just at one airport. The problem is compounded by human error or hardware malfunctions. It is not just false identification that is at stake. With the DoD having implemented biometric targeting in its drone fleet, human targets can be positively identified before being bombed. Any false positives in this case end up having life or death consequences.

Consider also the murderer who can use facial recognition software to identify and target his or her victim in advance, or the pedophile who can do the same to identify that kid playing on the swing set in the park. The application for this software for terrorists is stark. No more need to check in with the home office in Raqqa or Mogadishu about whether the targeting information is correct—a phone app can do that for them. Consider the true story of a gang member who attended a graduation ceremony for hundreds of new cadets among the Australian Federal Police, in 2011. He snapped face pictures of all the new graduates to build a facial recognition database so that fellow gangsters would be able to easily identify any officer engaged in an undercover operation against the gangs. What is to stop anyone from doing the same against a corporation or government?[330] The possibilities seem endless.

Hacking Irises

Although a variety of smart device manufacturers will swear that it is impossible to hack iris-driven security software, hackers have, of course, done just that. Researchers from the CCC have shown in a video how to bypass a scanner's protections to unlock a device. Using an easy to make "dummy-eye", a smartphone was fooled into believing that it was seeing the eye of its legitimate owner. Anyone who has a photo of the legitimate owner can unlock the phone without much difficulty, they claim. The folks at the CCC believe _using traditional PIN-protection is actually a safer approach than using body features for authentication. Those smartphone manufacturers who proudly proclaim integration of their iris recognition authentication system with their payment system (such as Apple Pay or Samsung Pay) are actually enabling savvy hackers to access the phone's data and the mobile wallet at the same time._

Iris recognition in general is in the process of breaking into the mass market, with a variety of access control systems being installed at a growing list of places and applications. But the CCC maintains that the security risk to users from iris recognition is even greater than with fingerprints. In some circumstances, a high-resolution picture from the Internet is sufficient to capture an iris as well. The easiest way for a thief to capture iris pictures is with a digital camera in night-shot mode or with the infrared filter removed. In the infrared light spectrum—normally filtered in cameras—the fine, normally hard to distinguish details of the iris of dark eyes are easily identifiable. If all iris structures are visible, the iris picture can be printed on to a laser printer. To emulate the curvature of a real eye's surface, a normal contact lens can be placed on top of the print, which successfully fools the iris recognition system into acting as though the real eye were in front of the camera.[331] A rather low-tech way of cracking what is supposed to be a high-tech security protocol, but effective.

I Think, Therefore Scan my Brain Stem

When in the 17th century French philosopher René Descartes said, "I think, therefore I am," he probably never imagined that in the 21st century such words would prove to be the answer to a security question. In 2009, the Orwellian sounding HUMABIO (Human Monitoring and Authentication using Biodynamic Indicators and Behavioral Analysis) became a well-funded EU research project that sought to combine sensor technology with the latest in biometrics to find reliable and unobtrusive ways to identify people quickly. One of its proposed methods was to scan individuals' brain stems to gain insight into how they think (and, presumably, what kind of behavior they may therefore elicit).

This raises the question of where to draw a line (if a line can even be drawn) between 'intelligence gathering', 'surveillance', and 'security protocols' versus 'mind reading' or purely intrusive activities that cross every conceivable line. What HUMABIO and a variety of other firms that have sprung up since have in 'mind' is to monitor peoples' brains. Scanning a brain and monitoring electrical signals or blood flow is indeed an attempt to read someone's mind. Could such technology be the final frontier in security checks?

If every other form of biometric security can be 'fooled', why not a brain scan? And, just what *are* the chances of defeating a fingerprint, iris, voice, and brain scan simultaneously? That would obviously be rather difficult (but, of course, not impossible). Intelligence agencies, law enforcement, and security companies would presumably use brain scans as part of a multi-tiered security protocol, which is part of what HUMABIO was attempting, and it has run several successful tests of combined biometric security checks. As an example, a freight truck simulator used EEG (brain scan on the scalp) and ECG (heart rhythm) monitoring, face recognition cameras, voice checking microphones and a sensing seat to verify a driver's identity. All three trials were shown to be effective.

In order for some biometric tests to be successful, it is important to understand when they stop working. Voice recognition and iris scans probably will not work on someone who is weeping, and fingerprint scans will not work when fingers are wet. Likewise, most gait measurements require a subject to walk at a steady pace. Understanding such thresholds is critical, for it is certainly possible for multiple layers of scanning to fail at the same time. When that happens, one protocol can take over when another fails to work. When someone is too stressed out or emotional, the results of a brain scan will no doubt become skewed. Similarly, if a person is upset and that is recognized on a facial scan, does it necessarily mean he or she is a terrorist or plans to kill someone? As biometric security checks become more advanced, they will be able to learn more about us in a few seconds than we might otherwise learn about another person over the course of years.[332]

Coming to an Airport Near You

In 2018, Apple and Samsung will reportedly allow passcodes, fingerprints, and retinal scanning to function in unison, as these companies have also come to understand that a multi-layered security system would make it more difficult for hackers to hack.[333] A number of airlines have also started testing (and using) multiple forms of scans to verify the identity of employees and passengers. In 2017, JetBlue Airways and Delta Air Lines tested facial- and fingerprint-recognition technology at two US airports, to replace boarding passes. The JetBlue program matched passenger photos to their passport or visa photos (which raises a potential security gap when fake passports and visas that have been previously approved are presented for verification). Delta may eventually replace boarding passes with fingerprint scans. The testing highlights efforts by carriers to speed customers through congested airports while increasing security. KLM also began using face-scanning technology in 2017 for boarding at Amsterdam's Schiphol Airport, and Delta was experimenting with a self-serve process for checking bags at one airport using facial recognition.

JetBlue passengers were able to participate without enrolling or registering in advance. A custom-designed camera took a photo of passengers and transmitted it to US authorities to compare against databases of passport, visa, and immigration images. A display above the camera notified travelers when they could board—the first such integration of biometric authorization between the USG and an airline. Delta tested a system to enable passengers to also check a bag and board a flight using their fingerprint instead of an identification card and boarding pass. Pre-clearance company Clear also expanded its passenger processing at major US airports with lanes using fingerprints or iris scans to check members' identities, which can be used to eliminate the need for initial identity checks and boarding passes.[334]

Biometrics already plays a significant role in our lives. It adds additional layers of security and provides an extra degree of comfort to those who believe in taking as many precautions as possible to avoid becoming a victim of virtual terrorists. On one hand, we should welcome its development and increasingly widespread use. On the other hand, critics and skeptics would say it is yet another means for governments and corporations to gather and retain the most personal, and most intimate, information about each one of us. Proponents and opponents are both right and both wrong, of course, but what is clear is that biometrics can only grow as a security protocol and fact of modern life. For now, at least, the pluses outweigh the minuses.

Artificial Intelligence

Artificial Intelligence (AI) broadly refers to the study and creation of information systems capable of performing tasks that resemble human problem-solving capabilities, using computer algorithms to do things that would normally require human intelligence—such as speech recognition, visual perception, and decision-making. Computers and software are naturally not self-aware, emotional, or intelligent the way human beings are. They are, rather, tools that carry out functionalities encoded in them, which are inherited from the intelligence of their human programmers.[335]

Algorithms already play increasingly active roles in a growing range of businesses and governments. Computer-aided diagnostics help physicians interpret ultrasound and MRI results, and do the same to identify crime suspects through facial recognition and fingerprint-specific software. AI e-discovery software can sift through millions of pretrial documents and rank them for potential evidentiary value much faster than a human would ever be able to do, and for a fraction of the cost. There is a lot of potential value to be gained by using AI for a seemingly endless array of purposes, but, by the same token, AI's existence and widespread use has also opened the door for virtual terrorists to hack, steal, malign, and sow fear.

What Say You, Mr. Watson?

In 2016, it is estimated that 4.2 billion records were exposed globally in more than 4,000 known security breaches (many more remained unreported). That is a lot of data to keep track of. Before AI became widely used, most businesses, governments, and security firms had the ability to analyze 10 percent of the data at their disposal. IBM has applied AI to security in the form of its Watson "cognitive computing" platform. The company has taught Watson to read through vast quantities of security research, with some 60,000 security-related blog posts published every month and 10,000 reports being produced each year. The company has scores of customers using Watson as part of their security intelligence and analytics platform.

The program becomes smarter with every piece of information it consumes and is able to provide detailed insights on specific threats and how such campaigns evolve. IBM believes that Watson performs 60 times faster than a human investigator and can reduce the time spent on complex analysis of an incident from an hour to less than a minute. While machine learning and AI speed up the laborious process of sorting through data, quantum computing (which makes direct use of quantum-mechanical phenomena such as superposition and entanglement to perform data operations[336]) will eventually be able to look at every data permutation simultaneously. Whereas common digital computing requires that data be encoded into *binary digits* (bits), each of which is always in one of two definite states (zeros or ones), quantum computation uses *quantum bits*, which can be in superposition (sub-atomic level) states.[337] That is a fancy of way of saying that digital computers represent data as ones or zeros, but to a quantum computer, these can be both zeros and ones, or neither at the same time.[338]

Some scientists who work in the AI field believe that *AI robots will be living and working with us within the next decade.* Autonomous animated avatars are already being created, such as "Baby X", a virtual infant that learns through experience and can "feel" emotions. Adult avatars can be plugged into existing platforms like Watson, essentially putting a face on a chatbot. Within a decade, humans may well be interacting with lifelike emotionally responsive AI robots, very similar to the premise of the HBO series "Westworld" and the film *I, Robot*. However, before that becomes a reality robotics will need to catch up to AI technology.[339]

The Rise of Homo Deus

Israeli Historian Yuval Noah Harari has chronicled how Homo sapiens ("wise man") is a temporary creature that will soon to be replaced by Homo deus ("god man"), believing that, within a century or two, Homo sapiens, as we have known ourselves to be for thousands of years, will disappear. That is because we will use technology to upgrade ourselves into something which is far more different from us than we are different from Neanderthals. Breakthroughs in biotechnology, including gene-editing methods such as CRISPR, hint at the power we will soon have to change our genes, our bodies, and perhaps even our brains.

AI may soon allow us to build brain-computer interfaces that will blur the line between man and machine. We are already moving in that direction, as we depend on our smartphones for a staggering number of the decisions we make each day. Harari believes that in 2050 our smartphones will be indistinguishable from us, literally being embedded in our bodies via biometric sensors that will monitor our heart rate, blood pressure, and brain activity 24 hours a day. By constantly analyzing the data generated, our smartphones may come to know our desires, likes, and dislikes even better than we think we do.

Amazon already proclaims to know our taste in books and music better than we do. Harari believes that people are already delegating more responsibility to AI by, for example, merging their smartphones with their social media accounts. He contends that smart devices are intelligent entities that constantly study us, adapt to our unique personality, and actively shape our worldview as well as our innermost desires.[340]

In 2017, the police force in Dubai enrolled its first robotic officer, with plans for robots to account for up to a quarter of the city's police force by 2030. Wearing a police cap and moving on wheels, the robot features a computer touch-screen on its chest that can be used to report a crime or inquire about speeding tickets. The robots are mostly to be deployed at tourist spots, equipped with a camera that transmits live images to the police force's operations center and identifies suspects wanted by police with its facial recognition software.[341] A Silicon Valley-based firm has taken this a step further by having created entirely autonomous vehicles that guide themselves through complex environments. The vehicles are armed with 16 microphones, speakers, a camera, 360-degree video capability, two-way audio, thermal imaging, real-time human interaction, and an interactive link with IBM Watson to provide 24/7 real-time monitoring capabilities.[342]

Since law enforcement and intelligence agencies use AI to ramp up their capabilities, there is no reason to believe the virtual terrorists would not want to do the same thing—and they are. Imagine a world where Watson is hijacked and its cognitive capabilities are used to hack into government computers, engage in murder for hire, or distribute child pornography. It may seem far-fetched, but no more so than in 1987, when the film *RoboCop* envisioned a superhuman cyborg policing the streets of Detroit. Thirty years later, it is nearly a reality.

As Stephen Hawking noted, in 2014, "Whereas the short-term impact of AI depends on who controls it, the long-term impact depends on whether it can be controlled at all". He believes we are on the cusp of the kinds of AI that were previously exclusive to science fiction films. In 2014, Google purchased Deep Mind Technologies (an AI company) and in 2016, it picked up Robotics maker Boston Dynamics. The amount of money that Google and other commercial companies will continue to pour into robotics and AI could create a world in which smart robots could indeed roam our streets, *I, Robot* style.[343]

Smart Bodies and Augmented Realities

Apple created a paradigm shift with the launch of the iPhone in 2007. Ten years later, it is estimated that 44 percent of the world's population owned a smartphone[344]—in 2017, they were as natural a part of our lives as ordinary cell phones

336

were in 2006. We quickly adapt to change. Yet, as rapidly as the technology (and our comfort levels with it) have evolved, in 2027 it may not be hard to imagine that the suite of apps and services that today revolve around the typical smartphone will have migrated to other, even more convenient and capable smart devices, giving us "smart bodies", with devices and sensors residing on our wrists, in our ears, on our faces, and perhaps elsewhere on our bodies.

Apple is diving deep into "augmented reality"—in a self-imposed race against time with the other large social media and Internet companies—to be able to overlay digital images onto a person's view of the world. Interfacing the digital world with our smart homes, smart cars, and even smart cities will constitute a new way to interact with computers. Apple hopes to make the Siri of the future capable of doing nearly everything an iPhone does currently through its touch interface.

Apple and other firms in the digital space are likely to release smart eyeglasses that are almost unnoticeable and have a tiny display in the lenses that is neatly concealed in the frame. They would be easily operated with a few fairly inconspicuous touch gestures, eye movements, or voice commands[345] and could convincingly supplement our visual and auditory reality, delivering information at what is deemed to be an appropriate time and place. Instead of using your phone to get away from the world, you would use it to engage with the world in a much deeper and more meaningful way. We are already catapulting our way toward this brave new augmented reality. A variety of our smart devices (and associated apps) are involved in many of our daily tasks, ranging from our health and home security to our home appliances and banking. Armed with the predictive power of AI, Apple and firms like it seek to become the "default interface" to our lives.

Imagine having our daily lives structured and planned out in advance, with calendars automatically being filled using existing AI scheduling software, directing us from one task to another, and suggesting the fastest form of transportation to get us to the desired destination (ridesharing, mass transit, or a flying car), and booking it for us in advance. Take it a step further; AI may one day recommend the ideal place for you to have your afternoon coffee because it has selected a person who is looking for a new boyfriend or girlfriend, is also having coffee there, and matches what you have stated you are looking for in a mate.

Apple and its competitors will by then have crafted a world of tradeoffs: *If you want your life enhanced by AI you will have to submit to constant surveillance—by your devices and by the tech giants themselves. These companies are betting that hundreds of millions of their customers will happily comply, whether to say they have the latest in technology or simply for the convenience of not having to think about it all. These companies will, of course, swear they will encrypt your data and keep it confidential, but then, these are the same companies whose ToS require you to hand them the keys to your life in the process.*[346]

By creating augmented reality, these companies may also be (wittingly or unwittingly) creating entire societies who cannot think for themselves—just as so many students in today's world cannot read, write, or sign their own names on a piece of paper—because of their overreliance on and fixation with smart devices. *While a future rich with possibility and "vision", a future dominated by augmented reality also portends further erosion of what passes for "privacy" in this era.*

Amnesty International Secretary General Salil Shetty believes checks and balances must be in place, especially because no one truly understands the implications of many of the algorithms that are being written. AI technology is already being used in the US for "predictive policing", which has rights groups calling for enhanced regulation. For example, one concern is that algorithms based on historic trends could reinforce existing biases against people of certain ethnicities. Shetty is particularly concerned about military use of AI in weapons (so-called "killer robots") and other potential applications.[347] There are just so many unknown unknowns with augmented reality that it is difficult to determine where to even begin to examine implications, pass laws, and anticipate future ramifications.

Autonomous Malware

While the debate about AI and augmented reality rages, virtual terrorists are getting smarter and thinking of new ways to benefit from both, creating methods to operate autonomously in this brave new world. Malware is being designed with adaptive, success-based learning to improve the success and efficacy of cyberattacks. *This coming generation of malware will be situation-aware, meaning that it will understand the environment it is in and make calculated decisions about what to do next, behaving like a human attacker: performing reconnaissance, identifying targets, choosing methods of attack, and intelligently evading detection.*

This next generation of malware uses code that is a precursor to AI, replacing traditional "if not this, then that" code logic with more complex decision-making trees. Autonomous malware operates much like branch prediction technology, designed to guess which branch of a decision tree a transaction will take before it is executed. A branch predictor keeps track of whether or not a branch is taken, so when it encounters a conditional action that it has seen before, it makes a prediction so that, over time, the software becomes more efficient.

Autonomous malware is guided by the collection and analysis of 'offensive intelligence', such as types of devices deployed in a network to segment traffic flow, applications being used, transaction details, or time of day transactions occur. The longer a threat can persist inside a host, the more adept it becomes at operating independently, blending into its environment, selecting tools based on the platform it is targeting and, eventually, taking counter-measures based on the security tools in place.

Cross-platform autonomous malware designed to operate on and between a variety of mobile devices is also being developed. Such cross-platform "transformers" include a variety of exploit and payload tools that can operate across different environments. This evolving variant of autonomous malware includes a learning component that gathers offensive intelligence about where it has been deployed (including the platform on which it has been loaded), then selects, assembles, and executes an attack against its target.

Transformer malware is being used to target cross-platform applications with the goal of infecting and spreading across multiple platforms, thereby expanding the threat surface and making detection and resolution more difficult. Once a vulnerable target has been identified, these tools can also cause code failure and then exploit that vulnerability to inject code, collect data, and persist undetected.

Autonomous malware can have a devastating effect on our connected devices and, as a result, our ability to perform daily tasks we usually take for granted. Fighting against it will require highly integrated and intelligent security technologies that can see across platforms, correlate threat intelligence, and automatically synchronize a coordinated response. AI and machine learning will prove invaluable in this role, ultimately enabling IBNS that can automatically translate business requirements and apply them to the entire cybersecurity infrastructure.[348]

AI and Cybersecurity

If machines can be taught to think like humans, they can also be tricked like humans. AI is itself becoming a target, with hackers attempting to exploit machine learning by gradually teaching a security system that unusual behavior is normal (known as "behavioral drift"). AI can also be used by hackers to fake human voices and create video images that could let criminals into a network. There are a host of other ways that virtual terrorists could exploit AI for their nefarious purposes.

In order for the cybersecurity industry to get the most out of AI, it should be able to recognize what machines do best and what people do best. It should also gravitate toward finding the sweet spot between unsupervised and supervised machine learning, so that businesses and governments can fully benefit from their existing knowledge of current threat vectors and combine it with the ability to detect new attacks and uncover new vulnerabilities. Advances in AI can provide new tools for threat hunters, helping them protect new devices and networks even before a threat is classified by a human researcher. Machine learning techniques such as unsupervised learning and continuous retraining can keep us a step ahead of virtual terrorists.[349]

IBM has taught Watson to scour through cybersecurity incident reports written in natural language in a bid to help companies and cybersecurity researchers better detect and ward off breaches. Called Watson for Cybersecurity, the project comes with an app called IBM QRadar Advisor with Watson, which enables cybersecurity professionals to consult Watson's vast cybersecurity knowledge. The app draws information from multiple resources, including cybersecurity blogs, websites, and research papers, considerably shortening the amount of time required to find relevant clues. IBM has also introduced a Watson-powered chatbot that can advise customers of its global X-Force Command Center on cybersecurity issues.

As part of a new research project, code-named Havyn, IBM will attempt to develop a voice-powered security assistant leveraging Watson's conversation technology to respond to verbal commands and natural language requests from security analysts. Havyn will provide real-time information about newly detected threats as well as past incidents, and give guidance about the steps required to restore the security of affected networks. Watson makes concealment efforts more difficult by quickly analyzing multiple streams of data and comparing them with the latest security attack intelligence to provide a more complete picture of the threat. Watson also generates reports on these threats in minutes, which greatly speeds the time between detecting a potential event and a security team's ability to respond.[350]

IBNS provides pervasive visibility across an entire distributed network and enables integrated security solutions to automatically adapt to changing network configurations, shifting business needs with a synchronized response to threats. IBNS is not a product or a market; it is a piece of networking software that helps to plan, design and operate networks to improve their availability and agility. Another way to describe it is the lifecycle management software for networking infrastructure.

The system takes a higher-level business policy as input from end users, converts it to the necessary network configuration, then generates and validates the resulting design and configuration for correctness. The system can configure appropriate network changes across existing network infrastructure and ingest real-time network status for systems under its administrative control. Since it is protocol-agnostic, the system continuously validates (in real time) that the original business intent is being met and can take corrective actions (such as blocking traffic, modifying network capacity or notifying) when the desired intent is not met.[351] IBNS can also dynamically partition network segments, isolate affected devices and remove malware.

AI and machine learning are becoming significant allies in cybersecurity. Machine learning is being bolstered by predictive applications to help safeguard networks. New security measures and countermeasures can also be provisioned or updated automatically as new devices, workloads, and services are deployed or moved from anywhere to anywhere in a network—from endpoints to the cloud. Tightly integrated and automated security enables a comprehensive threat response far greater than the sum of the individual security solutions protecting the network.

One of the biggest challenges of using AI and machine learning lies in the caliber of intelligence. Cyberthreat intelligence is highly prone to false positives due to the volatile nature of the IoT. Threats can change within seconds —a machine can be clean one second, infected the next, and back to clean again. Enhancing the quality of threat intelligence is critically important as IT teams pass more control to AI to do the work that humans otherwise would do. It is ultimately an exercise in trust, balancing operational control. As is the case with any relationship, as it matures, AI and machine learning applications for cybersecurity will become more and more effective.

Since a cybersecurity skills gap persists, products and services must be built with greater automation to correlate threat intelligence to determine the level of risk while automatically synchronizing coordinated responses to threats. In the future, AI in cybersecurity will constantly adapt to the growing attack surface, but for now we are connecting the dots, sharing data and applying that data to systems. Humans make these complex decisions, which require "intelligent" correlation through human intelligence, but in the future, a mature AI system could be capable of making such complex decisions on its own. Total automation is not possible, so humans and machines must find a way to work together to maximize the outcome.[352]

With that in mind, some cities have already begun to deploy AI technologies for public safety and security. By 2030, the typical North American city will rely heavily upon them, including cameras for surveillance, which can also detect anomalies pointing to a possible crime, and predictive policing applications. AI tools may also prove useful in helping police manage crime scenes for search and rescue events by helping commanders prioritize tasks and allocate resources, though these tools are not yet ready for automating such activities. Improvements in machine learning, in general, and transfer learning in particular (to facilitate enhanced learning in new scenarios based on similarities with past scenarios) may facilitate such systems.

The cameras deployed almost everywhere in the world today tend to be more useful for helping solve crimes than preventing them. This is due to the generally low quality of event identification from videos and the lack of manpower to review massive video streams. As AI for this domain improves, it will better assist crime prevention and prosecution through greater accuracy of event classification and efficient automatic processing of video to detect anomalies. These improvements could lead to even more widespread surveillance. The New York Police Department's CompStat was the first tool pointing toward predictive policing, and many police departments now use it.

Machine learning significantly enhances the ability to predict where and when crimes are more likely to happen, and who may commit them. Well-deployed AI prediction tools have the potential to actually remove or reduce human bias, rather than reinforce it, since AI techniques can be used to develop intelligent simulations for training law enforcement personnel. While international criminal organizations and terrorists from different countries are busy colluding, police forces from different countries still face difficulty in joining forces to fight them. The EU, through the Horizon 2020 program, supports such attempts in projects such as LawTrain. The next step will be to move from simulation to actual investigations, by providing tools that support such collaborations.

AI can assist in social network analysis to prevent those at risk from being radicalized by the IS or other violent groups. Law enforcement agencies are increasingly interested in trying to detect plans for disruptive events from social media, and also monitor activity in large gatherings of people to analyze security. Significant work on crowd simulations is being done to determine how crowds can be controlled. The TSA, US Coast Guard, and the many other security agencies that currently rely on AI will likely increase their reliance to enable significant improvements in efficiency.

AI techniques in vision, speech, and gait analysis can aid interviewers, interrogators, and security guards in detecting possible deception and criminal behavior. The TSA currently has an ambitious project to redo airport security nationwide. Called DARMS, the system is designed to improve airport security by relying on personal information to tailor security based on a person's risk categorization, and the flights being taken. The future vision for this project is a tunnel that checks people's security as they walk through it. Developers of this technology need to be careful to avoid building in bias (such as about a person's risk level category) through use of datasets that reflect prior bias.

A recent multi-year study comparing privacy regulation in four European countries and the US yielded counter-intuitive results. Those countries, such as Spain and France, with strict and detailed regulations bred a "compliance mentality" within corporations, which had the effect of discouraging both innovation and robust privacy protections. Rather than taking responsibility for privacy protection internally and developing a professional staff to foster it in business processes, or engaging with privacy advocates or academics outside their walls, these companies viewed privacy as a compliance activity. Their focus was on avoiding fines or punishments, rather than to proactively design technology and adapt practices to protect privacy.

A vigorous and informed debate about how to best steer AI in ways that enrich our lives and society, while encouraging creativity, is an urgent need. Since future AI technologies and their effects cannot be foreseen with perfect clarity, policies will need to be continually re-evaluated in the context of observed societal challenges and evidence from deployed systems. Recent advances are largely due to the growth and analysis of large data sets enabled by the Internet, advances in sensory technologies, and applications of deep learning. While encouraging innovation, policies and processes should address ethical, privacy, and security implications, and should be made to ensure that the benefits of AI technologies will be spread broadly and fairly.[353]

The Future of AI and Cybersecurity

Many cybersecurity pundits have lost faith in traditional malware and antivirus software tools because they are only stopping an estimated 15 to 20 percent of malicious code. AI and cognitive computing offer a distinct advantage for protecting valuable data, since *AI gathers intelligence through learning as it anticipates the next attack on security, allowing for immediate and effective threat responses.* Given that AI can be used for good or evil purposes, embedding controls on the use of this technology may be effective for a time, but they will eventually be penetrated. The insight and prediction capabilities provided by AI will change the current landscape of threats and begin to level the playing field.

Cyberspace is the ultimate 3D chessboard, with layers upon layers of moves and vulnerabilities, creating exponential threats that traditional thinking is simply not equipped to handle. Albert Einstein famously said, "We cannot solve our problems with the same level of thinking that created them".[354] The use of AI allows us to take our thinking on cybersecurity to that next level and identify more advanced problems. Cognitive technology gives us new insights into current and future threats, allowing greater speed and precision in our response.

One of the biggest challenges is asking the right questions of the data. We collect so much, so fast, that soon we are overwhelmed. Inside that massive amount of data are the answers—the needles in the haystack. *Tomorrow's approach to asking the right questions will no longer be about making the haystack smaller to find that needle but rather about using AI and cognitive computing as bigger magnets to increase our chances of finding it.*[355]

Along with the positive transformational changes that await us in the biometric, AI, and autonomous reality universe lurks the dark vision that Virtual Terrorism plans to cast upon it. If we are successful in staying a step ahead of the virtual terrorists in the decades to come, that new universe may prove to be utopian. If we fail to stay a step ahead, it is sure to turn into a dystopian nightmare.

14. <u>Space</u>

In 2014, students at Technion-Israel Institute of Technology hacked in to the Waze GPS system and registered thousands of fake Waze users using an automated scripting program they had written, designed to impersonate smartphones. The students then connected those virtual (and fake) smartphone users to another application that reported falsified GPS coordinates to the Waze system, making all Waze users at the time seem as if they were legitimately moving about the city. The sock puppets then intentionally submitted thousands of reports to Waze about being stuck in traffic at false coordinates. Waze ended up doing exactly what it was supposed to do, and rerouted thousands of legitimate Waze users away from a traffic jam that did not exist, causing tremendous gridlock[356] and illustrating just how simple it is to cause havoc with GPS systems.

As is the case with other forms of Virtual Terrorism, those seeking to do harm to space-based systems come in a variety of shapes and sizes, ranging from states seeking to establish military supremacy, to cybercriminals hoping for financial gain, to terrorist groups hacking into satellites, and drones to individuals just having a bit of fun. They are using an array of increasingly sophisticated tools and behaviors to get what they seek, from jamming and spoofing to outright theft of data. Not long ago, space was the domain of governments and militaries; today, it is the domain of anyone with the skill to hack.

On one hand, space represents the final frontier for virtual terrorists—it is the final pathway to get to the cyber finish line, depending on what one's objectives may be. The increasing number of individual satellites and satellite constellations provide a greater number of entry points and represent a world of unforeseen opportunity, which is a great source of temptation for virtual terrorists. There is greater connectedness through and between communication pathways among satellites in orbit, which offer autonomous communication routes to billions of devices. One of the negative byproducts of that is a reduction in national security and defense capabilities on the part of governments and militaries, with diminished powers of observation and navigation, and lower degrees of confidence about security and reliability over satellites and satellite-based tasks.

Since many of the technologies that enable cyberattack capabilities in space are within the grasp of most states (no matter how small or poor) as well as non-state actors, in one sense, space levels the strategic playing field and creates hitherto unparalleled opportunities for small, belligerent governments or terrorist groups to instigate high impact attacks in space. As an example, in October 2014, a cyberattack on the US weather satellites system demonstrated the cyber vulnerabilities of strategic space-based assets. While military satellites are generally well protected against such attacks (depending on their age, orbit, and access), this is often not the case for most commercial satellites, even with dual use capabilities for either commercial or military purposes.

Given what satellites are and where they operate, they exhibit vulnerabilities that either have much in common with land-based targets or are unique. Such vulnerabilities include ground stations, solar panels, electronic transmissions, as well as commands that can instruct satellites to collide with one another, modify the trajectory of missiles, or instruct either to self-destruct. *Any satellite that can change orbit can be considered a space weapon. Since many of the possible cyber scenarios in space have yet to occur, cybersecurity experts, military commanders, and policy makers do not fully understand the range of potential consequences that could result.*[357] Space is both the final frontier (to borrow a phrase from *Star Trek*) and the great unknown. *It is the unknowns associated with the cyberwarfare in space that pose the greatest threat from the perspective of governments and militaries.*

Cyber Era Battleship Diplomacy

In a 2017 radio interview, Dr. Peter Vincent Pry, executive director of the Task Force on National and Homeland Security and the chief of staff of the Congressional EMP Commission, revealed that two North Korean satellites were orbiting the US at trajectories that are optimized for a surprise EMP attack. He was referring to the KMS 3-2 and KMS-4 earth observation satellites launched by North Korea in April 2012 and February 2016, respectively. Pry warned that _the purpose of the satellites was to position North Korea to be able to play a cyberage version of battleship diplomacy—with one of the two satellites always being close to being in orbit directly over the US at any point in time, if a bilateral crisis erupts, Kim Jong-Un can threaten the US by taking a page from the Soviet era plan to attack the US with an EMP as part of a larger surprise assault aimed at crippling the US military._

As previously discussed, during the Cold War the Russians had a plan to conduct a surprise EMP attack against the US by disguising a warhead as a satellite. Their thinking was that a satellite's trajectory is different from that of an intercontinental ballistic missile (ICBM) trajectory that is aimed at a city. An ICBM launch is usually based on a lower energy, 45-degree angle that follows a classic ballistic trajectory. A rocket fired for purposes of a satellite launch has a different trajectory and military personnel who monitor such events usually assume it is for peaceful purposes. The Soviets' idea was to put a nuclear weapon on a satellite, launch it on a satellite trajectory toward the south (so it would be flying away from the US), send it in orbit over the South Pole, and come up on the other side of the earth so that it approached the US from the south.

During the Cold War—and still today—the US does not have ballistic missile early radar systems looking south. Given that all of the world's nuclear powers are in the northern hemisphere, the US military did not believe it was necessary to have national missile defenses directed toward the southern hemisphere. According to Pry, the Soviets were primarily interested in paralyzing America's strategic forces, strategic command, and control and communications so that its military command could not communicate with its forces. In doing so, the hope was that they would then have sufficient time to launch a mass attack across the North Pole to blow up US ICBMs. In essence, kill them once with the EMP, then blast US bases by using their long-range missiles.

349

By contrast, North Korea does not have enough missiles with sufficient sophistication to blow up US missiles or bomber bases, so it presumably seeks to implement just the initial EMP part of the original Soviet plan. As noted earlier, doing so could severely disrupt America's electricity grid, telecommunications, transportation network, and other forms of critical infrastructure. *Although the global media is fond of highlighting North Korea's many missile launch failures—at least some of which are no doubt due to US cyberattacks—when viewed through the lens of potential preparations for an EMP attack, its launches should actually be viewed as successes.* After all, two of its satellites circle the earth and, in spite of its many launch failures, the country continues to make significant progress in its missile programs.

False reassurance has been given to the world that North Korea has not "demonstrated" that it can miniaturize a nuclear warhead small enough for missile delivery or build a reentry vehicle for an ICBM capable of penetrating the atmosphere to blast a US city. Yet *any nation that has built nuclear weapons and long-range missiles, as North Korea has done, can easily overcome the comparatively simpler technological challenge of warhead miniaturization and reentry vehicle design.* Kim Jong-Un has been photographed posing with what appears to be a genuine miniaturized nuclear warhead for ballistic missiles. North Korea has two classes of ICBMs—the road mobile KN-08 and the KN-14—*both of which appear to be equipped with sophisticated reentry vehicles.*

In 2011, the Director of the Defense Intelligence Agency (DIA) testified before the US Senate Armed Services Committee that North Korea had weaponized its nuclear devices into warheads for arming ballistic missiles. In 2015, the Commander of North American Aerospace Defense (NORAD) warned that *the intelligence community had assessed that the KN-08 mobile ICBM could strike the US with a nuclear warhead*. Also in 2015, former senior national security officials of the Reagan and Clinton administrations warned that *North Korea should be regarded as capable of delivering a small nuclear warhead, by satellite, specially designed to make a high-altitude EMP attack against the US*. According to the Congressional EMP Commission, *a single warhead delivered by a North Korean satellite could blackout the national electric grid and other life-sustaining critical infrastructures for more than a year, threatening mass starvation and potential societal collapse. The two North Korean satellites that orbit over the US are on trajectories consistent with surprise EMP attack.*[358]

On April 30, 2017, South Korean officials told local media that North Korea's test of a medium-range missile the day before was not a failure, as widely reported in the world press, because it was deliberately detonated at an altitude of 72 kilometers—*the optimum burst height for a 10-kiloton warhead for the purpose of making an EMP explosion. The missile was fired on a lofted trajectory, to maximize, not its range, but to reach a high-altitude as quickly as possible, where it was successfully fused and detonated—testing everything except an actual nuclear warhead.*[359] If you do the math on that, it makes a lot of sense and may explain why neither the US, South Korea nor China have taken military action against North Korea, despite its numerous nuclear tests and provocations.

When outgoing US president Obama told incoming president Trump that North Korea would be his most serious foreign policy challenge, this must have been at least part of what he meant. This serious threat should spur current and successive US administrations to launch a program to move swiftly to harden defenses against EMP attack (if that is possible). Apart from enhancing missile defenses, the US should consider reviving the Strategic Defense Initiative (SDI), originally recommended under President Reagan, to address such threats. Space-based missile defenses could still render nuclear missiles and EMP-threatening satellites obsolete, and the technology available to accomplish that is much better today than it was in the 1980s, when SDI was first publicly debated.

The Outer Space Weapons Race

Satellites will play a crucial role in any satellite-enabled country's ability to mount a robust offense or defense in the wars of the future, so satellite-enabled countries are naturally making their opponents' satellites a primary target. For that reason, the entire network of US military and intelligence satellites is in the process of being controlled through a single command center, jointly operated by the DoD and the broader intelligence community. The new center will help defend these satellites from attack by ensuring that all US military and intelligence satellites are visible and controllable. If an adversary tries to deny the USG access to its satellites, the government wants to be able to respond in an integrated and coordinated manner.

Space and cyberspace were named as the primary focus for fighting future wars by the Chinese PLA in its guiding military strategy announced in 2016. China's real goal is apparently to gain control of the Earth–Moon system, a concept that has also been around since the Cold War between the US and Soviet Union. While the US decided in the 1960s and 1970s that long-term survival on the Moon was technologically impossible, the Chinese have committed themselves to that goal, but its ambitions for space missions are not just about science; *China is developing assets for its space programs that will enable it to military control parts of space.*

China sees space warfare as its best chance to directly compete with the US militarily, since it has no blue water navy, nor anywhere near the assets and firepower capability that the US military has. Rather than trying to match the US Navy and Air Force, China believes it could gain an advantage through production of specialized missiles, spacecraft, and platforms to send to the moon. *Many Chinese military analysts see space warfare as inevitable, and argue that since it will become the center of gravity in future wars it must be seized and controlled so as to achieve space supremacy.*

As part of a push to develop weapons meant to cripple the core strengths of the US military, in 2007, China destroyed one of its own weather satellites using a SC-19 anti-satellite (ASAT) missile. In 2013, the country claimed it had launched a "sounding" (research) rocket, but it was later revealed to have been China's Dong Ning-2 ASAT missile, and in 2014, Beijing did the same, portraying it at the time as an "anti-intercept test". *China's subsequent ASAT tests have used targets at lower altitudes. The US is particularly vulnerable to such weapons because of its reliance on systems that use low-earth orbit, which is a primary reason why NASA is forbidden from cooperating with China in space. China is developing a larger missile defense system that some analysts expect to be deployed by the early 2020s.*[360]

Chinese scientists have also achieved success in their development of a high-power microwave (HPM) weapon, a form of directed energy weapon that combines "soft kill" (electronic countermeasures that alter the electromagnetic, acoustic or other signature of a target, thereby changing the tracking and sensing behavior of an incoming threat) and "hard kill" (measures that physically counterattack an incoming threat, thereby altering or destroying its payload in such a way that the intended effect on the target is severely impeded[361]) capabilities through the disruption or even destruction of enemy electronics systems. HPM is a type of weapon that possesses unique advantages in speed, range, accuracy, flexibility, and reusability. The PLA's future HPM weapons could have multiple defensive and offensive functions that would enhance its combat capabilities. HPM systems are able to destroy electronic equipment, and in an age when most combat systems rely on electronics, such weapons could change the way wars are fought.

The PLA's breakthrough in HPM weapons reflects a track record of consistent progress over the course of decades. Until the past several years, the decades-long research on HPM weapons had, apparently, reached a dead end, until the US Air Force Research Laboratory successfully developed its Counter-electronics High-Powered Microwave Advanced Missile Project, which could target an enemy's electronics from an aircraft or missile. While the full extent of current US program is, of course, classified, the PLA's reported advance in the development of HPM weapons appears to indicate that Chinese capabilities have the potential to keep pace with those of the US in disruptive military and space technology.

The eventual fielding of the PLA's HPM weapons will serve as a critical force multiplier for its war-fighting capabilities. In the near term, deployment of this weapon could be as a ship-borne anti-missile system (or a way to reinforce China's air defense systems). Such a weapon system has the potential to undermine the efficacy of even the most advanced US missiles, such as the Long Range Anti-Ship Missile under development. Used on its own, and especially if it were used in conjunction with Chinese ASAT weapons (or incorporated with missiles to overcome enemy air defenses), HPM weapons can likely degrade and/or damage the electronics of an incoming missile by interfering with data links, GPS receivers, and other guidance mechanisms.[362]

This shift toward the areas of cyberwarfare, electronic warfare, and space warfare using autonomous weapons was formally introduced through the Chinese military's Strategic Support Force (SSF) branch in 2015. The SSF brings the military's new weapons under one roof and demonstrates a bold move toward the weaponization of outer space and broad information capabilities. During the Cold War, the US, UK, and Soviet Union signed the Outer Space Treaty (in 1967), which was either ratified by or acceded to by 105 countries (including China). It set in place laws regarding the use of outer space and banned any nation from stationing nuclear warheads, chemical or biological weapons in space. However, *the Treaty does not prohibit the placement of conventional weapons in orbit, so such weapons as kinetic bombardment (i.e. attacking Earth with a projectile) are not strictly prohibited.*[363]

In addition to HPW, China's military is developing powerful lasers and electromagnetic railguns for use in a future war involving space-based attacks on satellites. Laser attack systems have significant advantages over more conventional weapons—including those with fast response speed, robust counter-interference performance and high target destruction rates—especially for space-based ASAT systems. An ASAT attack in space would employ ground-based radar to identify a target satellite, a special camera to provide precision targeting, and a deployable membrane telescope that would focus the laser beam on the target satellite. Chinese researchers have proposed building a 5-ton chemical laser that will be stationed in low-earth orbit as a combat platform capable of destroying satellites in orbit. Given the amount of funding devoted to that objective by the Chinese military, the satellite-killing laser could be deployed as soon as *2023*.

Beijing clearly wants the world to believe that it can rapidly militarize space. Developing dedicated space combat systems is in line with China's long-term goal of achieving global strategic ascendency. China's space program is dual-use, supporting both civilian and military needs. For example, China's Shenzhou and Tiangong manned spacecraft were used to perform military missions; its coming space station and plans for a future base on the moon also will have military applications. The combat space station could attack key US satellites, preventing the US from communicating with its military forces and interfering with its ability to conduct surveillance, blinding the US military in the event of war.

In 2015, the PLA published the book *Light War*, which assigned a central role to fighting future wars using lasers. The book argues that *future warfare will be dominated by combining Big Data analytics using cyber warriors armed with AI, robot lasers, and directed energy weapons.* The Chinese effort could neutralize decades of investment by the US in its own directed-energy weapons, which are also expected to be deployed in the early 2020s (high-powered compact laser guns are slated for deployment in the 2030s). China's disclosures about the coming "weaponization of space" should greatly concern US and allied defense planners. *The US may soon have no choice but to change its long-held policy of not deploying arms in space.*[364]

Russia appears to be making a similar move with the creation, in 2015, of a new branch of the Russian armed forces—the Aerospace Forces—which brought its air force and Aerospace Defense Forces under a unified command. The focus of the Russian joint command center is somewhat different from the US, however. In addition to space forces, it will also oversee the Russian air force and its anti-missile defenses so as to defend Russian airspace from airborne and space-borne attacks. The Russian government said at the time that a key reason for proceeding with the Aerospace Forces was that Russia, the US, and China were all working on ASAT weaponry that could bring war into space, prompting the imperative of new defensive strategies.[365]

Quantum Entanglement, Anyone?

355

To control this bold new world of space warfare, the Chinese government seeks to build an entirely new kind of Internet that is completely secure and impervious to hackers. In 2017, Chinese scientists set a new distance record for beaming a pair of entangled particles—photons of light that behave like twins and experience the exact same things simultaneously, even though they are separated by great distances. The principle is called quantum entanglement, which is one of the subatomic world's strangest phenomena. China smashed quantum entanglement's previous distance record. In a groundbreaking experiment, a laser on a satellite orbiting 480 kilometers above the earth produced entangled photons that were transmitted to two different ground-based stations 1200 kilometers apart, without breaking the link between the photons. That distance was 10 times greater than the previous record for entanglement and was the first time that entangled photons had been generated in space.[366]

By launching a group of quantum-enabled satellites, China hopes to create a super-secure network that uses an encryption technique based on the principles of a field known as quantum communication. While traditional forms of encryption rely on mathematical functions that are very difficult to be reversed, scientists have demonstrated a far better way to transmit secret data, by demonstrating encryption techniques that rely on the law of physics rather than mathematical complexity (called quantum key distribution). Without getting too technical, for the process to work, laser beams send "quantum information" held in a "quantum system" to receivers, which work together to find a protocol to secure the communication.

In a 2016 experiment, a 600-kilogram Chinese satellite was launched and a crystal at the center of the spacecraft produced pairs of entangled photons which were used like a laser beam imbued with information. Once in orbit, the satellite sent its partners entangled photons to bases on the ground in Beijing and Vienna (Austria being a partner in the launch) to create a secret key used to access the information carried in the transmission. *The reason it cannot be hacked is because the information carried in the quantum state of a particle cannot be measured or cloned without destroying the information itself.* While, as of 2016, it could be proven that quantum encryption works in a city-sized radius (or at most between two nearby cities), China believes the atmosphere in space will allow the photons to travel further without disruption because in space there is nothing to attenuate light.

Quantum technology is a major focus of China's five-year economic development plan. While other space agencies have been experimenting with similar technology, none has seen the level of financial support being provided by Beijing. Although China has not disclosed how much money it has spent on quantum research, its funding for basic research, which includes quantum physics, was US$101 billion in 2015; by contrast, in 2005, it spent less than US$2 billion on quantum research. Scientists in the US, Canada, Europe, and Japan are also rushing to exploit the power of particle physics to create truly clandestine communication, but China's launch puts them far ahead of their global counterparts.[367] *As evidence that the Chinese government is peering far into the future, it plans to create an entire system of quantum-enabled, satellite-based communication that relies on entanglement.*

<u>Hacking Satellites</u>

Many of the world's existing satellites are decades old, intended to function for perhaps a few years, but many of them failed to fail. That is great from a data collection perspective but, because their computer systems are also decades old, they make tempting targets for cyberattacks. Space agencies all over the world are naturally trying to protect their satellites and their operations, more generally, against cyberattack, which is no easy task. The c

bpol	default	

ybersecurity effort at NASA ranges from maintaining e-mail systems at the Agency's Washington, DC headquarters to guarding US networks in Russia, where Americans work in tandem with Russian crews together at the International Space Station (ISS). The Agency also must protect enormous amounts of in-house scientific data and the control systems at its 20 research centers, laboratories, and other facilities in the US.

Among NASA's cyber concerns are hackers wanting to breach communications between its ground-based operations and one of its 65 spacecraft transmitting research data. Its nightmare is a direct cyberattack on its satellites. In 2016, NASA reported 1,484 "cyber incidents", including hundreds of attacks executed from websites or web-based applications, as well as the loss or theft of computing devices. Its cybersecurity teams are working to "harden" old ICSs, such as those used to launch spacecraft.[368] In an era of budget cuts, and where an increasing number of questions are routinely raised about the perceived 'value' of space exploration, NASA has its hands full trying to maintain its raison d'être as well as its cybersecurity.

All satellite operators have special cybersecurity-related challenges. For satellite Internet providers, whose satellites cover a wider geographical area than standard ISPs (often extending more than 1,000 miles), and whose services often span multiple countries and continents, tracking the location of a computer using a satellite IP address can be somewhat difficult. By using satellite links, it is nearly impossible for hackers to be discovered. To hack a satellite, all that is technically required is a satellite dish, some cable, and a satellite modem (which costs about $1,000).

One of the most widespread and least expensive types of satellite connectivity is downstream-only, which people will sometimes use for faster downloads, since satellite connections tend to provide larger bandwidth than some other types of Internet connection. Traffic coming out of a user's computer will go through a dial-up or other form of connection, while traffic coming in goes through the satellite connection. Since such satellite communication is not encrypted, hackers can point an antenna at the traffic to intercept the data or determine the IP address of a legitimate satellite user in order to hijack it.

Such vulnerabilities in the satellite system were made public at a security conference in 2009 but the hackers appear to have been using the vulnerabilities to hijack satellite connections since at least 2007. Kaspersky researchers found a sample of their malware that appears to have been compiled that year. The malware sample contained two hardcoded IP addresses for communicating with a command server, one of which was an address that belonged to a German satellite Internet provider.

To use a hijacked satellite connection for exfiltrating data, the attacker first infects a targeted computer with malware that contains a hardcoded domain name for his or her command server. Instead of the domain name using a static IP address, the hackers use what is known as Dynamic DNS hosting, which allows them to change the IP address for a domain at will. The attacker then uses an antenna to pick up satellite traffic in a region and collects a list of IP addresses belonging to legitimate satellite users. The attacker can then configure the domain name for the command server to use one of the satellite IP addresses. The malware on infected computers will then contact the legitimate satellite Internet user's IP address to initiate a transmission control protocol/IP connection but that user's machine will drop the connection since the communication is not intended for it. The same request will also go to the attacker's command-and-control computer, however, which will be using the same IP address and will reply to the infected machine and establish a communication channel to receive data siphoned from that machine.

Any data that gets siphoned from the infected machine will also go to the innocent user's system but that system will simply drop it. The legitimate satellite user will not notice that his satellite connection has been hijacked unless he checks the log files and notices that packets are being dropped by his satellite modem. The user will see some requests that he did not ask for but it will just look like Internet noise rather than suspicious traffic. The method is not reliable for long-term exfiltration of data, since these satellite Internet connections are one-way and can be very unreliable. The attacker will also lose the satellite connection once the innocent user whose IP address that has been hijacked goes offline. That is why hackers only tend to use it on the most high-profile targets, when anonymity is essential.

Kaspersky researchers have seen hackers communicating through satellite connections around the world, but most of their activity was concentrated in the Middle East and Africa, in countries such as the Congo, Lebanon, Nigeria, Somalia, and the United Arab Emirates. It was not the first time the researchers had seen groups using satellite connections for command servers. Hackers have used so many different satellite IP addresses that it is clear they have been hijacking them from legitimate users. If adopted by criminal gangs in the future, such techniques will make it harder for researchers, law enforcement agencies, and governments to track command servers and shut them down.[369]

Fun with GPS

The Global Positioning System is a space-based, low orbit constellation of 24 navigational satellites that provides location information anywhere on Earth. It is an 'invisible utility' that we rely on for a broad range of things, including getting from point A to point B in our cars, delivering packages, managing public safety, air traffic control, and missile guidance. GPS is a superb technological innovation but the signals most of us receive to achieve GPS guidance are very weak, somewhat akin to viewing a car headlight from thousands of miles away. As a result of limited power supplies on satellites, the signals cannot be any stronger than they already are and can easily be overpowered by broadcasting noise on the same frequency.

It used to be the case that only militaries had the technological capability to disrupt GPS signals. Governments and militaries still that do that, with great regularity, of course, but as previously noted, individuals with no particular technological prowess also have the ability to disrupt GPS signals at airports and towns at will. Though illegal in the US, GPS jammers are widely available online, inexpensive, and easy to use. Collateral damage is becoming an increasing problem, with anyone in the vicinity of several hundred feet of a jammer being impacted when they are operational. It is not just cars or trucks that pass someone on the road who may be jamming signals but many others who can and do interrupt critical business and government operations. As an example, a London truck driver making deliveries while jamming GPS signals (so that his company would not know where he was at any given point in time) ended up severely disrupting stock trades at one of the locations where he was making a delivery.

Spoofing occurs when someone (or a computer program) masquerades as someone else by falsifying data—this has become a big problem with GPS. Given how weak GPS signals are, spoofers can relatively easily fool navigational devices, overpowering a legitimate signal with a stronger, counterfeit signal. Once done, virtual terrorists can take control of any GPS receiver and connect it to a low-cost simulator capable of recreating any route desired on a Google Earth map, for example. Emitting phony signals can send an oil tanker careening into a bridge or direct an army convoy into enemy territory.

In 2014, students at Technion-Israel Institute of Technology hacked in to the Waze GPS system and registered thousands of fake Waze users using an automated scripting program they had written, designed to impersonate smartphones. The students then connected those virtual (and fake) smartphone users to another application that reported falsified GPS coordinates to the Waze system, making all Waze users at the time seem as if they were legitimately moving about the city. The sock puppets then intentionally submitted thousands of reports to Waze about being stuck in traffic at false coordinates. Waze ended up doing exactly what it was supposed to do, and rerouted thousands of legitimate Waze users away from a traffic jam that did not exist, causing tremendous gridlock and illustrating just how simple it is to cause havoc with GPS systems.

Consider the implications of such capability for cyberterrorists and cybercriminals in outer space. In 2008, the Lashkar-e-Taiba terrorist group used satellite technology to produce imagery and conduct communications during its attacks in Mumbai, and Shia insurgents in Iraq have manipulated cheap Russian software intended to steal satellite TV signals to hack the drone video feeds from US satellites. Hackers in Brazil have used high-performance antennas to turn US Navy satellites into their own personal citizens band radios, to send coded messages to organized crime groups.

Spacecraft have also already been hacked. Also in 2008, a Russian cosmonaut brought an infected laptop to the ISS and spread the W32.Gammima.AG virus to ISS operational computer systems as well as several Windows XP laptops on board. Another cosmonaut accidentally infected the ISS another time, with the Stuxnet virus, by plugging a USB stick into the space station's computer network. These incidents were accidental. Imagine what could happen if someone were to deliberately sabotage the ISS or satellites before they are launched.[370]

A Common Framework for Cybersecurity in Space

It is apparent that outer space is evolving as an important frontier in cyberwarfare but very few rules govern best practices or international law in space. A current and widely accepted framework for governing space is sorely needed. The first step toward creating a common framework for cybersecurity in space requires agreement on a set of principles by which strategy can be guided and risk assessed. An 'actor-neutral' approach can help ensure that energy and resources are applied promptly and efficiently, and where they can be of most benefit in responses to the threats.

Space technology has created a global common good: the barriers to entry are low and inexpensive access to space capability has begun to take hold in global markets. Since cyber vulnerabilities cannot be eliminated, they must to be managed. A risk-management-based approach to cybersecurity in space would assess cybersecurity on the basis of cost-effectiveness and proportionality, with potential benefits being weighed against appropriate costs and penalties, including insurance premiums and future expenses, so that procurement systems can be put in place. Risk agility is a critical ingredient so that, as cybersecurity threats change, priorities can be recast. If ever there was a case to be made for global risk agility, it is in space.

Cybersecurity policy in space clearly needs to extend beyond its current state of affairs, which is riddled with gaps, inconsistencies, and vulnerabilities. A natural point of departure would be alignment with ongoing or future efforts designed to strengthen critical national infrastructure. That implies a meaningful exercise in long-term planning and budgeting. A bottom-up, reactive approach to this subject will not work. That approach has been tried over the past two decades and has been shown to fail, one attempt after another. A space cyber regime should reach beyond a tick-the-box legislative mentality that provides false comfort while not really addressing the problem and allowing adversaries to get further and further ahead.

Cybersecurity policy for space should be based on an agreed set of operational and strategic principles, with the following objectives:

- To turn the intersection of space and cyberspace from a permissive, ungoverned environment into a self-governing network;

- To encourage a comprehensive and inclusive understanding of cybersecurity across the user community;

- To facilitate and assure legitimate use of the information, communications, and technology infrastructure supported by space technologies; and

- To raise the costs of use by illicit actors.

In 2006, the then-US National Security, Space Management and Organization conducted a comprehensive survey of approaches used by commercial operators and integrators to protect satellite communication networks against electronic, physical and cyberattacks. The survey identified a set of seven 'best practices' for information sharing and analysis, as well as responses to intentional jamming, physical attacks, cyber/network threats, and other hazards. Enhancement of these proposals by the UK Space Agency and others increased the number of best practice categories, which could form the basis of the proposed space cyber regime.

Among the best practices under consideration were raising awareness, encouraging vigilance, identifying dependencies, recognizing vulnerabilities, building in resilience and measured responses, future-proofing hardware and software, creating procurement strategies, identifying regulatory requirements, and sharing experience. If this sounds mostly like common sense, it is, but such an approach is much more complex than meets the eye and will require decades of work to get it done right.

An over-reliance on technical fixes is why cybersecurity controls failed to make an effective impact on cyberthreats in the late 1990s and early 2000s. Highly regulated institutional responses such as government-led approaches are likely to lack the agility and flexibility required for these cybersecurity capabilities. Developing institutionalized organizational standards, particularly with regard to collaboration, knowledge exchange, and innovation are more likely to encourage the type of risk agility, creativity and speed of response required to tackle cybersecurity in space head on. An international multi-stakeholder space cybersecurity regime based on an international community of the willing, and including shared risk assessments and threat responses, is likely to provide the best opportunity for developing a sectoral response to match the range of threats.

By developing an international multi-stakeholder cybersecurity regime, the space industry could play an increasingly influential role in developing international standards and establishing a strong sustainable knowledge base in the cybersecurity domain. The group, which could grow over time to include any state concerned with space cyber risks, would identify actions that can develop the skills, knowledge, and collaborative mechanisms needed to catalyze greater resilience in the international space infrastructure.

In 2016, Chatham House produced a comprehensive study[371] of space and cybersecurity with explicit recommendations for what needs to happen in order to create a framework to achieve cybersecurity in space. The study is worthy of the topic, as are its recommendations. The question is whether governments, militaries, businesses, and individuals have the incentive and fortitude to implement them:

Raising Awareness

- Ascertain the minimum levels of knowledge required to develop an instinct for cybersecurity throughout the supply chain.

- Identify communications platforms that can be used to develop a common collaborative environment.

- Decide on communications platforms and paths, languages, lexicon and right of access.

- Agree on whether the authority should be regional or international, and how the authority should function.

- Develop an educational infrastructure that can spread throughout the internationalized supply chain into the user communities and adjacent sectors.

- Delineate what governments can do to help, such as providing threat briefings on a trust basis.

- Establish ways to maintain concepts of trust and operational security in a very broad and potentially large community.

- Agree on the qualifications needed to join a community of interest, and how to ensure that all members of the community add value.

- Establish a virtual knowledge platform with agreed security levels and operational redundancy.

Encouraging Vigilance

- Ascertain specific needs in terms of identifying symptoms of an attack or preceding reconnaissance.

- Provide threat briefings to explain what vigilance is needed.

- Train experts in how to notice unusual activity, how to verify suspicions and alert the community identifying and mapping dependencies.

Identifying and Mapping Dependencies

- Establish procedures for identifying dependencies within relevant timescales.

- Assess dependencies for criticality and lack of redundancy.

- Identify ecosystem connections that are driven by commercial considerations and configured for agility.

- Develop a sustainable, near-real-time, cloud-based system for mapping space information and communication technology configurations.

Recognizing Vulnerabilities

- Develop and maintain a risk matrix by matching vulnerabilities to threats, paying attention to the alignment of commercial and national infrastructure vulnerabilities and regularly updating the matrix.

- Identify which vulnerabilities will not be commercially compelling to resolve and ensure that regulators are aware of them.

Building in Resilience and Measured Reponses

- Agree what levels of resilience are required and how to ensure these are regularly revisited and updated.

- Find the right mix of market and governmental risk and reward judgments.

- Develop a funding stream for increased resilience and new technologies to achieve critical infrastructure levels of protection at both national and international levels.

- Build in incentives for investment in cyber resilience in satellite vehicles for cases where the value of the satellite and payload is comparatively low.

- Develop regulatory controls and standards (including templates as needed) for critical national and international systems, including minimum acceptable availability levels.

- Ensure a reporting mechanism is established to identify changes in critical network configurations with monitoring and regulatory facilities.

- Delegate cyber controls into the supply chain at agreed standards so as to facilitate investment.

- Develop well-understood penalties for non-compliance under established legal frameworks.

- Work with the insurance sector to increase incentives.

Hardware and Software Future-Proofing

- Develop approaches to future-proofing of existing hardware and software, given the often long life cycle of satellites and the problems of obsolescence in some ground systems.

- Invest in new 'hack-proof' or 'hack-resistant' technologies, including 'blue-sky' approaches such as quantum technologies for communication.

Procurement Strategies

- Develop cooperative mechanisms whereby cybersecurity in space is made equivalent to physical safety in space and is not part of the commercially competitive agenda.

- Identify the procurement processes and legislative frameworks that should be used for public procurement in an international supply chain.

- Draw up security-conscious procurement strategies that match the speed of the market.

- Develop industry standards so that cybersecurity rigor can be ensured (and insured) through the entire supply stack, from the highest boardroom level all the way down to microchip level, with penalties for default.

- Establish clarity with regard to implementing national and international controls such as on international trafficking in arms regulations vis-à-vis the development and sharing of cybersecurity technology.

Regulatory Requirements

- Develop an international discussion about how the regime might function as an international community of the willing, and its relationship with international bodies.

- Develop the regime in the form of a 'general obligation to cooperate' mechanism, deciding whether it should be a regulated or non-regulated information management environment, or both—and whether industry, academia, or government should lead or whether a multi-stakeholder approach could be more effective.

- Balance regulated and non-regulated instruments within the regime.

- Incorporate mechanisms beyond the regulated environments so that organizations are not inhibited from sharing knowledge and ensure that this is understood by the regulatory bodies.

- Install mechanisms that enable legislative and regulatory requirements to be passed back to national and international authorities as needed.

Sharing Experience

- Establish mechanisms for communications processes to share experience and knowledge, including agreeing to a common lexicon.

- Demonstrate that participation in the regime leads to significant advantage whereas nonparticipation is detrimental.

- Build confidence in the process so that traditional military reluctance to share technical data and threat information is overcome (this is particularly important given the considerable number of overlaps in civil and military capabilities).

- Develop understanding within military authorities about the need for light-touch regulation in the commercial domain and increase the comfort level for military authorities to work in, and contribute to, a low-regulation environment.

- Establish mechanisms for analysis and sharing of sensitive information.

- Implement established practices for international quality control.

- Develop collaborative mechanisms required for raising awareness and operational responses.

- Determine which communities should have access to the shared experience data.

- Identify an impartial player who can monitor inputs and outputs and share information safely and securely.

- Develop incentives for sharing information across the divides.

Establishment of Good Practice

- Aggregate good practice into a single system of guidance.

- Adapt working models for good practice and bring in mechanisms specific to the cyberspace community of interest.

- Agree on models for risk management.

- Set up mechanisms to determine the appropriate current and future requirements for cybersecurity in the various satellite missions.[372]

That is quite a list. *What are the chances that even half of it can be implemented in the next decade? Probably not good, but if the global community of nations does not begin to seriously address these issues, as time passes, doing so will become an insurmountable task with less and less likelihood of success.* Perhaps this list presents already impossible objectives, but there is really no excuse for not marshalling the resources necessary to convene a serious global legislative and governance task force to tackle the problem of cybersecurity in space.

Space really *is* the final frontier of cybersecurity. If ever there were an argument to be made about the efficacy and wisdom of adopting a proactive stance toward establishing cyber resiliency, it is for outer space. The direction that the cyber space race is heading is rather worrisome. As was the case with the nuclear arms race, those nations and militaries that succeed in achieving the first mover advantage by creating visionary technologies to conquer cyber risk in space stand to gain a potentially long-term comparative advantage vis-à-vis their adversaries. All of the world's major powers are heading in this direction. To the victor go the spoils, which, in this case, could be military supremacy for decades to come.

As we will see in Chapter 15, there are a plethora of legal challenges that prevent legitimate actors in cyberspace from operating with the support of an efficient, effective regulatory regime in the mix. Given how difficult it has proven to be to get countries to operate within the framework of the existing legal regime governing cyberspace and the evolutionary nature of cyber risk in outer space, the likelihood of achieving a state of legal and operational parity among nations appears to be limited at best. Those nations—in particular, China, Russia, and the US—which have already achieved an advanced status on the path toward military supremacy in outer space will undoubtedly be reluctant to give away too much at the bargaining table in future multilateral negotiations. This will further hamper efforts to better define the cyber landscape in outer space and apply a modicum of best practices going forward.

15. Legal Aspects

As the world's most comprehensive and advanced legal framework for protecting privacy and addressing data breaches, the General Data Protection Regulation (GDPR) will strengthen and unify data protection for all individuals within the EU. When it becomes effective in May 2018, it will give control of personal data back to citizens and residents, and simplify the regulatory environment for international business by unifying the regulation within the EU, replacing a data protection directive from 1995. The GDPR extends the scope of the EU data protection law to all foreign companies processing data of EU residents. It also provides for harmonization of data protection regulations throughout the EU, making it easier for non-European companies to comply with these regulations. It comes with a strict data protection compliance cost, however, with severe penalties of up to 4 percent of worldwide turnover (the UK Parliament's version contains increased fines of up to 5 percent).[373]

A Call to Arms

In the wake of the third high profile terror attack in England in the first half of 2017, UK Prime Minister Theresa May called for enactment of a new set of international laws designed to govern cyberspace, acknowledging that YouTube had played a role in the London Bridge attacks. Her manifesto pledged to regulate the Internet, including forcing Internet providers to participate in counter-extremism drives. It came after the introduction of the UK's Investigatory Powers Act of 2016—dubbed the "Snooper's Charter"—which expanded the powers of spy agencies and the Government over the Internet. The Act required ISPs to maintain a list of visited websites for all Internet users for one year and gave intelligence agencies more powers to intercept online communications. Police can access stored browsing histories without any warrant or court order.[374]

It was unfortunate that the Prime Minister's actions were reactive rather than proactive, as is so typically the case, but she was right to encourage the world's governments to join the UK in enacting such laws. While a step in the right direction, such laws are unlikely to make much of a difference, for virtual terrorists operate in an anonymous and borderless world in which the rule of law mostly does not apply. For such laws to work, the individuals they seek to apprehend must, in the first instance, be identified, and as has been proven countless times in recent years, the perpetrators of cyberterrorism are as adept at hiding behind the Internet as their cybercriminal counterparts.

More often than not, neither the individuals nor groups nor governments who are responsible for Virtual Terrorism are ever identified or apprehended. Just as quickly as a method of identifying them is deployed, the parties responsible adapt, change identity, adopt of new modus operandi, and continue their reign of terror. The Prime Minister recognized the importance of addressing the role that social media plays in how cyberterrorists communicate with one another and their recruits. Social media companies have also now come to realize the critical role they play by unwittingly supporting cyberterrorism. Many of them want to do something about it and are at last devoting substantially greater resources in an effort to combat it.

There are a plethora of challenges standing in their way, however. Among them is the sheer volume of messages and videos generated—hundreds of millions each day. There are no algorithms currently available that can identify every potential terrorist message or video, and the social media firms are often reliant on their users to report problem messaging. By the time they are able to respond, the messages have been disseminated and consumed. Even if such algorithms did exist, there is no realistic way for law enforcement and intelligence agencies to be able to act on all of them in a timely and effective manner. Even if they could, *virtual terrorists change their IP addresses, locations, identities, and personas with such regularity, and so quickly, that they can basically act at will, confident that they will never be caught.*

There are good reasons why so few meaningful laws exist to govern the Internet. If there were an easy way to address the problem, many more such laws would presumably have been implemented years ago. Cyberspace is a fast moving and ever-changing landscape that caters to criminality, and illegal and outrageous behavior. No set of laws is going to change that, but it would be wrong not to devote greater resources to strengthen the international legal regime in an attempt to do so. Failure to move in that direction will mean that the world's nations will simply fall further and further behind the cyber curve.

It is ironic that this clarion call would come from the UK, which has come to epitomize the surveillance state. The British people have made a tacit agreement with their government: they agree to accept an intrusive surveillance regime in return for being kept safe. As good as the government is at doing its best to keep its side of the bargain, the chips are stacked against both the government and its people, for their enemy is as cunning, creative, adaptive, and persistent as any enemy ever was. While there is no alternative to implementing an even tougher range of security protocols in such an environment, the world should be realistic about what can be achieved, how quickly, and how effectively from a legal perspective, in this Era of Virtual Terrorism.[375]

Power to the People?

The EU will implement the most dramatic law of its kind governing data in 2018. The GDPR will strengthen and unify data protection for all individuals within the EU. When it becomes effective, it will give control of personal data back to citizens and residents and simplify the regulatory environment for international business by unifying the regulation within the EU, replacing a data protection directive from 1995. The GDPR extends the scope of the EU data protection law to all foreign companies processing data of EU residents. It also provides for harmonization of the data protection regulations throughout the EU, making it easier for non-European companies to comply with these regulations. It comes with a strict data protection compliance cost, however, with severe penalties of up to 4 percent of worldwide turnover (the UK Parliament's version contains increased fines up to 5 percent).[376]

Contrast that with the direction the US is going. In the last months of Barack Obama's presidency, the then-Democratic-led FCC prepared guidelines that created unprecedented protections for the personal information that Americans put into cyberspace. The Internet data rules created under the FCC would have permitted ISPs to sell consumers' browsing data—but only with explicit permission by way of consumers "opting in" to their data being sold to third parties. *In 2017, President Trump reversed all that and signed a bill that puts everything any Americans do on the Internet, and all the data generated in the process, on the table for Internet providers to sell to whomever they choose—with or without consumer consent*. If you call a car dealership, it is against the law for phone companies to sell information about your vehicle and your interest in selling it, but if you try to sell your car online, the company you pay each month for your Internet connection can now sell that information.

In the past, Internet users could selectively decide whether to use the services of Facebook or Google, or abstain from using them if they wished to safeguard their personal information.[377] That is no longer the case. As previously noted, *the ToS we all unwittingly agree to when we use Internet-related services give these companies permission to basically do whatever they want with the information (and images) we voluntarily give to them—which was bad enough. Now, they have permission to sell it to whomever they please. The recipients of that information are, in turn, free to do with it whatever they choose to do with that information and that process may now continue ad nauseam.*

There is strange legal (and moral and ethical) dichotomy at play here, which is indicative of some of the larger questions that 'the law' (to the extent that it exists) is at pains to address on the subject of cybersecurity. This raises a number of questions, such as, are there any boundaries that apply to cyberspace? In order for any law to be meaningful, the individual(s) perpetrating a crime must be identifiable and the law itself must be enforceable. In a world without boundaries, where virtual terrorists operate across borders at will and anonymously, can any law be truly meaningful? Even if and when a perpetrator may be identified, caught, and prosecuted, how meaningful can a law against Virtual

Terrorism be if it catches a fraction of one percent of the lawbreakers? That is, of course, a question that also applies for more terrestrial crimes.

As we will now see, some progress has been made in an effort to craft laws with meaning and teeth to battle Virtual Terrorism but they remain evolutionary, muddled, inadequate, and behind the curve. If ever there was a case to be made for staying ahead of the curve, it would be in the legal realm because laws take a long time to create, implement, and enforce. As it stands today, virtual terrorists can count on staying ahead of the curve for many years to come because the progress that has been made pales in comparison to the scourge being fought.

The Law of Armed Conflict

A useful place to start in deciphering what is possible and what is fantasy in terms of how the law may be made to apply to virtual terrorists in the future is to take a look at how it has applied to armed conflict. The term "armed attack" remains open to interpretation with respect to cyberattacks. The so-called "Law of War" (also known as the Law of Armed Conflict, embodied in the Geneva and Hague Conventions and the UN Charter) may in some circumstances apply to cyberattacks, but without attempts by nation-states to apply it, or specific agreement on its applicability, its relevance remains unclear.

The Law's application would appear clearest in situations where a cyberattack causes physical damage, such as disruption of critical infrastructure. The more consequences impinge on critical national interests, the more they will contribute to the depiction of a cyberattack as a use of force. The sooner consequences manifest themselves, the less opportunity states have to seek peaceful accommodation of a dispute or to otherwise forestall their harmful effects. Therefore, states harbor a greater concern about immediate consequences than those that are delayed or build slowly over time. Economic coercion may involve no intrusion at all (trade with a targeted state is simply cut off), whereas in combat the forces of one state cross into another in violation of its sovereignty. Although highly invasive, espionage does not constitute a use of force (or armed attack) under international law, absent a nonconsensual physical incursion of the target state's territory.

The more quantifiable and identifiable a set of consequences, the more a state's interest will be deemed to have been affected. This is particularly challenging in a cyber event, where damage, economic or otherwise, is difficult to quantify. *Economic coercion or hardship does not qualify under international law as an armed attack. In international law, acts which are not forbidden are permitted; absent an explicit prohibition, an act is presumptively legitimate.* For instance, it is generally accepted that international law governing the use of force does not prohibit propaganda, psychological warfare, or espionage. To the extent such activities are conducted through cyber actions, they are presumptively legitimate and legal.

The law of state responsibility governs when a state is responsible for cyberattacks. However, that responsibility lies along a continuum, from operations conducted by a state itself to those in which it is merely involved in some fashion. The closer the nexus between a state and the attack, the more likely other states will be inclined to characterize them as uses of force, for the greater the risk posed to international stability. Attributing the level of state involvement to a cyberattack can be particularly challenging. The basic principles encompassed in The Hague Conventions regarding the application of armed forces are those of military necessity, proportionality, humanity, and chivalry. *If a nation's military is conducting cyber operations, according to these principles, it may be said to be engaging in cyberwarfare under the law.*[378]

The US View

In 2012, the US State Department first took a public position on whether cyber activities could constitute a use of force—under Article 2(4) of the UN Charter and customary international law—stating that cyber activities that proximately result in death, injury, or significant destruction would likely be viewed as a use of force. The examples offered at the time included triggering a meltdown at a nuclear plant, opening a dam and causing flood damage, or causing airplanes to crash by interfering with air traffic control. *By focusing on the ends achieved rather than the means with which they are carried out, this definition of cyberwarfare fits within existing international legal frameworks.*

If an actor employs a cyberweapon to produce kinetic effects that might warrant firepower under other circumstances, then the use of that cyberweapon also rises to the level of the use of force. The USG recognized that cyberattacks without kinetic effects are also an element of armed conflict under certain circumstances, however. Cyberattacks on information networks in the course of an ongoing armed conflict would be governed by the same principles of proportionality that apply to other actions under the law of armed conflict. These principles include retaliation in response to a cyberattack with a proportional use of kinetic force.

In addition, it was deemed that computer network activities that amount to an armed attack or imminent threat thereof may trigger a nation's right to self-defense under Article 51 of the UN Charter. The USG's 2011 International Strategy for Cyberspace affirmed that, when warranted, the US will respond to hostile acts in cyberspace as it would to any other threat. The US reserved the right to use all means necessary —diplomatic, military, and economic—as appropriate and consistent with applicable law, exhausting all options before military force would be used.[379]

Despite this, in the case of the alleged Russian hacking of the 2016 US presidential electoral process, the Obama administration did not use anywhere close to all of the tools available in its tool kit. This example illustrates well how realpolitik and other considerations can impact and ultimately severely weaken what laws (or theories about how the law should be applied in the real world) do exist to combat Virtual Terrorism. The Obama administration was well aware of what the Russians had already done and were continuing to do during the election campaign (based on apparently overwhelming intelligence-based evidence), but its concern that the Russians could have chosen to more directly interfere with the electoral process prompted Obama to opt to 'send a message' to Vladimir Putin, by sending 35 Russian diplomats home and closing two Russian compounds, along with economic sanctions that were so narrowly targeted that even those who helped design them describe their impact as largely symbolic. The response indicates that the USG did not know the degree of Russia's capability in this sphere, which makes sense.

Less reported at the time, however, was that Obama also approved a covert measure that authorized planting cyber weapons in Russia's infrastructure—the digital equivalent of bombs that could be detonated if the US found itself in an escalating exchange with Moscow. The project, which Obama approved in a covert-action finding, was still in its planning stages when Obama left office. It was left up to President Trump to decide whether to use that capability, and few expected him to do so, given all of the allegations and controversy swirling around the Trump campaign and presidency regarding possible collusion with Russia during the campaign and into the Trump presidency. The series of warnings the USG delivered to Putin apparently prompted Moscow to abandon any plans of further aggression, such as sabotage of US voting systems.[380]

The US Congress as an Impediment

It is ironic that Obama chose such a tepid response to the alleged Russian hacking, because in 2015, he had proposed sweeping new cybersecurity legislation designed to establish alignment of some existing state data breach laws while closing legal loopholes to enable the government to pursue cybercriminals who steal and sell the identities of Americans. The US lawmaking process is famously convoluted and riddled with 'special' interests, which accounts for much of the reason so little appears to get done in Washington. Such complexity extends to the state level as well, however, with nearly every US state having a unique data breach notification law, making it confusing and costly for companies to notify customers of data breaches.

Obama's bill—the Personal Data Notification and Protection Act—was an honest attempt to make some real progress and hold organizations accountable for data breaches. It would have:

- Required certain businesses that use, access, transmit, store, dispose of, or collect sensitive personally identifiable information about more than 10,000 individuals during any 12-month period to notify those whose information was believed to have been accessed or acquired through a discovered security breach;

- Directed businesses to notify affected individuals and major media outlets within 30 days if the number of affected residents of a state exceeds 5,000;

- Required the DHS to designate a federal government entity to receive notices about security incidents, threats, and vulnerabilities;

- Directed businesses to notify a DHS-designated entity —and required that entity to then notify the US Secret Service (USSS), the FBI, and the FTC—if a security breach affected more than 5,000 individuals, federal employees or contractors involved in national security or law enforcement, or a database contained the sensitive information of more than 500,000 individuals;

- Amended the federal criminal code to extend extraterritorially the application of penalties for fraud offenses involving an access device issued, owned, managed, or controlled by a financial institution, credit card system member, or other entity organized under the laws of the US or any US state or territory; and

- Removed a condition under existing law that subjected a person to such penalties only if the underlying articles, property, or proceeds are held within or have transferred through US jurisdiction.[381]

As was the case with previous pieces of legislation whose purpose was to fortify US cyber response capabilities, the bill was introduced in 2015, sent to a Congressional committee, and never again saw the light of day.

So, just why does the US Congress have such a difficult time passing legislation that is so sorely needed and should be such a priority for the security of the nation? After years of intensive efforts under the Obama administration, *the reason appears to have been differences over how much liability protection to grant businesses in order to encourage them to share cyberthreat information.* The argument against granting the private sector broad liability protection was that businesses could potentially exploit it to collude on other matters. Supporters of more targeted liability protection (mainly Democrats) contended it would provide sufficient protection to enable businesses to share cyberthreat information, but proponents of broad liability protection (mainly Republicans) argued that businesses would not feel adequately protected if they were granted only limited liability because their lawyers would caution them that they could still be subject to legal action.[382]

After four years of legal and legislative wrangling, in 2015, the US Congress finally passed the Cybersecurity Act of 2015 (formerly, the Cybersecurity Information Sharing Act) as part of the omnibus spending bill. The Act gave companies the ability to share cybersecurity information with federal agencies (including the NSA), providing liability protection and antitrust exemption for those sharing the information. It called for information sharing portals to be set up with agencies like the FBI and the ODNI so that companies provide information directly to law enforcement and intelligence agencies instead of going through the DHS and the court vetting system. It allowed the use of specific threat data by law enforcement without specific court approval, when there is a known, specific threat.

The legislation had been highly controversial (of course), with detractors arguing that it could allow organizations to circumvent privacy norms and civil liberties, including the requirement for warrants regarding surveillance. There was no specific mention of warrantless wiretapping and the like as part of the bill's language but opponents were concerned that the language was sufficiently vague, and lacked specific exclusions, which provided a loophole for just such snooping. Following its passage, security experts and civil society groups wrote to Congress arguing to strongly oppose it because of its weak privacy protections and opposing the Republican leadership's choice to refuse to hold a stand-alone vote, instead forcing it into law as part of the must-pass omnibus spending bill. In the end, it was left up to the private sector to build an information infrastructure that promotes security while preserving trust.

While the Act was a useful starting point and should perhaps be considered a victory for 'progress' in the area of US cybersecurity, Congress needs to do much more, such as reforming the outdated 1986 Computer Fraud and Abuse Act and the 1996 Digital Millennium Copyright Act, to ensure that security researchers are able to identify and responsibly disclose vulnerabilities without fear of prosecution or civil liability.[383] There remains much to do. Since this is an instance when government cannot get the job done on its own, the private sector may ultimately prove to be the key missing ingredient and the catalyst for making a difference, though there are plenty of challenges and conflictive self-interests associated with doing so.

The Fragility of Public-Private Partnerships

If achieving a modicum of collaboration between the private and public sectors to achieve cybersecurity is a challenge on an individual country level, it is a massive undertaking multilaterally. The role, reach, duties, and capabilities of each collaborating party combine with legal permissions and constraints to create an obstacle course that stands in the way of achieving objectives. Many participants in PPPs end up asking themselves where the line should be drawn between collaborating and pursuing a solo path. Inconsistencies in approach and capabilities and relative pluses and minuses to going down one path or another abound.

One of those obstacles is conflicting laws and policies. Cross-border data transfer restrictions greatly limit international efforts to detect and thwart cyberattacks because international companies must comply with multiple and sometimes conflicting local, national, or supranational data protection laws. The 2014 European Court of Justice's landmark decision involving Google and the Spanish Data

Protection Authority highlights the significant potential consequences of the extra-territorial application of EU data protection laws. The court found that Google was subject to Spanish data protection law, was obligated to delete web search results that link to web pages containing accurate (but outdated) information regarding a person, and upon an individual's request invoking his or her "right to be forgotten," must also delete search results linking even truthful information about a person that is prejudicial or contrary to the wish to be forgotten over time. The same restrictions do not apply elsewhere in the world, which creates a compliance headache.

Although the PPP platform for cybersecurity is embryonic and evolving, and there are many questions regarding how best to progress in a seamless and fruitful manner, some companies are quite willing to step up to the plate. A number of innovative PPP models have emerged, which gives hope for a more meaningful paradigm in the future. For collaboration to succeed there must be safeguards in place to encourage parties on all sides to share information in a way that, to the greatest extent possible, protects confidentiality and competitive concerns.

Granting limited security clearances to key corporate actors and embedding private sector actors in government-operated cybersecurity centers beyond those that already exist in the DHS is useful. But changes must take place that institutionalize the processes by which the public and private sectors can cooperate. Institutional forms of cooperation must be tailored to fit the exact nature of the cyberthreat. Clarifying the laws regarding what unilateral action companies can take to defend themselves against cyberattacks would help to define the parameters of legitimate, private-sector responses to those attacks.

Among the hesitations in the private sector against forming PPPs are issues of trust, control, and disclosure. Companies often doubt whether they should involve a government after a cyberattack, as this implies granting the government access to the company's private data. Even in the case of a serious breach, many companies remain reluctant to directly involve the public sector if they fear that government involvement would only escalate the severity of the situation. In order to foster a sense of trust, some PPP's in the Netherlands have created a secure network of information that the government cannot directly access without the express consent of the companies involved. One model has members of the public and private sectors working together on a joint cybersecurity panel to develop trust and promote cooperation and dialogue.

Another hesitation to engaging in PPPs is the complex regulatory and legal landscape surrounding cybersecurity. In the event of a breach, companies may need to go even further than standard SEC disclosure obligations. Private companies may need to disclose 'potential' risks or cyberattacks to state governments, the DOJ, or plaintiffs who may be affected by a cyberthreat, depending on the scope of the attack. The majority of US states have adopted legislation that requires government agencies to disclose to citizens any breaches of personal information. Thus, in establishing a PPP, the public sector must find a balance between cooperation with the private sector and holding them accountable in the event of a breach.

Once a private company involves a government agency in investigating a cyberattack, the company typically fears losing autonomy over their own investigation. Some companies are also hesitant to share information with governments; since governments are generally not able to share much of their data as a result of national security concerns, many companies feel that information sharing will end up being a one-way street. They also worry that handing over sensitive information may damage their reputation, or that the information will not be treated completely confidentially.[384]

The World Economic Forum has proposed a number of recommendations for developing PPPs in the cyber arena. Among them are strategies for establishing more real time information sharing systems, developing a uniform rule of law for cybercrime, and encouraging national law enforcement agencies to more actively engage in cybersecurity PPPs to improve coordination between the public and private sectors. Capacity building, including targeted training for law-enforcement, prosecutors, and judges, is necessary to ensure all parties are kept abreast of technological developments and have the requisite knowledge and skills to deal with the constantly evolving cyber landscape.[385]

Taking the Lead

The USG has taken the lead in reaching out to other governments to help craft stronger multilateral responses to cyberattacks. The DDoS attacks on American banks in 2012 —the largest DDoS attack at the time, orchestrated by a group calling itself the Izz ad-Din al-Qassam Cyber Fighters (believed to be originating from Iran)—disrupted service to the online banking portals of a number of major US financial institutions. In response, the USG took the unprecedented step of appealing (diplomatically and technologically) to 120 countries to help cut off computer traffic at nodes around the world, thereby mitigating the threat.

Since then, multilateral approaches to tackling the problem have occurred with some regularity. In 2014, the DOJ led global operations to disrupt two massive and sophisticated cybercrime schemes related to the "Gameover Zeus" botnet and "Cryptolocker" ransomware, which affected hundreds of thousands of computer users around the world. US law enforcement coordinated with counterparts in more than ten countries, and with numerous private sector industry experts in the US. The government has created many task forces and inter-agency groups to facilitate robust information sharing within the government, and between the government and private sector, on an ongoing basis.

The DoD's Cyber Crime Center is a national center focusing on addressing forensics, investigative training, research, and analytics impacting government agencies and private companies operating in the defense sector. The DHS's CERT plays a leading role in international information sharing, and the DOJ's Computer Crime and Intellectual Property Section works with prosecutors and agents nationally and overseas, as well as with companies and governments, to investigate and prosecute cybercrime.

The Electronic Crimes Task Force (ECTF) groups have for more than a decade provided significant advances in public-private information sharing. For example, the ECTFs at the

USSS—which focus on identifying and locating international cybercriminals connected to cyber intrusions, bank fraud, data breaches, and other cybercrimes—have achieved significant success in detecting and apprehending numerous international cybercriminals. Additionally, the USSS Cyber Intelligence Section has worked with law enforcement partners worldwide to secure the arrest of cybercriminals responsible for the theft of hundreds of millions of credit card numbers. These initiatives are usually most effective when there is robust information sharing and cooperation between the government and the private sector.[386]

The Multilateral Response

According to the Vienna Convention on the Law of Treaties (known as the "Treaty on Treaties"), the text of a treaty may be expanded, either explicitly or implicitly, to address new circumstances; existing legislation may therefore be amended, and most of the international counterterrorism conventions can be applied to cyberterrorism. Although the UN has published charters on war and terrorism, it has not yet created a comprehensive convention that covers all acts of terrorism. However, there are 17 specific conventions and major legal instruments which deal with terrorist activities (between 1963 to 2010) including the:

- 1980 Convention on the Physical Protection of Nuclear Material,

- 1991 Convention on the Marking of Plastic Explosives for the Purpose of Detection,

- 1997 International Convention for the Suppression of Terrorist Bombings,

- 1999 International Convention for the Suppression of the Financing of Terrorism, and

- 2005 International Convention for the Suppression of Acts of Nuclear Terrorism.[387]

In looking at the progression of these Conventions, it is interesting to note how they advanced from preventing "unlawful acts" to "suppressing terrorism". The body has held numerous forums and reports on cyberterrorism but as of 2017 had not established a Convention on the subject.

That said, in 2011, the UN established the International Multilateral Partnership Against Cyberthreats (IMPACT), the first UN-backed cybersecurity alliance, which functions as a key partner of the ITU. IMPACT was also the first comprehensive PPP formed specifically to combat cyberthreats, and brings together governments, business and academia. With more than 150 countries taking part in the ITU-IMPACT coalition, IMPACT is tasked by the ITU with providing cybersecurity assistance and support to ITU's 193 Member States and other organizations within the UN system.

IMPACT's Global Response Center acts as a global cyberthreat resource center and provides emergency responses to facilitate identification of cyberthreats and sharing of resources to assist ITU-UN Member States. IMPACT's Electronically Secure Collaborative Application Platform for Experts connects those responsible for cybersecurity from more than 140 countries and provides a response mechanism for ITU-IMPACT partner countries. Three other divisions provide consulting and training services, scholarships, reports, and expertise to governments, industry, and academia in partner countries.[388] Also in 2011, the UN launched the African Center for Cyber Law and Cybercrime Prevention to monitor cyberspace and cybercrime in African jurisdictions.

Interpol began its efforts to improve its counter-cybercrime capacity at the international level very early, beginning with a 1981 survey of members on cyber-criminal law that recognized dilemmas in application of existing legislation. Based on the recognition of the legal gaps between countries, legal frameworks, and types of crimes, Interpol expanded its task to include both law enforcement and legal harmonization. One of the main crimes Interpol addresses head on is financial and high-tech crimes such as currency counterfeiting, money laundering, intellectual property crime, payment card fraud, computer virus attacks, and cyberterrorism. Interpol cooperates with law enforcement authorities all over the world and has created a variety of working groups to benefit from regional expertise in Africa, Asia, Europe and the US. It established the Interpol Global Complex in Singapore, in 2014, as a focal point to work and foster global cooperation among law enforcement agencies.[389]

Other multilateral entities—among them the Association of Southeast Asian Nations (ASEAN), the ASEAN Regional Forum, and Asia-Pacific Economic Cooperation—have sought to address cyberterrorism in the legal sphere, with varying degrees of success. The earliest among them was the EU in 2001, with its Convention on Cybercrime (also known as the Budapest Convention on Cybercrime). It was the first international treaty seeking to address Internet and computer crime by harmonizing national laws, improving investigative techniques and increasing cooperation among nations. It is also illustrative of how difficult it can be to achieve unified coordination against cyberterrorism. As of 2016, 52 states had ratified the Convention, but some important countries such as Brazil and India declined to adopt it on the grounds that they did not participate in its drafting. Russia opposes it, claiming that adoption would violate Russian sovereignty, and has usually refused to cooperate in law enforcement investigations relating to cybercrime.[390]

The GDPR as a Possible Global Framework

As noted earlier, the GDPR is the world's most comprehensive and advanced legal framework for protecting privacy and addressing data breaches. It could serve as the foundation for a possible global framework to achieve the same, so it is worth taking a deeper dive into what it is and how it works. The biggest change to the regulatory landscape of data privacy associated with the GDPR is its extended jurisdiction—*it applies to all companies processing the personal data of individuals residing in the EU, regardless of the company's location.* Previously, territorial applicability of the directive was ambiguous and referred to data process 'in the context of an establishment'. This topic has arisen in a number of high profile court cases.

The GPDR will apply to the processing of personal data by controllers and processors in the EU, regardless of whether the processing takes place in the EU or not. The GDPR will also apply to the processing of personal data in the EU by a controller or processor not established in the EU, where the activities relate to offering goods or services to EU citizens (irrespective of whether payment is required) and the monitoring of behavior that takes place within the EU. Non-EU businesses processing the data of EU citizens must also appoint a representative in the EU.

The conditions for consent have been strengthened under the regime. *Companies will no longer be able to use long and illegible terms and conditions. Any request for consent must be given in an intelligible and easily accessible form, with the purpose for data processing directly attached to that consent. Going forward, consent must be clear and distinguishable from other matters, and provided in an intelligible and easily accessible form, using clear and plain language. It must be as easy to withdraw consent as it is to give it.*

Breach notification will become mandatory in all member states where a data breach is likely to "result in a risk for the rights and freedoms of individuals". This must be done within 72 hours of first having become aware of the breach. Data processors will also be required to notify their customers "without undue delay" after first becoming aware of a data breach. Part of the expanded rights of data subjects outlined by the GDPR will also be their right to obtain from the data 'controller' confirmation as to whether or not personal data concerning them is being processed, where, and for what purpose. The data controller must further provide a copy of the personal data, free of charge, in an electronic format. This is a dramatic shift to data transparency and empowerment of data subjects.

Also known as Data Erasure, the "right to be forgotten" entitles the data subject to have the data controller erase his or her personal data, cease further dissemination of the data, and potentially have third parties halt processing of the data. The conditions for erasure include data that is no longer deemed relevant to the original purpose for processing, or a data subject withdrawing consent. It should also be noted that this right requires controllers to compare subjects' rights to "the public interest in the availability of the data" when considering such requests.

Privacy by Design as a concept has existed for years but it is only just becoming part of a legal requirement with the GDPR. At its core, Privacy by Design calls for the inclusion of data protection from the onset of the designing of systems, rather than as an addition to their design. Data controllers can hold and process only the data absolutely necessary for the completion of their duties, as well as limiting access to personal data to those needing to act in the course of processing. The GDPR also introduces data portability—the right for a data subject to receive the personal data concerning them and have the right to transmit that data to another controller.

Controllers have only been required to notify their data processing activities with local data protection administrators (DPA), which for large multinationals can be a bureaucratic nightmare, especially since most EU Member States have different notification requirements. Under the GDPR, it will not be necessary to submit notifications or registrations to each local DPA of data processing activities, nor will it be a requirement to notify or obtain approval for transfers based on model contract clauses. Instead, there will be internal record keeping requirements and DPA appointments will become mandatory only for those controllers and processors whose core activities consist of processing operations which require regular and systematic monitoring of data subjects on a large scale, or of special categories of data, or data relating to criminal convictions and offenses.

In the future, DPAs must be appointed on the basis of professional qualities and, in particular, expert knowledge on data protection law and practices. They can be a staff member or an external service provider and must be provided with appropriate resources to carry out their tasks and maintain their expert knowledge. They will be required to report directly to the highest level of management and cannot carry out any other tasks that could result in a conflict of interest.

Under the GDPR, organizations in breach of its guidelines can be fined up to 4 percent of annual global turnover or €20 million (whichever is greater). This is the maximum fine that can be imposed for the most serious infringements, such as not having sufficient customer consent to process data or violating the core of Privacy by Design concepts. There is a tiered approach to fines (e.g. a company can be fined 2 percent for not having their records in order, not notifying the supervising authority and data subject about a breach, or not conducting impact assessments). These rules apply to both controllers and processors—meaning 'clouds' will not be exempt from GDPR enforcement.[391]

There are some truly revolutionary aspects of the GDPR— both from the perspective of the data user and the data provider or processor. Its rollout will be an experiment. Either it will prove to be mostly successful and prompt global companies to modify their data handling methods in some fundamental ways, or it will turn out to be a Kafkaesque, bureaucratic, enforcement nightmare. Global firms are taking the pending implementation of the new rules seriously, and it will undoubtedly cost companies a lot of money to be in full compliance with the new rules. The real challenge will be whether the EU has a monitoring and enforcement mechanism that is up to par with the GDPR, whether and how individuals will report infringements, and whether any of it will make a real difference at the end of the day. Kudos go to the EU for even attempting it.

China's Alternative Glimpse into the Future

As a contrast to the GDPR, which seeks to protect individual rights and reign in the actions of large corporates, China's Cybersecurity Law gives an alternative vision about how nations may choose to apply the law toward cyberspace in the future. The law, which took effect in June 2017, is applicable to almost all businesses in China that manage their own e-mail or other data networks, and includes "critical sectors" of the Chinese economy that encompass businesses involved in communications, information services, energy, transport, water, financial services, public services, and electronic government services. Any company that is a supplier or partner with firms in these sectors may also be subject to the law.

The law requires network operators to cooperate with Chinese crime or security investigators and allow full access to data and unspecified "technical support" to the authorities upon request. The law also imposes mandatory testing and certification of computer equipment for critical sector network operators. These tests and certifications require network operators to formulate internal security management systems and implement network security protections, adopt measures to prevent viruses or unspecified forms of cyberattacks, monitor and record the safety of a network, and undertake data classification, back-ups of important data, and encryption.

On one hand, these security measures form part of what might otherwise be considered 'best practice' recommendations for firms that gather and store important company and client data. On the other hand, the law requires network operators in critical sectors to store within China all data that is gathered or produced by the network operator in the country. The law also requires business information and data on Chinese citizens gathered within China to be kept on domestic servers and not transferred abroad without permission. It includes a ban on the export of any economic, technological, or scientific data that could pose a threat to national security or the public interest (with a broad interpretation of what that might be).

International law firms have warned that companies could be asked to provide source code, encryption, or other crucial information for review by the government, increasing the risk of this information being lost, passed on to local competitors, or kept and used by the government itself. Article 9 of the law states that "network operators must obey social norms and commercial ethics, be honest and credible, perform obligations to protect network security, accept supervision from the government and public, and bear social responsibility". The vagueness of this provision, as well as undefined concepts of national security and public interest contained within the law, increases the government's grounds to make wide assertions about the need for investigation, and reduces a foreign company's ability to contest a government demand for data access. Spot checks can be initiated at the request of the government or a trade association, meaning domestic competitors can request spot checks on foreign firms.

To comply with the data localization requirements, foreign firms will have to either invest in new data servers in China—which would be subject to government spot checks—or incur new costs to hire a local server provider (such as Huawei, Tencent, or Alibaba, which have spent billions of dollars in recent years establishing domestic data centers). The substantial investment by these Chinese technology firms is one of the reasons critics of the new law believe it is partly designed to bolster the domestic Chinese data management and telecommunications industry against global competitors. An alternative explanation is that the requirement is a legal move by Beijing to bring data under Chinese jurisdiction to make it easier to prosecute entities seen as violating China's Internet laws.[392]

Prior to implementation of the law, a foreign firm would monitor its energy turbines in China from its headquarters, using its real-time global data to optimize operations, and a provider of global online education would send data on Chinese users overseas to allow them to access its courses abroad. Now such firms must reconfigure their IT systems to keep such data inside China. Critics worry that the new law could be a Trojan horse designed to promote China's aggressive policy of indigenous innovation. As previously noted, doing so prompted Microsoft to enter into a local joint venture and reveal its source code to officials in order to sell a local version of its Windows operating system. Other foreign technology firms worry that they will be forced to divulge intellectual property to government inspectors, with no knowledge of or control over what may happen to the data once it is released.[393]

In July 2017, Apple announced it was setting up its first data center in Guizhou, China (in partnership with Guizhou-Cloud Big Data Industry Co. Ltd.) in order to comply with the new Cybersecurity Law. Apple put a public relations face on the move, stating that it would allow the company to improve the speed and reliability of its products and services, while also complying with China's new regulations, which require cloud services be operated by Chinese companies. Apple was the first foreign firm to announce amendments to its data storage for China following the implementation of the new law. It insisted that no "backdoors" would be created into any of its systems.[394] That month Apple also silently removed VPN apps from its app store in China, which had given Chinese citizens the ability to access the unfiltered Internet.

While at first glance the Law appears to give the Chinese government and Chinese companies a built-in advantage—given that interest in investing in China is strong and is likely to remain so well into the future because of the size of the domestic marketplace—China's companies and its consumers may lose out in the end. While many of the companies that operate in China will accede to 'moving legal goal posts' by implementing the Cybersecurity Law and enforcing increasingly burdensome regulatory requirements, some foreign firms will no doubt be pushed to the brink, decide they have had enough, and leave the country. If that occurs, it will hurt Chinese consumers by creating a less vibrant and less competitive marketplace.

China's Cybersecurity Law is masquerading as an attempt to enhance cybersecurity but it is so much more. *The danger is that other countries may adopt a similar approach, in a brazen attempt to gain commercial advantage for indigenous firms, while clearly crossing a legal and regulatory boundary that far surpasses what is required to be considered consistent with best practices.* So, there are two sides of the cybersecurity legal pendulum—the Chinese version and the EU version. Given the evolutionary state of the Virtual Terrorism landscape, the reactive nature of the legal regime, and that best practices constitute a moving target, *it is anyone's guess in which direction the cyber legal sphere will move in the longer term. Based on where Virtual Terrorism appears to be heading, the Chinese model may well prevail, and the majority of companies may eventually succumb to the new normal.*

16. **Protection**

> Software developers only know what it is they are *supposed* to be protecting against after a new form of malware has been deployed, identified, and a way is found to block it. The Petya malware that swept the world in 2017 is a useful case in point. After the attack, it was learned that hackers penetrated the network of the small Ukrainian software firm (MeDoc) which sold a piece of accounting software used by approximately 80 percent of Ukraine's businesses. By injecting a tweaked version of a file into updates of that software, they were able to start spreading backdoored versions of it weeks before Petya was deployed throughout Ukraine, injecting Petya through the MeDoc system's entry points. In the process, it was learned that innocent software updates could be used to silently spread the malware.[395]

Apart from raising awareness about Virtual Terrorism, devoting more resources toward combating it, enacting more effective laws, and attempting to turn the tide to remain in front of the curve rather than behind it, what else can governments, businesses, and individuals do to protect themselves? Creating a more holistic approach to the problem is a start, becoming proactive (instead of reactive) in thinking about how to address the problem, implementing routine cybersecurity audits, and creating teams of individuals dedicated solely to the problem inside organizations. To do so, budgets need to be adjusted to devote more financial and human assets to addressing the issue across the board. Security and privacy risk mapping, benchmarking, and scenario planning should become standard components of a cyber risk management protocol.

The list of what can be done is a long one, but *what is also needed is a change in how we think about Virtual Terrorism and other forms of man-made risk*. Less known and understood types of risk only tend to get on our radar in a meaningful way after the fact. Not only do we need to become more forward thinking on this subject, but we should presume that Virtual Terrorism will become as common in our collective psyche and lexicon as other forms of terrorism have become, after many decades of enduring it and trying to do something about it. Governments, corporations and individuals are really only starting to understand what Virtual Terrorism is, and what its potential impact can be. If we fail to fight this battle swiftly, with bravado, and effectively, it will soon be impacting us all in even more unforeseen ways and will become even more difficult to combat.

Passive versus Active Defense

As is the case with so many things, we have a choice about how we can tackle Virtual Terrorism. *We can either be fearful or aggressive, reactive or proactive, or in denial versus forward leaning.* Adopting a "passive defense" implies using technologies and products (for example, firewalls, cryptography, intrusion detection) and procedures (such as reconstitution and recovery) to protect IT assets. Some forms of passive defense may be dynamic (i.e. stopping an attack in progress) but, by definition, passive defense does not generally impose serious risk or penalty upon the attacker. By contrast, "active defense" imposes serious risk or penalty on the attacker because of the pursuit of aggressive identification, investigation and prosecution, or preemptive counter attacks.

By deploying passive measures, which are by nature reactive in orientation, attackers are free to continue the assault until they either succeed or decide to move on to the next target. Given the vulnerabilities of most cyber systems, the low cost of most attacks, and the ability of attackers to strike anonymously, a skilled and determined attacker is more likely to succeed than fail. Some defensive actions (such as stopping an attack in progress) can be pursued with both passive and active means—a defender might passively plug a vulnerability in real time while actively seeking to locate the source of an attack.

The idea is to design a system to be secure from an attack from the beginning. If done so that it is visible to a would-be attacker, cyberattacks could be prevented because they would be perceived to be futile (or if launched, would cause little or no damage). The problem is that *the vast majority of IT systems were not designed with security in mind.* As a result, there is an enormous legacy of insecure systems that are in use and security protocols may conflict with organizational needs, which can be costly to introduce and may result in reduced efficiency and functionality. Most organizations are also not incentivized to redesign systems to be much more secure unless the equivalent of a digital 9/11 were to occur.[396]

The Private Sector's Challenge

Governments have a different order of magnitude of resources, tools, and capabilities to utilize in order to attempt to achieve cyber resiliency than most businesses do, hence they routinely engage in cyber strategic planning and exercises to ensure their people and systems are performing as expected. That is regrettably not generally the case in the private sector, where *many decision makers lack awareness, fail to devote sufficient assets to address the problem, and continue to believe that cyberattacks will happen to some other firm rather than theirs.* To create effective safeguards against cyber risk, businesses must have the right priorities, policies, protocols, and tools at their disposal.

For an organizational approach to cybersecurity to have a reasonable chance of success, decision makers must prioritize security and have clear and established metrics for assessing the effectiveness of a security program. Security practices should be regularly reviewed and have strong ties to prevention and mitigation. To minimize the impact of security breaches, employees must report security failures and issues when they occur. It is also crucial for security processes and procedures to be clearly communicated and well understood.

One area of concern that extends broadly across all stages of organizational defense is the problem of insiders who have authorized access to data with the potential for abuse that can cause great harm. *Insiders account for a majority of successful penetrations for criminal purposes.* The two most general ways of dealing with infiltration are through deep pre-employment investigations (something that most non-government entities are neither capable of doing nor permitted to do in many countries) and through stronger forms of containment and compartmentalization of access within an organization.

The best detection methods for minimizing the impact of breaches are those that allow organizations to spot security weaknesses before they become full-blown incidents, so it is important to have a good system for categorizing incident-related information. Well-documented processes and procedures for incident response and tracking are key to effective breach mitigation. Organizations also need strong protocols to manage their response to crises. All of these drivers and safeguards are interconnected and interdependent. Security teams must analyze where their weaknesses are, calculate where investments in security must be made, and they should ideally be mandated by decision makers to do what must be done to secure the firm.

The primary objective is to eliminate the unconstrained operational space of adversaries by making attackers' presence known. Security teams should be gathering information about the latest threats and vulnerabilities, ensuring they have complete control over access to their networks, and developing consistent response practices and procedures. Integrated security architecture is critical, providing real time insight into threats, as well as into automated detection and defense which are essential for improving threat detection. In doing so, businesses can begin the process of ensuring they have comprehensive controls and mitigations in place to address any security gaps.[397]

According to IBM, *hackers compromised about 9 billion digital data records between 2013 and 2016, with about a third being medical records. Just 4 percent of that data was encrypted, but even encrypted data often ends up being compromised since many organizations do not deploy hacker-proof cryptography.* IBM has taken a major leap forward in cryptography. It's IBM "Z" encrypts virtually all data, making it much more difficult for criminals to identify worthwhile targets. The Z mainframe computer locks data down with public 256-bit AES encryption—the same robust protocol used in the ubiquitous SSL and TLS web encryption standards, and used by the USG for protecting classified data. Z can encrypt up to

13 gigabytes of data per second per chip, with roughly 24 chips per mainframe (depending on the configuration), a 400 percent increase in silicon-dedicated specifically to cryptographic processes, with more than 6 billion transistors dedicated to cryptography.

IBM Z keeps data encrypted at all times unless it is being actively processed and even then it is only briefly decrypted, while conducting computations, before being encrypted again. A single one of its Z mainframes can process 12 billion transactions per day, while dramatically reducing the number of administrators who can access raw readable data, which means that hackers have fewer targets they can pursue in order to gain privileged credentials to access a system. Z users can access the data they need for daily work without exposing large swaths of data they will not be using. While a very encouraging development, if history is any guide, it is probably just a matter of time until virtual terrorists find a way to 'break' Z's encryption capabilities. It is also unclear how widely Z will be adopted by the business community, since only large businesses tend to rely on mainframes, and Z is expensive to use.[398]

All businesses—regardless of their size or sector—can engage in some commonly accepted practices. The degree to which they are pursued is, again, a function of resources. But a business need not be unduly burdened to implement some of what follows. If a business were to implement all of these recommendations, its chance of being crippled by a cyberattack would be greatly diminished.

Credential Dumps

"Credential dumps" are files containing leaked e-mail addresses or usernames and passwords. After such information is collected, threat actors typically use it in credential-stuffing attacks against other sites, or mine them for usernames and passwords matching any given organization. As such, these lists allow hackers to target specific organizations, log in to their systems, and steal, modify, or delete sensitive corporate data. While these types of attacks are common, they tend to occur more frequently within the healthcare and legal sectors. In order to help proactively mitigate the risks posed by credential dumps, organizations should consider implementing two-factor authentication, ensuring the security team is able to monitor and search all employee logins by IP address, and work with a reputable third-party vendor to monitor the Dark Web (and Surface Web) for credential dumps containing any mentions of domain names owned or managed by the organization.

If a match is found, it is critical to identify and validate whether the affected individual works at the organization, whether the password meets complexity requirements, and whether any remote logins from unusual networks have been observed. If the subject is an employee, the account must be immediately locked and a forensic analysis of the employee's laptop or workstation should be performed to identify malware. If the employee's password does not match the requirements, additional steps typically include resetting passwords on all third-party sites where the credentials were used, and ensuring that all employees refrain from using their corporate e-mail addresses on third-party websites.

DDoS

Most DDoS attacks typically last from one to six hours, during which time the affected websites may lose partial or complete functionality. The most important steps to take in mitigating a DDoS attack include advance preparation, minimizing the necessary number of responders, and documenting the event to be in a position to share information about it with appropriate parties. In preparation for DDoS attacks, organizations are strongly encouraged to create an Incident Response (IR) plan, which should be stored in such a way that it is available even in the event of a network outage. The IR plan should be tested monthly or quarterly and should include:

- Emergency contact information for all key staff;

- Contact information for carriers, on-call network engineers, and DDoS providers;

- A chain of command or designated single decision-maker with ample expertise;

- A list of all entry points for the network and the staff responsible for each (if there are many networks, identify the services that go through each one);

- Document all IR tests in an incident tracking system;

- During IR tests, simulate a response with every relevant group on a call (ask about their capabilities and how they would respond to an event);

- Document all potential mitigation strategies;

- Set expectations across all teams regarding response timing (most DDoS events will require a minimum of 45-90 minutes to mitigate); and

- Open a bridge call for technical first-responders only (immediately document who is on the call and who is making decisions).

Phishing

Phishing e-mails typically solicit recipients to click on a link or open an attachment. If the recipient complies, malware may execute on their system and inflict a range of damages, which can include stealing usernames and passwords, encrypting the recipient's files with ransomware, and taking control over the infected computer via remote-access applications. While organization-wide awareness of phishing is integral to prevention, organizations should also consider taking the following precautions:

- Deploy antivirus software on *all* user workstations;

- Ensure all workstations are patched frequently;

- Block all attachments, all unwanted attachments, or use an online file exchange service;

- "Whitelist" attachment types that would be normally expected within a business context (such as .doc, .xls, and .pdf);

- Deploy application whitelisting (i.e. only approved apps may be used);

- Disable or remove Internet Explorer and use Google Chrome (considered more secure);

- Deploy ad blocking tools;

- Use a commercial proxy server to block malicious sites;

- Use a third-party service to train users about how to recognize phishing e-mails;

- Force all outbound web traffic to cross a proxy server so that it is logged and blocked by the service;

- Use an alternate PDF reader instead of Adobe; and

- Create a human resources (HR) policy advising that risky behavior on the network may result in repercussions (including termination).

In the event that a user has clicked on a link or executed an attachment, and phishing is suspected or confirmed, organizations should determine whether forensics are warranted and possible. If the answer is yes, conduct a forensic analysis on the workstation as well as proxy logs. If forensics are not possible, wipe and re image the user's workstation using a recent backup. Do not simply restore files; rather, *restore the entire operating system*. Identify how the file or link was received and put blocks on the e-mail system and proxy server to prevent further infections. Provide remedial training for staff members who open malicious links.

Ransomware

Destructive malware will most often take the form of ransomware, which is frequently executed on an organization's network via phishing. As noted earlier, after a user clicks on a malware link or opens a malicious e-mail attachment, the ransomware executes by encrypting all important files on the workstation—or, in some cases, multiple drives, networks, or critical systems—until a ransom is paid. Ransomware is common across all industry verticals and can be particularly disastrous for organizations that rely on access to such information. In order to prevent and prepare for ransomware infections, organizations should take the following precautions:

- Ensure that all workstations and servers have appropriate backups in place (not just a sync to a server);

- Have a pool of spare, offline devices ready if it is necessary to replace a user's workstation or server;

- Collect intelligence about major destructive malware events at other organizations and distribute intelligence to backup teams;

- Practice recovering a system from a backup on a recurring basis (monthly is recommended);

- Use network segmentation/isolation to protect high-risk or high-impact portions of the network (such as HR, Finance, and IT); and

- Use the services of a third-party vendor to simulate phishing and train users not to click on links or open attachments.

If a malware infection and/or ransomware encryption does occur, organizations should respond by utilizing the services of a forensics firm for major events impacting multiple systems. Be prepared to power off servers immediately if an attack is spreading across multiple systems and identify any sensitive documents on the system that may have been exfiltrated. Reset any impacted users' credentials and provide remedial information security training for employees who clicked on links or opened malicious attachments. Socialize general information about the event within the organization to raise employee awareness and notify regulators and/or law enforcement as required.[399]

Medical Devices

It is not enough to adopt the right approach to achieving cybersecurity for your own business because those efforts may be undercut by the defects inherent in third-party service providers or in the devices you may depend on to operate your business. Using the highly vulnerable medical services community as an example, if the manufacturers of medical devices do not exercise a similar degree of cyber resiliency, your own efforts may be severely undercut. For this reason, medical devices should be isolated inside a secure network zone, which is protected by an internal firewall that will only allow access to specific services and IP addresses. Ideally (and recognizing that this may not be practicable), medical devices should be completely isolated inside a network that is not connected to the external Internet.

At a minimum, health care providers should implement a strategy to rapidly integrate and deploy software and hardware fixes provided by the manufacturer to their medical devices, and a strategy to procure medical devices from any vendor only after a review with the manufacturer that focuses on the cybersecurity processes and protections. Quarterly reviews should be conducted with all medical device manufacturers. Older devices should be retired as soon as possible and only those new devices with your firm's cybersecurity protocol should replace them.

Medical device manufacturers must have a documented test process to determine if any of their devices are infected and a documented standard process to remediate the problem when malware and cyberattackers have infiltrated the device. Manufacturers should include specific language about the detection, remediation, and refurbishment of any medical devices sold to health care institutions which are then infected by malware. Only 'one-way' memory sticks should be used to preserve the air gap and encryption should be used wherever possible.[400]

Cyber Risk Insurance

The private sector has become accustomed to relying on a variety of risk management tools that the public sector generally either does not pursue or is unable to use, by virtue of their organizational size or because of the classified nature of their work. The insurance industry has been busy developing products to help meet the cybersecurity needs of the private sector, and cyber risk insurance (CRI) has been developed in recent years. CRI remains in a relatively embryonic state, based on how new this type of insurance is, the willingness of insurers to assume limited forms of risk associated with cyberattacks and on the relatively small size of the CRI market, when compared with other forms of insurance.

CRI is estimated to generate perhaps $3 to 4 billion worth of premiums, a small fraction of the more than $500 billion in premiums written only by US insurers in 2015. As the 'hot' new product, as might be expected, dozens of underwriters now offer CRI, and it has been estimated that its sales will grow to as much as $20 billion by 2020. As is the case with many forms of specialty insurance, some consumers are true believers in the product, while others either do not perceive a need for it or do not believe it adds much value.

Insurers naturally prefer to dive into a data-rich pool before assuming large potential liabilities in any class of insurance, but some areas of coverage do not lend themselves to that. The absence of historical data on cyber losses has made it difficult to build predictive models to assess the probability of loss. Insurers have not been selling CRI long enough, or on a large enough scale, to be able to generate their own mass of data. There is also no centralized source of information about cyber events for insurers to rely on and loss data is limited and unreliable, based on how new the field is and the fact that many attacks go unreported.

The 'moving target' nature of cyber risk also poses real challenges. As soon as insurers get comfortable with one form of cyber risk and start to believe they understand it, cyberattackers develop new operational methodologies, which requires a brand new set of assumptions, coverage parameters, loss scenarios, and sets of permissions for what can be reinsured. Given the dynamic nature of the IoT, there is serious question as to whether insurers will be able to keep up with the continual metamorphosis of cyber risk, which has prompted some insurers to wonder whether it is a pool they even wish to swim in. Some insurers also wonder about their own cyber vulnerabilities and what would happen if they were to become the target of a cyberattack and were unable to operate as a result. What kind of message would that send to their CRI clients regarding the sanctity of their insurer's cybersecurity?

To remain competitive, some insurance underwriters offer CRI as endorsements to standard property and liability policies in order to attract and retain insureds, sometimes with only minor or no increase in premiums. Ratings agencies have raised concern about whether these insurers understand the risk they are assuming, and whether they may be accumulating substantial but underfunded exposure on their books.

For their part, CRI consumers have difficulty quantifying what their likely exposure is. Just what would the impact of a cyberattack be on a firm's operations? How does a firm reliant on data determine its exposure, much less its potential loss, in the event of an attack? Very few firms have any real notion of the value of their data, much less its future value. How much insurance do they need, and are insurers willing to provide coverage for data, as well as physical assets? Is taking out coverage seen as a net plus or a net minus for the value of a company, given that the amount of CRI coverage is generally capped at low limits of liability? CRI products are far from standardized. How is a buyer to know what is best for them, and is what is best for them today likely to remain the case in the future, given how dynamic the marketplace is? These will remain perennial issues with no single correct answer.

Another consideration is that so few CRI claims have made their way through the legal landscape that there is real question about how 'the law' will judge various forms of losses. How does state law mesh with federal law when neither are well developed or 'battle tested'? What about losses in more than one national jurisdiction—will one take precedence over the other? The answers to such questions will, of course, take many years to sort themselves out. That will not stop some consumers from purchasing coverage, believing they are better off with it than having to explain why they did not have it in place when a loss occurs.

The CRI market is ripe for disruption, even as it is busy disrupting. Just as the traditional property-catastrophe insurance market was disrupted by catastrophe bonds and other insurance-linked securities, it is not hard to imagine how "cyber bonds" could one day be floated to help larger organizations transfer their exposure to investors in the capital markets. Similarly, cyber risk retention groups could be created to cover groups of small to midsize companies. Cyber captives may also be launched on- and off-shore to facilitate self-insurance and offer buyers direct access to the reinsurance market. Given how fast moving the insurance marketplace has become and the cyber risk marketplace already is, these types of risk management solutions, which were once considered out of the box, may become mainstream and preferred solutions going forward.

An enduring challenge for the insurance industry will be how to model for cyber risk losses. All but the newest forms of insurance have rich data pools to select from, even if there have been great differences in the timing and scope of losses, such as for weather-related events.[401] A cyber disaster comparable in scale to a major hurricane cannot be modeled because it has not happened yet, but many of the points already raised make a modeling exercise doubly difficult when it does actually occur.

The four-hour outage of Amazon's S3 cloud storage system (which was not the result of a cyberattack), in 2017, cost S&P 500 companies an estimated $150 million. Lloyd's analyzed a hypothetical scenario in which a blackout in the northeastern US left 93 million people without power and concluded that such an event could cost insurers between $21 billion and $71 billion, illustrating how challenging it is to pinpoint the cost of such risks.

There are some important differences between modeling natural catastrophes and cyber catastrophes, foremost among them being the fact that humans drive cyber events rather than meteorological laws. While storms, earthquakes, and volcanic eruptions defy accurate prediction as naturally occurring phenomena, hackers' motivations, tactics, and targets do the same. However, insurers can "map" the locations where valuable data are stored[402], and a new methodology of valuing what data is worth has been created (the Enterprise value of Data[403]) which should result in greater predictive capability in the near-term.

A decision about whether to purchase CRI coverage will be different for each consumer. It does add value and is usually better than not having the degree of comfort that insurance provides. The average risk manager will surely want to be able to say to his or her superior that CRI is in place, when asked. However, consumers can be forgiven for being at least a little leery of the product, given its evolutionary status; then again, that has been the case for every insurance product when it was new. What will remain a question mark is just how CRI will evolve, how claims will be addressed, whether the law will catch up to the coverage, and whether cyberattackers will make such coverage largely irrelevant at the end of the day.

The Pentagon's Cyberwarfare Strategy

The most sensitive of USG agencies have for some time continually fortified their cybersecurity programs, and it will surprise no one to learn that the Pentagon has been a long-time leader in doing so. In 2015, the Pentagon released a new strategy that for the first time explicitly discussed the circumstances under which cyberweapons could be used against an attacker, naming the countries it believed presented the greatest threat: China, Iran, North Korea, and Russia. At the core of the revised cyber strategy was a hierarchy of cyberattacks, ranging from those that US companies should maintain responsibility for and should be capable of fending off to approximately 2 percent of attacks on American data systems that may be of such significance that they would require a governmental response. The strategy called for an appropriate US military response via cyberoperations to disrupt an adversary's military related networks or infrastructure, so as to protect US interests.

Most USG cyberattacks on adversaries have historically been covert operations, classified, and deliberately not publicized.

407

At the heart of the diplomatic, economic, and threatened military responses is the concept of deterrence—which the US had a far easier time establishing in the nuclear arena than it has had in cyberspace, where attribution is elusive. The new strategy acknowledged that deterrence was, at least in part, a function of perception. The objective is to convince a potential adversary that it will suffer unacceptable costs if it conducts an attack on the US, decreasing the likelihood that a potential adversary will attack. Of course, for that approach to succeed, the US must be able to declare or display effective response capabilities to deter an adversary from initiating an attack, which it may be reluctant to do. It must also develop effective defensive capabilities to deny a potential attack from succeeding and strengthen the resilience of US systems to withstand an attack.[404]

In a comprehensive review of the resilience of military systems toward cyberthreats, a DoD task force made sweeping recommendations for how the US military may become better prepared to thwart future cyberattacks. It called for deeper intelligence collection about adversaries' offensive software and hardware tools, including identification and understanding of adversarial cyber weapon development organizations, tools, leadership, and intentions, as well as development of targeting information to support initiatives to counter cyber weaponization. There was a recognition of the need to move beyond tabletop exercises and develop the capacity to conduct many (potentially hundreds or more) simultaneous, synchronized offensive cyber operations while defending against a like number of cyberattacks.

The task force further recommended establishing an enterprise security architecture that would give the DoD the ability to segment its network, provide continuous monitoring and situational awareness, automate patch and threat management functions, and provide out-of-band command and control for most sensitive systems. It pointed out that little consideration had been devoted to military system design focused on providing test points that can report system health and operation, which needed to change.

The Department was directed to develop methods to evolve trusted copies of operating software for systems that ensured only the desired changes were made in the "gold copy" and to leverage commercial technologies to automate portions of network maintenance and "real-time" mitigation of detected malware. Perhaps most importantly, the task force sought a change in the DoD's culture regarding cybersecurity by establishing a department-wide policy to enhance communication and education programs.

The DoD was urged to change its focus to cyberspace, acknowledging that, unlike other facets of military doctrine, cyber actors often bear little cost to engaging in risky behavior. It was recommended that the Department establish a plan that comprised operational rules and expectations for the secure use of DoD networks and systems, training programs, a small team of experts to monitor and test breaches in policy, and establish clear punitive consequences for breaches of cyber policy. Legacy computer systems that were unable to meet new standards of cybersecurity were to be isolated or replaced.[405] It is heartening when such a large institution takes a good hard look at itself and can be honest about its cyber deficiencies, and what needs to be done to correct them. If that can be done inside the Pentagon, there should be no organization on Earth that cannot do the same.

What OPM Did to Fortify its Defenses

In Chapter 1 we reviewed some of the things that the OPM had done wrong, which led to its disastrous data breach. It was a case study in what *not* to do and its impacts will continue to be felt for many years. Although it has not been widely acknowledged in the media, since 2014 there has been a truly impressive effort by the agency to fortify its cybersecurity. The OPM's transformation is useful to review as a case study, for it demonstrates just what is required to go from an organizational cybersecurity wasteland to a model for other large public-sector organizations to emulate.

The OPM's senior leadership drew up a master plan shortly after the breach was uncovered and (relatively swiftly for a government agency), implemented 23 concrete steps to improve its data security:

409

1. Two-factor Strong Authentication was implemented for all privileged users, and the percentage of unprivileged users with the same authentication was increased. The OPM became a leader in requiring the utilization of a Personal Identity Verification card (or alternative form of multi-factor authentication) to significantly reduce the risk of adversaries penetrating federal networks and systems.

2. Remote access for network administrators was severely restricted.

3. Only legitimate business connections were allowed to have access to the Internet.

4. New hardware and software was deployed, including 14 essential tools to secure the network. The OPM continues to deploy additional security tools to improve its cybersecurity posture, including those that mask and redact data.

5. Anti-malware software was distributed across the organization to protect and prevent the deployment or execution of cybercrime tools that could compromise the agency's networks.

6. Security Assessment and Authorization was upgraded for multiple systems.

7. A 24/7 Security Operations Center was created and staffed by certified professionals to monitor the network for security alerts.

8. Continuous monitoring was implemented to enhance the ability to identify and respond in real time to cyberthreats.

9. More firewalls were installed to enable the agency to filter network traffic.

10. Centralized security management and accountability was introduced into the Office of the CIO, which was staffed with fully trained security professionals.

11. A comprehensive review of IT security clause contracts was reviewed to ensure that appropriate oversight and protocols are in place.

12. A Risk Executive function was introduced to ensure risk mitigation at the organizational, business process, and information system levels (this included development of a Risk Executive Charter and Risk Registry Template).

13. Cybersecurity awareness training was mandated for the entire workforce.

14. The OPM collaborated with agency partners to share, learn and standardize best practices, and to ensure information security policies are rigorous and cost-effective, based on a risk assessment methodology that considers both current and potential threats.

15. The intelligence community and other stakeholders were brought in to identify high value cyber targets within the OPM network and mitigate target vulnerabilities to the extent practicable.

16. Law enforcement and other agencies worked with the OPM to shore up existing security protocols, enhance system security, and detect and thwart evolving and persistent threats.

17. Management and technology experts were brought in from around the government to help manage IR, provide advice on further actions, and ensure that Congress and the public are kept current on ongoing efforts.

18. The OPM helped other agencies hire IT leaders to ensure they can acquire the personnel needed to combat evolving cyberthreats.

19. Resources were devoted to network remediation and stabilization to modernize the OPM's IT footprint. From Fiscal Year 2014 to 2015, OPM nearly tripled its investment in IT modernization effort, from $31 million to $87 million. The funding for 2016 paid for maintenance of a sustained security operations center to provide critical

oversight of the OPM's security posture and real-time 24/7 monitoring of network servers to detect and respond to malicious activity. It also included support for stronger firewalls and storage devices for capturing security log information used for analysis in IR.

20. The OPM will continue standardizing operating systems and applications throughout the agency, with the ultimate goal of implementing configuration baselines for all operating platforms being used. Once these baselines are in place, OPM will conduct routine compliance scans against them to identify any security vulnerabilities that may still exist.

21. The OPM is still in the process of developing, documenting, and implementing enhanced oversight procedures for ensuring that a system test is fully executed for each contractor-operated system.

22. The agency is reviewing the number of approved privileged users, and taking steps to minimize their numbers, limit the functions they can perform, the duration of time they can be logged in, the functions that can performed remotely, and ensuring that all privileged user activity occurs while users are logged on.

23. Finally, portfolio management was improved by hiring a dedicated IT portfolio manager to lead its IT transformation efforts and ensure that security and performance requirements are addressed across the enterprise.

These actions put the OPM in a much stronger and more secure posture than it was in when the breach occurred. As a result of the cybersecurity enhancements described above, the OPM was able to detect sophisticated malicious activity that continues to plague its networks. The agency has taken a number of additional actions to strengthen its cybersecurity even further, among them:

- Expanding continuous monitoring of contractor systems.

- Ensuring access to contractor systems to ensure that the OPM and law enforcement agencies can access data and conduct effective and immediate response in the case of any future cyber incidents.

- Reviewing encryption of databases to determine whether additional encryption is possible.

- Reaching out to leading private sector companies to leverage their experience.

- Incrementally engineering a modern network capable of significantly increased security controls.

- Establishing regular employee and contractor training to ensure that every individual is doing their part to protect the agency's sensitive data. Going forward, this training will be required on a bi-annual basis.

- Putting in place clear protocols and plans of actions prepared in advance to manage IR.

The OPM has taken aggressive steps to improve security protocols, set up continuous monitoring of its systems, and other measures that have established the agency as a leader in federal cybersecurity procedures.[406] Its dramatic cybersecurity transformation is a credit to its leaders and employees. If the rest of the USG is able to implement similar safeguards, the type of breach it endured in 2014 will hopefully never happen again. Similar cybersecurity transformations are occurring throughout the USG.

Best Practices

Fortunately, in this new and evolving world of Virtual Terrorism, there are a range of best practices that individuals, businesses, and governments can turn to in an attempt to protect themselves against virtual terrorists. Many of them are common sense and some are easy to implement, while others require sophisticated IT infrastructure. The point of going down the road of attempting to turn the tide is to embrace an ecosystem of protection that cascades from organizational culture to decision maker to the IT department and on down to the end user of data. Engaging in best practices implies comprehension of the scope of the problem and a willingness to do what it takes to fight back.

Defensive Systems: Multiple, overlapping, and mutually supportive defensive systems should be deployed to guard against single point failures in any specific technology or protection method. This should include regularly updated firewalls as well as gateway antivirus, intrusion detection or protection systems, website vulnerability with malware protection, and web security gateway solutions throughout the network. Implement smart data governance practices in your organization so that you know what business data is being stored on cloud services.

Encryption: Implement and enforce a security policy whereby any sensitive data is encrypted at rest and in transit. Ensure that customer data is encrypted as well and that passwords are strong. *Important passwords, such as those for users with high privileges, should be at least 8-10 characters long (preferably longer) and include a mixture of letters, numbers, and special characters.* Encourage users to avoid reusing the same passwords on multiple websites. Sharing passwords with others should be forbidden. Delete unused credentials and profiles and limit the number of administrative-level profiles created.

E-mail: Educate employees on the dangers posed by spear phishing e-mails, including exercising caution around e-mails from unfamiliar sources more generally, and the dangers of opening attachments that have not been solicited. *Be leery of any that look suspicious or appear to be too good to be true, and any Microsoft Office e-mail attachment that advises you to enable macros to view its content. Unless you are absolutely sure that it is a genuine e-mail from a trusted source, do not enable macros and instead immediately delete the e-mail. Do not reply to suspicious e-mails and do not give out sensitive information.* Report suspicious or obviously bogus e-mails to the proper authorities. Never use links in an e-mail to connect to a website unless you are sure it is genuine. *Type URLs directly into the address bar to ensure you are connecting to a legitimate site and not one with an address that simply looks similar.*

Software: Always keep your security software up to date to protect yourself against any new malware variants and keep your operating system and other software constantly updated (daily, if not multiple times per day, since multiple updates occur each day). Software updates will frequently include patches for newly discovered security vulnerabilities that could be exploited by attackers.

Websites: Regularly assess your website for any vulnerabilities—scan it daily to check for malware and secure your websites against MITM attacks. Choose SSL Certificates with Extended Validation to verify protection and display the green browser address bar to website users. Display recognized "trust" marks in highly visible locations on your website, and be picky about displaying plugins. The software you use to manage your website may come with vulnerabilities included. The more third-party software you use, the greater your attack surface, so only deploy what is absolutely necessary.

Additional actions to take:

- Research the capabilities and security features of an IoT device before purchase and perform an audit of IoT devices used on your network.

- Regularly backup any files stored on your computer or any other devices (weekly, and preferably, daily).

- On mobile devices, refrain from downloading apps from unfamiliar sites and only install apps from trusted sources.

- Sign up to alerts from your bank so that you will be alerted if any suspicious transactions are made on your account.

- Change the default credentials on devices, and regularly check the manufacturer's website for firmware updates.

- Disable features and services that are not required.

- Modify the default privacy and security settings of IoT devices according to your requirements. Disable or protect remote access to devices when not needed.

- *Use wired connections instead of wireless where possible.*

- Ensure that a hardware outage does not result in an unsecure state of the device.

- Install a suitable mobile security app to protect your device and data.

- Ensure that the cloud service you use regularly backs up your files.[407]

The list of potential safeguards is almost endless—these are but a few of the most common recommendations. We must be able to say to ourselves that we have at least tried to do everything within our power to protect against virtual terrorists. Those organizations that fail to take these basic precautions are likely to end up regretting it, but the truth is, that if a hacker intends to attack you or your firm, they will, and chances are, they will be successful.

Lessons from Petya

You can do everything on that list and still remain vulnerable, because software developers only know what it is they are supposed to be protecting against after a new form of malware has been deployed, identified, and a way is found to block it. The Petya malware that swept the world in 2017 is a useful case in point. The attack was different from the WannaCry virus unleashed a few weeks earlier in several ways. Although ostensibly referred to as a form of ransomware, Petya was ultimately more accurately described

416

as a form of *sabotage* rather than an attempt to generate revenue. It is estimated that less than $10,000 in ransom was actually paid as a result of the attack, at least in part because the e-mail link that ransom was supposed to be paid to was taken offline shortly after the attack. *Petya was ultimately intended to steal passwords and destroy data*, and, unlike WannaCry, Petya had no kill switch, so it represented a much more insidious threat. With the arrival of Petya, *more "blended" cyberattacks (combining ransomware with "wiper" or other forms of attack) should be expected, mixing elements of different threat vectors in new ways.*

After the attack, it was learned that hackers penetrated the network of a small Ukrainian software firm (MeDoc) which sold a piece of accounting software used by approximately 80 percent of Ukraine's businesses. By injecting a tweaked version of a file into updates of that software, they were able to start spreading backdoored versions of it weeks before Petya was deployed throughout Ukraine, injecting Petya through the MeDoc system's entry points. In the process, it was learned that innocent software updates could be used to silently spread the malware.

Kaspersky Labs subsequently said it had seen two other examples in the year prior to the release of Petya of malware delivered via software updates to carry out sophisticated infections. In one case, perpetrators used updates for a popular piece of software to breach financial institutions. In another, hackers corrupted the update mechanism for a form of ATM software sold by an American company to be able to hack cash machines. *Similar attacks should be expected in the future by infecting the supply chain that links dispersed computer systems together.*

In the Petya case, hackers first breached another unnamed software firm and used its VPN connections to other companies to plant ransomware on a handful of targets. Only later did the hackers move on to MeDoc as a malware delivery tool. One reason hackers are turning to software updates as an inroad into vulnerable computers may be the growing use of "whitelisting" as a security measure, which, as noted above, strictly limits what can be installed on a computer to only "approved" programs. *A basic security precaution that every modern developer should use to prevent their software updates from being corrupted is "codesigning", which requires that any new code added to an application be signed with an unforgeable cryptographic key. MeDoc did not implement codesigning, which would have allowed any hacker that can intercept software updates to act as a MITM and alter them to include a backdoor.*

The hackers were deep enough into MeDoc's network that they likely could have stolen the cryptographic key and signed the malicious update themselves, or even added their backdoor directly into the source code before it would be compiled into an executable program, signed, and distributed. None of this should dissuade anyone from updating and patching their software or using software that updates automatically.

Codesigning no doubt makes compromising software updates far more difficult, requiring much deeper access to a target company for hackers to corrupt its code. That means codesigned software that is downloaded or updated from Google's Play Store or the Apple App Store is far safer and thus significantly harder to compromise than a piece of software like MeDoc, distributed by a family-run company without codesigning. But even the App Store's security is not impenetrable. In 2015, hackers distributed infected developer software that inserted malicious code into hundreds of iPhone apps in the App Store that were likely installed on millions of devices, despite Apple's strict codesigning implementation.

What this all means is that on highly sensitive networks such as the type of critical infrastructure disabled by Petya, even "trusted" applications cannot be fully trusted. Systems administrators need to segment and compartmentalize their networks, restrict the privileges of even whitelisted software, and retain backups in case of any ransomware outbreak.[408] In the Era of Virtual Terrorism, no one can afford to believe they will not be targeted or that hackers will not be successful in attacking even the best protected system. That is why this book is dedicated to everyone who has either been hacked, or will be, because chances are, at some point in time, you will be hacked.

17. <u>The Future</u>

> A big reason why the cybersecurity landscape is so bad is that too few people and organizations take it seriously. That might have been forgiven when the Internet was the new thing but, *today, the consequences of failing to get it right are known and the failure to do so is simply dereliction of duty.* It is clear that minimum universal standards need to be established to help ensure that the entire product manufacturing and sales process—from the beginning of the supply chain through to the end user— implements an adequate and ethical cybersecurity protocol. If that were the case, the software industry would no longer be able to walk away from liability for hacking. If courts do not force the liability issue, public opinion eventually will. It is a shame that it may take that to focus the collective mind on the problem.[409]

The Dark Web is Taking a Darker Turn

A black market being run by international cybercrime syndicates on the Dark Web points toward an ominous future for sensitive information and could redefine how the cyber forensics industry will need to adapt to new realities going forward. By using previously stolen information from organizational insiders and hacker mercenaries, a range of actors appear to be subcontracting cybercriminal groups around the world to provide access to information they do not have. The black marketplace they have created is known as Comarkets (or "Criminal Market") and was formerly known as "Babylon APT". CMarket functions on the Dark Web and contains *a public marketplace, invite-only sub-markets, and hacker-for-hire services available to potentially breach any network in any country.* The site is apparently run by hackers from multiple countries and was formed because other Dark Web marketplaces have become too likely to draw the attention of law enforcement and intelligence agencies.

When cybersecurity experts trace the origin of a cyberattack, they typically review the tools used, which type of hacking group would likely have been interested in the target, and which other cyberattacks used similar tools or had related criminal interests. That model is being turned upside down by CMarket, which illustrates just how significantly global cartels, organized crime networks, cybercrime syndicates, and governments overlap and create a counter narrative that plays by a different set of rules. Russian hackers had breached data from a terrorist group and were planning to sell it to government authorities but, instead, chose to wait for the terrorists to carry out their attack, knowing that waiting to release the information after the attack had occurred would increase the value and therefore the price of the data.

Some data for sale in CMarket is geared specifically towards government interests, including databases from some of the world's largest and most sophisticated intelligence and military agencies (which implies that some members of the CMarket are active personnel in these organizations). Data from research organizations, universities, infrastructure-related ICS, sensitive identification and security access systems, as well as information associated with elections are all being sold on CMarket. Data related to active national investigations, hospital data bases, personal identification information, industrial espionage, and other information of interest to cybercriminals also form part of the CMarket mosaic.

Through CMarket, hacked information from other hackers, intelligence from governments, and stolen information from competing cybercriminal organizations are all being sold to one another, painting a sinister picture of the path the Dark Web has already taken. One can only imagine how insidious the Dark Web will become in the future. The willingness of organizational insiders to sell their data is an Achilles heel of the Internet, but is only one contributing factor that has enabled CMarket to exist and thrive. Should CMarket be taken down by law enforcement one day, as AlphaBay was, it will undoubtedly be the case that another version of it will quickly be created to take its place.[410]

Focusing the Collective Mind

As we have seen, virtual terrorists have the ability to stay a perpetual step ahead their opponents and require seemingly endless resources to combat them. In 2016, more than $18 billion was spent on cybersecurity, and it has been estimated that nearly a trillion dollars more will have been spent by 2022 trying to make organizations and individuals more cyber resilient. Despite this, Virtual Terrorism is clearly getting worse. With data breaches at an all-time high, virtual terrorists are becoming more ferocious and the toll they take is rising to ever greater heights. Could it be that the words "cyber" and "security" are a contradiction in terms?

We are fighting battles on multiple fronts and all of them require ingenuity, resources, and seemingly endless perseverance to win. Unprecedented amounts of data are now online and it is doubling every three years, which means that today's cybersecurity challenges will seem easy by comparison with what awaits us in the near future. We do not necessarily understand our data—its value, its sensitivity, who has access to it, or how to classify it. That needs to change.

There are surprisingly few regulations that force companies to take reasonable steps to protect their data. We tend to value convenience of access over our data versus cumbersome security access measures; too many people are willing to risk a data breach over a little inconvenience. Too many organizations select hosting providers, encryption methodologies, and sophisticated cybersecurity tools before they truly understand what they should be protecting and what they are purchasing. They often spend tens or hundreds of thousands of dollars on sophisticated cybersecurity tools but fail to educate their employees about basic security measures.[411]

The IoT has thrust upon us a computerized world that is slowly taking over more and more of what makes modern societies and businesses function, from road signs and cars to medical devices and airplanes. Bulletproof security is often an afterthought in the production process. Hackers have proven they are able to take control over just about anything. The Internet-driven black market for computerized extortion, stolen goods, and hacking-for-hire is booming. In 2017, Google was already managing approximately 2 billion lines of source code and the average computer program had 14 vulnerabilities, each of them being a potential illicit entry point. It is easy to quickly get discouraged that the task that confronts us seems insurmountable and that the game is already over.

A big reason why the cybersecurity landscape is so bad is that too few people and organizations take it seriously. That might have been forgiven when the Internet was the new thing, but today the consequences of failing to get it right are known, and the failure to do so is simply dereliction of duty. It is clear that minimum universal standards need to be established to help ensure that the entire product manufacturing and sales process—from the beginning of the supply chain through to the end user—implements an adequate and ethical cybersecurity protocol. If that were the case, the software industry would no longer be able to walk away from liability for hacking. If courts do not force the liability issue, public opinion eventually will. It is a shame that it may take that to focus the collective mind on the problem.[412]

In 2016, the Pew Research Center and Elon University's Imagining the Internet Center canvassed more than 1,500 technology experts, scholars, corporate practitioners, and government leaders about how they see the future of the IoT. While respondents expressed a range of opinions, from deep concern to disappointment to resignation to optimism, most agreed that people are generally empowered by networked communication technologies. Some expressed concern about the risk of an altered power dynamic between state-level actors, elites and "regular" citizens—a natural outgrowth of a heightened state of cybersecurity more generally.

Most of the experts predicted that the exchange of information and sharing of diverse ideologies over the next decade will create new challenges, as hundreds of millions more people around the world become connected to the Internet for the first time. One of the biggest challenges will be finding an appropriate balance between protecting anonymity and enforcing consequences for abusive behavior.[413] The effort to create a safer and equalized Internet will inevitably push bad actors into more-hidden operational channels (such as Tor). It should be expected that the perpetrators of Virtual Terrorism will attempt to counter enhanced cyber resiliency among their targets by adapting accordingly, setting the stage for a battle that will surely be ongoing for decades to come.

The Cyber Resiliency Curve

In the judgment of a number of cybersecurity professionals, both the public and private sectors remain far behind the cyber resiliency curve. There has been a great deal of resistance against the objective of achieving cyber resiliency in part because it is a relatively new concept and so many people and organizations do not understand it. Many firms do not have a cyber strategy and attempt to 'buy' their way out of a problem after the fact, rather than adopting a holistic strategy. Those firms that have the right tools often do not properly implement them, fail to make resiliency a part of their organizational DNA, harden their work force, or do other things that would give them a better ability to fight back.

Several studies have revealed that the vast majority of cyber breaches occur in software systems that are more than 10 years old. The solution is generally simple—to patch the vulnerability—but too many people fail to exercise even the most basic cyber due diligence, as the WannaCry and Petya viruses of 2017 attest. There is also resistance among some organizations about being on the 'leading edge'—they do not want to be the early adopters. Once a best practice standard becomes apparent, organizations tend to move toward it in droves.

According to Greg Touhill, the former (and first) CISO of the USG, the biggest surprise he encountered in his job was how many senior decision-makers in the government were completely oblivious to cyber risk (in his experience, private sector critical infrastructure providers have a similar degree of ignorance). He was pleasantly surprised to find that civilian decision-makers in the USG were receptive to his suggestions. When he started as CISO in the Obama administration, only 32 percent of the USG used multi-factor authentication; 8 months later it was 90 percent. Touhill thinks we will see more 'managed' cybersecurity services in the future, with smaller IT departments doing more outsourcing.

Mike Brown, a former Director of Cybersecurity Coordination for the DHS, believes that the USG needs to do a lot more to achieve what may be considered a cohesive, strategic approach to cybersecurity. He does not think the USG has presented a consistent articulation for what its cyber strategy should be, or what its expectations are for measurable results. In his opinion, some areas of the DHS are better in some cybersecurity practices than the DoD or any other parts of government, and vice versa, pointing to a lack of consistency.

It seems clear that most organizations will remain reactive rather than proactive and hesitate to "run toward the light" to embrace strict cybersecurity protocols. That is partly due to human and organizational nature. After all, getting it right is a rather time and resource consuming proposition. Fortunately, the landscape of options is far better in 2017 than it was in the past, with a literal smorgasbord of experts and service providers ready to assist those organizations who reach out for help.

Future Technologies

As mesmerizing as the explosion of bold new technologies has been over the past couple of decades, the future promises to make them pale by comparison. A tremendous range of such technologies are already under development in areas such as nanotechnology, biotechnology, robotics and AI. Along with it will come new opportunities for propelling the human race audaciously into the future, as well as expanded room to maneuver for those with more malicious intentions. Just as the cost of getting things done in cyberspace will become faster and cheaper, Virtual Terrorism will become easier to achieve, particularly for those with the technological skill to take advantage of the changes that await us.

Synthetic biology will make it easier to produce biological agents in home laboratories, cyborg insects will be able to spread bio-agents and poisons, and tiny robots a few millimeters in size will be mass-produced in swarms (able to join other swarms to produce armies of tiny robots). Weapons will become smaller, cheaper, easier to obtain, and more easily hidden. The cost of 3D printers will become low enough to permit broad usage and could result in covert weapon production. Biometric systems will be expanded to include not just face, iris, voice, or hand recognition, but vein patterns and hand geometry. Along with such enhanced risks will come enhanced means of protection, such as safeguards against computer viruses that automatically begin the hunt for perpetrators the moment a cyber intrusion begins and the ability to collect DNA markers from suspicious mail.

Part of the price for this advance in technology will be more erosion of privacy, a loss of trust in government, and increased public anxiety. To the extent that cyberattacks on critical infrastructure become successful (as will undoubtedly become the case), bio attacks occur, or EMP is unleashed, the degree to which public opinion of government stops being eroded will depend on how successful it can become in responding to such attacks. As has already been discussed in detail, most of the world's governments have a long way to go before they may hope to be able to say that (if, indeed, they desire to, and many will not).

It may not be too difficult to imagine a world, as envisioned in the 2002 film *Minority Report*, wherein crime (including cybercrime and cyberterrorism) can be predicted, using advanced algorithms and AI. Some may consider such an eventuality the birth of a true police state, while others may just be thankful that the technology exists. Such capability would certainly create ample opportunity for systemic abuse. Imagine what kind of fun hackers would have by creating false accusations of future crimes or turning law enforcement on itself.

We may not realize it, but everyone is a stakeholder in a cybersecure future, whether a perpetrator, victim, law enforcement official, intelligence officer, or prison guard. This raises many questions, such as, assuming we do create a better mousetrap, where will the money be found to support it, what kind of impact will that have on the judicial and penal systems, and will the public require limitations on future compromises to civil liberties? These would all be nice questions to have to answer, but the truth is that arriving at a more effective means of combating Virtual Terrorism, and dealing with its aftermath, imply delving into uncharted waters with no clear path into the future.[414]

A Dystopian 1984 Future?

Being watched by the government and competitors, having data sold without permission, and the constant threat of cyberattacks—one could be forgiven for wondering just what the future holds for anyone concerned about privacy and the sanctity of data. Many would argue that tech developers have a responsibility to prevent a dystopian *1984* future from becoming a reality. In George Orwell's *1984*, technology was being used to monitor, control, and dictate individual action. Orwell imagined a world in which people distracted themselves without any meaning or purpose. In the future, computing will be defined by the choices that developers make and the impact those choices have on the world.

There is much discussion in the tech world about what AI will mean for society, especially since it is quickly driving change that could eliminate jobs. Microsoft is presently infusing all of its products and services with AI and enabling those who develop on its platform to imbue creations with customized capabilities. Microsoft research has gone deep into areas such as machine learning, speech recognition, and enabling machines to recognize what they "see". *Amazon, Apple, Google, and IBM have also been aggressively pursuing AI as a business model whose primary focus is to mine personal information using AI to sell things.*

The benefits and potential perils of AI have already been discussed. Microsoft lets developers customize gesture commands and voice recognition instead of making them conform to settings in "off-the-shelf" AI. Devices such as smart surveillance cameras, smartphones, or factory floor machines could become part of "edge computing", with the coordination of cloud power and intelligent edge devices improving productivity and safety on the ground. The company sees the future as a "smart cloud", with mobile devices taking back seats to digital assistants that follow people from device to device.[415]

426

If that is the future, *the smart cloud could become dark quickly, as it is certain that hackers and cybercriminals will find a way to hijack it for their own benefit.* In 2017, new AI software took a still image of a person and an audio clip, using them to create a doctored video of the person speaking the audio and creating realistically fake videos. These systems focus on changing the shape of the mouth but eventually they will also be able to change facial expressions and posture, which would essentially make AI a "tool" for artists. Soon enough, we will have difficulty distinguishing between real and fake video (fake news on steroids). Experts are already able to create fake videos that are virtually indistinguishable from genuine videos. Existing AI tools are making the process so quick and easy that, eventually, almost anyone will be able to do it.[416]

Hackers can already introduce faults in sensitive products such as drones that are produced by 3D printers, according to researchers from Ben-Gurion University of the Negev, South Alabama University and Singapore University of Technology and Design, who warned that "bugs" produced in computers could cause them to crash or otherwise be destroyed. The team produced a YouTube video in which they destroyed a $1,000 drone by breaking into a computer, identifying the drafting file of the drone and introducing defects that cannot be detected by visual examination. During flight tests, the defective propeller broke when the drone ascended. As a result, it crashed to the ground and was destroyed.

As of 2015, the 3D printing industry was estimated to be worth in excess of $5 billion, with one third of all objects produced by the technology serving as functional parts. More than 100 industries already use 3D printing, including for the production of aviation engines and in the defense industry. Imagine the challenge of identifying and keeping track of all the 3D-produced hardware already produced, much less to be produced. It has potential impact on national security, the economy, and even lives. *3D printing has already attracted the attention of cyberterrorists and will become of greater interest with time.[417] It is not hard to imagine virtual terrorists seeking to sabotage an entire range of sensitive 3D products, given how relatively easy it may become to do.*

Digital Social Control

The Chinese Communist Party appears to be on its way to creating its own futuristic dystopia—what it calls a "social-credit system"—which aims to rate and manage the social and political behavior of its citizens. It is not yet clear how extensive the system will be, whether it will even work, nor if it can withstand the criticism it will inevitably receive, but an outline is complete and some of the building blocks are in place. All signs are that China has begun the most ambitious experiment in digital social control in the world.

A pilot scheme in Suining county (in Jiangsu province, north of Shanghai) gives clues about what such a system might mean in practice. In 2010, the local government began awarding people points for good behavior (such as winning a national honor of some kind) and deducted points for everything from minor traffic offenses to illegally petitioning authorities for assistance. Those who scored highest were eligible for rewards such as fast-track promotion at work or being able to jump the queue for public housing. Amid a public backlash, the project turned out to be a failure.

Despite that, the CCP and government seemed undaunted, issuing plans for a nationwide social credit system, with about 30 local governments collecting data that would support it, as of 2016. The plan appears hugely ambitious, aiming to explicitly influence the behavior of the whole of Chinese society. The project is a response to one of the Party's biggest problems: the collapse of confidence in public institutions and the need to keep track of the changing views and interests of China's population (without letting them vote, of course).

Almost every Chinese citizen has a *hukou* (household registration) document that determines where they can get public services. Wholesale surveillance (increasingly digital) is a central pillar of CCP rule. A system of block-by-block surveillance called "grid management" is being set up in several parts of the country. Newer forms of monitoring involve the ubiquitous use of CCTV cameras (China has overtaken the US as the country with the largest number of CCTV devices).

As Internet use has grown, so have China's comprehensive controls in cyberspace—from the Great Firewall (the system that blocks access to tens of thousands of websites) to the Golden Shield (an extensive online surveillance system) and the Great Cannon (a tool to attack hostile websites). The scale of the data collection effort suggests that the long-term aim is to keep track of the transactions made, websites visited, and messages sent by all of China's 700 million Internet users. Given that the NSA can already collect 42 billion Internet records per month and 5 billion mobile phone location records each day, China's data collection ambitions should not prove too challenging.

To undertake such surveillance work, the government must match the owners of devices with the digital footprints they leave behind, so laws passed in 2012 and 2016 require Internet firms to retain their customers' names and other personal information (it is unclear how censors plan to tackle VPNs, which mask a user's IP address). The list at the heart of the social credit system is called the "judgment defaulter's list", composed of those who have defied a court order. People on the list can be prevented from buying tickets to travel, sell, buy, or build a house, enroll their children in elite fee-paying schools, join or be promoted in the Party and army, or receive honors and titles. If the defaulter is a company it may not issue shares or bonds, accept foreign investment, or work on government projects.

By August 2016, defaulters had already been stopped from buying airline tickets about 5 million times. Other types of "untrustworthy behavior" meriting attention include conduct that seriously undermines normal social order, cyberspace transmissions, and endangering national defense interests. Such broad categories imply the system could be used to punish dissent, expressions of opinion, and perceived threats to security. Regulations on video games say that individuals or firms that violate the rules could be blacklisted and inscribed in the social credit database. The social credit project could well become a 360-degree digital surveillance panopticon.

Although Western governments, companies, data-brokers, and marketing companies all hold vast quantities of personal information without causing serious harm to civil liberties, China treats personal information differently. In conventional democracies, laws limit what companies may do with it and the extent to which governments can get their hands on it. China's National Security Law and the new Cybersecurity Law give the government unrestricted access to almost all personal data. Civil liberty advocates who might protest are increasingly thrown in jail, and companies that hold data (such as Alibaba, Baidu, and Tencent) routinely obey government demands to access data.

While Big data systems in democracies are not designed for social control, China's is, and since its leaders consider the interest of the CCP and society to be one in the same, instruments of social control can be used for political purposes. In 2016, the Party asked China Electronics Technology Group (one of the country's largest defense contractors) to develop software to predict terrorist risks on the basis of people's job records, financial background, consumption habits, hobbies, and data collected from surveillance cameras. Sifting through data ostensibly to seek terrorists can easily morph into hunting down dissidents. Western intelligence agencies have tried to use data mining schemes to identify individual terrorists but have generally failed because of an excess of false positives.

Can such a vast social credit system actually work? The Chinese face two big technical hurdles: the quality of the data and the sensitivity of the instruments to analyze it. Big data projects everywhere—such as the attempt by Britain's National Health Service to create a nationwide medical database—have stumbled over the issue of how to prevent incorrect information from contaminating the system. Problems associated with the processing and interpreting of bad data would be even more onerous in a country of 1.4 billion people. Analyzing all that data would no doubt be an issue, and such a repository of data would also provide incentives for cybercriminals to steal or alter information.

Acknowledging such challenges, the Chinese government has allowed an unusual amount of discussion about them in state-run media. A 2016 high-level "social credit summit" in Shanghai talked about how scores can be checked and mistakes rectified. Much about the social credit system remains unclear. The government has apparently not yet determined whether it wants to use the system primarily to crack down on crooks or greatly enhance its surveillance state, but the government has already created the capacity for a *1984*-esque national system of social control. Many of the elements are already in place: the databases, digital surveillance, system of reward and punishment, and the "state knows what is best for you" paternalism. All that remains is for the government to join the pieces together. When that is done, China will have the world's first digital totalitarian state.[418]

<u>Building a Better Mousetrap</u>

Astonishing as it may seem, Microsoft's Windows operating system still powers more than 95 percent of the world's desktop computers. As of 2014, 95 percent of all ATMs in the US were still running the Windows XP system (which was the entry point for the WannaCry virus, and for which Microsoft had ceased providing security updates). As a result, with a single piece of malware, hackers have the ability to cause an entire software system to fail uniformly. Why else could more than 1 billion passwords be stolen at one time, or more than a dozen financial institutions be attacked at once? There is certainly an argument to be made that software systems should be able to self-detect defects and self-repair them. At a minimum, *it should be made law that, upon first identification of a vulnerability or defect, the manufacturer becomes obligated to notify every single user of that system.*

By the same token, we need enhanced and more resilient means of protecting our information. Cyber resiliency implies adeptness in crafting a response and dexterity in determining which way is best to rapidly recover degraded technological capabilities. Part of the problem is that machines and systems are not designed to fail gracefully; when they fail, it is often total in scope. As AI, robotics, nanotechnology, and other highly disruptive technologies become even more commonplace, the potential for cataclysmic failure and system-wide disruption will grow exponentially.[419]

What we really need is a new form of operating system that matches the exponential changes occurring around us. One entity that is doing just that is the OS Fund, which partners with entrepreneurs who are rewriting the operating systems of life. Its founder notes that with the Fund's powerful tools of creation—including 3D printing, genomics, machine intelligence, robotics, software, and synthetic biology—they have the ability to create the kind of world people could previously only dream of.[420] That is exactly the type of thinking needed to use today's technology to beat virtual terrorists at their own game.

Nate Silver, of the 538 blog, said in 2015 that our lackadaisical approach to cybersecurity and the profound technological vulnerabilities that lay before us has been akin to applying sunscreen and claiming it can protect us against nuclear meltdown.[421] This is an apt analogy that should be like a cold slap in the face to everyone who opposes virtual terrorists. As others have also recommended, we need to create the cyber equivalent of the Manhattan Project, to put together the best minds from the private and public sectors, academia, and civil society to create a framework for combatting Virtual Terrorism in the 21st century. There may be some resistance to such an effort being spearheaded by a government so perhaps leading minds and cash-rich organizations from the private sector could take the lead in creating it. We need to collectively transcend away from linear thinking about cybersecurity and toward a multidimensional mindset to address a multifaceted problem.

Intelligence Agencies as IT Start-up Investors

A number of intelligence agencies have invested in IT start-ups to be on the cutting edge of emerging technologies and maintain a competitive advantage. In the US, the CIA has been doing just that through In-Q-Tel and is believed to have invested hundreds of millions of dollars into scores of companies since 1999. Israel has a well-deserved reputation as a high-tech hub, and its foreign intelligence agency, the Mossad, has not been shy about wanting to take advantage of all the intellectual capital available in the country. Many of the new high-tech companies in Israel have been founded by individuals who were previously part of Unit 8200—Israel's equivalent of Britain's GCHQ or America's NSA—a "signals intelligence" agency which has moved heavily into the cyber sphere since the late 1990s.[422]

In 2017, the Mossad teamed up with California-based Sequoia Capital, one of the world's top venture capital firms, to form Libertad, a technological innovation fund. The Mossad wants to encourage innovation and creation of groundbreaking technology to realize its research and development challenges. In Internet intelligence, it wants to be part of innovative technologies for automatic identification of personality characteristics based on online behavior and activity, using methods based on statistics, machine learning, and other areas.[423]

Libertad is looking for innovative robotic technologies in the fields of flexible robotics, biomimetics (synthetic methods for mimicking biochemical processes), miniaturized systems, and silencing solutions. In the energy field, it seeks the latest technologies in Energy Harvesting and Self-Powered Systems, which result in increased performance and miniaturization capabilities. It pursues superior encryption information at high speed using unconventional, groundbreaking methods. Almost any area of data collection, interpretation, analysis, and application is potentially of interest.[424]

While the idea of intelligence agencies investing in the private sector is hardly new, there will be much more of it to come in the future. Governments understand that they cannot possibly own all of their countries' intellectual firepower, and that much of it naturally gravitates to the private sector. Staying ahead of the curve in the cyber arena involves money as much as it does any other ingredient, and the money to invest in national intelligence schemes can come from anywhere, so expect the trend to continue. Although we cannot know for certain, it is reasonable to assume that much of the money powering today's IT startups may already be coming from intelligence agencies, even if the recipients may not know it.

The Chaos Computer Club

433

Imagine an organization that advocates for more transparency in government, freedom of information, and supports the principles of the hacker ethic (sharing data and information responsibly). Such an organization has existed since 1981 in Germany. Known as the Chaos Computer Club (CCC), it is Europe's largest association of hackers, with 5,500 registered members, some of whom run cybersecurity for banks and advise policymakers. The CCC is widely considered to be one of the most influential digital organizations in the world, where discussions about democracy intersect with digital rights. Members of the CCC have publicized a number of important information security issues and frequently criticize new legislation and products with weak information security that endangers citizen rights or the privacy of users.[425]

What may have started as a group of activists has turned into a popular, powerful, tech-focused watch dog group. By exposing weaknesses in German government, banking, and other computer systems, the CCC has helped make them more resistant to attack. In 2006, CCC members claimed that the computers the country used to tally its votes were so vulnerable to tampering they could be programmed to play chess. One month after acquiring one of the government's voting computers, the group reprogrammed it to do just that, which prompted Germany's Federal Constitutional Court to forbid the use of voting computers in the future.

The CCC has not been shy in its approach to challenging authority or publicizing its exploits, all in the name of the common good. Apart from the previously mentioned antic with Wolfgang Schäuble (Germany's previous Interior Minister), the group has exposed major security flaws in a variety of electronic systems, including cell phone encryption and biometric identification. Since, at times, the object of the CCC's 'citizen watchdog' approach to the hacking ethic has been the German government, the two have found themselves on opposite sides of the fence. In 2011, the CCC exposed German government use of Trojan malware to spy on its citizens.

The group's annual conference—the Chaos Communication Conference—draws more than 12,000 people each year.[426] It is a tribute to German society (and its government, of course) that the CCC has thrived for decades to become the phenomenon that it is today. What is curious is why so few other such organizations exist elsewhere in the world. While acknowledging that many of the world's country's would never permit a CCC to exist in the first place, the dozens of other free democracies around the world would appear ripe for the birth of similar organizations.

The World Cybersecurity Organization

The global community already has a plethora of organizations devoted to the public good, ranging from the UN to the World Bank to the World Health Organization. These organizations were created as a result of a common acknowledgement of a problem, the will and determination to do something about, and a willingness to devote substantial resources to addressing it on the part of the world's governments. If ever there was a compelling case to be made for creating a new global body today, it would be to for the World Cybersecurity Organization (WCO). The problem is global in scope and requires a global solution.

The WCO could provide much needed focus on global education about Virtual Terrorism, identifying threats, sharing information about the latest hacking techniques, distributing software updates, and sending teams of specialists to address incidents that threaten national economies and security. If billions of people could claim basic education about how to combat Virtual Terrorism, half the battle would already be won, but that would only go so far. The ability to share protection information freely across borders—just as hackers do—could help level the playing field.

An important part of the WCO's mandate could also be to help craft a set of universal laws designed to combat cybercrime and hacking. That may be the only way to commence the badly needed effort for a set of globally applicable laws to fight it. Part of what such laws might entail is coming to agreement on what would constitute a crime, as well as having a common agreement on how jurisdiction would be applied and enforced. Although many countries compete in the cyber arena for supremacy, they also all fight a common enemy. There has to be a way to find a meeting of the minds among the world's leaders to create the WCO. There is so much to do, and so little time to waste.

<u>Final Thoughts</u>

This book has covered a lot of ground, ranging from the perils of the Dark Web and social media to evolving technologies associated with drones, robots, and AI. What all these topics have in common is that they form a mosaic for the most important emerging threat of our time—Virtual Terrorism—which either already has, or will, impact everyone on the planet in due course. *It is a call to action for government and business leaders, NGOs, and individuals of all stripes to not only become aware of the most transcendent phenomenon of our time but to make our knowledge of Virtual Terrorism a part of our daily consciousness, for it is all around us all of the time, and its impact upon us can only grow with time.*

Too few organizations have devoted the time, thought, and resources necessary to truly understand Virtual Terrorism or to combat it with the right approach, tools, and outlook. If we are ever to get out ahead of the problem, proactivity must take the place of reactivity, budget allocation "reserves" in case of a cyberattack must be replaced by annual line items devoted to fighting it, and a backward-looking orientation to the past should be exchanged for an outlook that is forever forward leaning. The stakes are enormous.

In the future, cyberattacks will become more opportunistic, difficult to detect, and more potent, because system interconnectivity will encourage them. The impact of attacks may continue to go undetected for long periods of time and have even longer-term effects. The day will inevitably come when virtual terrorists are successful in attacking critical infrastructure with lasting impact, when a bioterror attack is unleashed from behind a keyboard, and when national economies are brought to their knees because cyberattacks on banking and telecommunication systems do so much damage that they cannot quickly recover. Given how swiftly the cyber sphere has developed and how rapidly it continues to grow, our worst fears may unfortunately come true.

Although it will take a herculean effort to win this battle, it can be won, but it starts with achieving cyber resiliency from the individual through to the governmental level. We have no choice but to take this fight to all the virtual terrorists who threaten our way of life, and to do it now.

Notes

Chapter One

[1] Hern, Alex, "Hackers publish private photos from cosmetic surgery clinic", *The Guardian*, May 31, 2017, accessed July 18, 2017, https://www.theguardian.com/technology/2017/may/31/hackers-publish-private-photos-cosmetic-surgery-clinic-bitcoin-ransom-payments.

[2] Boden, Pete, "The Emerging Era of Cyber Defense and Cybercrime", *Microsoft Secure Blog*, accessed July 18, 2017, https://blogs.microsoft.com/microsoftsecure/2016/01/27/the-emerging-era-of-cyber-defense-and-cybercrime/.

[3] Ibid.

[4]"Global drug market approaching scale of $4trn oil & gas industry – Russian drug czar", *RT International*, accessed July 18, 2017, https://www.rt.com/business/252057-global-drug-market-size/.

[5] Hoffman, Bruce, *Inside Terrorism*, 2 ed., (New York: Columbia University Press, 2006), p. 40.

[6] Clarke, Richard A., and Robert K. Knake, *Cyber War: The Next Threat to National Security and What to Do About It*, (New York: Ecco, 2012), p. 228.

[7] Philipp, Joshua, "CHINA SECURITY: Chinese Electronics Force You to Abide by Chinese Censorship", *The Epoch Times*, January 12, 2016, accessed July 18, 2017, http://www.theepochtimes.com/n3/1939162-china-security-chinese-electronics-force-you-to-abide-by-chinese-censorship/.

[8] Much of the material presented in this section was derived from the Institute for Economics and Peace, *Global Terrorism Index 2014: Measuring and Understanding the Impact of Terrorism,* 2014, accessed November 25, 2015, http://economicsandpeace.org/wp-content/uploads/2015/06/Global-Terrorism-Index-Report-2014.pdf.

[9] Institute for Economics and Peace, *Global Terrorism Index 2015: Measuring and Understanding the Impact of Terrorism,*

2015, accessed November 25, 2015, http://economicsandpeace.org/wp-content/uploads/2015/11/Global-Terrorism-Index-2015.pdf.

[10] Institute for Economics and Peace, *Global Terrorism Index 2014: Measuring and Understanding the Impact of Terrorism,* 2014, accessed November 25, 2015, http://economicsandpeace.org/wp-content/uploads/2015/06/Global-Terrorism-Index-Report-2014.pdf. Additional statistics in this section were derived from the Index.

[11] Institute for Economics and Peace, *Global Terrorism Index 2015.*

[12] Ibid.

[13] Stiglitz, J. and L.J. Bilmes, *The Three Trillion Dollar War: The True Cost of the Iraq Conflict,* (New York: W.W. Norton & Company, 2008), accessed November 25, 2015, http://threetrilliondollarwar.org.

[14] This section adapted from Wagner, D. and Dante Disparte, *Global Risk Agility and Decision Making,* (London: Palgrave Macmillan, 2016), pp. 124-131.

[15] What is cyberterrorism? Even experts can't agree. Harvard Law Record. Victoria Baranetsky. November 5, 2009.

[16] Shamah, David, "Latest viruses could mean 'end of world as we know it' says man who discovered Flame", *The Times of Israel,* June 6, 2012, accessed July 26, 2017, http://www.timesofisrael.com/experts-we-lost-the-cyber-war-now-were-in-the-era-of-cyber-terror/.

[17] "Cyberterrorism" in *Battleground: Government and Politics,* ed. Sara Hower et al. (1st ed.) (Santa Barbara, CA: Greenwood, 2011), pp. 140–149.

[18] Denning, Dorothy E., "A View of Cyberterrorism Five Years Later" in *Internet Security: Hacking, Counterhacking, and Society,* ed. K.E. Himma, (Sudbury, MA: Jones and Bartlett Publishers, 2007), accessed July 26, 2017, http://faculty.nps.edu/dedennin/publications/Cyberterror percent202006.pdf, p. 4.

[19] "Hybrid War – does it even exist?", *NATO Review Magazine,* accessed July 18, 2017, http://www.nato.int/docu/review/2015/Also-in-2015/hybrid-modern-future-warfare-russia-ukraine/EN/.

[20] "Hybrid Warfare", *Wikipedia,* accessed April 8, 2017, https://en.wikipedia.org/wiki/Hybrid_warfare.

[21] Eronen, Pasi, "Russian Hybrid Warfare: How to Confront a New Challenge to the West", (Washington, DC: FDD Press, 2016), accessed July 26, 2017, http://www.defenddemocracy.org/content/uploads/documents/Russian_Hybrid_Warfare.pdf.

[22] Reeves, Shane, "The Viability of the Law of Armed Conflict in the Age of Hybrid Warfare", *Lawfare*, accessed July 21, 2017, https://www.lawfareblog.com/viability-law-armed-conflict-age-hybrid-warfare.

[23] "Office of Personnel Management data breach", *Wikipedia*, accessed July 21, 2017, https://en.wikipedia.org/wiki/Office_of_Personnel_Management_data_breach.

[24] Philipp, Joshua, "You're on File: Exclusive Inside Story on China's Database of Americans", *The Epoch Times*, accessed July 21, 2017, http://www.theepochtimes.com/n3/1973047-youre-on-file-exclusive-inside-story-on-chinas-database-of-americans/?utm_expid=.5zxdwnfjSHaLe_IPrO6c5w.0&utm_referrer=.

[25] Office of the Inspector General, "Semiannual Report to Congress: October 1, 2014 - March 31, 2015", *United States Office of Personnel Management*, accessed July 25, 2017, https://www.opm.gov/news/reports-publications/semi-annual-reports/sar52.pdf, p. 23.

[26] Committee on Oversight and Government Reform: U.S. House of Representatives: 114th Congress, "The OPM Data Breach: How the Government Jeopardized Our National Security for More than a Generation", *Oversight and Government Reform*, September 7, 2016, accessed July 25, 2017, https://oversight.house.gov/wp-content/uploads/2016/09/The-OPM-Data-Breach-How-the-Government-Jeopardized-Our-National-Security-for-More-than-a-Generation.pdf.

[27] "Latest WikiLeaks release shows how the CIA uses computer code to hide the origins of its hacking attacks and 'disguise them as Russian or Chinese activity'", *Daily Mail*, accessed July 21, 2017, http://www.dailymail.co.uk/news/article-4367746/WikiLeaks-says-CIA-disguised-hacking-Russian-activity.html.

[28] The bill was introduced on January 21, 2015 but not enacted. See: "H.R. 451 (114th): Safe and Secure Federal

Websites Act of 2015", *Govtrack*, accessed July 26, 2017, https://www.goVirtual Terrorismrack.us/congress/bills/114/hr451.

[29] The bill was passed by the US House of Representatives on July 7, 2016 but did not pass in the Senate. See: "H.R. 4361 (114th): Government Reform and Improvement Act of 2016,) *Govtrack*, accessed July 26, 2017, https://www.goVirtualTerrorismrack.us/congress/bills/114/hr43 61.

[30] The bill was introduced in Congress on May 25, 2016, but was not enacted. See: "H.R. 4361 (114th): Government Reform and Improvement Act of 2016,) *Govtrack*, accessed July 26, 2017, https://www.goVirtualTerrorismrack.us/congress/bills/114/hr43 61.

[31] Starks, Tim, "House report: Massive OPM breaches a 'failure' of leadership", *Politico*, accessed July 21, 2017, http://www.politico.com/story/2016/09/opm-cyber-hacks-house-report-227817.

[32] Ponemon Institute and Unisys, "Critical Infrastructure: Security Preparedness and Maturity", *Ponemon Institute*, July 2014, accessed July 26, 2017, https://www.hunton.com/files/upload/Unisys_Report_Critical_I nfrastructure_Cybersecurity.pdf, p. 4.

[33] Report to the Committee on Homeland Security, House of Representatives, "Critical Infrastructure Protection: Sector-Specific Agencies Need to Better Measure Cybersecurity Progress", *GAO*, November 2015, accessed July 26, 2017, http://www.gao.gov/assets/680/673779.pdf.

[34] Theohary, Catherine A. and John W. Rollins, "Cyberwarfare and Cyberterrorism: In Brief", *Congressional Research Service*, March 27, 2015, accessed July 26, 2017, https://fas.org/sgp/crs/natsec/R43955.pdf, pp. 2-3.

[35] "Winston Churchill", *Wikiquote*, accessed July 21, 2017, https://en.wikiquote.org/wiki/Winston_Churchill.

Chapter Two

[36] Bilefsky, Dan, "Hackers Use New Tactic at Austrian Hotel: Locking the Doors", *The New York Times*, accessed July 26, 2017,

https://www.nytimes.com/2017/01/30/world/europe/hotel-austria-bitcoin-ransom.html.

[37] "Personal Details of Nearly 200 million US Citizens Exposed", *BBC News*, accessed July 21, 2017, http://www.bbc.com/news/technology-40331215.

[38] "The World's Most Valuable Resource Is No Longer Oil, but Data", *The Economist*, May 6, 2017, accessed July 26, 2017, https://www.economist.com/news/leaders/21721656-data-economy-demands-new-approach-antitrust-rules-worlds-most-valuable-resource.

[39] Timberg, Craig, "U.S. to relinquish remaining control over the Internet", *The Washington Post*, accessed July 21, 2017, https://www.washingtonpost.com/business/technology/us-to-relinquish-remaining-control-over-the-Internet/2014/03/14/0c7472d0-abb5-11e3-adbc-888c8010c799_story.html?utm_term=.7c671e2d69a9.

[40] Farrell, Maria, "Quietly, symbolically, US control of the internet was just ended", *The Guardian*, retrieved July 21, 2017, https://www.theguardian.com/technology/2016/mar/14/icann-Internet-control-domain-names-iana.

[41] "Montevideo Statement on the Future of Internet Cooperation", *Wikipedia*, accessed July 21, 2017, https://en.wikipedia.org/wiki/Montevideo_Statement_on_the_Future_of_Internet_Cooperation.

[42] Desanctis, Alexandra, "The U.S. Must Not Allow Russia and China to Threaten Global Internet Freedom", *National Review*, accessed July 21, 2017, http://www.nationalreview.com/article/440257/global-Internet-freedom-us-icann-oversight-vital-check-china-and-russia.

[43] "Freedom on the Net", *Freedom House*, November 2016, accessed July 26, 2017, https:u//freedomhouse.org/sites/default/files/FOTN_2016_BOOKLET_FINAL.pdf.

[44] Segal, Adam, "Final Thoughts on China's World Internet Conference", *Council on Foreign Relations*, accessed July 21, 2017, http://blogs.cfr.org/cyber/2015/12/21/final-thoughts-on-chinas-world-Internet-conference-2/.

[45] Llansó, Emma, "Adoption of Traffic Sniffing Standard Fans WCIT Flames", *CDT*, November 28, 2012, accessed July 21, 2017, https://cdt.org/blog/adoption-of-traffic-sniffing-standard-fans-wcit-flames/.

[46] Philipp, Joshua, "CHINA SECURITY: Under Veil of Cybersecurity, China Looks to Govern Global Internet", *The Epoch Times*, accessed July 21, 2017, http://www.theepochtimes.com/n3/2006286-china-security-under-veil-of-cybersecurity-china-looks-to-govern-the-global-Internet/?utm_expid=.5zxdwnfjSHaLe_IPrO6c5w.0&utm_refer rer=http percent3A percent2F percent2Fwww.theepochtimes.com percent2Fn3 percent2Fauthor percent2Fjoshua-philipp percent2Fpage percent2F5 percent2F.

[47] VCloudNews, "Every Day Big Data Statistics – 2.5 Quintillion Bytes of Data Created Daily", *V&C*, accessed July 21, 2017, http://www.vcloudnews.com/every-day-big-data-statistics-2-5-quintillion-bytes-of-data-created-daily/.

[48] Philipp, Joshua, "DARPA Is Creating a New Internet, Around Search", *The Epoch Times*, accessed July 21, 2017, http://www.theepochtimes.com/n3/1401628-darpa-is-creating-a-new-Internet-based-around-search/.

[49] Shen, Wade, "Memex", *DARPA*, accessed July 21, 2017, http://www.darpa.mil/program/memex.

[50] Ibid.

[51] "Internet Relay Chat", *Wikipedia*, accessed July 21, 2017, https://en.wikipedia.org/wiki/Internet_Relay_Chat.

[52] Mendieta, Luis, "Shedding Some Light on the Dark Web", *Anomoli*, accessed July 21, 2017, https://www.anomali.com/blog/shedding-some-light-on-the-dark-web?utm_source=hs_e-mail&utm_medium=e-mail&utm_content=50580699&_hsenc=p2ANqtz-_EoYfN-19LKb9Dt5Kic4r5wG3DXQydERZZ6lVILiez_hZ-ZcpNXoEsXK84krrtE8veoE7WSRzLUX_4xdzmlb9dIQ6SBWu Uqglh1He1YVugjls-YQ0&_hsmi=50580700.

[53] Biddle, Sam, "The NSA Leak is Real, Snowden Documents Confirm", *The Intercept*, August 19, 2016, accessed July 21, 2017, https://theintercept.com/2016/08/19/the-nsa-was-hacked-snowden-documents-confirm/.

[54] Biddle, Sam, "Leaked NSA Malware Threatens Windows Users Around the World", *The Intercept*, April 14, 2017, accessed July 21, 2017, https://theintercept.com/2017/04/14/leaked-nsa-malware-threatens-windows-users-around-the-world/

[55] Philipp, Joshua, "How a Video Game Villain Led Researchers to the Man Behind 'The Shadow Brokers'", *The*

Epoch Times, accessed July 21, 2017, http://www.theepochtimes.com/n3/2197900-how-a-video-game-villain-led-researchers-to-the-man-behind-the-shadow-brokers/?utm_expid=.5zxdwnfjSHaLe_IPrO6c5w.0&utm_refer rer=https percent3A percent2F percent2Foutlook.live.com percent2F.

[56] Goodin, Dan, "NSA-leaking Shadow Brokers just dumped its most damaging release yet", *ArsTechnica*, accessed July 21, 2017, https://arstechnica.com/security/2017/04/nsa-leaking-shadow-brokers-just-dumped-its-most-damaging-release-yet/.

[57] Philipp, Joshua, "ISIS Wants to Enable Serial Killers by Hacking Surveillance Cameras", *The Epoch Times*, accessed July 21, 2017, http://www.theepochtimes.com/n3/2179764-IS-wants-to-enable-serial-killers-by-manipulating-surveillance-cameras/?utm_expid=.5zxdwnfjSHaLe_IPrO6c5w.0&utm_refe rrer=http percent3A percent2F percent2Fwww.theepochtimes.com percent2Fn3 percent2Fauthor percent2Fjoshua-philipp percent2Fpage percent2F2 percent2F.

[58] Burke, Samuel, "Massive cyberattack turned ordinary devices into weapons", *CNN*, October 22, 2016, accessed July 21, 2017, http://money.cnn.com/2016/10/22/technology/cyberattack-dyn-ddos/.

[59] Homeland Security News Wire, "Remote-controlled terrorism", *Homeland Security News Wire*, February 7, 2017, accessed July 21, 2017, http://www.homelandsecuritynewswire.com/dr20170207-remotecontrolled-terrorism.

[60] Philipp, Joshua, "Hospital Data Being Held for Ransom by Hackers Will Be a 2016 Epidemic, Expert Warns", *The Epoch Times*, February 18, 2016, accessed July 21 2017, http://www.theepochtimes.com/n3/1969848-hospital-data-being-held-to-ransom-by-hackers-will-be-a-2016-epidemic-warns-expert/.

[61] TrapX Security, "TrapX Labs Discovers New Medical Hijack Attacks Targeting Hospital Devices", *TrapX Security*, accessed July 21, 2017, https://trapx.com/trapx-labs-discovers-new-medical-hijack-attacks-targeting-hospital-devices-2/.

[62] "Hospital computers across Britain shut down by

cyberattack, hackers demanding ransom", *RT*, May 12, 2017, accessed July 21, 2017, https://www.rt.com/uk/388115-nhs-hospitals-cyberattack/.

[63] TrapX Research Labs, "Anatomy of Attack: MEDJACK.2: Hospitals Under Siege", *TrapX*, 2016, accessed July 21, 2017, http://deceive.trapx.com/rs/929-JEW-675/images/AOA_Report_TrapX_MEDJACK.2.pdf?aliId=3059857

[64] Thompson, Cadie, "A hacker figured out a way to almost completely control GM cars with OnStar", *Business Insider*, July 30, 2015, accessed July 26, 2017, http://www.businessinsider.com/hackers-device-can-take-over-gm-cars-with-onstar-system-2015-7.

[65] Thompson, Cadie, "The 29-year-old hacker who was able to take control over GM cars tells us how easy it was to pull off", *Business Insider*, July 30, 2015, accessed July 21, 2017, http://www.businessinsider.com/gm-onstar-hacker-reveals-just-how-easy-it-was-to-attack-car-2015-7.

[66] Gartner, "Gartner Says By 2020, a Quarter Billion Connected Vehicles Will Enable New In-Vehicle Services and Automated Driving Capabilities", *Gartner*, January 26, 2015, http://www.gartner.com/newsroom/id/2970017.

[67] Greenberg, Andy, "Hackers Remotely Kill a Jeep on the Highway – With Me in it". *Wired*, July 21, 2015, accessed July 21, 2017, https://www.wired.com/2015/07/hackers-remotely-kill-jeep-highway/.

[68] Cook, James, "A flaw in BMW and Rolls Royce cars lets hackers unlock the doors", *Business Insider*, February 2, 2015, accessed July 21, 2017, http://www.businessinsider.com/bmw-and-rolls-royce-cars-hacked-2015-2.

[69] Thompson, Cadie, "The Jeep hack was only the beginning smart car breaches", *Business Insider*, July 22, 2015, accessed July 21, 2017, http://www.businessinsider.com/smart-cars-are-vulnerable-to-hackers-2015-7.

[70] Kovacs, Eduard, "Trains Vulnerable to Hacker Attacks: Researchers", *Security Week*, December 29, 2015, accessed July 21, 2017, http://www.securityweek.com/trains-vulnerable-hacker-attacks-researchers.

[71] "How ISIS Terrorists May Have Used PlayStation 4 to Discuss and Plan Attacks", *Forbes*, November 14, 2015,

accessed July 21, 2017,
https://www.forbes.com/sites/insertcoin/2015/11/14/why-the-paris-IS-terrorists-used-ps4-to-plan-attacks/#474bcbb27055.

[72] "Hacking blamed for emergency sirens blaring across Dallas early Saturday", *Dallas News*, August 4, 2017, accessed July 21, 2017, https://www.dallasnews.com/news/dallas/2017/04/08/emergency-sirens-blare-across-dallas-county-despite-clear-weather.

[73] "Hacking Aircraft. Remote Control", *The Economist*, November 4, 2014, accessed July 21, 2017, http://www.economist.com/blogs/gulliver/2014/11/hacking-aircraft.

[74] "Berlin to boost aviation safety amid fears hackers can hijack warplanes", *RT*, July 13, 2017, accessed July 21, 2017, https://www.rt.com/news/396178-germany-hackers-hijack-warplanes/.

[75] British American Security Information Council, "Hacking UK Trident: A Growing Threat", *BASIC*, June 2017, accessed July 26, 2017, http://www.basicint.org/sites/default/files/HACKING percent20UKpercent20TRIDENT.pdf?source=techstories.org.

[76] Curtis, Sophie, "Is your sex toy spying on you? New hack lets cyber crooks take control of your VIBRATOR", *Mirror*, August 11, 2016, accessed July 21, 2017, http://www.mirror.co.uk/tech/your-sex-toy-spying-you-8611446.

[77] Bilefsky, "Hackers Use New Tactic at Austrian Hotel", *The New York Times,* January 30, 2017, accessed July 31, 2017, https://www.nytimes.com/2017/01/30/world/europe/hotel-austria-bitcoin-ransom.html.

[78] Johnson, Tim, "Hack of new season of 'Orange is the New Black' portends a looming TV crisis", *McClatchy DC Bureau*, April 30, 2017, accessed July 21, 2017, http://www.mcclatchydc.com/news/nation-world/national/national-security/article147720299.html.

[79] Temperton, James, "One nation under CCTV: the future of automated surveillance", *Wired*, August 17, 2017, accessed July 21, 2017, http://www.wired.co.uk/article/one-nation-under-cctv.

[80] Marc Goodman, *Future Crimes: Inside the Digital Underground and the Battle for Our Connected World,* (2nd ed.) (USA: Anchor, 2015) pp. 305-308.

Chapter Three

[81] Philipp, Joshua, "CHINA SECURITY: Chinese Electronics Force You to Abide by Chinese Censorship", *The Epoch Times*, January 12, 2016, accessed July 21, 2017, http://www.theepochtimes.com/n3/1939162-china-security-chinese-electronics-force-you-to-abide-by-chinese-censorship/.

[82] "Paradiplomacy", *Wikipedia*, accessed July 21, 2017, https://en.wikipedia.org/wiki/Paradiplomacy.

[83] Clarke, Richard A. and Robert K. Knake, *Cyber War: The Next Threat to National Security and What to Do About it,* (Harper Collins, 2010), pp. 50-58.

[84] Philipp, Joshua, "Extensive Network of Secret Chinese Military Units Attack US on Daily Basis", *The Epoch Times*, November 21, 2014, accessed July 21, 2017, http://www.theepochtimes.com/n3/1094262-chinas-silent-war-on-the-us/.

[85] Philipp, Joshua, "How Silencing China's Dissidents Led to Stealing the West's Secrets", *The Epoch Times*, January 30, 2015, accessed July 21, 2017, http://www.theepochtimes.com/n3/1230816-how-silencing-chinas-dissidents-led-to-stealing-the-wests-secrets/.

[86] Philipp, Joshua, "EXCLUSIVE: How Hacking and Espionage Fuel China's Growth", *The Epoch Times*, September 10, 2015, accessed July 21, 2017, http://www.theepochtimes.com/n3/1737917-investigative-report-china-theft-incorporated/.

[87] Philipp, Joshua, "China's Fingerprints Are All Over Spy Operation Targeting Japan", *The Epoch Times*, August 24, 2015, accessed July 21, 2017, http://www.theepochtimes.com/n3/1734669-chinas-fingerprints-are-all-over-spy-operation-targeting-japan/.

[88] Windrem, Robert, "Exclusive: Secret NSA Map Shows China Cyber Attacks on U.S. Targets", *NBC News*, July 30, 2015, accessed July 21, 2017, http://www.nbcnews.com/news/us-news/exclusive-secret-nsa-map-shows-chinacyberattacks-us-targets-n401211.

[89] Philipp, Joshua, "US-China Cyberpact: A Deal Built on Distrust", *The Epoch Times*, September 29, 2015, accessed July 21, 2017, http://www.theepochtimes.com/n3/1777875-a-

deal-built-on-distrust/.

[90] Philipp, Joshua, "CHINA SECURITY: Cyber Agreement Could Help China Perfect Cybertheft", *The Epoch Times*, October 20, 2015, accessed July 21, 2017, http://www.theepochtimes.com/n3/1876649-china-security-cyber-agreement-could-help-china-perfect-cybertheft/.

[91] Philipp, Joshua, "Obama Warns of Cyberwar During Comments on Chinese Hackers", *The Epoch Times*, September 16, 2015, accessed July 21, 2017, http://www.theepochtimes.com/n3/1753476-obama-warns-of-cyberwar-during-comments-on-chinese-hackers/.

[92] Philipp, Joshua, "CHINA SECURITY: Chinese Electronics Force You to Abide by Chinese Censorship".

[93] Haas, Benjamin, "China moves to block internet VPNs from 2018", *The Guardian*, July 11, 2015, accessed July 21, 2017, https://www.theguardian.com/world/2017/jul/11/china-moves-to-block-Internet-vpns-from-2018.

[94] Director of National Intelligence, "Background to "Assessing Russian Activities and Intentions in Recent US Elections: The Analytic Process and Cyber Incident Attribution", *DNI*, January 6, 2017, accessed July 21, 2017, https://www.dni.gov/files/documents/ICA_2017_01.pdf.

[95] Dreyfuss, Ben, "The Intercept Discloses Top-Secret NSA Document on Russia Aimed at US Voting System", *Mother Jones*, June 5, 2017, accessed July 21, 2017, http://www.motherjones.com/politics/2017/06/intercept-nsa-document-russia-hack/.

[96] Smith, David and Jon Swaine, "Russian agents hacked US voting system manufacturer before US election – report", *The Guardian*, June 5, 2017, accessed July 21, 2017, https://www.theguardian.com/technology/2017/jun/05/russia-us-election-hack-voting-system-nsa-report.

[97] "Russia Collusion Investigations Struggle to Find Evidence", *The Epoch Times*, April 6, 2017, accessed July 21, 2017, http://www.theepochtimes.com/n3/2239820-russia-collusion-investigations-struggle-to-find-evidence-2/.

[98] Syal, Rajeev, "Brexit: foreign states may have interfered in vote, report says", *The Guardian*, April 12, 2017, accessed July 21, 2017, https://www.theguardian.com/politics/2017/apr/12/foreign-states-may-have-interfered-in-brexit-vote-report-says.

[99] "Macron campaign says it is the victim of massive,

coordinated hacking campaign", *CNBC*, May 5, 2017, accessed July 21, 2017, http://www.cnbc.com/2017/05/05/macron-campaign-says-it-is-the-victim-of-massive-coordinated-hacking-campaign-reuters.html.

[100] Nossiter, Adam, David E. Sanger, and Nicole Perlroth, "Hackers Came, but the French Were Prepared", *The New York Times*, May 9, 2017, accessed July 21, 2017, https://www.nytimes.com/2017/05/09/world/europe/hackers-came-but-the-french-were-prepared.html?rref=collection percent2Fsectioncollection percent2Fworld&action=click&contentCollection=world&regio n=rank&module=package&version=highlights&contentPlacem ent=1&pgtype=sectionfront&_r=2.

[101] Windrem, Robert, "Timeline: Ten Years of Russian Cyber Attacks on Other Nations", *NBC News*, December 18, 2017, accessed July 21, 2017, http://www.nbcnews.com/storyline/hacking-in-america/timeline-ten-years-russian-cyberattacks-other-nations-n697111.

[102] The Guardian, "US intelligence chiefs have doubts about cybersecurity firm over its Russian roots", *The Guardian*, May 11, 2017, accessed July 21, 2017, https://www.theguardian.com/us-news/2017/may/11/kaspersky-labs-cybersecurity-us-senate-intelligence.

[103] Chivvis, Christopher S., "How to Deter Foreign Cyberattacks on U.S. Elections", *Rand Corporation*, January 5, 2017, accessed July 21, 2017, https://www.rand.org/blog/2017/01/how-to-deter-foreign-cyberattacks-on-us-elections.html.

[104] Connable, Ben, Jason H. Campbell, and Dan Madden, "Stretching and Exploiting Thresholds for High-Order War: How Russia, China, and Iran Are Eroding American Influence Using Time-Tested Measures Short of War", (Santa Monica, CA: Rand Corporation, 2016), accessed July 21, 2017, http://www.rand.org/pubs/research_reports/RR1003.html.

[105] Philipp, Joshua, "US Adversaries Are Using 'Short of War' Conflicts to Undermine the United States Says RAND", *The Epoch Times*, May 31, 2016, accessed July 21, 2017, http://www.theepochtimes.com/n3/2080137-us-adversaries-are-using-short-of-war-conflicts-to-undermine-the-united-

states-says-
rand/?utm_expid=.5zxdwnfjSHaLe_IPrO6c5w.0&utm_referrer
=http%3A%2F%2Fwww.theepochtimes.com%2Fn3%2Fautho
r%2Fjoshua-philipp%2Fpage%2F4%2F.
[106] "Like letting Tomahawk missiles get stolen: Microsoft
slams NSA mishandling of exploits", *RT*, May 14, 2017,
accessed July 21, 2017, https://www.rt.com/usa/388374-
microsoft-ransomware-tomahawk-attack/.
[107] "Leaked NSA exploit blamed for global ransomware
cyberattack", *RT*, May 12, 2017, accessed July 21, 2017,
https://www.rt.com/usa/388187-leaked-nsa-exploit-
ransomware/.
[108] "WannaCry ransomware shares code with North Korea-
linked malware – researchers", *RT*, May 16, 2017, accessed
July 21, 2017, https://www.rt.com/news/388492-wannacry-
ransomware-code-north-korea/.
[109] Ablon, Lillian and Timothy Bogart. "Zero Days, Thousands
of Nights: The Life and Time of Zero-Day Vulnerabilities and
Their Exploits". (Santa Monica, CA: RAND Corporation,
2017), accessed July 21, 2017,
http://www.rand.org/pubs/research_reports/RR1751.html.
[110] Gilbert, David, "Cyber Arms Race", *Vice News*, May 26,
2017, accessed July 21, 2017,
https://news.vice.com/story/the-u-s-government-is-stockpiling-
lists-of-zero-day-software-bugs-that-let-it-hack-into-iphones.
[111] Electronic Frontier Foundation (EFF), "Exhibit B:
Commercial and Government Information Technology and
Industrial Control Product or System Vulnerabilities Equities
Policy and Process", *EFF*, January 14, 2016, accessed July
21, 2017, https://www.eff.org/document/vulnerabilities-
equities-process-january-2016.
[112] "#Vault7: 'CIA malware plants Gremlins' on Microsoft
machines – WikiLeaks", *RT*, May 12, 2017, accessed July 21,
2017, https://www.rt.com/viral/388075-wikileaks-cia-microsoft-
malware/.
[113] "Cherry Blossom", *WikiLeaks*, accessed July 21, 2017,
https://wikileaks.org/vault7/#Cherry Blossom.
[114] "#Vault7: WikiLeaks reveals CIA 'Scribbles' tool can track
whistleblowers & foreign spies", *RT*, April 28, 2017, accessed
July 21, 2017,
https://www.rt.com/news/386433-wikileaks-cia-scribbles-
microsoft-office/.

[115] "Latest WikiLeaks release shows how the CIA uses computer code to hide the origins of its hacking attacks and 'disguise them as Russian or Chinese activity'", *Daily Mail*, March 31, 2017, accessed July 21, 2017, http://www.dailymail.co.uk/news/article-4367746/WikiLeaks-says-CIA-disguised-hacking-Russian-activity.html.

[116] Greenwald, Glenn and Ewan MacAskill, "NSA Prism program taps in to user data of Apple, Google and others", *The Guardian*, June 7, 2013, accessed July 21, 2017, https://www.theguardian.com/world/2013/jun/06/us-tech-giants-nsa-data.

[117] American Civil Liberties Union (ACLU), "Brief of Fisc Amicus Curiae Amy Jeffress", *ACLU*, October 16, 2015, released April 11, 2017, accessed July 21, 2017, https://www.aclu.org/foia-document/brief-fisc-amicus-curiae-amy-jeffress.

[118] "President Obama's team sought NSA intel on thousands of Americans during the 2016 election", *Circa*, May 3, 2017, accessed July 21, 2017, http://circa.com/politics/president-obamas-team-sought-nsa-intel-on-thousands-of-americans-during-the-2016-election.

[119] Sanger, David E. and William J. Broad. "Trump Inherits a Secret Cyberwar Against North Korean Missiles", *The New York Times*, March 4, 2017, accessed July 21, 2017, https://www.nytimes.com/2017/03/04/world/asia/north-korea-missile-program-sabotage.html?_r=2.

[120] "Ghost Fleet", *GhostFleetBook.com*, accessed July 21, 2017, https://www.ghostfleetbook.com/the-book/.

[121] Philipp, Joshua, "Why a Novel on War with China has the Pentagon Talking", *The Epoch Times*, July 28, 2015, accessed July 21, 2017, http://www.theepochtimes.com/n3/1648090-why-a-novel-on-war-with-china-has-the-pentagon-talking/.

[122] Fravel, M. Taylor, "China's New Military Strategy: Winning Informationized Local Wars", *China Brief* Volume: 15 issue: 13, July 2, 2015, accessed July 21, 2017, https://jamestown.org/program/chinas-new-military-strategy-winning-informationized-local-wars/.

[123] Philipp, Joshua, "Chinese Military Officially Shifts Focus to Cyberwarfare and Space Warfare", *The Epoch Times*, June 26, 2015, accessed July 21, 2017, http://www.theepochtimes.com/n3/1407686-chinese-military-

officially-shifts-focus-to-cyberwarfare-and-space-warfare/?expvar=004&utm_expid=.5zxdwnfjSHaLe_IPrO6c5w.1&utm_referrer.

[124] "Russian military admits significant cyber-war effort", *BBC*, February 23, 2017, accessed July 21, 2017, http://www.bbc.com/news/world-europe-39062663.

Chapter Four

[125] Philipp, Joshua, "CHINA SECURITY: What Can Be Done to Stop Chinese Economic Theft?", *The Epoch Times*, April 9, 2016, accessed July 21, 2017, http://www.theepochtimes.com/n3/1944921-china-security-what-can-be-done-to-stop-chinese-economic-theft/

[126] "The Hiscox Cyber Readiness Report 2017", *Hiscox*, 2017, accessed July 26, 2017, http://www.hiscox.com/cyber-readiness-report.pdf.

[127] Graham, Luke, "Cybercrime costs the global economy $450 billion: CEO", *CNBC*, February 7, 2017, accessed July 21, 2017, http://www.cnbc.com/2017/02/07/cybercrime-costs-the-global-economy-450-billion-ceo.html.

[128] Philipp, Joshua, "Half of Corporate 'Targeted Continuously' by Hackers: IT Professionals", *The Epoch Times*, July 2, 2015, accessed July 21, 2017, http://www.theepochtimes.com/n3/1414037-half-of-corporate-networks-targeted-continuously-by-hackers-it-professionals/.

[129] Philipp, Joshua, "Businesses Wrangling With Cyberattacks Have Reached the Final Stage of Grief", *The Epoch Times*, October 2, 2015, accessed July 21, 2017, http://www.theepochtimes.com/n3/1854758-businesses-wrangling-with-cyberattacks-have-reached-the-final-stage-of-grief/.

[130] Goodman, *Future Crimes*, pp. 41-42.

[131] Philipp, Joshua, "China's New Industrial War", *The Epoch Times*, March 16, 2017, accessed July 21, 2017, http://www.theepochtimes.com/n3/2232139-chinas-new-industrial-war-2/?utm_expid=.5zxdwnfjSHaLe_IPrO6c5w.0&utm_referrer=https percent3A percent2F percent2Foutlook.live.com percent2F.

[132] Philipp, Joshua, "CHINA SECURITY: What CAN BE Done

to Stop Chinese Economic Theft?".

[133] Philipp, Joshua, "CHINA SECURITY: IBM Shows Chinese Agents Its Source Code", *The Epoch Times*, October 19, 2015, accessed July 21, 2017, http://www.theepochtimes.com/n3/1881004-china-security-ibm-shows-chinese-agents-its-source-code/.

[134] Philipp, Joshua, "US Navy Cruisers and Destroyers Look to Ditch Lenovo Servers", *The Epoch Times*, May 7, 2015, accessed July 21, 2017, http://www.theepochtimes.com/n3/1348839-us-navy-cruisers-and-destroyers-look-to-ditch-lenovo-servers/.

[135] "HP Partners with Tsinghua to Create a Chinese Technology Powerhouse", *HP*, May 21, 2015, accessed July 21, 2017, http://www8.hp.com/us/en/hp-news/press-release.html?wireId=1950801#.WRxxM2jyvic.

[136] Yuan Yang, "China's Cyber Security Law Rattles Multinationals", *Financial Times*, May 30, 2017, accessed July 21, 2017, https://www.ft.com/content/b302269c-44ff-11e7-8519-9f94ee97d996.

[137] Baraniuk, Chris, "Why Printers add secret tracking dots", *BBC*, June 7, 2017, accessed July 21, 2017, http://www.bbc.com/future/story/20170607-why-printers-add-secret-tracking-dots.

[138] "Copy Machines, a Security Risk?", *CBS*, April 19, 2010, accessed July 21, 2017, http://www.cbsnews.com/videos/copy-machines-a-security-risk/?lumiereId=50086489&videoId=6738ccae-8bdf-11e2-9400-029118418759&cbsId=6412572&site=cbsnews.

[139] Goodman, *Future Crimes*, pp. 323-328.

[140] Leary, Judy, "The Biggest Data Breaches in 2016", *Identity Force*, accessed July 21, 2017, https://www.identityforce.com/blog/2016-data-breaches.

[141] Roettgers, Janko, "Netflix Hackers Could Have Three Dozen Additional TV Shows, Films from Other Networks and Studios", *Variety*, April 30, 2017, http://variety.com/2017/digital/news/netflix-hackers-additional-shows-movies-1202404171/.

[142] Roettgers, Janko, "'Orange Is the New Black' Leak Shows: Hollywood Cybersecurity Lives and Dies with Third-Party Vendors", *Variety,* April, 29, 2017, accessed July 21, 2017, http://variety.com/2017/digital/news/oitnb-leak-hack-hollywood-security-1202403886/.

[143] Osborne, Charlie. "St. Jude Medical releases security patches for vulnerable cardiac devices", *Zero Day*, accessed July 21, 2017, http://www.zdnet.com/article/st-jude-releases-security-patches-for-vulnerable-cardiac-devices/.

[144] Inagaki, Kana, "Cyber encryption is out of sight for camera makers", *Financial Times*, May 24, 2017, accessed May 25, 2017, https://www.ft.com/content/373fefea-2424-11e7-a34a-538b4cb30025.

[145] "What is Tor Browser?", *Tor, Tor Project*, accessed July 21, 2017, https://www.torproject.org/projects/torbrowser.html.en.

[146] Solon, Olivia, "Here's how to protect your internet browsing data now that it's for sale", *The Guardian*, March 30, 2017, accessed July 21, 2017, https://www.theguardian.com/technology/2017/mar/30/privacy-protection-web-browsing-history-data-congress.

[147] Computer Crime and Intellectual Property Section Criminal Division, "Prosecuting Computer Crimes", *Office of Legal Education Executive Office for United States Attorneys*, accessed July 21, 2017, https://www.justice.gov/sites/default/files/criminal-ccips/legacy/2015/01/14/ccmanual.pdf.

[148] "House Bill Would Give Companies Some Leeway To Hack Back", *Nextgov*, March 3, 2017, accessed July 21, 2017, http://www.nextgov.com/cybersecurity/2017/03/house-bill-would-give-companies-some-leeway-hack-back/135892/.

[149] Caldwell, Leslie R., "Department Releases Intake and Charging Policy for Computer Crime Matters", *The United States Department of Justice Archives*, October 25, 2016, accessed July 21, 2017, https://www.justice.gov/archives/opa/blog/department-releases-intake-and-charging-policy-computer-crime-matters.

[150] Etzioni, Amitai, "The Private Sector: A Reluctant Partner in Cybersecurity", *The George Washington University*, December 19, 2014, accessed July 21, 2017, https://icps.gwu.edu/private-sector-reluctant-partner-cybersecurity.

[151] Cyber Threat Intelligence Integration Center, "What We Do", *Office of the Director of National Intelligence*, accessed July 21, 2017, https://www.dni.gov/index.php/ctiic-what-we-do.

[152] Garrie, Daniel, "The Need for Private-Public Partnerships

Against Cyber Threats – Why a Good Offense May be Our Best Defense", *The Huffington Post*, January 1, 2016, accessed July 21, 2017, http://www.huffingtonpost.com/daniel-garrie/the-soft-power-war-IS-d_b_8818866.html.

[153] Raduege, Harry D., Jr., "The Public/Private Cooperation We Need on Cyber Security", *Harvard Business Review*, June 18, 2013, accessed July 21, 2017, https://hbr.org/2013/06/the-publicprivate-cooperation.

[154] Marriage, Madison, "WannaCry worm is a wakeup call for investors", *Financial Times*, May 24, 2017, accessed July 21, 2017, https://www.ft.com/content/5ba47f70-2426-11e7-a34a-538b4cb30025.

Chapter Five

[155] Goodman, *Future Crimes*, p. 240.

[156] Terrelonge III, Leroy, "Cybercrime Economy: An Analysis of Cybercriminal Communication Strategies", *Flashpoint*, April 19, 2017, accessed July 21, 2017, https://www.flashpoint-intel.com/blog/cybercrime/cybercriminal-communication-strategies/.

[157] Perlroth, Nicole, "With New Digital Tools, Even Nonexperts Can Wage Cyberattacks", *The New York Times*, May 13, 2017, accessed July 21, 2017, https://www.nytimes.com/2017/05/13/technology/hack-ransomware-scam-cyberattacks.html?rref=collection percent2Fsectioncollection percent2Fworld&action=click&contentCollection=world&region=stream&module=stream_unit&version=latest&contentPlacement=1&pgtype=sectionfront&_r=0.

[158] Morgan, Steve, "Hackerpocalypse: A Cybercrime Revelation", *Cybersecurity Ventures*, accessed July 23, 2017, http://cybersecurityventures.com/hackerpocalypse-cybercrime-report-2016/.

[159] Ablon, Lillian, Martin C. Lisicki, and Andrea A. Golay, "Markets for Cybercrime Tools and Stolen Data", (Santa Monica, CA: RAND Corporation, 2014), accessed July 23, 2017, http://www.rand.org/content/dam/rand/pubs/research_reports/RR600/RR610/RAND_RR610.pdf, p. 23.

[160] "Gamification", *Wikipedia*, accessed July 23, 2017, https://en.wikipedia.org/wiki/Gamification.

[161] Coin Desk, *Bitcoin*, accessed May 23, 2017, http://www.coindesk.com/price/.

[162] Charles, Brooke Satti, "ISIS. Are they Using Bitcoins to Fund Criminal Activities?", *Security Intelligence*, October 29, 2014, accessed July 23, 2017, https://securityintelligence.com/IS-are-they-using-bitcoins-to-fund-criminal-activities/.

[163] Goodman, *Future Crimes*, pp. 218-223, 230-231, 238-244, 255-277.

[164] "FBI ran 23 Dark Web child porn sites to gather visitor info", *RT*, November 12, 2016, accessed July 23, 2017, https://www.rt.com/usa/366567-fbi-child-porn-sites/.

[165] "Judge rejects EFF claim that FBI's using malware to catch child porn viewers was unconstitutional", *RT*, March 24, 2016, accessed July 23, 2017, https://www.rt.com/usa/337065-court-rejects-eff-fbi/.

[166] "900 suspected pedophiles arrested as 'darknet' child porn kingpin jailed for 30 yrs", *RT*, May 6, 2017, accessed July 23, 2017, https://www.rt.com/news/387317-pedophile-ring-arrested-playpen/.

[167] McGoogan, Cara, "Dark web browser Tor is overwhelming used crime, says study", *The Telegraph*, February 2, 2016, accessed July 23, 2017, http://www.telegraph.co.uk/technology/2016/02/02/dark-web-browser-tor-is-overwhelmingly-used-for-crime-says-study/.

[168] Greenberg, Andy, "It's About to Get Even Easier to Hide on the Dark Web", *Wired*, January 20, 2017, accessed July 23, 2017, https://www.wired.com/2017/01/get-even-easier-hide-dark-web/.

[169] Moore, Daniel and Thomas Rid, "Cryptopolitik and the Darknet", International Institute for Strategic Studies (IISS), *Survival: Global Politics and Strategy* (58): 7-38, January 19, 2016, accessed July 23, 2017, https://www.iiss.org/en/publications/survival/sections/2016-5e13/survival--global-politics-and-strategy-february-march-2016-44d5/58-1-02-moore-and-rid-9204.

[170] Global Economic Symposium, "Cybercrime, Cybersecurity, and the Future of the Internet", Symposium 2010, accessed July 21, 2017, http://www.global-economic-symposium.org/knowledgebase/the-global-polity/cybercrime-

cybersecurity-and-the-future-of-the-Internet.

[171] Wainwright, Robert, "Proposal – Dealing with Cyber Crime – Challenges and Solutions", Global Economic Symposium, 2010, accessed July 23, 2017, http://www.global-economic-symposium.org/knowledgebase/the-global-polity/cybercrime-cybersecurity-and-the-future-of-the-Internet/proposals/dealing-with-cybercrime-2013-challenges-and-solutions.

Chapter Six

[172] Gartenstein, Daveed, Ross Blackman, and Madeleine Blackman, "ISIL's Virtual Planners: A Critical Terrorist Innovation", *War on The Rocks*, January 4, 2017, accessed July 23, 2017, https://warontherocks.com/2017/01/ISs-virtual-planners-a-critical-terrorist-innovation/.

[173] Pew Research Center, "The Future of World Religions: Population Growth Projections, 2010-2050", *Pew Research Center*, April 2, 2015, accessed July 23, 2017, http://www.pewforum.org/2015/04/02/religious-projections-2010-2050/#beyond-the-year-2050.

[174] Kirby, Brendan, "Islam on Track to Overtake Christianity as World's No. 1 Religion", *Polizette*, May 29, 2017, accessed July 24, 2017, http://www.lifezette.com/polizette/islam-track-overtake-christianity-worlds-no-1-religion/.

[175] United Nations Department of Economic and Social Affairs, "World population projected to reach 9.7 billion by 2050", *United Nations*, July 29, 2015, accessed July 24, 2017, http://www.un.org/en/development/desa/news/population/2015-report.html.

[176] Rudgard, Olivia, "Islam will be largest religion in the world by 2070, says report", *The Telegraph*, March 1, 2017, accessed July 24, 2017, http://www.telegraph.co.uk/news/2017/03/01/islam-will-largest-religion-world-2070-says-report/.

[177] Doyle, Harrison, "New Tools, New Vulnerabilities: The Emerging Cyber-Terrorism Dyad", *Cyber Defense Review*. August 27, 2015, accessed July 24, 2017, http://cyberdefensereview.army.mil/The-Journal/Article-Display/Article/1136007/new-tools-new-vulnerabilities-the-emerging-cyberterrorism-dyad/.

[178] Votel, General Joseph L., LTC Christina Bembenek, Charles Hans, Jeffery Mouton, and Amanda Spencer, "Virtual Caliphate: Defeating ISIL on the Physical Battlefield is Not Enough", *CNAS*, January 12, 2017, accessed July 24, 2017, https://www.cnas.org/publications/reports/virtual-caliphate.

[179] Winter, Charles. "Documenting the Virtual 'Caliphate'", *Quilliam*, October 2015, accessed July 26, 2017, http://www.quilliaminternational.com/wp-content/uploads/2015/10/FINAL-documenting-the-virtual-caliphate.pdf.

[180] Miller, Greg and Scott Higham, "In a propaganda war against ISIS, the U.S. tried to play by the enemy's rules", *The Washington Post*, May 8, 2017, accessed July 24, 2017, https://www.washingtonpost.com/world/national-security/in-a-propaganda-war-us-tried-to-play-by-the-enemys-rules/2015/05/08/6eb6b732-e52f-11e4-81ea-0649268f729e_story.html?utm_term=.133f8348970e.

[181] Pengelly, Martin, "Defense secretary Mattis says US policy against ISIS is now 'annihilation'", *The Guardian*, May 28, 2017, accessed July 24, 2017, https://www.theguardian.com/us-news/2017/may/28/james-mattis-defense-secretary-us-IS-annihilation.

[182] Gartenstein-Ross and Blackman, "Isil's Virtual Planners: A Critical Terrorist Innovation", *War on the Rocks*, January 4, 2017, accessed July 21, 2017, https://warontherocks.com/2017/01/ISs-virtual-planners-a-critical-terrorist-innovation/.

[183] Philipp, Joshua, "IS Online Recruiters Traced to Russia, Eastern Europe", *The Epoch Times*, August 6, 2015, accessed July 24, 2017, http://www.theepochtimes.com/n3/1708303-IS-online-recruiters-traced-to-russia-eastern-europe/.

[184] Philipp, Joshua, "Hacker Leaks Hundreds of IP Addresses, Phonebooks of ISIS Recruiters", *The Epoch Times*, August 30, 2016, accessed July 24, 2017, http://www.theepochtimes.com/n3/2147589-hacker-leaks-hundreds-of-ip-addresses-phonebooks-of-isis-recruiters/?utm_expid=.5zxdwnfjSHaLe_IPrO6c5w.0&utm_referrer=http%3A%2F%2Fwww.theepochtimes.com%2Fn3%2Fauthor%2Fjoshua-philipp%2Fpage%2F3%2F.

[185] Zech, Steven T., "Virtual Vigilantes: "Anonymous" Cyber-Attacks Against the Islamic State", *Political Violence at a*

Glance, April 7, 2015, accessed July 24, 2017, https://politicalviolenceataglance.org/2015/04/07/virtual-vigilantes-anonymous-cyberattacks-against-the-islamic-state/.
[186] Hesterman, Jennifer L., "Cyber vigilantes: Citizen hackers go to war against terrorists", *PoliceOne.com*, September 1, 2010, accessed July 24, 2017, https://www.policeone.com/terrorism/articles/3295107-Cyber-vigilantes-Citizen-hackers-go-to-war-against-terrorists/.
[187] Awan, Akil N., "The Virtual Jihad: An Increasingly Legitimate Form of Warfare", *Combating Terrorism Center*, accessed July 24, 2017, https://www.ctc.usma.edu/posts/the-virtual-jihad-an-increasingly-legitimate-form-of-warfare.
[188] Van Ginkel LL.M. and Dr. Bibi T., "Responding to Cyber Jihad: Towards an Effective Counter Narrative", *ICCT*, March 2015, accessed July 24, 2017, https://www.icct.nl/download/file/ICCT-van-Ginkel-Responding-To-Cyber-Jihad-Towards-An-Effective-Counter-Narrative-March2015.pdf.
[189] Byers, Andrew and Tara Mooney, "Winning the Cyberwar Against ISIS", *Foreign Affairs*, May 5, 2017, accessed July 24, 2017, https://www.foreignaffairs.com/articles/middle-east/2017-05-05/winning-cyberwar-against-IS.
[190] Doyle, Harrison, "New Tools, New Vulnerabilities: The Emerging Cyber-Terrorism Dyad", *Cyber Defense Review,* August 27, 2015, accessed July 24, 2017, http://cyberdefensereview.army.mil/The-Journal/Article-Display/Article/1136007/new-tools-new-vulnerabilities-the-emerging-cyberterrorism-dyad/.

Chapter Seven

[191] Goodman, *Future Crimes*, p. 72.
[192] Johnston, Stuart J., "Microsoft Survey: Online 'Reputation' Counts", InternetNews.com, January 27, 2010, accessed July 24, 2017, http://www.Internetnews.com/webcontent/article.php/3861241/Microsoft+Survey+Online+Reputation+Counts.htm.
[193] Siegler, MG, "Eric Schmidt: Every 2 Days We Create as Much Information as We Did up to 2003", *TechCrunch*, August 4, 2010, accessed July 24, 2017, https://techcrunch.com/2010/08/04/schmidt-data/.

[194] "Big Data Analytics", *IBM*, accessed July 24, 2017, https://www-01.ibm.com/software/data/bigdata/what-is-big-data.html.

[195] Goodman, *Future Crimes*, pp. 72-73, 82-100, 109-120.

[196] Hunt, Elle, "'Revenge porn': one in five report they have been victims in Australian survey", *The Guardian*, May 7, 2017, accessed July 24, 2017, https://www.theguardian.com/world/2017/may/08/revenge-porn-research-one-in-five-australians-have-been-victims.

[197] Hopkins, Nick and Olivia Solon, "Facebook flooded with 'sextortion' and revenge porn, files reveal", *The Guardian*, May 22, 2017, accessed July 24, 2017, https://www.theguardian.com/news/2017/may/22/facebook-flooded-with-sextortion-and-revenge-porn-files-reveal.

[198] Goodman, *Future Crimes*, pp. 123-127, 163-166.

[199] Jolly, Bradley, "The bizarre 'click farm' of 10,000 phones that give FAKE 'likes' to our most-loved apps", *Mirror*, May 15, 2017, accessed July 24, 2017, http://www.mirror.co.uk/news/world-news/bizarre-click-farm-10000-phones-10419403.

[200] Wagner, Daniel, "What the Islamic State is Teaching the West About Social Media", *The Huffington Post*, March 23, 2015, accessed July 24, 2017, http://www.huffingtonpost.com/daniel-wagner/what-the-islamic-state-is-teaching-the-west-about-social-media_b_6918384.html.

[201] Philipp, Joshua, "Anti-Terrorist Hacker Group Reveals 40 ISIS Websites Protected by US Tech Firm", *The Epoch Times*, November 6, 2015, accessed July 24, 2017, http://www.theepochtimes.com/n3/1892477-anti-terrorist-hacker-group-reveals-40-isis-websites-protected-by-us-tech-firm/.

[202] Philipp, Joshua, "Hacker Exposes 97 ISIS Websites, as Anonymous Targets Terrorists Online", *The Epoch Times*, November 20, 2015, accessed July 27, 2017, http://www.theepochtimes.com/n3/1903879-hacker-exposes-97-isis-websites-as-anonymous-targets-terrorists-online.

[203] Philipp, Joshua, "Hackers Trace Locations of ISIS CyberCaliphate, Say Their Cyberattacks Are Fake", *The Epoch Times*, November 12, 2015, accessed July 24, 2017, http://www.theepochtimes.com/n3/1898608-hackers-trace-locations-of-isis-cybercaliphate-say-their-cyberattacks-are-

fake/.

204 Goodman, *Future Crimes*, pp. 204-206.

205 Saenz, Aaron, "Al Qaeda In Azeroth? Terrorism Recruiting and Training in Virtual Worlds", *Singularity Hub*, August 24, 2011, accessed July 24, 2017, https://singularityhub.com/2011/08/24/al-qaeda-in-azeroth-terrorism-recruiting-and-training-in-virtual-worlds/.

206 De, Deepanwita, "The rising war against virtual terrorism", *The Dialogue*, September 25, 2016, accessed July 24, 2017, http://www.thedialogue.co/rising-war-virtual-terrorism/.

207 Berger, J.M. and Heather Perez, "The Islamic State's Diminishing Returns on Twitter: How suspensions are limiting the social networks of English-speaking ISIS supporters", *George Washington University Program on Extremism*, February 2016, accessed July 27, 2017, https://cchs.gwu.edu/sites/cchs.gwu.edu/files/downloads/Berger_Occasional percent20Paper.pdf.

208 Philipp, Joshua, "Hackers Say Twitter Isn't Telling the Whole Story About Anti-Terror Fight", *The Epoch Times*, March 4, 2016, accessed July 24, 2017, http://www.theepochtimes.com/n3/1983519-hackers-say-twitter-isnt-telling-the-whole-story-about-anti-terror-fight/.

209 Greenemeier, Larry, "When Hatred Goes Viral: Inside Social Media's Efforts to Combat Terrorism". *Scientific American*, May 24, 2017, accessed July 24, 2017, https://www.scientificamerican.com/article/when-hatred-goes-viral-inside-social-medias-efforts-to-combat-terrorism/.

210 Winter, Charlie, "Documenting the Virtual 'Caliphate'", *Quilliam Foundation*, October 2015, accessed July 24, 2017, http://www.quilliaminternational.com/wp-content/uploads/2015/10/FINAL-documenting-the-virtual-caliphate.pdf.

211 Ibid.

212 Koerner, Brendan, "Why ISIS is Winning the Social Media War", *Wired*, March 2016, accessed July 24, 2017, https://www.wired.com/2016/03/isis-winning-social-media-war-heres-beat/.

213 Kharpal, Andy, "Google outlines 4 steps to tackle terrorist-related content on YouTube", *CNBC*, June 19, 2017, accessed July 24, 2017, http://www.cnbc.com/2017/06/19/google-youtube-tackles-terrorist-videos.html.

[214] "Hacking Social Media. Threats & Vulnerabilities – Threats & Anti-threats Strategies for Social Networking Websites", *Hakin9*, accessed July 24, 2017, https://hakin9.org/hacking-social-media-threats-vulnerabilities-threats-anti-threats-strategies-for-social-networking-websites/.

[215] Office of the Director of National Intelligence, "3D Cyberspace Spillover: Where Virtual Worlds Get Real", SHARP, (Washington, DC: Office of the Director of National Intelligence, 2008), various pages, https://fas.org/irp/eprint/virtual.pdf.

Chapter Eight

[216] Whipple, Austin, "Hacker psychology: Understanding the 4 emotions of social engineering", *Network World*, May 13, 2016, accessed July 24, 2017, http://www.networkworld.com/article/3070455/cloud-security/hacker-psychology-understanding-the-4-emotions-of-social-engineering.html.

[217] "Coward", *Dictionary.com*, accessed July 24, 2017, http://www.dictionary.com/browse/coward.

[218] Antonius, Daniel, "How the Fear of Terrorism Drives Corporate and National Culture", *Security Magazine*, November 5, 2015, accessed July 24, 2017, http://www.securitymagazine.com/articles/84902-how-the-fear-of-terrorism-drives-corporate-and-national-culture.

[219] John Horgan, *The Psychology of Terrorism*, (New York: Routledge, 2014), pp. 20-21.

[220] Whipple, "Hacker psychology: Understanding the 4 emotions of social engineering".

[221] Philipp, Joshua, "New Al-Qaeda Document Calls for Fueling Hatred to Instigate Violence", *The Epoch Times*, September 21, 2016, accessed July 24, 2017, http://www.theepochtimes.com/n3/2160167-new-al-qaeda-document-calls-for-fueling-hatred-to-instigate-violence/?utm_expid=.5zxdwnfjSHaLe_IPrO6c5w.0&utm_refe rrer=http percent3A percent2F percent2Fwww.theep.

[222] Gross, Michael L., Daphna Canetti, and Dana R. Vashdi, "Cyberterrorism: its effects on psychological well-being, public confidence and political attitudes", *Journal of Cyber Security* 3(1) (2017): 49–58, accessed July 24, 2017,

https://academic.oup.com/cybersecurity/article/3/1/49/299913
5/Cyberterrorism-its-effects-on-psychological-well.

[223] Philipp, Joshua, "The Silent War Against America's
Image", *The Epoch Times*, September 7, 2016, accessed July
24, 2017, http://www.theepochtimes.com/n3/2151976-the-
silent-war-against-americas-image-
2/?utm_expid=.5zxdwnfjSHaLe_IPrO6c5w.0&utm_referrer=htt
p percent3A percent2F percent2Fwww.theepochtimes.com
percent2Fn3 percent2Fauthor percent2Fjoshua-philipp
percent2Fpage percent2F3 percent2F.

[224] Gross, Michael L., Daphna Canetti, and Israel Waismel-
Manor, "Immune from Cyber-Fire? The Psychological &
Physiological Effects of Cyberwar", *Binary Bullets: The Ethics
of Cyberwarfare,* 2016, 157-76, accessed July 27, 2017,
http://poli.haifa.ac.il/~mgross/images/publications/Immunefro
mcyberfirerevised.pdf.

[225] Ibid.

[226] Nixon, Charisse L, "Current perspectives: the impact of
cyberbullying on adolescent health", *NCBI*, August 1, 2014,
accessed July 27, 2017,
https://www.ncbi.nlm.nih.gov/pmc/articles/PMC4126576/.

[227] Ibid.

[228] "The Breaking News Consumer's Handbook", *WNYC*,
September 20, 2013, accessed July 27, 2017,
http://www.wnyc.org/story/breaking-news-consumers-
handbook-pdf/.

[229] McClure, Laura, "How to tell fake news from real news",
TEDEd, January 12, 2017, accessed July 27, 2017,
http://blog.ed.ted.com/2017/01/12/how-to-tell-fake-news-from-
real-news/.

[230] Sharkov, Damien, "Russian Government Launches
Western 'Fake News' Tracker", *Newsweek*, February 22,
2017, accessed July 27, 2017,
http://www.newsweek.com/russian-government-launches-
western-fake-news-tracker-559524.

[231] "A Very Montenegrin Coup", *Aljazeera*, March 2, 2017,
http://www.aljazeera.com/programmes/peopleandpower/2017
/03/montenegrin-coup-170302060130440.html.

[232] Watts, Clint, "Inside Russia's Fake News Playbook", *Daily
Beast*, April 27, 2017, accessed July 27, 2017,
http://www.thedailybeast.com/inside-russias-fake-news-
playbook.

[233] Perez, Evan and Shimon Prokupecz, "CNN Exclusive: US suspects Russian hackers planted fake news behind Qatar crisis", *CNN*, June 7, 2017, accessed July 27, 2017, http://www.cnn.com/2017/06/06/politics/russian-hackers-planted-fake-news-qatar-crisis/index.html.

[234] Horgan, *The Psychology of Terrorism,* pp. 13, 22.

[235] "Coping With Psychological Warfare at Home", *WebMD*, accessed July 27, 2017, http://www.webmd.com/mental-health/features/coping-with-psychological-warfare-home#1.

Chapter Nine

[236] Weiss, Joe, "Industrial control systems: The holy grail of cyberwar", *The Christian Science Monitor*, March 24, 2017, accessed July 27, 2017, http://www.csmonitor.com/World/Passcode/Passcode-Voices/2017/0324/Industrial-control-systems-The-holy-grail-of-cyberwar?cmpid=gigya-fb.

[237] Zetter, Kim, "Inside the Cunning, Unprecedented Hack of Ukraine's Power Grid", *Wired*, March 3, 2016, accessed July 27, 2017, https://www.wired.com/2016/03/inside-cunning-unprecedented-hack-ukraines-power-grid/.

[238] Ibid.

[239] Brenner, Bill, "2003 Blackout: An Early Lesson in Planetary Scale?", *Akamai*, accessed July 27, 2017, https://blogs.akamai.com/2013/08/2003-blackout-an-early-lesson-in-planetary-scale.html.

[240] "(Known) SCADA Attacks Over the Years", *Fortinet*, February 12, 2015, accessed July 21, 2017, https://blog.fortinet.com/2015/02/12/known-scada-attacks-over-the-years.

[241] "Global Energy Cyberattacks: "Night Dragon", *McAfee*, February 10, 2011, accessed July 27, 2017, http://www.mcafee.com/us/resources/white-papers/wp-global-energy-cyberattacks-night-dragon.pdf.

[242] Williams, Katie Bo, "Report: Iran Hacked into a New York Dam in 2013", *The Hill*, December 21, 2015, accessed July 27, 2017, http://thehill.com/policy/cybersecurity/263898-report-iran-hacked-into-a-new-york-dam-in-2013.

[243] Goodman, *Cybercrimes*, pp. 27-30.

[244] Wagner, Daniel, "The Growing Threat of Cyber-Attacks on

Critical Infrastructure", *The Huffington Post*, May 24, 2016, accessed July 27, 2017, http://www.huffingtonpost.com/daniel-wagner/the-growing-threat-of-cyb_b_10114374.html.

[245] Pelroth, Nicole, "Hackers Are Targeting Nuclear Facilities, Homeland Security Dept. and F.B.I. Say", *The New York Times*, July 6, 2017, accessed July 27, 2017, https://mobile.nytimes.com/2017/07/06/technology/nuclear-plant-hack-report.html?referer=http://drudgereport.com/.

[246] Nakashima, Ellen, "Russia has Developed a Cyberweapon that Can Disrupt Power Grids, According to New Research", *The Washington Post*, June 12, 2017, accessed July 27, 2017, https://www.washingtonpost.com/world/national-security/russia-has-developed-a-cyber-weapon-that-can-disrupt-power-grids-according-to-new-research/2017/06/11/b91b773e-4eed-11e7-91eb-9611861a988f_story.html?utm_term=.9e4daecad05e.

[247] "Crashoverride: Analysis of the Threat of Electric Grid Operations", *Dragos*, accessed July 27, 2017, https://dragos.com/blog/crashoverride/CrashOverride-01.pdf.

[248] "Inflection Point: Sandworm Team and the Ukrainian Power Outages", *FireEye, Inflection Point*, 2016, accessed July 27, 2017, https://www2.fireeye.com/WBNR-Inflection-Point.html?utm_source=webinar&utm_medium=blog&utm_campaign=ICS-iSIGHT.

[249] "How a Power Grid Got Hacked", *Fifth Domain Cyber*, January 29, 2017, accessed July 21, 2017, http://fifthdomain.com/2017/01/29/how-a-power-grid-got-hacked/.

[250] "Report of the Commission to Assess the Threat to the United States from Electromagnetic Pulse (EMP) Attack", *Critical National Infrastructures*, April 2008, accessed July 27, 2017, http://www.empcommission.org/docs/A2473-EMP_Commission-7MB.pdf.

[251] Emanuelson, Jerry, "E1, E2 and E3", *Futurescience*, accessed July 27, 2017, http://www.futurescience.com/emp/E1-E2-E3.html.

[252] Kelly-Detwiler, Peter, "Failure to Protect U.S. Against Electromagnetic Pulse Threat Could Make 9/11 Look Trivial Someday", *Forbes*, July 31, 2014, accessed July 27, 2017, https://www.forbes.com/sites/peterdetwiler/2014/07/31/protecting-the-u-s-against-the-electromagnetic-pulse-threat-a-

continued-failure-of-leadership-could-make-911-look-trivial-someday/#2b09a5717a14.

253 Weiss, "Industrial control systems: The holy grail of cyberwar".

254 "Critical Infrastructure: Security Preparedness and Maturity", *Ponemon Institute & Unisys*, July 2014, accessed July 27, 2017,
http://images.outreach.unisys.com/Web/UnisysCorporation/percent7B3f7a3970-c2eb-4281-9e46-988f9048d4d1
percent7D_14-0316_Unisys_Ponemon_Study.pdf?elq=bbe092c04b9644828
f55c738ffaaafcb&elqCampaignId.

255 Ibid.

256 "Your guide to policies, information and services", *European Commission*, accessed July 25, 2017,
https://ec.europa.eu/digital-single-market/en/cybersecurity.

257 Wagner, Daniel, "The Growing Threat of Cyber-Attacks on Critical Infrastructure".

258 Natter, Ari and Mark Chediak, "US Grid in 'Imminent Danger' From Cyber-Attack, Study Says", *Bloomberg*, January 6, 2017, accessed July 25, 2017,
https://www.bloomberg.com/news/articles/2017-01-06/grid-in-imminent-danger-from-cyber-threats-energy-report-says.

259 Wagner, Daniel, "The Growing Threat of Virtual Terrorism", *International Policy Digest*, March 20, 2017, accessed July 25, 2017, https://intpolicydigest.org/2017/03/20/the-growing-threat-of-virtual-terrorism/.

260 Osborn, Kris, "DARPA tasks BAE with workaround to secure the power grid in event of massive attack", *Defense Systems*, April 13, 2017, accessed July 25, 2017,
https://defensesystems.com/articles/2017/04/13/grid.aspx.

261 Anand, Priya, "The 'mind-boggling' risks your city faces from cyber attackers", *MarketWatch*, January 20, 2016, accessed July 25, 2017,
http://www.marketwatch.com/story/the-mind-boggling-risks-your-city-faces-from-cyberattackers-2016-01-04.

262 Cerrudo, Cesar, "An Emerging US (and World) Threat: Cities Wide Open to Cyber Attacks", *IOActive*, 2015, accessed July 25, 2017,
https://ioactive.com/pdfs/IOActive_HackingCitiesPaper_Cesar Cerrudo.pdf.

263 Anand, "The 'mind-boggling' risks your city faces from

cyber attackers".

[264] Visner, Samuel Sanders, "The Cybersecurity of the Infrastructure – A Challenge and an Opportunity", *The Hill*, March 2, 2017, accessed July 25, 2017, http://thehill.com/blogs/congress-blog/technology/321987-the-cybersecurity-of-the-infrastructure-of-the-united-states.

Chapter Ten

[265] Goodman, *Future Crimes*, pp. 187-188.
[266] Sanger, David E., "Bank Hackers Steal Millions via Malware", *The New York Times*, February 14, 2015, accessed July 25, 2017, https://www.nytimes.com/2015/02/15/world/bank-hackers-steal-millions-via-malware.html?mcubz=1&_r=1.
[267] Chozick, Amy, "Bloomberg Admits Terminal Snooping", *The New York Times*, May 13, 2013, accessed July 25, 2017, http://www.nytimes.com/2013/05/13/business/media/bloomberg-admits-terminal-snooping.html.
[268] Goodman, *Future Crimes*, pp. 174, 183, 187-188.
[269] "Banks are hiding their cyberattacks", *Business Insider*, October 14, 2016, accessed July 25, 2017, http://www.businessinsider.com/banks-are-hiding-cyberattacks-2016-10.
[270] Burne, Katy and Robin Sidel, "Hackers Ran Through Holes in Swift's Network", *MSN*, April 30, 2017, accessed July 25, 2017, https://www.msn.com/en-us/money/markets/hackers-ran-through-holes-in-SWIFTs-network/ar-BBAz12y.
[271] Frenkel, Sheera, "Hackers Find 'Ideal Testing Ground' for Attacks: Developing Countries", *The New York Times*, July 2, 2017, accessed July 25, 2017, https://mobile.nytimes.com/2017/07/02/technology/hackers-find-ideal-testing-ground-for-attacks-developing-countries.html?referer=https://www.linkedin.com/.
[272] "Hacking Threat Increasingly Targeting Smaller Financial Firms", *Brink*, April 19, 2017, accessed July 25, 2017, http://www.brinknews.com/hacking-threat-increasingly-targeting-smaller-financial-firms/.
[273] Steinberg, Julie, "Was North Korea Behind the Hacking of a Bank in India?", *The Wall Street Journal*, April 10, 2017, accessed July 25, 2017,

https://www.wsj.com/articles/cybertheft-attempt-on-indian-bank-resembles-bangladesh-heist-1491816614.

[274] Mozur, Paul and Choe Sang-Hun, "North Korea's Rising Ambition Seen in Bid to Breach Global Banks", *The New York Times*, March 25, 2017, accessed July 25, 2017, https://www.nytimes.com/2017/03/25/technology/north-korea-hackers-global-banks.html?hp&action=click&pgtype=Homepage&clickSource=story-heading&module=first-column-region&region=top-news&WT.nav=top-news&_r=3.

[275] "2017 Trustwave Global Security Report", *Trustwave*, 2017, accessed July 25, 2017, https://www2.trustwave.com/rs/815-RFM-693/images/2016 percent20Trustwave percent20Global percent20Security percent20Report.pdf.

[276] "New Ponemon Study on Malware Detection & Prevention Released", *Ponemon Institute*, March 18, 2016, accessed July 25, 2017, http://www.ponemon.org/blog/new-ponemon-study-on-malware-detection-prevention-released.

[277] Mongeau, Scott, "Can Financial Institutions Protect Themselves Against Hacking Attacks?", *FEI*, December 6, 2016, accessed July 25, 2017, http://daily.financialexecutives.org/can-financial-institutions-protect-hacking-attacks/.

[278] Koranyi, Balazs, "G20 to jointly fight bank sector hacking", *Reuters*, March 17, 2017, accessed July 25, 2017, http://www.reuters.com/article/us-g20-germany-cyber-idUSKBN16O2F0.

[279] Solon, Olivia, "Snapchat's new map feature raises fears of stalking and bullying", *The Guardian*, June 23, 2017, accessed July 25, 2017, https://www.theguardian.com/technology/2017/jun/23/snapchat-maps-privacy-safety-concerns.

[280] Binghamton University, "Your smartwatch is giving away your ATM PIN", *Science News*, July 6, 2016, accessed July 25, 2017, https://www.sciencedaily.com/releases/2016/07/160706131951.htm.

[281] Goodman, *Future Crimes*, pp. 136-140.

[282] "Threat Intelligence Report for the Telecommunications Industry", *Kapersky Security Intelligence*, accessed July 25, 2017,

https://securelist.com/files/2016/08/Kaspersky_Telecom_Thre
ats_2016.pdf.
[283] Dignan, Larry, "Your Biggest Cybersecurity Weakness Is
Your Phone", *Harvard Business Review*, September 22,
2016, accessed July 25, 2017, https://hbr.org/2016/09/your-
biggest-cybersecurity-weakness-is-your-phone.
[284] Ruggiero, Paul and Jon Foote, "Cyber Threats to Mobile
Phones", *United States Computer Emergency Readiness
Team (US-CERT)*, accessed July 25, 2017, https://www.us-
cert.gov/sites/default/files/publications/cyber_threats-
to_mobile_phones.pdf.

Chapter Eleven

[285] Knapton, Sarah, "DIY 'garage' scientists could unleash
genetically-edited organisms into wild, warn experts", *The
Telegraph*, September 30, 2016, accessed July 25, 2017,
http://www.telegraph.co.uk/science/2016/09/30/diy-garage-
scientists-could-unleash-genetically-edited-organisms/.
[286] "Overview of Potential Agents of Biological Terrorism", *SIU
School of Medicine*, accessed July 25, 2017,
http://www.siumed.edu/im/overview-potential-agents-
biological-terrorism.html#bio.
[287] Knapton, Sarah, "Bill Gates: Terrorists could wipe out 30
million people by weaponizing a disease such as smallpox",
The Telegraph, 19 April, 2017, accessed July 25, 2017,
http://www.telegraph.co.uk/science/2017/04/19/bill-gates-
terrorists-could-wipe-30-million-people-weaponising/.
[288] Knapton, "DIY 'garage' scientists could unleash
genetically-edited organisms into wild, warn experts".
[289] Ibid.
[290] Mowatt-Larssen, Rolf, "Al Qaeda's Pursuit of Weapons of
Mass Destruction", *Foreign Policy*, January 25, 2010,
accessed July 25, 2017,
http://foreignpolicy.com/2010/01/25/al-qaedas-pursuit-of-
weapons-of-mass-destruction/.
[291] McFadyen, Siobhan, "Animal testicle bombs are a
dangerous step towards ISIS biological warfare, says expert",
Express, May 6, 2016, accessed July 25, 2017,
http://www.express.co.uk/news/world/667874/isis-daesh-
biological-warfare-dirty-bomb-animal-testicles-brussels.

[292] Amiga, Aimee and Ruth Schuster, "EU Report: ISIS Could Commit Chemical or Biological Terror Attack in West", *Haaretz*, accessed July 25, 2017, http://www.haaretz.com/middle-east-news/isis/1.691157.

[293] "ISIS Terrorist Cell Dismantled in Morocco 'Planned to Use Biological Weapons'", *Morocco World News*, February 19, 2016, accessed July 25, 2017, https://www.moroccoworldnews.com/2016/02/180240/isis-terrorist-cell-dismantled-in-morocco-planned-to-use-biological-weapons/.

[294] "Cyber, biological, crypto: Hybrid terrorism at work", *C4isrnet*, May 30, 2017, accessed July 25, 2017, http://www.c4isrnet.com/articles/cyber-biological-crypto-hybrid-terrorism-at-work.

[295] Acharya, Amrit P. and Arabinda Acharya, "Cyberterrorism and Biotechnology", *Foreign Affairs*, June 1, 2017, accessed July 25, 2017, https://www.foreignaffairs.com/articles/world/2017-06-01/cyberterrorism-and-biotechnology.

[296] Goodman, Marc and Andrew Hessel, "The Bio-crime Prophecy: DNA Hacking the Biggest Opportunity Since Cyber Attacks", *Wired*, May 23, 2013, accessed July 25, 2017, http://www.wired.co.uk/article/the-bio-crime-prophecy.

[297] Rosen, Joseph M., C. Everett Koop, and Eliot B. Grigg, "Cybercare: A System for Confronting Bioterrorism", *Engineering and Homeland Security,* 32(1) (2002), accessed July 25, 2017, https://www.nae.edu/19582/Bridge/EngineeringandHomelandSecurity/CybercareASystemforConfrontingBioterrorism.aspx.

[298] "Lessons Learned from TOPOFF 4 – 9385", *WMSYM*, March 1-5, 2009, accessed July 25, 2017, http://www.wmsym.org/archives/2009/pdfs/9385.pdf.

[299] Vicinanzo, Amanda, "Biological Terrorist Attack on US an 'Urgent and Serious Threat'", *Homeland Security Today*, April 23, 2015, accessed July 25, 2017, http://www.hstoday.us/single-article/biological-terrorist-attack-on-us-an-urgent-and-serious-threat/0ce6ebf3524d83c537b1f4f0cc578547.html.

[300] Sell, Tara Kirk and Matthew Watson, "Federal Agency Biodefense Funding, FY2013-FY2014", *NCBI*, accessed July 25, 2017, https://www.ncbi.nlm.nih.gov/pmc/articles/PMC3778993/.

[301] "Zika to Cost Latin American, Caribbean Region up to $18B from 2015-2016, with Poorer Nations Hit Hardest, UNDP/IFRC Report Shows", *KFF*, April 7, 2017, accessed July 25, 2017, http://www.kff.org/news-summary/zika-to-cost-latin-american-caribbean-region-up-to-18b-from-2015-2017-with-poorer-nations-hit-hardest-undpifrc-report-shows/.

[302] "The Economic Impact of the 2014 Ebola Epidemic: Short and Medium Term Estimates for West Africa", *The World Bank*, October 8, 2014, accessed July 25, 2017, http://www.worldbank.org/en/region/afr/publication/the-economic-impact-of-the-2014-ebola-epidemic-short-and-medium-term-estimates-for-west-africa.

[303] Ridge, Tom and Dante Disparte, "The World Needs a DARPA-Style Project to Prevent Pandemics", *Harvard Business Review*, accessed July 25, 2017, https://hbr.org/2017/04/the-world-needs-a-darpa-style-project-to-prevent-pandemics.

[304] "Biodefense Indicators: One Year Later, Events Outpacing Federal Efforts to Defend the Nation: A Bipartisan Report of the Blue Ribbon Study Panel on Biodefense", *Blue Ribbon Study Panel on Biodefense*, December 2016.

[305] "Use of Chemical, Biological, Radiological and Nuclear Weapons by Non-State Actors", *Chatham House*: The Royal Institute of International Affairs, 2016.

Chapter Twelve

[306] Greenberg, Andy, "Malware Lets a Drone Steal Data by Watching a Computer's Blinking LED", *Wired*, February 22, 2017, accessed July 25, 2017, https://www.wired.com/2017/02/malware-sends-stolen-data-drone-just-pcs-blinking-led/.

[307] Jiang, Sijia and Jim Finkle, "China's Xiongmai to recall up to 10,000 webcams after hack", *Reuters*, October 25, 2016, accessed July 25, 2017, http://www.reuters.com/article/us-cyberattacks-china-idUSKCN12P1TT.

[308] Here Come the Drones – and Their Security Holes", *Nextgov*, February 24, 2017, accessed July 25, 2017, http://www.nextgov.com/cybersecurity/2017/02/here-come-dronesand-their-security-holes/135703/.

[309] Zetter, Kim, "Hacker Lexicon: What is an Air Gap?", *Wired*,

December 8, 2014, accessed July 25, 2017,
https://www.wired.com/2014/12/hacker-lexicon-air-gap/.
[310] Greenberg, "Malware Lets a Drone Steal Data by
Watching a Computer's Blinking LED".
[311] Curtis, Sophie, "'Dronejackings' and home hacking among
top cyber security threats for 2017", *Mirror*, November 29,
2016, accessed July 25, 2017,
http://www.mirror.co.uk/tech/dronejackings-home-hacking-
among-top-9354003.
[312] Franceschi-Bicchiera, Lorenzo, "Drone Hijacking? That's
Just the Start of GPS Troubles", *Wired*, July 6, 2012,
accessed July 25, 2017,
https://www.wired.com/2012/07/drone-hijacking/.
[313] Atherton, Kelsey D., "West Point Cadets are Shooting
Down Drones with Cyber Rifles", *Popular Science*, June 15,
2016, accessed July 25, 2017, http://www.popsci.com/west-
point-cadets-shoot-drones-cyber-rifle#page-8.
[314] "Cyber Security Patrol: How Attackers Can Use a Drone
Carrying a Smartphone to Gain Access to Unsecured
Wireless Printers", *iTrust: Centre for Research in Cyber
Security*, accessed July 25, 2017,
https://itrust.sutd.edu.sg/research/projects/cyber-security-
patrol/.
[315] Campbell, Cate Scott, "PODCAST: This is Why Computer
Science Rocks", *Forbes*, April 25, 2017, accessed July 25,
2017,
https://www.forbes.com/sites/thomasbrewster/2017/04/25/vul
nerable-quadcopter-drone-hacked-by-ut-dallas-cyber-
researchers/#75c2f6fa1037.
[316] Stewart, Scott, "Beyond the Buzz: Assessing the Terrorist
Drone Threat", *Stratfor,* February 9, 2017, accessed July 25,
2017, https://www.stratfor.com/weekly/beyond-buzz-
assessing-terrorist-drone-
threat?id=be1ddd5371&uuid=79ca77a7-5abc-40df-92ba-
f7c692232711.
[317] Hambling, David, "Could ISIS Really Attack the West with
a Dirty Drone?", *Popular Mechanics*, April 8, 2016, accessed
July 25, 2017,
http://www.popularmechanics.com/military/weapons/a20334/I
S-dirty-drone/.
[318] Katz, Rita, "How ISIS Maximizes the Terror from its Killer
Drones", *Daily Beast*, May 3, 2017, accessed July 25, 2017,

http://www.thedailybeast.com/how-IS-maximizes-the-terror-from-its-killer-drones.

[319] Warrick, Joby, "Use of Weaponized Drones by IS Spurs Terrorism", *Washington Post*, February 21, 2017, accessed July 25, 2017, https://www.washingtonpost.com/world/national-security/use-of-weaponized-drones-by-IS-spurs-terrorism-fears/2017/02/21/9d83d51e-f382-11e6-8d72-263470bf0401_story.html?utm_term=.c200476e279c.

[320] Rassler, Don, Muhammad al-Ubaydi, and Vera Mironova, "CTC Perspectives – The Islamic State's Drone Documents: Management, Acquisitions, and DIY Tradecraft", *Combating Terrorism Center*, June 21, 2016, accessed July 25, 2017, https://www.ctc.usma.edu/posts/ctc-perspectives-the-islamic-states-drone-documents-management-acquisitions-and-diy-tradecraft.

[321] Federal Aviation Administration, "Press Release – DOT and FAA Finalize Rules for Small Unmanned Aircraft Systems", *Federal Aviation Administration*, accessed July 25, 2017, https://www.faa.gov/news/press_releases/news_story.cfm?newsId=20515.

[322] "Blockchain", *Wikipedia*, accessed July 25, 2017, https://en.m.wikipedia.org/wiki/Blockchain.

[323] Chantz, Hy, "Using Blockchain to address Drone Cybersecurity", *Security Intelligence*, August 25, 2016, accessed July 25, 2017, https://securityintelligence.com/using-blockchain-to-address-drone-cybersecurity/.

[324] Cerrudo, Cesar, and Lucas Apa, "Hacking Robots Before Skynet", *IOActive*, 2017, accessed July 25, 2017, https://ioactive.com/pdfs/Hacking-Robots-Before-Skynet.pdf.

[325] Ibid.

Chapter Thirteen

[326] Maney, Kevin, "Can Hackers Be Stopped? The State of Defense in the Private Sector", *Newsweek*, November 2, 2016, accessed July 25, 2017, http://www.newsweek.com/2016/11/11/war-against-hacking-cybercrime-515935.html.

[327] Goodman, *Future Crimes*, pp. 345-346.

[328] The Economist, "India's ID System is reshaping ties between state and citizens", *The Economist*, April 12, 2017, accessed July 25, 2017, http://www.economist.com/news/asia/21720609-long-they-have-mobile-signal-indias-id-system-reshaping-ties-between-state-and-citizens.

[329] Goodman, Marc, "You Can't Replace Your Fingerprints", *Slate*, accessed July 25, 2017, http://www.slate.com/articles/technology/future_tense/2015/02/future_crimes_excerpt_how_hackers_can_steal_fingerprints_and_more.html.

[330] Goodman, *Future Crimes*, pp. 347-360.

[331] 46halbe, "Chaos Computer Clubs breaks iris recognition system of the Samsung Galaxy S8", *Chaos Computer Club*, May 22, 2017, accessed July 25, 2017, https://www.ccc.de/en/updates/2017/iriden.

[332] Saenz, Aaron, "Security Checks Reaching Towards Your Brain", *Singularity Hub*, May 14, 2009, accessed July 25, 2017, https://singularityhub.com/2009/05/14/security-checks-reaching-towards-your-brain/#.WU0CNrpFygk.

[333] Rodriguez, Monica, "Why Smartphones Are Now Adding Iris Scanners", *Motherboard*, August 1, 2016, accessed July 25, 2017, https://motherboard.vice.com/en_us/article/bmv5dm/iris-scanners-smartphones-galaxy-note.

[334] Schlangenstein, Mary, "JetBlue and Delta Test Biometric Scanning to Replace Boarding Passes", *Bloomberg*, May 31, 2017, accessed July 25, 2017, https://www.bloomberg.com/news/articles/2017-05-31/jetblue-tests-using-face-recognition-to-scrap-boarding-passes.

[335] Goodman, *Future Crimes*, p. 406.

[336] Gerschenfeld, Neil, and Isaac L. Chuang, "Quantum Computing with Molecules", *Scientific American*, June 1998, accessed July 25, 2017, http://cba.mit.edu/docs/papers/98.06.sciqc.pdf

[337] "Quantum Computing", *Wikipedia*, accessed July 25, 2017, https://en.wikipedia.org/wiki/Quantum_computing.

[338] Bond, Shannon, "Artificial intelligence and quantum computing aid cybercrime fight", *Financial Times*, May 24, 2017, accessed July 26, 2017, https://www.ft.com/content/1b9bdc4c-2422-11e7-a34a-

538b4cb30025.

[339] McGee, Chantel, "The man who built a virtual nervous system explains how humans will interact with machines in ten years", *CNBC*, May 21, 2017, accessed July 26, 2017 http://www.cnbc.com/2017/05/21/mark-sagar-how-humans-will-interact-with-machines-in-ten-years.html.

[340] Falk, Dan, "Godlike 'Homo Deus' Could Replace Humans as Tech Evolves", *NBC*, May 31, 2017, accessed July 26, 2017, https://www.nbcnews.com/mach/technology/godlike-homo-deus-could-replace-humans-tech-evolves-n757971.

[341] "First robotic cop joins Dubai police", *Yahoo*, accessed July 26, 2017, https://www.yahoo.com/tech/first-robotic-cop-joins-dubai-police-092135132.html.

[342] Knight Scope, accessed July 26, 2017, http://www.knightscope.com/.

[343] Kolodny, Carina, "Stephen Hawking Is Terrified of Artificial Intelligence", *The Huffington Post*, May 5, 2014, accessed July 26, 2017, http://www.huffingtonpost.com/2014/05/05/stephen-hawking-artificial-intelligence_n_5267481.html.

[344] Sui, Linda, "44% of World Population Will Own Smartphones in 2017", *Strategy Analytics*, December 21, 2016, accessed July 26, 2017, https://www.strategyanalytics.com/strategy-analytics/blogs/smart-phones/2016/12/21/44-of-world-population-will-own-smartphones-in-2017#.WVATGGjyvic.

[345] Metz, Rachel, "Google Glass Is Dead; Long Live Smart Glasses", *MIT Technology Review*, November 26, 2014, accessed July 26, 2017, https://www.technologyreview.com/s/532691/google-glass-is-dead-long-live-smart-glasses/.

[346] Mims, Christopher, "In 10 Years, Your iPhone Won't Be a Phone Anymore", *The Wall Street Journal*, June 15, 2017, accessed July 26, 2017, https://www.wsj.com/articles/in-10-years-your-iphone-wont-be-a-phone-anymore-1498395600.

[347] Larson, Nina, "AI 'good for the world'…says ultra-lifelike robot", *Phys.Org*, June 8, 2017, https://phys.org/news/2017-06-ai-good-world-ultra-lifelike-robot.html.

[348] Manky, Derek, "Artificial Intelligence: Cybersecurity Friend or Foe?", *Dark Reading*, May 11, 2017, accessed July 26, 2017, http://www.darkreading.com/threat-intelligence/artificial-intelligence-cybersecurity-friend-or-foe-/a/d-id/1328838.

[349] Ismali, Nick, "The importance of creating a cyber security culture", *Information Age*, April 8, 2017, accessed July 26, 2017, http://www.information-age.com/importance-creating-cyber-security-culture-123465778/.

[350] Pultarova, Tereza, "IBM's artificially intelligent Watson computer set to tackle cybercrime", *Engineering and Technology*, February 13, 2017, accessed July 26, 2017, https://eandt.theiet.org/content/articles/2017/02/ibms-artificially-intelligent-watson-computer-set-to-tackle-cybercrime/.

[351] Lerner, Andrew, "Intent-based Networking", *Gartner*, February 7, 2017, accessed July 26, 2017, http://blogs.gartner.com/andrew-lerner/2017/02/07/intent-based-networking/.

[352] Manky, Derek, "Extreme Makeover: AI & Network Cybersecurity", *Dark Reading*, May 10, 2017, accessed July 26, 2017, http://www.darkreading.com/threat-intelligence/extreme-makeover-ai-and-network-cybersecurity-/a/d-id/1328837.

[353] "Artificial Intelligence and Life in 2030: One Hundred Year Study on Artificial Intelligence: Report of the 2015 Study Panel", *Stanford*, September 2016, accessed July 26, 2017, https://ai100.stanford.edu/sites/default/files/ai100report10032016fnl_singles.pdf.

[354] "Albert Einstein Quotes", *Brainy quote*, accessed July 26, 2017, https://www.brainyquote.com/quotes/quotes/a/alberteins121993.html.

[355] "Winning the Cyber War with AI & Cognitive Computing: The Experts' View", *AI Business*, September 9, 2016, accessed July 26, 2017, http://aibusiness.org/winning-the-cyber-war-with-ai-cognitive-computing-the-experts-view/.

Chapter Fourteen

[356] Goodman, *Future Crimes*, pp. 188-195, 433-435.

[357] Livingstone, David and Patricia Lewis, "Space, the Final Frontier for Cybersecurity?", *International Security Department*, September 2016, accessed July 26, 2017, https://www.chathamhouse.org/sites/files/chathamhouse/publi

cations/research/2016-09-22-space-final-frontier-cybersecurity-livingstone-lewis.pdf.

[358] Woolsey, James R., and Vincent Pry, "How North Korea could kill up to 90% of Americans", *The Hill*, March 29, 2017, accessed July 26, 2017, http://thehill.com/blogs/pundits-blog/defense/326094-how-north-korea-could-kill-up-to-90-percent-of-americans-at-any.

[359] Klein, Aaron, "Exclusive – Congressional Expert: North Korea Prepping EMP Catastrophe Aimed at U.S. Homefront", *Breitbart*, May 8, 2017, accessed July 26, 2017, http://www.breitbart.com/jerusalem/2017/05/08/exclusive-congressional-expert-north-korea-prepping-emp-warfare-aimed-u-s-homefront/.

[360] Philipp, Joshua, "China Covers Up Anti-Satellite Test, Again", *The Epoch Times*, August 3, 2014, accessed July 26, 2017, http://www.theepochtimes.com/n3/838700-china-covers-up-anti-satellite-test-again/.

[361] "Active protection system", *Wikipedia*, accessed July 26, 2017, https://en.wikipedia.org/wiki/Active_protection_system.

[362] Kania, Elsa B., "The PLA's Potential Breakthrough in High-Power Microwave Weapons", *The Diplomat*, March 11, 2017, accessed July 26, 2017, http://thediplomat.com/2017/03/the-plas-potential-breakthrough-in-high-power-microwave-weapons/.

[363] Philipp, Joshua, "China Makes Advances in Space Lasers, Microwave Weapons", *The Epoch Times*, March 22, 2017, accessed July 26, 2017, http://www.theepochtimes.com/n3/2234510-china-advances-assassins-mace-warfare-program/.

[364] Gertz, Bill, "How China's Mad Scientists Plan to Shock America's Military: Super Lasers, Railguns, and Microwave Weapons", *The National Interest*, March 10, 2017, accessed July 26, 2017, http://nationalinterest.org/blog/the-buzz/how-chinas-mad-scientists-plan-shock-americas-military-super-19737.

[365] Philipp, Joshua, "World Powers Are Preparing for Space Warfare", *The Epoch Times*, September 6, 2015, accessed July 26, 2017, http://www.theepochtimes.com/n3/1741095-world-powers-are-preparing-for-space-warfare/.

[366] Whigham, Nick, "China sets new record for quantum entanglement to build new communication network", *News.com*, accessed July 26, 2017,

http://www.news.com.au/technology/science/space/china-sets-new-record-for-quantum-entanglement-en-route-to-build-new-communication-network/news-story/e528da0cf68b2e63bbe093cab49ec507.

[367] Whigham, "China takes major step in creating a global network for quantum communication".

[368] Syeed, Nafeesa, "Outer-Space Hacking a Top Concern for NASA's Cybersecurity Chief", *Bloomberg*, April 12, 2017, accessed July 26, 2017, https://www.bloomberg.com/news/articles/2017-04-12/outer-space-hacking-a-top-concern-for-nasa-s-cybersecurity-chief.

[369] Zetter, Kim, "Russian Spy Gang Hijacks Satellite Links to Steal Data", *Wired*, September 9, 2015, accessed July 26, 2017, https://www.wired.com/2015/09/turla-russian-espionage-gang-hijacks-satellite-connections-to-steal-data/.

[370] Goodman, *Future Crimes*, pp. 188-195, 433-435.

[371] Livingstone and Lewis, "Space, the Final Frontier for Cybersecurity?".

[372] Ibid.

Chapter Fifteen

[373] "General Data Protection Regulation", *Wikipedia*, accessed July 26, 2017, https://en.wikipedia.org/wiki/General_Data_Protection_Regulation.

[374] Stone, Jon, "Theresa May says the internet must now be regulated following London Bridge terror attack", *Independent*, June 4, 2017, accessed July 26, 2017, http://www.independent.co.uk/news/uk/politics/theresa-may-Internet-regulated-london-bridge-terror-attack-google-facebook-whatsapp-borough-security-a7771896.html.

[375] Wagner, Daniel, "Why Theresa May's call to arms on terrorism via social media could be blocked by reality", *South China Morning Post*, June 6, 2017, accessed July 26, 2017, http://www.scmp.com/comment/insight-opinion/article/2097066/why-theresa-mays-call-arms-terrorism-social-media-could-be.

[376] "General Data Protection Regulation", *Wikipedia*.

[377] Taparata, Evan, "President Trump, how is letting internet providers sell consumers' browsing data in the public

interest?", *PRI*, April 16, 2017, accessed July 26, 2017, https://www.pri.org/stories/2017-04-16/president-trump-how-letting-Internet-providers-sell-consumers-browsing-data.

[378] Theohary, Catherine A. and John W. Rollins, "Cyberwarfare and Cyberterrorism: In Brief", *Congressional Research Service*, March 27, 2016, accessed July 26, 2017, https://fas.org/sgp/crs/natsec/R43955.pdf, pp. 3-5.

[379] Theohary and Rollins, "Cyberwarfare and Cyberterrorism: In Brief", p. 3.

[380] Miller, Greg, Ellen Nakashima, and Adam Entous, "Obama's secret struggle to punish Russia for Putin's election assault", *The Washington Post*, June 23, 2017, accessed July 26, 2017, https://www.washingtonpost.com/graphics/2017/world/national-security/obama-putin-election-hacking/?utm_term=.92e293fdf2a2.

[381] 114th Congress (2015-2016), "H.R.1704 – Personal Data Notification and Protection Act of 2015", *Congress.Gov*, accessed July 26, 2017,https://www.congress.gov/bill/114th-congress/house-bill/1704.

[382] Chabrow, Eric, "Why Congress Can't Pass Cyber Law", *Bank Info Security*, March 27, 2014, accessed July 26, 2017, http://www.bankinfosecurity.com/blogs/congress-cant-pass-key-cyber-bill-p-1644.

[383] Seals, Tara, "US Congress Passes Controversial Info-Sharing Bill", *Info Security*, December 21, 2015, accessed July 26, 2017, https://www.infosecurity-magazine.com/news/us-congress-passes-controversial/.

[384] "A Look into Public Private Partnerships for Cybersecurity", *Penn Wharton: University of Pennsylvania*, April 18, 2017, accessed July 26, 2017, https://publicpolicy.wharton.upenn.edu/live/news/1815-a-look-into-public-private-partnerships-for.

[385] "Recommendations for Public-Private Partnership against Cybercrime", *World Economic Forum*, January 2016, accessed July 26, 2017, http://www3.weforum.org/docs/WEF_Cybercrime_Principles.pdf.

[386] Germano, Judith H., "Cybersecurity Partnerships: A New Era of Public-Private Collaboration", *The Center on Law and Security*, October 2014, accessed July 26, 2017, http://www.lawandsecurity.org/wp-

content/uploads/2016/08/Cybersecurity.Partnerships-1.pdf.
[387] "Cyber Terrorism Challenges: The Need for a Global Response to a Multi-Jurisdictional Crime", ResearchGate, June 2013, accessed July 26, 2017, https://www.researchgate.net/publication/257101606.
[388] "International Multilateral Partnership Against Cyber Threats", *Wikipedia*, accessed July 26, 2017, https://en.wikipedia.org/wiki/International_Multilateral_Partnership_Against_Cyber_Threats.
[389] "Cyber Terrorism Challenges: The Need for a Global Response to a Multi-Jurisdictional Crime", ResearchGate.
[390] "Convention on Cybercrime", Wikipedia, accessed July 26, 2017, https://en.wikipedia.org/wiki/Convention_on_Cybercrime.
[391] "GDPR Key Changes", *EUGDPR*, accessed July 26, 2017, http://www.eugdpr.org/key-changes.html.
[392] Wagner, Jack, "China's Cybersecurity Law: What You Need to Know", *The Diplomat*, June 1, 2017, accessed July 26, 2017, http://thediplomat.com/2017/06/chinas-cybersecurity-law-what-you-need-to-know/.
[393] "China's new cyber-security law is worryingly vague", *The Economist,* June 1, 2017, accessed July 26, 2017, https://www.economist.com/news/business/21722873-its-rules-are-broad-ambiguous-and-bothersome-international-firms-chinas-new-cyber-security.
[394] "Apple sets up China data center to meet new cyber-security rules", *Reuters*, July 12, 2017, accessed July 26, 2017, https://www.reuters.com/article/us-china-apple-idUSKBN19X0D6.

Chapter Sixteen

[395] Greenberg, Andy, "The Petya Plague Exposes the Threat of Evil Software Updates", *Wired*, July 7, 2017, accessed July 26, 2017, https://www.wired.com/story/petya-plague-automatic-software-updates/.
[396] "5 Cyberterrorism and Security Measures", National Academy of Sciences, 2007, Science and Technology to Counter Terrorism: Proceedings of an Indo-U.S. Workshop, (Washington, DC: The National Academies Press), accessed July 27, 2017, https://www.nap.edu/read/11848/chapter/6.

[397] "2017 Annual Cyber Report", *Cisco*, accessed July 27, 2017, http://www.cisco.com/c/dam/m/digital/1198689/Cisco_2017_ACR_PDF.pdf, pp. 71-73.

[398] Newman, Lily Hay, "IBM's Plan to Encrypt Unthinkable Amounts of Sensitive Data", *Wired*, July 17, 2017, accessed July 27, 2017, https://www.wired.com/story/ibm-z-mainframe-encryption.

[399] Camacho, Chris and Pierre Lamy, "Best Practices for Addressing Four Common Threats", *Flashpoint*, February 28, 2017, accessed July 27, 2017, https://www.flashpoint-intel.com/blog/emerging-threats/blog-best-practices-common-threats/.

[400] TrapX Research Labs, "Anatomy of Attack: MEDJACK.2: Hospitals Under Siege".

[401] Friedman, Sam and Adam Thomas, "Demystifying Cyber Insurance Coverage", *Deloitte University Press*, February 23, 2017, accessed July 27, 2017, https://dupress.deloitte.com/dup-us-en/industry/financial-services/demystifying-cybersecurity-insurance.html.

[402] Orcutt, Mike, "Insurers Scramble to Put a Price on a Cyber Catastrophe", *MIT Technology Review*, April 6, 2017, accessed July 27, 2017, https://www.technologyreview.com/s/603937/insurers-scramble-to-put-a-price-on-a-cyber-catastrophe/?utm_source=MIT+Technology+Review&utm_campaign=8d6e364469-weekly_roundup_2017-04-06_edit&utm_medium=e-mail&utm_term=0_997ed6f472-8d6e364469-153822473&goal=0_997ed6f472-8d6e364469-153822473&mc_cid=8d6e364469&mc_eid=e360f5e8d9.

[403] Disparte, D. and Daniel Wagner, "Do You Know What Your Company's Data Is Worth?", *Harvard Business Review*, September 16, 2016, accessed July 27, 2017, https://hbr.org/2016/09/do-you-know-what-your-companys-data-is-worth.

[404] Sanger, David E., "Pentagon Announces New Strategy for Cyberwarfare", *The New York Times*, April 23, 2015, accessed July 27, 2017, https://www.nytimes.com/2015/04/24/us/politics/pentagon-announces-new-cyberwarfare-strategy.html?_r=2.

[405] Department of Defense, "Task Force Report: Resilient Military Systems and the Advanced Cyber Threat", *Defense*

Science Board, January 2013, accessed July 27, 2017, http://nsarchive.gwu.edu/NSAEBB/NSAEBB424/docs/Cyber-081.pdf.

[406] "Actions to Strengthen Cybersecurity and Protect Critical IT Systems", *US Office of Personnel Management*, June 2015, accessed July 27, 2017, https://www.opm.gov/cybersecurity/cybersecurity-incidents/opm-cybersecurity-action-report.pdf.

[407] "Internet Security Threat Report", *Symantec* (22), April 2017, accessed July 27, 2017, https://digitalhubshare.symantec.com/content/dam/Atlantis/campaigns-and-launches/FY17/Threat percent20Protection/ISTR22_Main-FINAL-APR24.pdf?aid=elq_&om_sem_kw=elq_17978467&om_ext_c id=biz_e-mail_elq_.

[408] Greenberg, "The Petya Plague Exposes the Threat of Evil Software Updates".

Chapter Seventeen

[409] "How to Manage the Computer Security Threat", *The Economist*, April 8, 2017, accessed July 30, 2017, https://www.economist.com/news/leaders/21720279-incentives-software-firms-take-security-seriously-are-too-weak-how-manage.

[410] Joshua Philipp, "Hackers Selling Access to Critical Infrastructure on Dark Net", *The Epoch Times*, July 27, 2017, accessed July 30, 2017, http://www.theepochtimes.com/n3/2272096-hackers-selling-access-to-critical-infrastructure-on-darknet-2/.

[411] Elliot, Grant, "With Billions Spent on Cybersecurity, Why Are Problems Getting Worse?", *Dark Reading*, May 23, 2017, accessed July 27, 2017, http://www.darkreading.com/application-security/with-billions-spent-on-cybersecurity-why-are- problems-getting-worse/a/d-id/1328896.

[412] The Economist, "How to Manage the Computer Security Threat".

[413] Raine, Lee, Janna Anderson, and Jonathan Albright, "The Future of Free Speech, Trolls, Anonymity, and Fake News Online", *Pew Research Center*, March 29, 2017, accessed

July 27, 2017, http://www.pewInternet.org/2017/03/29/the-future-of-free-speech-trolls-anonymity-and-fake-news-online/.
414 "Pre-Detection of Terrorism", *Millennium Project*, July 25, 2016, accessed July 27, 2017, http://www.millennium-project.org/millennium/NATOARW-Presentations/TG-EF-YS-Pre-Detection-NatoARW-July2016.pdf.
415 Chapman, Glenn, "Microsoft CEO: tech sector needs to prevent '1984' future", *Yahoo*, May 10, 2017, accessed July 27, 2017, https://www.yahoo.com/tech/microsoft-aims-artificial-intelligence-mainstream-150225467.html.
416 Revell, Timothy, "AI can doctor videos to put words in the mouths of speakers", *New Scientist*, May 19, 2017, accessed July 27, 2017, https://www.newscientist.com/article/2131716-ai-can-doctor-videos-to-put-words-in-the-mouths-of-speakers/.
417 Siegel-Itzkovich, Judy, "Can 3D Printing Attract Terrorist Hackers as Israeli Research Indicates?", *The Jerusalem Post*, October 26, 2016, accessed July 27, 2017, http://www.jpost.com/Business-and-Innovation/Health-and-Science/Can-3D-printing-attract-terrorist-hackers-as-Israeli-research-indicates-470895.
418 "China invents the digital totalitarian state", *The Economist*, December 17, 2016, accessed July 27, 2017, https://www.economist.com/news/briefing/21711902-worrying-implications-its-social-credit-project-china-invents-digital-totalitarian.
419 Goodman, *Future Crimes*, pp. 476-481.
420 OS Fund, "About", *OS Fund*, accessed July 27, 2017, http://osfund.co/about/.
421 Nate Silver, "The Signal and the Noise: Why So Many Predictions Fail, But Some Don't", (USA: Penguin, 2015), p. 29.
422 Corera, Gordon, "How Israel builds its high-tech start-ups", *BBC News*, October 14, 2016, accessed July 27, 2017, http://www.bbc.com/news/technology-37643758.
423 Keinon, Herb, "Israel's intelligence agency is going to start investing in high tech startups", *Business Insider*, June 27, 2017, accessed July 27, 2017, http://www.businessinsider.com/mossad-intel-startup-funding-2017-6.
424 "About", *Libertad Ventures*, accessed July 27, 2017, http://www.libertad.gov.il/eng/index.html.

[425] "Chaos Computer Club", *Wikipedia,* accessed July 27, 2017, https://en.wikipedia.org/wiki/Chaos_Computer_Club.

[426] "The Hackers Russia-Proofing Germany's Elections", *Bloomberg*, June 27, 2017, accessed July 27, 2017, https://www.bloomberg.com/news/features/2017-06-27/the-chaos-computer-club-is-fighting-to-save-democracy.

Index

consumers, 19, 25, 41, 47, 49, 73, 83, 116, 118, 186, 316, 325, 374, 404–5, 407

control systems, 20, 224, 238, 241

corporations, 20, 22, 68, 77, 100, 123, 125–26, 128–29, 244, 249, 329, 333, 344, 395

countries, 6–8, 26–27, 67–68, 81–82, 101–3, 105–7, 144–46, 226, 256–57, 279, 284, 287–88, 322–24, 386–87, 432–35; developing, 7–8, 322

CRI (cyber risk insurance), 403–5, 407

crimes, 29, 99, 102–3, 121, 182–83, 336, 343, 425, 435

CRISPR (Clustered, Regularly Interspaced, Short Palindromic Repeat), 274, 276, 281, 335

cryptocurrencies, 32, 143–44

cryptography, 10, 395, 397–98

CSAC (Cybersecurity Association of China), 28, 30

CSCC (Center for Strategic Counterterrorism Communications), 158

CSPs (content security policy), 269

CTIIC (Cyber Threat Intelligence Integration Center), 128

cyber arms race, 84

cyberattacks, 17, 21–22, 54–55, 64–65, 70–71, 99–104, 189, 209–12, 224–28, 241–45, 248–49, 254–56, 375–77, 382–84, 404–8; aircraft, 53–54, 226, 297, 307–8, 353; cars, 46–48, 53, 234, 283, 360, 421;credit card data, 34, 36, 201, 207, 315; IP address, 88, 113, 149, 187, 358–59, 399; personal information, 14, 34, 70, 106–7, 112–13, 137, 141, 197–99, 268, 344, 374, 383, 426, 429–30; phone numbers, 113, 165, 179, 189, 250, 254, 264, 267, 269; Social Security numbers, 14, 18, 108–11, 141, 179, 323, 325, 328;

cyberbullying, 212–14

cybercriminals, 41–42, 47, 132–38, 140–43, 147, 149–50, 201, 206–7, 250–51, 253, 263, 266–69, 323–24, 427, 430; international, 385

cybersecurity, 28–30, 99–100, 103–4, 123–26, 130–31, 242–43, 245–46, 340–42, 345, 362–64, 369–70, 393, 409, 421–22, 432; companies, 28; frameworks, 123; international network, 242; measures, 123–24, 127, 209, 249; standards, 128; tools, 421

cyberspace, 22, 25, 73, 75, 96, 98, 100, 153, 155–56, 158, 174, 370–71, 373–74, 377, 408–9

cyberterrorism, xxii–xxiii, 3, 170, 208–12, 214, 372, 385–87, 425; theft, 99, 104, 109, 134, 136; information, 380;

hack, 39–40, 46, 49, 51, 77, 80, 83, 85, 258, 261, 263, 296, 329, 332–33, 336; OwnStar, 46; Shadow Brokers, 37–40, 45, 83–84; The Dark Overlord, 57
Hezbollah, 11, 304, 306
hidden services, 146, 148–50
HMIs (human-machine interface), 228
HP (Hewlett-Packard), 105
HPM (high-power microwave), 353
Hybrid Warfare, 11–13, 63, 82

I

IANA (Internet Assigned Names Authority), 27
IBM, 104–5, 334, 341, 397–98, 426
IBNS, 340–42
ICANN (Internet Corporation for Assigned Names and Numbers), 25–29
ICC (Information Coordination Cell), 158–59
ICIC (Improving Critical Infrastructure Cybersecurity), 18–19, 241–42
ICS (Industrial Control Systems), 225–28, 230, 232, 240, 293, 297, 358
India, 25, 43, 50, 139, 186, 258, 321–23, 387
infrastructure, 8, 56, 100, 151, 223–24, 233, 245, 249, 259, 407, 413; critical, 18, 20, 121, 125, 127, 223, 226, 234, 238–39, 242–43, 249, 293, 297, 436
insecurity, personal, 209, 212
insiders, organizational, 419–20
insurance, 14, 404–7
intellectual property, 22, 63–64, 70, 102–4, 106–7, 175, 392
Internet, 25–32, 40–43, 59–60, 72–73, 147–48, 153–54, 171–72, 196–97, 207–9, 294–95, 297, 371–72, 374, 419–20, 422; activity, 87; global, 27–29; service providers, 42, 62
investigators, 134, 166–67, 229, 233–34, 251–52, 257, 259
investors, 7, 130–31, 406, 432
IP (Internet Protocol), 48, 75, 164–65, 257, 359, 372, 403
Iran, 11, 29, 81–82, 89, 94–95, 101, 148, 210, 220, 226, 237, 304, 384, 407
Iraq, 6, 154, 160, 165, 169, 191, 279, 303, 306, 361
IRCs (Internet Relay Chats), 32
IRS (Internal Revenue System), 141
Islamic extremists, 5, 152, 155
ISPs (Internet Service Provider), 41, 79, 117–18, 151, 168, 176, 183, 248, 266, 268

ISS (International Space Station), 357, 361–62
ITU (International Telecommunication Union), 26, 29, 386

J

Japan, 69–70, 116, 251, 324, 327, 357
jihad, virtual, 153, 170–71, 173

L

laboratories, 276, 278, 286, 291–94, 357
laws, 5, 9, 61, 90–92, 102, 104, 106–7, 121–24, 173, 181–82,
    354, 356, 372–79, 381–83, 390–93; counterterrorism,
    China's, 4; enforcement, 5, 8, 13, 30–31, 34, 140, 142,
    149–51, 295, 299, 328, 331, 379–80, 386, 419–20;
    international, 60, 64, 73, 362, 371, 376; new, 105, 117,
    392–93; rule of, 98, 122, 372; violating China's Internet,
    392
lawsuits, 102, 123, 126, 194
legislation, 2, 18, 119, 123–24, 129, 131, 235, 317, 379–80,
    385–86

M

machine learning, 334, 340, 342–43, 426, 433
Macron, Emmanuel (President), 76-78
malware, 34–35, 38, 41–46, 70–71, 80, 83–84, 145–46, 230–
    31, 250, 256–59, 262–63, 358–59, 399–400, 403, 417;
    Assassin, 87; autonomous, 338–40; BlackEnergy, 228,
    232–33; generation of, 339; mobile phone, 250, 253,
    261; RAT (remote access trojan), 36, 70, 251
medical devices, 44–46, 115, 403, 421
messaging, 157, 173, 187–88
microphones and cameras, 315
models, virtual planner, 160–62, 164
monitoring, 87, 118, 185, 191, 195, 221, 224, 282, 331, 367,
    388, 390, 412, 428; continuous, 408, 410, 412–13
Moscow, 77–79, 378
Muslims, 5, 152–53, 155, 171, 201, 207

N

national security, 91–93, 106–7, 121, 348, 379, 383, 391,
    427; abroad, 72; review, 106–7
nations, 61, 81, 84, 95, 97–98, 102, 104, 160, 243, 350, 369–
    70, 377, 380, 387, 390
NCSF (National Cybersecurity Framework), 18–19, 242

S

sanctions, 81, 102–3, 121, 124

satellites, 70, 282, 299, 347–52, 354, 356–58, 360, 362–63, 366–67; connections, 358–60; IP address, 358–60; legitimate users, 358–59

SCADA systems, 223–26, 228

scientists, 237, 265, 274, 276, 279, 281, 306, 327, 334, 356–57

SDI (Strategic Defense Initiative), 351

security, 8, 14, 18, 20–21, 41, 83–84, 114–15, 196–98, 229, 239–40, 242–43, 333–34, 343–45, 379–81, 396–97; companies, 70, 331; flaws, 46–48, 110, 115, 264; measures, 2, 116, 126, 293, 417; risks, 50–51, 196, 330; software, endpoint, 45–46;

SEN (Secure Emergency Network), 244–45

SEO (search engine optimization), 33–34

servers, 24, 32, 38, 40, 42, 62, 87–88, 90–91, 105, 111, 144, 148–49, 265, 267, 402; command, 359–60

smallpox, 275–77, 282, 285–87

smartphones, xxiv, 23, 89, 144, 186, 213, 234, 253, 261, 271, 301, 323, 329–30, 335–37, 426

SMS (Short Message Service), 50, 268

social control, 430–31; digital, 428

social credit system, 70, 428–31

social media, 156, 162, 165–67, 175, 178, 180–82, 184–87, 190–91, 194, 196–97, 199, 201, 207, 213, 221; accounts, 35–36, 169, 172, 181, 219, 335; companies, 177, 186, 192, 195, 372; passwords, 176; platforms, 171, 173, 177, 183, 192–93, 197; sites, 172, 175–76, 179–80, 187, 192, 232; users, 74, 173, 178, 184, 197–98

software, 15, 20, 38, 48–49, 84, 86, 127–28, 154, 192–94, 256, 271–72, 328–29, 333, 415, 417–18; bug, 247; facial recognition, 328–29, 336; glitches, 246, 318; Microsoft, 62, 83; systems, 132, 138; 423, 431; updates, 55, 316, 415, 417–18

Soviet Union, 236, 277, 352, 354

space, 69, 82, 96, 140, 234, 347–48, 352–57, 362–64, 367, 370; common framework for cybersecurity in, 362; outer, 96, 354, 361–62, 370; technologies, 353, 362–63; warfare, 96, 352, 354, 356

SSF (Strategic Support Force), 354

SSIDs (Service Set Identifiers), 302

Stuxnet, 223, 225, 227, 229–30, 238, 293

84616783R00292

Made in the USA
Lexington, KY
24 March 2018